The Rag Race

THE GOLDSTEIN-GOREN SERIES IN AMERICAN JEWISH HISTORY

General editor: Hasia R. Diner

We Remember with Reverence and Love: American Jews and the Myth of Silence after the Holocaust, 1945–1962
Hasia R. Diner

Is Diss a System? A Milt Gross Comic Reader
Edited by Ari Y. Kelman

All Together Different: Yiddish Socialists, Garment Workers, and the Labor Roots of Multiculturalism
Daniel Katz

Jews and Booze: Becoming American in the Age of Prohibition
Marni Davis

Jewish Radicals: A Documentary History
Tony Michels

1929: Mapping the Jewish World
Edited by Hasia R. Diner and Gennady Estraikh

An Unusual Relationship: Evangelical Christians and Jews
Yaakov Ariel

Unclean Lips: Obscenity, Jews, and American Literature
Josh Lambert

Hanukkah in America: A History
Dianne Ashton

The Rag Race: How Jews Sewed Their Way to Success in America and the British Empire
Adam D. Mendelsohn

The Rag Race

How Jews Sewed Their Way to Success in America and the British Empire

Adam D. Mendelsohn

NEW YORK UNIVERSITY PRESS
New York and London

NEW YORK UNIVERSITY PRESS
New York and London
www.nyupress.org

References to Internet websites (URLs) were accurate at the time of writing.
Neither the author nor New York University Press is responsible for URLs
that may have expired or changed since the manuscript was prepared.

Library of Congress Cataloging-in-Publication Data
Mendelsohn, Adam, 1979–
The rag race : how Jews sewed their way to success in America and the British Empire /
Adam D. Mendelsohn.
p.   cm. — (The Goldstein-Goren series in American Jewish history)
Includes bibliographical references and index.
ISBN 978-1-4798-4718-1 (cl : alk. paper)
1. Clothing trade—United States—History—19th century. 2. Clothing trade—
United States—History—20th century. 3. Jews—United States—Economic conditions—
History. 4. Jews—England—Economic conditions—History. 5. Success in business—
United States—History—19th century. 6. Success in business—United States—
History—20th century.   I. Title.
HD9940.U4M45 2014
331.6'3924073—dc23   2014018129

New York University Press books are printed on acid-free paper,
and their binding materials are chosen for strength and durability.
We strive to use environmentally responsible suppliers and materials
to the greatest extent possible in publishing our books.

Manufactured in the United States of America

10 9 8 7 6 5 4 3 2 1

Also available as an ebook

For Odette and Enid,
a model mother and a much-missed grandmother

CONTENTS

Introduction

The Rag Race

Why have Jews prospered so dramatically in the United States? Their ascent has been exceptional. Other ethnic groups have succeeded in America, but none quite like the Jews.[1] So what was the alchemy that transmuted them from economically abased immigrants to among America's most successful citizens? Were they successful because they were Jews or because of the particular circumstances they encountered in the United States? And can their recipe for success be distilled and reproduced by the nation's newest immigrants?

Most of those who address these questions today tread gingerly on turf first turned by an earlier generation more comfortable with racial and religious essentialism and determinism.[2] Instead of heredity, scholars are now more inclined to point to social and cultural capital—kinship networks, hard-won commercial expertise, attitudes toward education and commerce, supportive institutions, and group solidarity—as key to explaining the economic success of Jews.[3] Shying from earlier claims that Jews possess immutable and innate features derived from the primordial past (that *gelt* was in their genes) most historians and sociologists now assume that these traits and tendencies were acquired over time, like protective cladding against the dread chill of an inhospitable climate (the view that *gelt* is in their jeans).[4] Restrictions that had long kept Jews on the fringes of the formal economy in the medieval and early modern periods, so one version of this argument goes, compelled them to develop skills and a *mentalité* that stood them in good stead in America. Others emphasize adaptations of more recent origin. Jews who flocked to America's shores in the nineteenth century from central Europe, for example, had been exposed to public education and bourgeois values before their departure as a consequence of the tortuous process of Jewish emancipation in that region. Certainly the average Jew who migrated to the United States from German-speaking lands was more likely to be literate and numerate than the majority of his or her fellow travelers, and significantly more so than immigrants from Ireland.[5] Eastern European Jewish immigrants—much like their central European counterparts who preceded them to the New World—carried cultural cargo shaped by the distinct circumstances of the *shtetl*. This broad approach, which focuses in large part on the cultural and social baggage that immigrants toted across the Atlantic, is not without its critics. One recent study has cautioned against the assumption that immigrants from Russia were well prepared for labor in a modern industrial economy.[6] And others have more broadly questioned the relationship between cultural characteristics and economic performance.[7]

This book does not discount the significance of culture—the baggage immigrants carried—in determining the trajectory of Jewish immigrants in America. However, it places its emphasis elsewhere. It argues that the Jews who flocked to the United States during a century of mass migration that stretched from 1820 to 1924 were aided appreciably by their association with a particular corner of the American economy that they turned into a home of their own. Why does this emphasis matter? If their cultural heritage was, above all else, responsible for speeding their upward path, what precise field Jews clustered in, and the particular historical contingencies they encountered in America, would be of lesser importance. Their experience could then offer few lessons applicable to other immigrant groups not blessed with a similar cultural inheritance. In contrast, if economic niches play a significant role in shaping economic outcomes—filling the sails of some, blowing others toward the shoals—the experience of Jews is more instructive.

Ironically, in our present age when ethnic economic niches have proliferated, our eyes have been dulled to their importance and complexity. A rotating cast of ethnic entrepreneurs make cameos in the life of our cities as taxi drivers, umbrella sellers, movers, restaurateurs, and the occupants of myriad other corners of urban commerce. Bemused tourists and curious locals are not the only observers to have noticed these clusters of immigrant entrepreneurship. Yet while sociologists have intensively studied ethnic economies and immigrant niches, historians have been slower to consider their significance.[8] In recent years, however, several historians have begun to outline how, why, and to what effect Jews have clustered together in the modern economy.[9]

This book argues that for Jews in the United States, the rag trade proved to be a particularly good fit. From humble beginnings Jews rode the coat-tails of the clothing trade from the margins of economic life in the nine-teenth century to a position of unusual promise and prominence in the twentieth. As we will see, the intimate relationship that developed between Jews and the clothing trade had long-term consequences for both: the eco-nomic ascent of Jews in America cannot be fully comprehended without understanding the business of stitching and selling garments, and the gar-ment industry cannot be fully understood without following the thread of Jewish involvement in the *shmatte* (rag) business.[10]

But how can we know that the nature of the clothing trade per se played an instrumental role in the economic success of Jews in the United States? One way to assess its influence is through comparison, an approach that others have profitably pursued before.[11] Such analogies will always be imperfect. No other nation attracted nearly as many Jews in the nineteenth and early twentieth centuries as did the United States. And no matter how close in culture and custom, no two countries present immigrants with exactly the same opportunities and challenges. But what if we compared the history of Jewish involvement in the clothing trade in America with a parallel setting where Jews in the identical industry started the century at a considerable advantage? If ethnic culture functioned independently of other factors, we would expect to see Jews in this setting advancing at roughly the same rate as, if not faster than, those in America, in the gar-ment industry and in their overall economic standing.

The clothing trade in England offers exactly this point of comparison. Already in the early decades of the nineteenth century, Jews were well entrenched in London in a trade that began to grow explosively in scale and importance. By the middle of the century a handful had achieved a prominence as clothiers that was unimaginable to their counterparts in the United States. Yet for all their early advantages, Jews in England were outstripped by their American peers by 1881. The particular circumstances of Jewish involvement in the clothing industry in the United States con-spired to push them ahead in the intervening years. Although the scale and density of Jewish settlement in the United States relative to that in England during the period of eastern European mass migration perforce makes comparison more problematic after 1881, historical differences in how Jews entered and experienced the clothing trade before that date created a cascade of consequences for immigrant newcomers who followed them into the business. Historical divergences within the same industry on different sides of the Atlantic before 1881, in other words, contributed to very real differences in the social and economic outcomes for Jews in the United States and England in the twentieth century.

So What Was So Special about the Clothing Trade?

Given the arguments in this book about the importance of one particular economic niche to the Jewish experience, it pays close attention to how the garment industry changed over time and what these changes meant for Jews. The trajectory of the garment business, the most common occupation for Jewish immigrants, became interlaced with the trajectory of Jews, threading through their economic ascent across generations like a slip stitch. Jews first entered this business by historical happenstance rather than by prescience about its future potential, but the early foothold they established proved to be of decisive importance. As the clothing trade expanded and diversified, becoming one of the most significant consumer industries in the United States, this hitherto humble niche showered unanticipated opportunities on generations of Jewish immigrants and their children. When the clothing trade moved into the van of economic change, it became a vehicle for the dramatic ascent of Jews.

The nature of this niche mattered. From our present vantage point it is difficult to detect why it was once special, when many of its daring experiments in production, distribution, and retailing on a mass scale have long since become commonplace. Some of its inspired improvisations—grand emporia and mail-order catalogues, to name just two innovative ways of marketing new products and conducting business more efficiently—distract our attention from several structural features, largely hidden to outside observers, that proved congenial to Jews. The industry was simultaneously illuminated by the guttering candlelight of the past and the blazing gas lights of the future. Its resistance to change proved as important for Jewish history as did the room and rewards it offered to innovators involved in marketing and distribution. Counterintuitively, the garment industry remained a vital Jewish ethnic niche across decades and successive waves of immigration not because it was quick to modernize its methods of production but precisely because it was in large part slow to do so. Even as enterprising Jewish clothiers worked out new ways of carrying ever-larger quantities of clothing to an ever-larger market, the persistence of a labor-intensive mode of manufacturing supplied jobs to recently arrived Jewish immigrants. Since the production system in New York City favored small firms — entrepreneurs with relatively little money could corral a handful of workers to begin stitching clothing for them — there was opportunity for enterprise even among those who had only recently arrived in America. The uneven development of the clothing trade, characterized by continuous innovation among retailers and wholesalers and by gradual change among manufacturers, ensured a depth of Jewish participation that was unseen in other fields. A variety of other structural features intrinsic to the growth of the clothing industry in the United States — such as the emergence of new and underserved markets and the instability and unpredictability of demand within them — accentuated the advantages enjoyed by small Jewish firms.

En masse, Jews entered — and later escaped — an occupation that provided, relative to many of the potential alternatives for immigrants, a solid preparation for economic life in the twentieth century. First, it was an enabling occupation that supplied many of its occupants with rough-and-ready schooling in skills essential for rapid advancement in a modern economy, particularly sensitivity to the whims and wants of the market and practice in petty entrepreneurship. Second, by clustering in the clothing trade, Jews set the wheels of opportunity turning in a certain direction. In America the internal logic of the industry dictated that the fastest path to advancement lay in self-employment rather than in wage labor. Jews were shepherded toward an entrepreneurial path of economic development that was distinct from that of several contemporary immigrant groups that flocked to other fields. In part as a result, an unusually high percentage of Jewish immigrants and their children became proprietors of small businesses in the United States, a development of enormous consequence. In England, where the internal logic of the industry was somewhat different, Jews pursued proprietorship at a markedly lower rate and were slower to leave the working class.[12] Even within the garment industry, however, the opportunities available for entrepreneurial activity shifted over time. Jewish immigrants to America who took up tailoring were fortunate in their timing. Other groups that followed them into the trade later in the twentieth century found that it was a less supple springboard than it had been.[13] Third, the ethnic economy that Jews fashioned around clothing provided a point of access into a variety of related fields, including scrap metal, military contracting, property development, entertainment, and consumer goods. And as the garment industry expanded, it supported an ever-larger collection of lawyers, accountants, advertisers, designers, and other experts who were often immigrants or the children of immigrants themselves.

The clothing trade was certainly not the only pathway to prosperity. Indeed, it shared several features with other niches that attracted clusters of Jewish entrepreneurs. Such fields, generally in the commercial realm, tended to advantage those who created dense networks that interconnected producers, distributors, and purveyors. In several cases these fields were new, expanding at breakneck speed, or socially déclassé—therefore somewhat more open to those who were less intimidated by these considerations—as well as suitable for a proliferation of smaller enterprises. Few alternatives were more important for Jews in the mid-nineteenth century than the dry-goods business. For Jews the clothing business was joined at the hip to the dry-goods trade. Jewish peddlers were as likely to carry fancy goods (yard goods and trimmings) and notions (buttons, thread, and needles) as they were to tote clothing. Jewish garment manufacturers could access inexpensive cloth sold by kinsmen who were wholesalers and importers of dry goods. Some dabbled in both clothing and fabric or moved between the two. But even though Jews clustered (and prospered) in several other areas of the American economy, no single sector became so closely intertwined with such a large swath of the Jewish community over such a broad period of time as did the garment industry. Unlike dry goods, for example, the manufacturing side of the garment industry became as important to Jews as did retailing and wholesaling.

It would be erroneous, however, to assume that this special relationship between Jews and the clothing trade alone guaranteed Jewish success in the United States. Things need not have turned out as they did. The garment industry might have developed in a less amenable manner. And the favorable characteristics of the trade did not provide a predetermined or inevitable path to prosperity. Instead, as this book demonstrates, many

Jews were well positioned to take advantage of the opportunities that this field presented, but when they succeeded, they did so through resourcefulness, skill, and good fortune. Their luck was in part the offspring of their own energies, but hard work and perseverance did not guarantee success. Plenty failed or suffered reverses despite their best efforts.

Even as the garment industry positioned Jews well for the future, it also pushed them into a walk-on role in the modernization of capitalism. As manufacturers began to churn out ever-larger quantities of ready-made garments in the second half of the nineteenth century, the producers and purveyors of clothing played a pivotal role in refashioning Americans into mass consumers. Stylish new clothing, once out of the reach of all but the well-to-do (and those who were willing to steal from them), now heralded a consumer revolution. Through innovations in manufacturing, distribution, and marketing, those who made and sold garments introduced practices that transformed patterns of production and habits of consumption. The Jewish peddlers, clothiers, and manufacturers who became prime purveyors of inexpensive fashions were the precursors of Jews who, in later generations, thrived by keeping their finger on the popular pulse in a variety of consumer industries. Given the centrality of Jews to these changes in the garment industry, the most important role they played in the expansion of capitalism in the United States came not in the realm of investment banking but in the bottom-up changes wrought by garment makers and salespeople who competed to sell their stock in an expanding and evolving marketplace and in the labor activism of those who stitched and sewed much of America's clothing. The predominance of Jews in this one sector provided their community—both its commercial pioneers and its activists—with a prominence and role in the general economy beyond what their numbers would otherwise have given them. In few other areas of the modern economy were Jews so central. And few other occupations left as important a legacy for modern Jewish history in the New World.

From Castoffs to Center Stage

The garment industry did not possess a Jewish essence, nor was Jewish involvement in the field driven by any particularistic agenda. Prior to the 1920s, Jews in the United States were not pushed or penned into this field by antisemitic pressures. Yet by neither design nor intention, key sectors of

the business of manufacturing and selling new clothing came to be dominated by Jews. Their success in the garment business, therefore, presents
a conundrum. How and why did Jews corner parts of the clothing trade?
This book offers several intertwined explanations, but it focuses on three
themes: the fortuitous positioning of Jews in marginal occupations, primarily secondhand dealing and peddling; fundamental changes in the way
clothing was manufactured, distributed, and sold in the nineteenth century; and ethnic connections among Jews that eased the entry of newcomers into the field and could provide mutual benefit to those who sought to
do business in new and challenging markets.

To understand how this unlikely story of economic ascent began, we
will start where Jews did in the clothing trade in England and America: among the scavengers and hawkers who struggled to make a living
by collecting, patching, and reselling clothing cast off by others. In our
present age of material plenty, garments are expendable, purchased in
profusion, worn at whim, and entombed within a closet or cast off when
fallen from favor or fashion. Rare is the garment that enjoys a full second
life—resurrected as hand-me-downs, repurposed as "retro" or "vintage"
by thrift-store shoppers, or distributed as charity—once it has been discarded by the original owner. Such affordable abundance and profligacy
would have been almost unimaginable to consumers in an earlier age when
workaday clothing was carefully husbanded, passing between owners until
it was so worn that further patching and refashioning was impractical or
impossible. Even then the threadbare fabric usually retained sufficient
value to be collected and recycled. An entire economy, long since faded,
existed to extract the maximum return from the latter lives of garments
discarded by (or purloined from) their original owners. For much of the
nineteenth century the collection and sale of castoff clothing in New York
City and London was dominated by Jews.

For a time this occupation came to define Jews in the popular imagination. For writers, cartoonists, and popular poets, a sack of castoffs and
stack of rumpled hats became convenient shorthand for Jews: they were
the rag race. Those who created these often-mocking depictions could
little anticipate how, in turn, the rag race—the business of buying, selling, stitching, and sewing clothing—would aid the transformation of
Jewish life in the United States and England. Ragmen and street sellers
raucously hawked and bartered in ways that seemed out of step with the

The Jewish "old clo'" man became a frequent figure of fun in depictions of urban life and a fixture in the popular imagination, appearing as stock characters in children's books, in verse, and on the printed page. (Collection of the author)

new commercial norms of the middle class. Instead of setting a fixed price, they seemed to relish haggling. Instead of operating from fixed premises, they bought and sold wherever they could accost potential customers.[14] To some journalists and writers who described the secondhand trade to a broader audience, Chatham Street in New York and Petticoat Lane in London served as stages for a morality play in which debates about the nature and boundaries of the developing capitalist system were acted out with

Jewish ragmen, auctioneers, pawnbrokers, labor brokers, and sweatshop owners as protagonists. Jews were not necessarily chosen for this purpose because they outnumbered other groups involved in these fields—often they did not—or because of the distinctiveness of their economic behavior, which was often no different from that of their competitors. Rather, to borrow Claude Lévi-Strauss's felicitous phrase, they were singled out because they were "good to think [with]."[15] Paradoxically, this intense focus on ragmen blinded observers to the inroads made by Jews elsewhere in the clothing business, as well as to the complexity of the secondhand trade itself. Few saw or understood that the used-clothing market was transformed by, and deeply embedded within, modernity. During the first decades of the nineteenth century it became increasingly elaborate and systematic. Rather than a relic of a time before mass manufacturing, it flourished in tight symbiosis with the production and marketing of ready-made clothing. Old and new clothes were twin elements of an interdependent economy. Although some people did move seamlessly from hawking secondhand clothing to selling new garments, the market for rags and cast-offs long remained viable. And, as we will see, both became commodities for speculation and export to distant markets.[16]

Nineteenth-century stereotypes built on a much-older association of Jews with the clothing trade. Although in medieval Europe tailoring and drapery guilds often tried to cut Jews out of the market, Jewish tailors sought to bypass restrictions—on occasion creating their own guilds or clustering in subfields, such as the making of hats, that were sometimes free of these constraints—and continued to sell to Jewish and Christian clients when they could. Those Jewish craftsmen who stitched sumptuous finery, however, were only the brocade on a far coarser and larger ethnic enterprise. The collection and sale of careworn clothing long allowed impecunious Jews to maintain a tenuous grip on the lower rungs of the economic ladder. In medieval and early modern Europe, rag traders, secondhand-clothing dealers, and peddlers often operated outside the confines of guild control, occupying a niche held in low esteem.[17] The cost of fashionable fabric and the skilled labor of master and journeyman tailors meant that hand-sewn, made-to-measure garments were expensive. Tailors long resisted the methods of mass production. Those without the means to purchase hand-tailored jackets and pantaloons could make do with the preworn outfits proffered by peddlers and stall keepers in secondhand markets. Jews still hawked all manner of inexpensive articles to farmers and villagers in the countryside of western and central Europe in the early nineteenth century, and in some areas the peddling of clothing remained a staple occupation for decades longer.[18]

This attention to "old clo'" dealers is one of the ways this volume cuts, crimps, and reworks several pieces of the standard narrative of the economic history of Jews in England and the United States. The secondhand-garment trade has been largely absent from studies of Jewish labor and the immigrant experience. This is particularly the case in the United States.[19] This lapse is partly the product of the lack of interest of historians of American economic life in secondhand markets. Only recently have some begun to unpick the complex threads of a staple business of the urban underclass and a source of affordable goods to fill their wardrobes, pantries, and living spaces.[20] Several scholars have now shown that even for the poor clothing was much more than just something to cover the body. An outfit, even a secondhand one, could serve as a marker of social status, a reflection of identity, and the object of aspiration. The neglect of Jewish secondhand dealers in particular has in part been a product of the stigma once associated with them and their wares. Though doing substantial business, those who earned a living in this trade were seen as marginal participants within the larger economy. Well beyond the nineteenth century the "old clo'" dealer was often a figure of fun and a source of embarrassment. His reputation was bespattered by the taint of criminality, the stain of poverty, and a whiff of the Old World. The trade was viewed by some people as a vestige of a best-forgotten past. More broadly, this reticence reflects the relative neglect of Jewish economic life in America as a subject of serious study.[21]

If the buying and selling of castoff clothing has frayed and largely been forgotten, the sweatshop has been double-stitched into popular and scholarly memory of Jewish immigration. This book leans heavily on this rich scholarship about Jewish involvement in the garment industry after 1881. Few of these works, however, consider how an earlier history shaped later developments within this ethnic niche.[22] Hence, the bulk of this book deals with the period before 1880. For to begin a discussion of Jews and the clothing trade in America with the sweatshop is like presenting a stage play without its opening acts. Even though the upward mobility of eastern European Jewish immigrants and their children was far from pre-scripted, the role of earlier immigrants in opening the arena and designing the props essential for the success of the later drama has not been fully recognized. In devoting considerable attention to the period prior to mass migration of eastern European Jews, this book argues that patterns established between the 1830s and 1870s persisted well after central European migrants had been supplanted by a new cast of characters. In doing so, it further unpicks the now threadbare stage curtain that was once seen to separate these two streams of immigrants. And in emphasizing structural and ethnic continuities within the clothing trade, it refocuses attention on the importance and influence of the niche itself on successive waves of Jewish immigrants.

Over the course of the nineteenth century an ethnic economy built on castoff and cut-price clothing was tapered and transformed into one centered on the mass manufacture of cheap clothing in Leeds, London, the Lower East Side of New York, and numerous other towns great and small. Whole sections of the menswear trade that had previously been foreclosed to Jews were transformed by a series of technological, commercial, and social changes. (For reasons discussed later in this book, change came more slowly in the manufacturing and marketing of womenswear.)[23] By dint of good fortune and fortuitous timing, Jews worked within the clothing trade in the United States and England at a time when it provided a broadening set of opportunities. Demand for clothing both old and new accelerated in the settlement colonies of the British Empire, on plantations in the American South, in boomtowns on the frontier, and among workers with disposable income in soot-stained industrial cities. Merchants and manufacturers began to jettison familiar patterns of doing business for new ways of making and marketing men's clothing. The trade began to shift decisively from skilled tailoring by artisans and the extensive reuse of castoff garments to its modern techniques of mass production, mass marketing, and mass consumption. Jews found themselves fortuitously positioned during the decisive decades when the clothing trade was upended. In effect, they had a hand in creating a new industry. In England a small cohort of Jews with expertise in the used-clothing trade discovered that their unglamorous vocation gave them a major advantage when they entered the nascent ready-made garment industry. In the United States a scattering of peddlers, clerks, and petty shopkeepers seeded the first significant crop of Jewish-owned manufacturing and wholesaling firms to sprout on American soil. For most Jews these changes produced only modest success, but a few attained great prosperity. Still others found their livelihoods undercut by disruptive new methods and technologies.

Although numerous Jewish men and women worked independently to advance their own interests, the action of these individuals had collective consequences. Immigrant entrepreneurs were often tied to their kinsmen and compatriots through elaborate ethnic networks. These networks did not persist as vestigial remnants of a preimmigrant past; rather, they flourished as dynamic commercial mechanisms. In theory the benefits of such relationships should have eroded substantially over time. Jewish migrants settled in the United States and the British Empire during a period of profound economic transformation that made markets more complex and business more impersonal. Whereas once family connections, acquaintance, and proximity provided the glue that most often bound parties together in commercial exchanges, now modern institutions—banks, insurance companies, credit bureaus, and forwarding agents—facilitated business between strangers. On the surface these changes diminished the advantages enjoyed by members of ethnic networks. If a credit bureau could establish the trustworthiness of a perfect stranger in a distant city, and formal market and legal mechanisms could protect an investment, what need was there to rely on kinsmen or compatriots? If the value of trusted intermediaries rose in environments with few such institutions, surely the opposite was true of settings where such mechanisms were in place? Anonymous commerce between willing buyers and sellers was potentially more efficient and cost-effective than relying only on goods and services acquired from relatives and coreligionists. To those who sought to turn a profit, surely it was "ultimately the exchange itself that mattered, not the identity of those with whom they did business"?[24]

Jewish business networks flourished precisely because of the rapidity and scale of growth in the United States and the British Empire. Instead of serving as second-best mechanisms in an age of neutral markets, migrant business networks thrived in the interstices of an incompletely integrated and imperfect economic system that was expanding geographically and growing in complexity. Ethnic networks bridged city and countryside, metropole and colony, entrepôt and boomtown at a time when these were otherwise not seamlessly joined. These relationships were particularly advantageous in an industry where fashions changed quickly (thereby making the relay of speedy and reliable intelligence particularly valuable) as well as in markets where there was a prolonged "information float" (a lengthy delay between dispatching and receiving messages because of geographical isolation) and in regions where credit was harder to come by.

Those who participated in these networks also benefited from the vertical integration and horizontal reach that these connections offered. Success could beget success: successful entrepreneurs invested their money and experience in new ventures. Yet this ethnic ecosystem was never exclusive, hermetic, and unchanging. Non-Jews were drawn in as partners, employers, employees, suppliers, and customers. Participants changed over time as the interests of employers and partners shifted. Nor was this ecosystem an Arcadian paradise of altruistic cooperation. As in any other such system there were commensals who benefited from belonging but added little of value to others, mutualists who took and contributed in equal measure, and freeloaders who exploited the fruits of the system. Participants in networks fought, fell out, and occasionally cheated each other. The ecosystem was also segmented. Some subgroups came to carve out areas for themselves by specializing in particular roles and then recruiting others of similar background to join them. The relationship between Jewish immigrants from different backgrounds was not necessarily one of cooperation and trust. But in the aggregate, there were benefits to participation.

Without question, culture played an important role in sustaining the sense of common cause that underpinned the ethnic ecosystem, as well as in conditioning Jewish responses to American-style capitalism. A variety of features found in the Jewish immigrant population—literacy and numeracy, familiarity with itinerant trading and petty storekeeping, an openness to commercial endeavor, and several other seeds carried in the cultural cargo of those who crossed the Atlantic—germinated when exposed to fructifying soil. Some migrants arrived with direct knowledge of tailoring and the business of buying and selling clothing. But many more cultivated existing skills and acquired new ones once they settled in America and England. Over time, Jewish peddlers, clerks, petty shopkeepers, and even tailors developed a working knowledge of merchandising and finance, a familiarity with the wants of the market, and a network of contacts for distribution and credit. They transmuted the cultural capital they had brought with them into capital of the very real kind. Inherited cultural characteristics could also take on new meaning and importance in a fresh context. Among Jewish immigrants the business advantages of belonging to commercial networks were often intertwined with communal commitments. Cultural affinities bolstered economic interactions, and economic relationships enhanced a sense of cultural connectedness. Commercial relationships played an essential role in sustaining a sense of solidarity and common cause between Jewish communities dispersed over distance, and vice versa.[25]

The economic networks that linked the people involved in the garment trade were buffeted by larger historical forces. At moments of crisis, some networks failed entirely, dragging their web of participants into bankruptcy. Others dissolved when they outlived their usefulness, and still others prospered by adapting quickly to new opportunities. The organic mutability of networks—their stagnation, responsiveness to stressors, and adaptation—was most visible during moments of dramatic change. This book focuses on the impact of several disruptive developments that reshaped markets and altered the dynamics of the clothing trade: colonization and frontier settlement, financial panic, and war. But it also focuses on the quieter but no less significant processes that transformed the garment industry: the emergence of a mass consumer society and technological change. These developments have rarely been considered key waypoints in the development of Jewish life in America and England. However, to Jews in the clothing trade, several of these changes were crucial, and they arrived tightly bundled together in the years between 1830 and 1890. These decisive decades are the focus of much of this book.

We will begin in London, at a moment of equipoise between old and new in the garment industry. To those who earned their livelihoods by buying and selling castoff clothing, the future appeared promising. The used-clothing markets in the East End of the city attracted a cacophonous throng of thousands of eager customers every weekend. A handful of clothing exchanges had recently opened their doors to local and foreign buyers, making the sale, purchase, and export of clothing more efficient. This early period is best understood as a prelude for what was to come, and for this reason chapter 1 provides a panoramic *tour d'horizon* of an economic world on the cusp of change. Chapter 2 compares early Jewish involvement in the clothing trade in England and in the United States. Whereas in England the secondhand trade appeared to provide an advantageous platform for those who were inclined to experiment with new modes of producing and marketing clothing, in America collecting and reselling used clothing presented dimmer prospects for economic advancement. How, then, did Jews in the United States enter the business of making and selling new clothing? Chapter 3 shows that in America, peddling, clerking, and petty shopkeeping, rather than a familiarity with rags and tattered castoffs, were the keys to the kingdom of the clothing trade. Chapters 4 and 5 suggest that for all the efforts of Jews in America to catch up with their coreligionists across the Atlantic, they seemed, to outside observers at least, instead to be falling further behind when it came to the garment industry. Chapter 4 explores the early experiments in modern retailing and manufacturing of cheap ready-made clothing of Jewish entrepreneurs in England, who were well ahead of their counterparts in the United States. Chapter 5 examines the impact of the rapid growth of settler populations in South Africa, Canada, and especially Australia. New markets provided economies of scale for metropolitan producers and advantaged those—including a handful of Jews—who could integrate production, distribution, and retail. By 1850 it might appear that English Jews had an unassailable lead in the clothing industry over their kinsmen in America. Chapters 6, 7, and 8 explain how and why Jews in the United States were able to catch up with and then surpass those in England. Chapter 6 traces the evolution of Jewish involvement in the ready-made trade in the United States in the 1850s, paying particular attention to the many new opportunities presented by westward and southward expansion. Chapter 7 describes how the military economy created during the Civil War transformed the position of Jews in the US garment industry. Chapter 8 compares the expansive opportunities open to Jews involved in the clothing trade in America in the wake of the war with the more limited prospects of Jews in England. The conclusion explains why this earlier history matters for understanding Jewish economic mobility in the twentieth century. We will see that the garment industry became an enabling occupation for the shiploads of new immigrants who arrived in both England and America beginning in the 1880s, although it propelled them forward at different speeds. Building on the dynamic platform created by earlier generations of Jews, the eastern European newcomers who came to America advanced at a faster rate that those who settled into the ethnic niche established by Jews in England.

Such a future would have seemed unlikely—even fantastical—in 1843. A first-time visitor to London in that year might enter the metropolis feeling confident after having perused Cunningham's authoritative guide-book, anticipating a day spent admiring the imposing sites of the impe-rial capital.[26] Little, though, could prepare the newcomer for the urban cacophony that awaited. Vendors and hawkers demanded notice for their "pine apples, a penny a slice," "kearots," and "sparrowgrass" (asparagus) and called out to attract customers' attention: "Milk ho!" "Butcher!" and "Baker!" The old-clothes man, with his echoing chant of "old clo,'" hoarsely competed for attention. Amid the parade of novelties, the figure of the Jewish collector of castoff clothing would have been familiar to any visi-tor from a provincial town, where Jewish peddlers were common both as itinerant collectors of castoffs and as familiar figures in folklore. And if our traveler came from abroad, she or he may well have encountered such men before, albeit announcing their trade in a different tongue. In this regard it would seem to make little difference whether our visitor arrived in Lon-don at the beginning, middle, or end of the nineteenth century or even a century earlier. The Jewish ragman, toting the sack that was the mark of his tattered fraternity, was seemingly a constant in a trade that appeared to many outsiders not to have changed at all since the distant past. This book argues otherwise.

1

Goblin Market

London, 1843

Visitors to London in 1843 in search of urban adventure would have done well to alight at the new Fenchurch Street terminus of the London and Blackwall Railway. They would be far from alone, joining a jostling human herd that was disgorged into the streets and alleys close to the Thames. After orientating themselves amid the clamor of the crowds and steeling themselves against the puckering reek of the streets, they would begin pushing through lanes choked with pedestrians and horse-drawn omnibuses, cabs, and carts, stepping around debris and dung scattered underfoot, and moving swiftly past shopkeepers and the quick-fingered who hoped to relieve the unwary of their wallets. The fortunate visitors found a crossing sweeper who, hoping for a small coin as a reward, would clear a path for them through the muck and mud. Otherwise, they required a strong stomach and stout boots as they moved northward toward Spitalfields. The streets became serpentine, cast into shadows by decrepit houses stooped like pious men in prayer and shrouded by a sky ashen with smuts and smoke. The crowds massed anew as they neared their destination. The visitors would soon enter a tattered and multicolored maze of garments, lined at ground level with a parade of shoes and boots and sold at sagging stalls that teetered into Petticoat Lane, Sandys Row, Tripe Yard, Frying Pan Alley, Naked Boy Court, and Moses Square. At first sight the dangling dresses and jackets gave one newcomer "the impression that about an acre of the loveliest of Houndsditch had simultaneously committed suicide."[1] If not diverted by persistent hawkers and swarming street urchins, visitors would do well to follow the shuffling procession of footsore ragmen laden

A raucous Sunday morning in the East End. Thousands of customers descended on the area to shop and haggle, making nearby streets all but impassable and producing a fertile field for pickpockets and other petty criminals. (Collection of the author)

with sacks through the crowds to the alley that led to Phil's Buildings, to climb the stairs, to pay their halfpenny admission fee to the retired pugilist who acted as gatekeeper, and to enter the vast open-air market beyond. The interior was scarcely less crowded than the street outside. Here was the Clothes Exchange, established in that year of 1843 and already a site of pilgrimage for slum explorers, journalists, and tatterdemalion customers alike in the Dickensian heart of the East End of London.

Seven thousand square feet in size, the market served as a shabby emporium for rag collectors hoping to sell the clothing they had gathered in London, dealers and retailers buying garments to salvage and resell in Petticoat Lane and the provinces, and bargain hunters shopping to outfit themselves. A pungent fug hung over the Clothes Exchange, bursting forth anew whenever a ragman opened a ripe sack to reveal his daily harvest of castoff clothing. On Sunday, the busiest day at the market, five hundred sellers rented stalls in carefully demarcated spaces to display their wares. A cacophonous throng of customers, estimated at over ten thousand people, descended on the area to shop and haggle, making nearby streets all but impassable and producing a fertile field for pickpockets and other petty criminals. When the light was poor—not an uncommon problem since

London's skies were befouled by factories and coal fires—the mart was lit by oil flares. Our visitors might calm their jangled nerves with a fortifying glass of hot wine bought from a stand at the center of the mart or by something stronger from the Montefiore Arms tavern, which anchored one of its corners. Startled by (and relishing) the exotic scene, few casual visitors were attuned to the sophistication of the mart through which they wandered. The Clothes Exchange pulsed at the center of a circulatory system that sent tattered commodities coursing between the metropolis and distant limbs. And the seemingly chaotic mart was a central node in a Jewish economy that, at its height, stretched from Rag Fair, an impromptu bazaar in Melbourne during the Australian gold rush, to the slave plantations of the American South and the galloping frontier of the American West.[2] The Clothes Exchange and the broader ethnic marketplace to which it belonged were far from static and timeless vestiges of a distant past. Instead, they were dynamic, adapting to shifts in the London landscape, pressure from ethnic rivals, developments in the clothing trade, and changes in the Jewish community.

Yet the bargains secured in the Clothes Exchange were centuries in the making, late additions to a long history of Jewish participation in the collection and sale of castoff clothing and the equally long history of Houndsditch as a center of London's clothing market. The street had been home to old-clothes traders since at least the sixteenth century.[3] Although there were several other clothing and shoe markets dotted across London, Houndsditch and Rag Fair—a boisterous open-air market in Rosemary Lane (renamed Royal Mint Street in 1850), closer to the Thames and near Tower Hill—became the epicenter of a Jewish economy during the later decades of the eighteenth century.[4] Until the 1840s Rag Fair was the livelier of the two markets, a place where ragmen, dealers, and customers congregated to barter and haggle. In Aldgate, however, the clothing trade initially radiated outward from the dense alleyways and lanes around Cutler Street. Several observers later puzzled over the "very peculiar situation" of the market, noting that the street led only to the warehouses of the East India Company.[5] But the site had several advantages for clothing dealers. The alleyway was not a public street, a fact that hindered those who were intent on suppressing trade within its confines.[6] Although the East India Company was not pleased by the impromptu daily market that stoppered the street on most afternoons, it had trouble policing the area.[7] The site was also interstitched with the trade in textiles. India House, which sat at the far end of Cutler Street, served as a salesroom and auction venue for the East India Company. Although larger merchant houses dominated the purchase of the fine fabrics imported by the company from India, in the eighteenth century Jewish traders came to specialize in the purchase of textiles damaged in transit. At the auctions, prosperous Jewish traders from Amsterdam jostled with their Jewish counterparts of the "lower sort," some of whom had crossed the English Channel by mail boat to attend the sales.[8] Sellers of the crudely sewn shirts and pants dismissively known as "slops" bought cheap cloth to transform into prefabricated apparel for sailors. Jewish buyers were sufficiently important that the East India Company tried not to hold its public auctions on Jewish holidays. Dutch merchants carried cloth back to Amsterdam, which served as a distribution center for goods imported from the British Empire. From this humble seed grew an ethnic economy in the East End.

The Dutch traders who came to Aldgate in search of cheap fabric were, however, only one element in a more complicated and evolving ethnic economy. By the last quarter of the eighteenth century Jewish rag and clothing collectors were a fixture of street life in London. To the eye of the outsider they seemed to wander at random. But there is evidence that collectors walked a regular beat, trudging familiar streets with a pack or basket; proffering flowers, trinkets, crockery, and jewelry in exchange for worn garments; and converging in the afternoon at Rag Fair with their daily harvest of castoff clothing. The collectors were slaves to fashion, lugging to market items cast off by the middle and upper classes (or bartered for other goods by their servants) as outmoded or threadbare. Few of these itinerant collectors were women, although women were involved in the sale of used clothing and were prominent among clothes dealers.[9] In the popular imagination, these clothing collectors became visual representatives of Jewish life in the city, subject to disapproving sneers on the streets and opprobrium in the press.[10] One journalist jested that "carrying the bag, and crying 'oghclo,' seems to be a sort of noviciate or apprenticeship which all Hebrews are subjected to."[11] The clothing and rag collector shared the lowly status of the pawnbroker and the hawker and did not escape the taint of criminality attached to both. At the height of the trade, perhaps one to two thousand Jewish collectors walked the streets of London.[12]

Although exhausting, the work required no capital, little skill, and only the most basic proficiency in English. For many newcomers it was a temporary or transitional occupation performed until a more promising alternative appeared or until they graduated to dealing in the clothes collected by others. Hawking clothes was more than just physically taxing: among the Jews admitted to London's lunatic asylums, "clothes dealer" was the most frequently listed occupation.[13] To eke out a living, collectors and dealers relied on the value that clothing retained even after being discarded by its original owners. Tailored garments remained beyond the means of much of the population well into the nineteenth century. With tailored clothing out of reach and ready-made clothing relatively expensive, used clothing carried little stigma among the working classes. There was no shortage of purchasers. Castoff clothing was widely worn even after mass-manufactured garments became affordable to wage workers. Paradoxically, the growing number of those who were able to purchase new ready-made clothing ensured that the secondary market was well supplied with discarded garments.[14]

The clothing trade was part of a fertile economic ecosystem, its roots intertwined with several allied occupations including peddling, pawnbroking, and auctioneering. As historian Beverley Lemire has demonstrated, garments played an essential role in the household economy of the poor, serving as an alternative currency system and a savings mechanism. Even if some of those who bought clothes in Houndsditch were of somewhat higher social rank—clerks, for example, in search of the inexpensive black coats that became the uniform of their caste—the working poor constituted the single largest category of customers for castoff clothing.[15] Garments were redeemable for cash or kind, held their value well, and were easy to pawn. (For the same reasons, they remained a popular target for thieves.)[16] The poor often assessed new clothing for its pawnability, seeing it as a strategic reserve against hard times. A newly purchased article of clothing might be pawned immediately to cover other expenses, redeemed on the weekend, and then repawned week after week for smaller and smaller sums until its purchaser could afford to own it outright. Most Jewish pawnbrokers in the East End were involved in the "low trade," pursuing a high-volume and low-margin strategy. Much of their regular business followed a weekly cycle of pawning. Although the rate of interest was limited by law, these small loans were rendered profitable by the fee incurred for each transaction.[17] Since clothing and textiles were by far the largest category of items pledged as security, pawnbrokers frequently dabbled in the clothing trade by auctioning or selling forfeited garments.[18] In England many pawnbrokers had salesrooms for forfeited items. They also acted as petty bankers for small-scale retailers, selling cheap jewelry to hawkers and peddlers who could resell the items. Pawnbrokers were obliged by law to sell at public auction unredeemed items valued at more than ten shillings, a requirement that connected them with auctioneering.[19]

The Street Markets

The street markets in Houndsditch and Rosemary Lane specialized in the retail of cheap goods, including haberdashery, and were popular with hawkers and peddlers.[20] The London authorities had waged sporadic campaigns against street merchants since at least the early fourteenth century. In January 1700 "several inhabitants" of Rosemary Lane petitioned the county justice of the peace to outlaw "Ragg Fair." Using arguments that would recur for the next two centuries, they complained of "all manner of wickedness sport and debauchery" and "very great hindrance and disturbance" caused by those who congregated to buy and sell.[21] The county's response established a well-worn pattern, ordering constables to suppress the "unlawful and riotous mootings dayly" for the "buying and selling of old goods wearing apparel" and other articles.[22] The constables may have succeeded in the short term, but the traders soon returned. Complainants were forced to rely on private prosecution.[23] Several petitions were sent to the Lord Mayor in the 1730s. For example, the Company of Merchant-Taylors implored him to disperse those who clogged the thoroughfares by operating a "sort of Market or Fair, for the buying and selling of old raggs and cloths." Not only did this "Great Concourse of loose, idle and disorderly people" hinder the business of honest traders and provide an outlet for stolen goods, but it also placed customers at "great danger of being robbed and pilfered by rogues, thieves and pickpockets, who daily attend at such unlawful meetings." Although the complaints focused on criminality, merchants and shopkeepers may have been more concerned about street sellers drawing customers away from their stores.[24] The promised remedies had limited effect. Two years later, the East India Company complained that the "nusances" had only "continued and increased."[25] This pattern was repeated for decades. Constables would roust traders out after receiving complaints of streets "blocked up with Jews and old clothes." But as soon as the traders were displaced from one side of the street, they were "seen crowding together at the other, and their baggage was spread on the pavement with the greatest speed."[26]

The constables were hindered by a cumbersome legal code that made it difficult to fine transient traders who were skilled at evading penalties. Charles Pearson, the City Solicitor from 1839 until 1862, thought the law "worse than ineffective" in preventing hawking.[27] The street market in Houndsditch crossed police jurisdictions, which made enforcement all the more challenging.[28] The skirmishes between the city and clothing hawkers escalated at the end of the 1830s, when railway construction drove scores of dealers from Rosemary Lane to the already-cluttered areas of Spital-fields and Whitechapel. The laying of the Fenchurch Street line required the eviction of three thousand residents of the East End, many of them from the alleys and courts just north of Rosemary Lane.[29] Rather than eas-ing congestion in the overcrowded East End, frenetic railway construction exacerbated competition for living space as houses and tenements were torn down to make way for viaducts. The construction also had important economic consequences, changing traffic patterns and encouraging "small local traders whose markets collapsed in the rubble" to set up shop else-where in the East End.[30] Added to this internal migration was a swelling population of Irish seasonal and permanent migrants who encroached on marginal street trades that had once been dominated by Jews. There is some evidence that the children of Erin rapidly took over the hawking of nuts and oranges from the children of Aaron. Unsurprisingly, this process involved occasional skirmishes in the streets. Rag Fair seems to have been the first clothing market to succumb to Irish inroads, as migrant families moved into the neighborhood bordering the Thames. While the husbands and sons worked at the docks, the wives and daughters supplemented the family income by collecting and selling old clothes.[31]

This fierce competition between the Irish and the Jews appears to have accelerated the ethnic segmentation of the used-clothing business. Although Irish immigrants came to dominate the down-at-the-heel market for secondhand shoes ("translating," or remodeling, old shoes and boots and then reselling them at markets at Seven Dials and elsewhere), Jews apparently continued to dominate the more capital-intensive business of dealing in old clothes.[32] Nonetheless, observers believed the number of Jewish "old clo'" men had fallen dramatically from the beginning of the century to between five hundred and six hundred by 1850.[33] The popular and prolific journalist George Augustus Sala reflected nostalgically in 1852 that the "old, bearded, gabardined" ragman of his youth (only a decade or two before) was "nearly extinct," replaced by a new breed of "Young Israel" who wore modish "cut-away coats, and chains, and rings" and eschewed a beard for fashionable "curl known as the aggravator."[34] He was probably describing the growing visibility of flashier dealers relative to the humbler collectors. At the same time, other observers speculated that the apparent decline of Jewish hawkers reflected their emigration to the United States, although petty traders would have probably found it difficult to raise the money for a ticket across the Atlantic.[35]

Irish and Jewish clothing traders competed for customers, but both saw the constabulary as a common enemy. In the summer of 1839 the Commissioners of City Sewers declared street sellers in Cutler Street a "public nuisance," threatening to arrest and confiscate the property of anyone caught hawking there.[36] Despite these penalties, dealers continued to flock to the area. The combination of increased competition in the neighborhood, additional pressure from the local authorities, and periodic sweeps by the constabulary appear to have ignited an ethnic turf war. In 1841 these tensions seem to have erupted in Cutler Street, where Irish and Jewish clothing traders allegedly came to blows. According to one account, two hundred constables converged on the scene to restore order. The brawl supplied the Lord Mayor with the ammunition he needed to prohibit old-clothes dealers from operating in and around Cutler Street and to appoint additional officers to enforce the new regulation.[37]

The Marts

Although dealers soon returned to Cutler Street—and the local authorities renewed their efforts to suppress the trade—the Lord Mayor's decision was important for two reasons.[38] First, a coalition of dealers appointed an advocate to appeal the decision on their behalf, an early example of activism by Jewish petty traders. Second, the prospect of greater enforcement spurred at least three sets of entrepreneurs to change the marketing of used clothing. In 1842 they began to acquire property around

The bustling interior of the Clothes Exchange, the largest of the used-clothing marts in the East End. On weekdays the mart primarily served hawkers hoping to find garments that they could repair for resale. On Sundays the mart was given over to petty retail, with space for five hundred sellers to peddle their wares. (Collection of the author)

Houndsditch with the intention of opening clothing markets to house traders driven from the streets. All three may have been inspired by the move elsewhere toward building market halls, well-appointed structures intended to replace raucous street markets. Two religiously observant brothers, Lewis and Henry Isaacs, natives of Liverpool, purchased and leveled eight ramshackle houses abutting Still Alley—a narrow pathway notorious for its brothels, criminals, and poverty—to create an enclosed market that they grandiloquently named the Clothes Exchange.[39] The mart was a speculative venture. Neither man had any direct experience in the clothing business: Henry was a builder by trade, and Lewis was a cabinetmaker.[40] Their chief rivals, Abraham Simmons and Moses Levy, leased land in Cutler Street. The third mart, the Carter Street Exchange, opened in three or four disheveled houses nearby.[41] Together, these three enclosed marts could hold around six thousand customers, and they initiated a process of consolidation in the used-clothing business.[42] Each of them began to act as a clothing bourse, facilitating new levels of specialization and sophistication in the trade.

The Clothes Exchange was the largest of the marts. The Isaacs brothers were not particular about the business conducted on their premises—they provided space to dealers in "anything and everything"—as long as they were paid.[43] Nonetheless, they played an active role in managing the mart. Lewis Isaacs told a parliamentary committee, "I also regulate it; it is my own property, and I am there every day in the week."[44] The proprietors profited by renting space to dealers, charging sixpence to a shilling depending on the size of the stall. The Clothes Exchange had space for five hundred stalls, most of which were little more than a tarpaulin draped on the ground.[45] Although many hawkers sold clothing in the adjacent streets, the mart alone afforded protection from laws against Sunday trading to those who could afford to pay for stalls inside.[46] The Clothes Exchange bustled between nine in the morning and two in the afternoon on Sundays when, by the estimate of its owners, "between 2,000 and 3,000" buyers and sellers haggled over battered hats and tattered jackets.[47] The market was quieter during the rest of the week and closed on Saturdays. (In Houndsditch, the secondhand-clothing trade ground to a halt on the Jewish Sabbath; the mart did open when Jewish holidays fell on weekdays.)[48] The sellers were a motley mix. Ragmen converged on the market from far and wide, bringing with them the castoff clothing they had gathered during the week. Although some of the clothing they carried was picked over and purchased by members of the public, much of it was claimed by dealers and hawkers who eyed it for salvage. Castoff clothing bought by petty dealers and street sellers from ragmen one week would reappear in the market or on the streets, repaired and ready for resale at higher prices.[49]

The Clothes Exchange charged a halfpenny admission fee during the week. We know that in the late 1850s, if not before, the gate was manned by a former prizefighter who collected the coins in a leather purse that dangled from his neck. Despite his intimidating presence, the narrow entrance was choked with patrons "scrambling, and wedging, and pushing, and driving" to get in.[50] On weekdays the mart primarily served hawkers hoping to find garments that they could transform into "suitable and saleable garments, clean and altered" for resale on the streets and "merchant buyers on the look-out for bargains."[51] According to Lewis Isaacs, some of those who bought clothing at the market did so to supplement their regular income, stitching in their spare time to prepare recycled garments for resale.[52] On Sundays the mart was given over to petty retail. Whitechapel and Spitalfields were inundated with bargain hunters. Rather than lose this cost-conscious traffic, the Clothes Exchange did not charge an admission fee.[53]

Elizabeth Aaron, a general dealer who had traded at the exchange for many years, explained that she "never ask[ed] questions" of ragmen who brought her items for purchase. She routinely bought from those she "did not know" and did not think "it necessary to make inquiries" about the provenance of the garments she acquired. To her mind it was "usual in the market to purchase of a person you don't know, and without asking questions." Joseph Phillips, a dealer in old clothes, explained that "everybody is supposed to buy as cheap as they can, without any questions at all."[54] According to another dealer, "strangers" were "constantly in the habit of bringing things to the market for sale, every day, from all parts of the town." He was not acquainted with the people he dealt with "one time in a hundred."[55] Dealers bought and sold as astute speculators, calculating the resale value of the clothing they purchased and often quickly passing it along to other dealers. Elizabeth Aaron described how "during the day the same things will change hands sometimes two or three times." She herself served "many dealers in different parts of the globe" and presumably bought and sold with these diverse markets in mind. Joseph Phillips explained that careful record keeping at the exchange was impractical. If he and his competitors kept invoices, they would "have to take hundreds in a day," because they bought and sold "to a neighbour a minute afterwards."[56]

These unregulated arrangements suited bargain-hunting shoppers but not the constables and magistrates who struggled to police the marts. The speed and ease with which articles passed from hand to hand, with little thought given to their provenance, made it difficult to track stolen goods.[57] The police were right to worry—there is evidence in court records that criminals used the market to launder stolen clothing—yet their fears suggest an inflated sense of concern that reflected contemporary attitudes about criminality.[58] The press shared the perception that Whitechapel and Spitalfields were redoubts of thievery and fencing, an idea that was anything but new.[59] Even those who had a stake in the well-being of the clothing trade admitted that the market was a place of mischief and merrymaking for the criminally inclined. Henry Isaacs believed that there was a "great deal of dishonesty in the market," particularly "common theft" on Sundays. During the week there were cases of pilfering on a daily basis. With such constant traffic he thought it impossible "to ensure strict honesty."[60] The police were granted free access "to come in and ramble" through the Clothes Exchange.[61] They were certainly kept busy: there were "prosecutions without end."[62] Despite the presence of an additional eight to ten police officers in the mart on Sundays, Henry Isaacs believed that they had "no influence at all" on crime.[63] In 1850 his brother claimed to have detected a decline of crime in the mart.[64] However, this is not clearly borne out in court records.

Prim observers of the secondhand market—parliamentarians, policemen, and the press—appear to have been equally discomfited by the novelty of the commerce conducted in Houndsditch. The humble customers who descended to shop and haggle on Sundays were the petty pioneers of a new mode of commercial interaction. This was anonymous commerce transacted between buyers and sellers who gathered from afar to conduct business as if at a clothing bourse. More often than not, "the parties were strangers" to one another. Many of the sellers had no local ties. Lewis Isaacs expressed unease about this mode of business, complaining that the markets attracted "an immense number of strangers down, who ought not to be in that neighborhood, for the express purpose of disposing of goods."[65] He probably feared that the Sunday market in Petticoat Lane was taking business away from familiar storekeepers who were reliable customers at his mart and drawing traffic away from his own premises.[66] We cannot know whether he was merely echoing attitudes that would resonate at a parliamentary inquiry or sharing the views of his audience toward a form of commerce that was far removed from the trusting, sedate, and orderly ideal of the middle class. But his statements, which he recanted three years later, tapped a deep well of ambivalence about the temptations of Victorian consumerism.[67] These same anxieties were famously encapsulated by Christina Rossetti in "Goblin Market," a narrative poem written in 1859 that cautioned against the seduction of consumption. Since hawkers and stall holders were transient, customers rarely developed loyalties to any single seller. Trust and dependability were sacrificed in pursuit of a bargain. Nonetheless, the knowledge that transactions were fleeting and pragmatic planted "great doubt on the minds of a great many purchasers as to the article they get."[68] Traditional storekeepers depended on return traffic and thus needed to maintain a good reputation, but the markets provided no guarantees about the quality of the garments bought and sold.[69] Henry Isaacs, echoing his brother's disquiet, complained that unlike the Sunday markets, traditional shopkeepers "were more particular in their mode of trading" and "traded for a connexion; he gave value for the money he received, expecting to see his customer again; but that is not the case with the Sunday morning trading. They come down in crowds, in shoals, buyers from all quarters and sellers from every quarter; they buy in a crowd, and of course they get the best price they possibly can, not caring as to the value of the article, or either as to the article itself."[70]

Witnesses at parliamentary hearings on Sunday trading shared this discomfort with the mode of commerce conducted by street sellers in London. The witnesses considered the markets to be an insult to proper morality and manners. Robert Taylor, a guardian of the poor in Lambeth, shared these observers' disapproval. He complained of having to fight his way through the "very scum of society" on Sunday mornings on his way to church. This was not a scene appropriate for those with delicate sensibilities. He "would not allow [his] daughters" to wander through a street market even if hell-bent on reaching church on time. Some in the crowds, Taylor believed, took "a pride in insulting" respectable men such as himself.[71] Not only did he and others disapprove of Jews trading on the Christian Sabbath, but they also complained that the noise—a "confusion of tongues"—of Petticoat Lane drowned out the voice of the preacher in a nearby chapel. Taylor feared that the minions of Mammon held the upper hand in Houndsditch on Sundays.[72]

Instead of easing congestion in the streets, as some of the detractors of Whitechapel's and Spitalfield's street markets had hoped, "everything was sold just the same as before" on the pavements outside the marts. Houndsditch cemented its reputation as a vast clothing bazaar. Hawkers continued to "set out stalls or hawk goods in the middle of the street."[73] Now, however, there was a "double sale," as the success of the marts and street markets created a symbiotic and self-perpetuating dynamic that attracted growing numbers of buyers and sellers to the area.[74] On a typical Sunday the streets and alleys between Houndsditch and Petticoat Lane, an area less than a mile in circumference, were packed with an intestiniform intricacy with stalls, shops, and street sellers hawking used clothing. Curbside couturiers displayed their latest collections. In "Harrow-alley, Pitt-street, ... all the neighborhood form[ed] a mart."[75] These catwalks of the underclass catered to poorer shoppers less concerned with what was in vogue than with securing bargains.

The trade bequeathed a rich linguistic legacy. Old clothes, pegged to any upright surface to attract the attention of a passerby, were "wall flowers." A customer whose eye was caught by such a display might ask the stall holder to pluck an item from a towering rack so that it could be inspected more closely. If the stall holder was obliging, he or she would reach up and pass the "hand-me-down" from its perch. With the garment now in hand a keen-eyed customer would look for signs of hasty repair—bootblack that concealed stains, patches that told of rough use by a previous owner— all indications that the garment had been "clobbered" by a "clobberer," whose job it was to knock damaged clothing and boots back into shape for resale.[76] Jackets lined with "shoddy"—recycled wool, used in this case for insulation—would cause no alarm. But clothes patched or manufactured with "shoddy" fabric were sure to break down after only moderate wear. These methods of giving new life to old clothing were held up as evidence of trickery and deceit by clothing dealers, adding fresh color to the popular view that Jewish clothing dealers could not be trusted.[77]

Early on Sunday mornings, when much of the city had yet to stir, raggedy shoppers, the *Jewish Chronicle* reported, could be seen "wending their way from all parts of London towards Houndsditch."[78] Customers came from across the city, some with children in tow. Packs of sailors and navvies walked in from the nearby docks.[79] Others traveled from further afield. In 1850 Lewis Isaacs boasted that some shoppers traveled "a long distance": "I have known them to come from Gravesend, and to make a pleasure trip of it and a purchase trip as well; they come rather shabbily, and they dress themselves for about 4s. or 5s. [shillings], and return, vulgarly speaking, in first style."[80] Some shoppers left home at dawn to reach the market before it closed in the early afternoon, but most preferred a slower start to their Sunday. Although some customers began bargaining with sleepy stall holders as early as seven a.m., the market was at its liveliest an hour before noon. Several observers noted that workmen, generally paid their week's wages late on Saturday evening in pubs and taverns, did "not seem disposed to stir earlier on Sunday morning" after an evening of carousing.[81]

Working men and women made up the majority of the Sunday traffic in Houndsditch. The market filled an important niche for workers from the "mechanic down to the lowest labourer," who had little time in their six-day workweek to shop for clothing.[82] In effect, Sunday became "the great shopping-day of the working class."[83] Given that Sunday-trading laws fined stores that were open on that day, informal markets such as that in Petticoat Lane found an audience eager to shop and able to do so after payday.[84] The area was known for its bargains. A seller with promising merchandise was soon "surrounded by an eager crowd, as if he had the Koh-i-noor [diamond], and was going to part with it dirt cheap."[85] Even if the purchases were small, the scale of turnover was substantial. Lewis Isaacs estimated in 1850 that close to half a million pounds worth of shoes, shirts, handkerchiefs, and other garments were sold by secondhand dealers every year.[86] Several observers estimated that on a typical Sunday the streets around the exchanges were crowded with between ten thousand and twenty thousand visitors—the vast majority being Christians—who descended to shop and haggle.[87]

The Clothes Exchange and street sellers specialized in the retail trade, predominantly supplying local people. In contrast, the nearby mart operated by Simmons and Levy focused on the wholesale trade—naval and military supplies, portions of auction lots, retailers' unsold stock, and unredeemed pledges from pawnbrokers—and sent used garments and fabric further afield. Some of this clothing may have been dispatched to the north of England, where secondhand clothing was in great demand from urban wage workers.[88] According to one observer, this exchange also handled the export of about twelve bales of castoff clothing and fabric each week, mostly to Ireland and Holland but also to the Continent, the United States, and British colonies.[89] By one exaggerated estimate, "half the second hand habiliments of the empire" passed through the two exchanges at some point in their life cycle. The Irish traders who rented rooms close by were part of a cosmopolitan clientele that included buyers from France, Holland, Germany, Greece, Switzerland, and North Africa. One observer noted that each group specialized in a particular segment of the market, one purchasing great coats and police uniforms for export to Ireland, another exporting the scarlet tunics of the British infantry to Holland, and still others purchasing children's clothing and garments from hospitals in bulk.[90]

The Afterlife of Castoffs

The Clothes Exchange and its peers were the center of a vast system. They relied on several different sources of supply. Every weekday, hundreds of collectors trawled through London and brought their catch of castoff clothing to the marts. Although the number of garments each person netted was limited by the sack he or she carried and weariness of his or her feet, collectively they supplied a predictable amount of clothing. Most dealers subsisted off the steady but stale diet sold by these small fry. The arrival of a pawnbroker toting unredeemed pledges or of retailers, wholesalers, and manufacturers selling excess or soiled inventory could set off eddies of excitement in the already-turbulent marketplace. These sellers provided a much-bigger catch, scads of stock that was often easier to repair and more profitable to resell.[91] Although some dealers circumvented this centripetal system, advertising in London newspapers for wardrobes that they offered to collect directly from sellers, the bulk of the secondhand trade appears to have been conducted in the marts.[92]

Clothing was quickly channeled into a distribution system that aggregated, repaired, and then dispersed these items. According to Sala, three types of old clothing were collected and sorted. "First class" clothes were good enough to be "revivered, tricked, polished, teased, re-napped, and sold" in secondhand stores or pawned for as much as they would fetch. "Second class" clothing was exported in "great quantities" to the colonies, Ireland, the "South American Republics," and the United States. "Third class" clothing—"utterly tattered and torn"—was destined for the shredder and eventual refabrication for use in "plate-glass-shops, middlemen, sweaters, cheap clothes, and nasty."[93] This centrifugal system sent garments in bulk to distant markets (or to the pavements outside the marketplace), often to be distributed and sold by members of the sellers' ethnic group. The marts provided important economies of scale. In the absence of a sophisticated alternative distribution system, some manufacturers and wholesalers of new clothing and footwear brought their wares to the market to tap into these distribution channels. Some clothiers visited the market daily to purchase stock. It was not uncommon for storekeepers to display used and new clothing side by side, sometimes without differentiating between the two.[94]

The international dimension of the trade identified by Sala was not new. Walter Harrison reported in 1775 that some storekeepers around Rag Fair exported "great quantities, both of new and secondhand clothes, to foreign parts."[95] Some of these dealers appear to have sold to their kinsmen and other coreligionists overseas. This was almost certainly the case in shipments to Holland, where Ashkenazi Jews dominated the importing and selling of used clothing. From at least the last quarter of the eighteenth century "fishing boats brimful of Jews" crossed the English Channel from Amsterdam to buy damaged textiles and used clothes at auction in London. In turn, Dutch dealers exported fabric, old clothes, and rags eastward. The *smous* (peddler), peddling cloth and castoff clothing, was a common sight in the Dutch countryside. By the middle of the nineteenth century many formerly itinerant hawkers had opened drapery and clothing stores. Some also began to move into the mass manufacture of ready-made clothing. Yet used garments so dominated the Dutch market that the first manufacturers chose to sell their products as though they were secondhand.[96]

Much of the clothing bought by dealers who specialized in export in the early and mid-nineteenth century was destined for Ireland and the United States. The Isaacs brothers boasted that a "great many buyers of clothing and other things from Ireland, from the Continent, from America, and from all other quarters" frequented their mart.[97] Their claim was corroborated by those who visited or traded in the East End.[98] The clothing dealer Elizabeth Aaron was not unusual in describing how she served "many dealers in different parts of the globe."[99] James Ewing Ritchie, a journalist, put it more colorfully, imagining an elaborate romantic fantasy. He anticipated that the ruined boots he saw piled for sale "will be vamped up, and shall dance merrily to accompanying shillalaghs at Donnybrook fair; that resplendent vest, once the delight of Belgravia, in a few weeks will adorn Quashie as he serenades his Mary Blane beneath West Indian moons."[100]

The volume of exports is difficult to quantify. The journalist Henry Mayhew estimated that clothing worth fifteen hundred pounds was exported from London every week.[101] Official trade figures lumped "apparel, slops and negro clothing" together. In the 1830s by far the largest percentage of exported clothes went to the West Indies, followed by the United States. Much of this was probably slops — cheaply stitched new garments — intended for sale to plantation owners to outfit their slaves.

Holland and the German states were the largest purchasers in Europe. Gibraltar imported an unusually large quantity of clothing given its size, which suggests that it may have acted as a secondary distribution center for the eastern Mediterranean.[102] Comments by Sala suggest that the cosmopolitanism of the clothing trade was known to well-traveled Englishmen. He rhetorically asked his readers, "Who has not heard of Gibraltar old clothesmen, or of fights on board the Levant steamers between the Greeks and Jews, on disputed questions, relative to the value of cast-off caftans and burnouses?"[103] As we will see in chapter 2, this international trade had several important consequences for the Jewish economy, seeding Jewish involvement in the clothing trade in the United States and the colonies and providing Jews a point of entry into the manufacturing of new clothing for export.

Although the outlines of this international trade were apparent to some of the more acute observers of Jewish economic life in Whitechapel and Spitalfields, they would likely pass unnoticed by casual visitors overawed by the noise, color, and congestion of the East End. Once sated with the sights and sounds of the Clothes Exchange, our visitors in 1843 would retrace their steps, perhaps thrilled but certainly wearied by a day of urban adventure. Passing through the thinning crowds, their eyes might alight on a name recently made infamous by the *Times* of London, as we will see in chapter 4. At the corner of Aldgate and the Minories, a major intersection, stood the imposing shop of Elias Moses & Son. Here, almost halfway between the Clothes Exchange and the new Fenchurch Street railway terminal, stood the unlikely heir of Houndsditch's used-clothes marts. If its location revealed its roots in the past, its glowing gas lamps and inviting plate-glass windows clearly oriented it toward the future. Here was a glimpse into the future of the clothing trade.

But before we explore the future of Jews and the clothing trade in England, we will cross the Atlantic to survey the scene in America. A visitor to New York City from London in the 1840s, adrift in a great metropolis in the making, might have been comforted by seeing apparently familiar sights. In a place where so much was new and overwhelming, a glimpse of a Jewish rag dealer toting a sack of clothing might have provided assurance that all was not different in America. If our traveler were to follow that clothing collector away from Broadway toward the Five Points slum—a sure indication that the visitor was a brave or foolhardy urban adventurer—he or she would wind up on Chatham Street. After examining stalls and stores seemingly transported to New York City directly from Houndsditch, our visitor might think that for all of the contrasts between America's commercial capital and London, at least at the level of the street trades, the place and role of Jews was the same. How wrong he or she would be.

2

New York City

A Rag-Fair Sort of Place

"New York," wrote James Fenimore Cooper in 1846, was a "Rag-Fair sort of place." By the time he penned these words, the city had secured its position as the mercantile and financial capital of the United States. For all its commercial glories the city, Cooper marveled, had a "hobble-dehoy look" that reminded him of the tatterdemalion clothing mart of London. Despite the ballooning of its population by almost 750 percent since the beginning of the century—New York grew twice as fast as Liverpool and three times the rate of Manchester—sections of the metropolis retained the "country air" of a much-smaller town—and a neglected town at that. Cooper's recurrent complaint in his fiction about "wretched pavements" suggests an annoyance born of stumbles on the rutted roadways of the city. In contrast, the "life, bustle, noise, show and splendor" reminded Cooper's fellow writer Washington Irving of "one of the great European cities (Frankfort for instance) in the time of an annual fair—Here it is a fair almost all the year round." Other travelers, awed by the marble palaces of Broadway and the city's hive-like intensity, may have recalled Rag Fair only when they ventured into the filthy thoroughfares around Chatham Street on the southern edge of the clapboard slums of the Five Points district, where the roadways were crusted with refuse rolled flat by passing wagons and trampled underfoot by pedestrians.[1]

If Petticoat Lane had become synonymous with Jews and the street trade in old clothes in London by the mid-nineteenth century, Chatham Street was its New York counterpart. At first glance, a visitor from London might find the cheap-jack commerce transacted in this thoroughfare little different from that in Houndsditch. Starting in the 1830s, New Yorkers and visitors to the city began to complain about the volubility and vigor of Jewish salesmen who waylaid and wheedled passing pedestrians. Visitors protested that, as in London, passersby reportedly could "hardly walk Chatham-street, New York, without being asked to purchase, or else being taken by the arm, and half-coaxed, half-forced into one of their shops to make a purchase."[2] ("No thank you," Ragged Dick replied politely in a Horatio Alger tale to an invitation from a Chatham Street clothier to examine the clothing in his store, "as the fly said to the spider.")[3] It was no coincidence that complaints about Chatham Street grew at the same time that New York experienced a retailing revolution. Prior to the 1820s, New Yorkers were as likely to purchase goods directly from an importer's ship or an artisan's workshop as from a specialized shop. Now merchants, led by those in the dry-goods trade, competed to create an alluring shopping experience in specialist retail stores. Innovators won only momentary advantage by introducing ornate storefronts, plate-glass display windows, gas lighting, and armies of obsequious shop assistants before they were emulated by their rivals. As this new mode of retailing took hold, the disorderly and overeager "Chatham St manner of receiving a customer" became a cultural counterpoint in middle-class thinking about what constituted a refined shopping experience.[4] For the next decades descriptions of muddy and littered Chatham Street and its dingy storefronts, persistent proprietors, and overhang of flapping frock coats and pantaloons featured in accounts of New York by journalists, travelers, and belletrists. The neighborhood produced equal amounts of fascination and repulsion.[5] Customers and curious onlookers came to shop and goggle week round; one Jewish newspaper disapprovingly reported that commerce in the thoroughfare was not slowed by the Sabbath.[6] Although Baltimore and Philadelphia also had streets tightly packed with Jewish secondhand-clothing dealers, the old clo' dealers of Chatham Street became embedded in the popular imagination. This reputation was exported overseas. In the 1860s and 1870s foreigners in Canton, China, referred to a street lined with old-clothes vendors as the "Chatham Street" of the city.[7]

Not only would Chatham Street have looked familiar to a homesick visitor from London pining for the sights and smells of the East End, but it might also have sounded reassuringly similar. The barkers who competed for the attention of passersby did so with the kind of calls and outsized claims that tripped off the tongues of street sellers in Petticoat Lane. Some even did so in familiar accents. Among the earliest dealers in used clothing in Chatham Street were immigrants from England, including several Jews. There is some evidence that Jewish used-clothing dealers in London seeded the wind for their coreligionists in America. Of the five hundred Jews who lived in New York in 1825, when the city's population was 166,000, only a handful were involved in the clothing business. But all six of the Jewish clothiers in the city whose birthplace was recorded in census returns in 1830 were of English or Dutch origin. A similar pattern was evident in Baltimore, Charleston, New Orleans, Philadelphia, and Syracuse.[8] The immigrants may have acquired a familiarity with the trade in London or Amsterdam. In Mobile, Alabama, for example, Solomon I. Jones, a "Renovator, from London," announced to the readers of the *Register* in October 1830 that he was opening a store to pursue the "business of Dyeing and Scouring of clothing."[9] Other Jews may have benefited from access to shipments of used clothing dispatched by Jewish dealers in London.

In the United States, as in England, there was good reason for immigrants to specialize in the collection and sale of castoff clothing. A would-be secondhand trader required relatively little capital to open a stall or store, and none at all if he chose to begin by scouring the streets for discarded garments. This occupation also accorded with the expectations of the wider society: secondhand dealing was understood to come naturally to Jews. A statement by Michael Coogan, an Irish immigrant, in the *Irish-American* newspaper in 1853 suggests how such notions could play a part in perpetuating niches. Coogan and others assumed that Jews were ill adapted for other work: "What a laudable sight it would be to see a German Jew or a Dutchman mount a ladder with a hod of brick or mortar to a five- or six-story house. . . . No, they follow pursuits more congenial to their taste and capacity. One takes to his bag, basket, and crook, rag-picking and bone-gathering; the other to glazing, peddling, and swopping old clothes."[10] But because of the low barriers to entering the trade, other groups also tried their hand at it. Poverty rather than skill or prior experience made the trade tenable, although it can only have helped to have learned the rudiments of the trade from coethnics. Jews in New York competed with Irish rag dealers and junk sellers, whose stores clustered above Orange Street in Five Points. In Boston, a city that attracted relatively few Jews before the Civil War, the sale of secondhand clothing was dominated by African Americans, who operated a cluster of stores on Brattle Street.[11] In California Jews and Chinese competed, sometimes hotly.[12] For the most part there was plenty of opportunity to go around: the market for used clothing was substantial in the United States before the Civil War. Slops and secondhand clothing—the less salubrious underside of the clothing business—were inexpensive and accessible. Although readymade clothing and other mass-produced goods have often been identified as the agents of a consumer revolution in America, the role of secondhand goods in the expansion of consumption has not been widely recognized.

Even as the exoticism of Chatham Street and its denizens attracted thrill-seeking tourists—not unlike those who ventured into Houndsditch—its storekeepers benefited from a tide of visitors, temporary sojourners, and new residents who settled in the city. Some of the newcomers were on their way to other destinations: 69 percent of all immigrants to the United States in the four decades prior to the Civil War entered the country via New York. Others had left their parents' farms in the countryside in search of work and excitement. New York's population more than doubled between 1820 and 1835, as the opening of the Erie Canal secured its position as the new republic's greatest trading emporium. Over the next decades, railroads, river barges, and increasing numbers of ships—not just sailing ships but also steamships—expanded the reach of its merchants and manufacturers westward and southward. A "winter forest of masts and spars of sailing ships" loomed over South Street on the East River. More than a thousand vessels from 150 foreign ports docked in 1835; three thousand did so fifteen years later. By 1855 the city had more than doubled again in size, and over half of its six hundred thousand residents were immigrants. The population spilled out of lower Manhattan. The *Commercial Advertiser*'s plaint in 1825 that "Greenwich is no longer a country village . . . [and will soon] be known only as a part of the city, and the suburbs will be beyond it" looked both prescient and quaint three decades later, when homes, offices, and shops had swept as far north as Fiftieth Street on the West Side and Thirty-Sixth Street on the East.[13]

In a city overbrimmed with new urban life, there was a small measure of truth in the claim that Chatham Street hucksters targeted gullible greenhorns. Although some Chatham storekeepers who eyed the traffic of transients and travelers may have been unscrupulous, honest money could be made in transforming a newcomer whose duds marked him as different

The archetypal country bumpkin—P. Green from Arcadia, New York—fitted up by a Chatham Street clothier. Even the youngest salesman offers the silver-tongued assurances that the public came to associate with the street and its salesmen. Another salesman accosts passersby from the doorway. (Collection of the author)

into someone who could pass as a New Yorker. Nor were the traders on Chatham Street the only ones who were understood to take a predatory interest in out-of-towners. The stock description of Jewish hucksters cajoling customers into their stores formed part of a larger trope of bumpkins being tricked by weaselly urbanites. "Drummers" employed by wholesale and manufacturing firms were known to comb "boardinghouses, hotels, saloons, and theaters for out-of-town merchants, whom they then endeavored to lead back to their employers' showrooms."[14] Each new arrival who strolled down Chatham Street with dollars in his pocket was a prospective customer. As late at 1860 an observer noted that its clothes dealers were especially attentive to "countrymen, sailors, foreigners, [and] men in California hats."[15] (As we will see in chapter 5, their counterparts in Sydney were also on the lookout for those whose "gait, dress, speech, or complexion" revealed that they came "from the rural districts.")[16]

Like Spitalfields and Aldgate, the bustling neighborhood around Chatham Street was a patchwork of slop sellers, pawnbrokers, hawkers, and secondhand dealers selling to a working-class clientele. The proximity of pawnbrokers to petty retailers was not accidental; these were overlapping and complementary fields. Solomon Solomons, the part owner of a large pawnshop toured by a journalist in 1859, reported an average of 250 transactions a day, with clothing the most common item put up as security. He sold unredeemed pledges at auction.[17] Other pawnbrokers sold unclaimed clothing to dealers or dabbled in the clothing trade themselves by mending, cleaning, and then reselling forfeited garments. As in England, these interrelated occupations became closely associated in the public mind with criminality, particularly the fencing of stolen property and the staging of mock auctions that gulled bidders into purchasing baubles whose value was vastly inflated by the puffery of an auctioneer or by collusion with confederates in the audience.[18] The police also thought that secondhand dealers kept bad company. Officers in the municipal police force created in New York in 1844 were charged with reporting "all suspicious persons, all bawdy houses, receiving shops, pawn brokers' shops, junk shops, secondhand dealers, gaming houses, and all places where idlers, tipplers, gamblers and other disorderly suspicious persons may congregate."[19] In some cases these suspicions were not misplaced.

Just as New York's merchants adapted to the quickening pace of business in the city, so did its criminals adjust to the dynamism of a metropolis in the making. Among the most notorious and entrepreneurial of this new breed of professionals was Fredericka Mandelbaum. "Marm" Mandelbaum arrived in New York with her family from Hesse-Kassel in September 1850, when she was in her early twenties. Beginning as a peddler, she followed the route typical of Jewish immigrants, saving her profits to open a dry-goods store. Her career, however, took an atypical turn when she used the cloak of respectability provided by the store to conceal an increasingly elaborate criminal enterprise that eventually earned her the reputation of being the "Queen of Fences" in New York City.[20]

If some sectors of the public worried that used clothing might be stolen, others harbored a different set of concerns about the uncertain origins of the suits sold in Chatham Street. Recycled garments had long been seen as vectors of pestilence. In New York, a city where cholera killed thousands in 1832 and 1849, such fears were very real, but they extended beyond the medical field to reflect anxieties about social contamination.[21] Much as Petticoat Lane roused scolds in London, commerce in Chatham Street was seen to subvert several emerging middle-class social conventions. In a city of newcomers where clothing might otherwise provide a measure of differentiation between social classes, the garments sold by Chatham Street dealers gave people of modest means access to the fashions of their supposed social superiors. How, some worried, was one to tell who was a respectable member of the city's bourgeoisie when a frayed frock coat repaired to its former glory or recut to reflect modish styles at mean prices could speed a parvenu's progress? In the hands of a skilled tailor, a threadbare suit could be made to look new by cutting and resewing or by the strategic application of bootblack and other tricks of the trade. Along with enabling misrepresentation and deception, Chatham Street clothing dealers were charged with blurring the boundaries between new and old. Some of those who sold cheap ready-made apparel also bought worn garments to refurbish and sell. If homespun clothing was seen to be imbued with republican virtue, creating profits from castoffs may have seemed to subvert Jacksonian ideas about honest labor. Anxious members of the middle class worried not just about promiscuous social movement between classes and the circulation of ill-gotten objects but also about the unrestrained flow of "hordes of beggars—of unlicensed pedlars and hawkers—of prostitutes who nocturnally swarm in some [of] our frequented streets and public walks—and disorderly assemblages of youths" through the city. Such fears were understandable at a time when New York City had gained a reputation for immorality, and its slums were swollen with the poor. Those who sought peace of mind by demanding the imposition of order on a cityscape they perceived to be anomic often grouped clothing dealers and pawnbrokers with those whom they regarded as lawbreakers and troublemakers.[22]

Much as these complaints conformed to a pattern that would be familiar to a visitor from London, the basic conventions of the street trade in castoff clothing were also reassuringly similar. Itinerant collectors bought, begged, and bartered for old garments, sometimes swapping china and glassware for castoff clothing. As in England, few of the clothing collectors were women, but they were relatively well represented among the dealers. Once acquired, clothing was cleaned and "made over, some made smaller, some turned, some changed in form" within the household economy or sold to traders who arranged for its repair and resale. This process was labor intensive, the final product only profitable if stitched and sewn by an unpaid or low-wage workforce of wives, daughters, and impecunious immigrants. One female store owner interviewed by the social reformer Virginia Penny described employing two girls and three men to make worn clothes over for her store. She paid her female employees thirty-one cents a day for twelve hours of work—a rate of pay comparable to that of seamstresses but unfavorable when compared with a variety of other occupations identified by Penny.[23] As in London, this same labor system later became closely identified with the piecework production of new clothing. Repurposed articles—boys' cloth caps and women's shoes made of old coats and pants "so worn in parts as to be unsalable," coats "made of cloaks, bonnets of aprons, &c."—were sold in stores located in poor neighborhoods or at informal markets such as the one near Penn Square, where Philadelphians could see "ranged, on an open space, a large quantity of second-hand clothes, shoes, dresses, &c., for sale."[24] Reconditioned clothes found eager buyers. One storekeeper described the diversity of his clientele—"French, Irish, and negroes"—but noted that "Germans do not like to buy second-hand clothes," a claim that is difficult to corroborate.[25] At least thirty-eight such dealers plied their trade in New York in 1845, and there were a hundred by 1863. The spendthrift former first lady Mary Todd Lincoln attempted to sell her wardrobe to one of these dealers in 1867. Some dealers purchased used clothing for resale in the local market, but others bought it to ship in bales to buyers in the South and West.[26]

The Distinctive Features of Chatham Street—and Houndsditch

When ready to retreat after tiring of fending off the entreaties of agitated salesmen, our traveler from London would likely leave Five Points with the firm impression that Chatham Street was as consequential for Jews in the United States as Petticoat Lane was for those in England. Here, surely, was the center of an ethnic enterprise akin to that found in the East End. The very hustle of the street seemingly offered ample evidence of a way of life transplanted wholesale to the New World. Such a confident conclusion, reached after a brief reconnaissance, was, however, misplaced. The action found on Chatham Street belied a reality very different from that of London. The markets of Houndsditch may have been the root from which sprang future Jewish involvement in the garment industry in England, but Chatham Street offered thinner soil to would-be entrepreneurs with

grand ambitions in the garment industry. In spite of the surface similari-
ties between the raucous clothing markets in Petticoat Lane and Chatham
Street (and Harrison Street in Baltimore, South Street in Philadelphia,
and several other cities), in antebellum America the used-clothing trade
did not acquire the sophistication that it did in England. Jewish clothing
dealers and their gentile peers established a comparatively rudimentary
system of agglomeration and regional distribution before the Civil War;
there were no grand marts to rival the clothing exchanges of London. Why
was this the case?

Several factors worked against the systemization of the used-clothing
trade in mid-nineteenth-century America on the scale seen in London.
Secondhand garments were probably in shorter supply than in England—
a consequence of the influx of immigrant consumers whose needs outstripped their contribution to the pool of available apparel and of relatively
smaller middle and upper classes that parted with proportionately fewer
garments—making the economies of scale achieved by centralization in
England more difficult to attain and less cost-effective than in London. For
a viable trade in used garments ragmen needed ready access to a reliable
supply of quality castoffs that could be purchased cheaply, refurbished,
and sold at a profit. As the historian Michael Zakim has demonstrated,
in the early days of the American republic some citizens were still in the
thrall of homespun cloth and unpretentious clothing stitched at home,
apparel that conjured the self-reliance and frugality of the revolutionary
era. In 1810, for example, as much as two-thirds of the clothing worn by
Americans was stitched at home. This rougher clothing was less likely
to command healthy prices when recycled than the tailored finery that
was discarded by the far-larger upper classes of London society.[27] Dealers
in London benefited from the scale of the metropolitan market, which
supplied collectors with ample stock and buyers aplenty for refurbished
clothing, as well as from the city's strong commercial ties to the provinces,
Europe, the United States, and the colonies. It was no accident that the
markets in Rag Fair and in Houndsditch were close to the Thames and
the docks: bales of clothing could be quickly and cheaply exported or dispatched northward to other domestic destinations. Given the city's acces-
sibility to dealers in England and elsewhere, London became an entrepôt
for secondhand fashions. In contrast, geography worked against the consolidation of the used-clothing trade in the United States before the Civil

War. No single city dominated the trade as London did in England. The distance between cities, the expense of transportation, and strength of local demand militated against the shipment of clothing to a single city for processing.

Jews in America were also less well prepared to create an elaborate recycling system of the sort that functioned in England. By the 1840s Jews in London had dominated the trade in secondhand clothing for close to sixty years, but in the United States the ethnic niche had a much more recent origin. London had long had a large Jewish population—it was between fifteen thousand and twenty thousand strong in 1800—the majority of whom, as part of the city's underclass, engaged in a variety of forms of petty commerce. Over decades, London Jews created an elaborate and efficient system for accumulating, sorting, repairing, and distributing secondhand clothing, and only then did they make the leap to centralizing the trade in marts after encountering considerable pressure from the city constabulary. In New York, by contrast, most members of New York's small Jewish community were merchants and artisans prior to 1820.[28] Rather than build on an existing foundation, as did their peers in England, Jewish immigrants to the United States who gravitated to *shmattes* started afresh in the fringe economy. This difference had implications for the development of Jewish involvement in the clothing trade in both places. Many of the earliest Jewish manufacturers and retailers of new clothing in London were schooled in dealing with rags, castoffs, and slops. The vitality, scale, and sophistication of the secondhand trade in England provided a potentially advantageous platform for people inclined to experiment with new modes of producing and marketing clothing. But in America collecting and reselling used clothing offered comparatively dimmer prospects for advancement within the garment industry.

After our visitor hurried out of clamorous Chatham Street on the way back to his or her lodgings, he or she might have idled awhile among the more peaceful emporia that lined Broadway. Notorious for its noise and the "crush of its traffic"—"carts and omnibuses are daily at a dead-lock for half an hour"—the thoroughfare was becoming the "busiest and most luxuriant retail street in America."[29] Brightly lit stores, filled with imported and domestic cloth and fashionable clothing, may have reminded the visitor of those of New Oxford Street in London. To the eye of the casual observer the clothiers of Broadway betokened the future. Chatham Street, by contrast, seemed redolent of the past. The emporia of Broadway, moreover, seemed to be rendering the haggling of Chatham Street increasingly irrelevant. Broadway's stores sold ever-larger quantities of new clothing at prices tempting for many of those who might otherwise resort to the secondhand market. Given this trend, it would have been easy to assume that within a generation the Jewish rag dealer would be little more than the subject of nostalgia. Why fill one's wardrobe with the leavings of others when manufacturers and retailers had found a way to make inexpensive clothing accessible to the common man? The garment trade in America was seemingly leaving Chatham Street behind. And it seemed to be leaving Jews behind too. Unlike in London, Jews in New York City were not among the prominent clothiers and manufacturers who drove these changes. While the names above dingy storefronts in Chatham Street still revealed the conspicuous presence of Jews, few awnings on Broadway yet bore a Semitic stamp. So who were the early pioneers who remade the garment industry? And if Jews were not among their number, and the secondhand market provided them with a relatively poor springboard into the ready-made business in America, how did they come to later conquer the clothing trade?

New Directions in the Clothing Trade

The fate of the clothing industry in New York was tightly interlaced with that of the city's economy. Manufacturers in Manhattan benefited from their location—the city sat like a fat spider at the center of a dense web of commercial connections and transport routes that crisscrossed the country—but also suffered for it. Local merchants and manufacturers were within reach of the most dynamic consumer market in the nation, but the urban landscape was congested, with its streets clogged with draymen carrying goods from crowded wharves; the scuttle of clerks, messengers, and mechanics hurrying to and from work; and a ceaseless tide of visitors and residents that washed through its thoroughfares. Labor was abundant because of the immigrants who entered the United States via New York, but space and fuel were expensive. Foundries and factories moved to New Jersey and Connecticut. However, some sectors of the economy that depended on armies of low-wage workers but needed little in the way of expensive machinery thrived. The clothing trade was one of a handful of industries best suited to adapting to this challenging environment.[30]

The clothiers whose stores on Broadway might have impressed our traveler from London in the 1830s and 1840s had adopted a new style of doing business that would not have been possible even three decades earlier. In the first years of the nineteenth century, people in search of inexpensive, locally stitched ready-made garments in New York had few options beyond the twelve slop sellers who clustered on Water and Front Streets, close to the wharves that lined the East River. Their wares competed with slops imported from England—"Kersey Pea Jackets," "Fearnought Great Coats," and an assortment of shirts and trousers—regarded as inferior to tailored garments.[31] Men of means might instead choose to frequent a master tailor whose reputation and lengthy apprenticeship served as a guarantee of quality for his made-to-measure work. In truth, a supporting cast of apprentices and journeymen would probably complete much of the stitching and sewing behind the scenes at his workshop. The master paid a preset price for the piecework performed by journeymen, and it was easier to increase profit margins by acquiring cloth on better terms from dry-goods merchants than by negotiating with contractors who were protective of their prerogatives and pay. The quantity of clothing produced by these workshops was limited both by constraints on demand—that is, the size of the market for tailored garments—and by the time it took even a skilled and well-practiced hand to complete a sequence of tasks that began with taking a customer's measurements and ended only when the finished garment fit to satisfaction. Ironically, this regulated system unraveled at the very moment when the cost of fabric declined dramatically and the demand for clothing soared.

With the resumption of European trade at the end of the War of 1812, New York was flush with fabric imported from Europe. Seizing the opportunity to turn this bounty into quick profits, entrepreneurs opened a new kind of clothing store. Zakim has described how many of those who sold inexpensive made-to-measure and ready-made garments were cut from a different cloth than the master tailors who had previously monopolized much of the market. In fact, few of the pioneers of the new mode of production had any experience or expertise as tailors; many of them began their careers as accountants, clerks, and merchants. (Despite an elaborate mythology to the contrary, neither the four Brooks brothers nor their father were master tailors.) They were part of a broader movement of men of commerce out of international trade—which had been rendered riskier by the messy divorce of America from the British Empire—and into manufacturing. Instead of reproducing the system that had protected master tailors and their journeymen, this breed of upstarts, who fashioned themselves as merchant tailors and clothiers, looked to squeeze profit from a new way of organizing labor. In effect, they came to replicate a system of production that had long been used by slop sellers: keep prices low by drawing on a pool of workers—often women and recent immigrants—who were not protected by the regulations that shielded journeymen and apprentices. Instead of relying on the hands of a craftsman to fabricate an entire garment, the pioneers divided the production process into multiple repetitive tasks that could be performed as piecework. The work assigned to traditional tailors could be limited to the most skilled tasks; the rest could be performed by a workforce whose wages were more malleable. Production could be ramped up during periods of higher demand and slackened when orders were slow by tailoring the size of the workforce to the needs of the moment. Skilled work such as cutting continued to command decent wages, while routine tasks could be parsed as piecework into the hands of the poor.

The introduction of protective tariffs on imported clothing in 1816 and 1828 was intended to shore up the position of traditional workshops, but it did more to ensure the well-being of the middle and bottom ends of the market, where American-made slops and ready-mades faced less competition from abroad. This did not reduce the options available to consumers. In New York and other large urban centers, men soon had a dazzling array of choices of where to shop and what to wear. Should they sport a coatee, dress, frock, sack (or half sack), shad, pelto, office, or over-coat? A monkey, baboon, reefing, hip, or round jacket? Should they select pants made of superfine, thick, or thin fabric? (One clothier advertised twenty-two choices for thin pants alone.) In olive, brown, black, blue, drab, or fancy?[32]

This new way of doing business, indifferent to artisanship, interposed a number of new intermediaries between a customer and those who sewed his clothing. Under the old system, a master tailor would perform the twin roles of retailer and craftsman, cutting not just a deal with the customer but also the cloth that would dress him. But now a gulf separated clothiers and their shop assistants from those who assembled the suits that adorned the showroom. Although some retailers retained their own "inside work-shops" so that they could manufacture garments partly or wholly in-house, more contracted with wholesalers to fill their shelves and warehouses with jackets, suits, and trousers made to their specifications. This freed retailers to focus their energies on merchandising. Depending on the size of the order and the scale of the operation, a wholesaler might purchase cloth, arrange credit from the textile mill and the bank, produce a pattern and cut the fabric, set in-house needleworkers sewing, coordinate the work of "outworkers" (those not employed in-house), and market the completed garment. Or a wholesaler might simply divvy up an order among subcon-tractors. These in turn would act as labor brokers, distributing each of the tasks in the production process to needleworkers who either worked alongside one another in a shared temporary space (called garret shops) or turned their homes into work spaces. A manufacturer might begin the process in-house by purchasing and cutting cloth that was then farmed out to different sets of outworkers, who would sew pockets, hem, press, attach buttons, and perform any number of additional steps. The garment would be returned to the workshop for distribution. By 1855 outworkers made up an astonishing 91 percent of the workforce in the industry. This decentralized system favored small producers, who could rapidly respond to new orders and shifts in fashion by mobilizing the appropriate number of workers to complete a contract. Factories—saddled with wage work-ers, costly machinery, and other overhead costs whether or not they had work—were far less nimble and came to specialize in those sections of the trade where demand was more predictable.[33] Those who recruited outworkers, by contrast, needed little in the way of capital to bid for new orders but benefited from possessing a familiarity with and connections to the needleworkers who would take on piecework. In a city swollen with immigrants, this role often fell to those who were able to recruit other members of their ethnic group.[34]

A New Type of Needleworker

This approach to production created not only a new mode of labor but also a new kind of laborer. In 1820 a quarter or fewer of New York's total population of 123,706 were immigrants, but by 1855 more than half of the city's 629,904 residents were foreign-born. These newcomers supplanted native-born workers in the clothing trade. By 1855, 96 percent of all men employed in the industry were foreign-born. More than half were German, and a third were Irish. Over two-thirds of dressmakers and seamstresses were immigrants; here, Irish women predominated. Although other manufacturing trades had equivalent numbers of foreign-born workers, the clothing industry stood out by reason of its size. In 1855 clothing was the single largest industry in the city and, when menswear and dressmaking were combined, the second-largest source of employment behind domestic service. It was also the worst paid of the large industries in the city— cap and hat makers, for example, were paid on average more than twice as much—supplying the native-born with a strong incentive to find alternative employment. The gender shift in the industry was almost as striking. In 1855 there were more than three women working as seamstresses and dressmakers for every four men employed as garment workers. Five years later, women handily outnumbered men. Merchant tailors had strong incentives to use female labor. In 1850 the average seamstress might earn $6.50 a month, while her male counterparts (whose ranks included cutters who could be paid $15 a week) earned an average wage $13.60 a month. Such unequal rates of pay were not atypical: women were often paid a quarter to half the amount paid to men and then were expected to perform much of the dreariest work, such as stitching shirts and underwear. Despite this pay disparity, there was no shortage of women willing to take on this work, because of an absence of alternatives. William Bobo, a visitor from South Carolina, described how "hundreds of girls" lined up to collect bundles of precut pantaloons that they would sew at home. Before being given the consignment, each needed to provide a deposit for the cloth. When the work was done, the pantaloons would need to satisfy the critical eye of an inspector who could withhold payment—all this for the promise of miserly pay.[35]

These changes were neither immediate nor uncontested. Journeymen, whose wages were steadily undercut and whose status was shredded, banded together in the 1820s against the "bastardization" of artisanship— the use of seamstresses and other cost-saving techniques—and for the return of the previous labor regime, in which they had exercised control and enjoyed more esteem. Large strikes in 1835 and 1836 brought only temporary respite, and their gains were erased in 1837 when half of the craft workers in New York lost their jobs as a result of a profound economic panic. When tailors and journeymen struck again in 1850, the old system was but a faded memory.[36] Some master tailors adapted to the new order, stepping back from hands-on participation as artisans to become business-men whose stock in trade happened to be clothing. Foremen and contrac-tors took their place on the cutting-room floor, so that they could focus on competing for contracts, purchasing cloth, sourcing credit, and managing their low-wage workforce. Others retreated to the bespoke market, hop-ing to hold this inner keep of the clothing trade against the barbarians at the gate. Still more struggled to retain their place in the trade, even as they were run ragged by their lower-cost competitors and the value of their skills declined. Without a doubt, the workers recruited to stitch and sew as pieceworkers had it much worse. In the 1830s and 1840s the average real income of these laborers declined, even as the cost of living in New York increased. Some people stitched up to sixteen hours a day when there was work available in order to make ends meet, conscripting their spouses and children to toil beside them. When the short season came to an end— April and October were the busiest months—piecework and incomes dried up. George Foster, a reporter for the *New York Tribune*, borrowed a name for this "accursed system" from Henry Mayhew, a journalist who had popularized it in an exposé of similar conditions in London. They called it "sweating."[37]

The replacement of a regulated tailoring system with sweating ensured not only that garments could be produced more cheaply and in vastly increased volumes with standardized styles but also that those who entered the trade as manufacturers, wholesalers, retailers, and laborers need not have served lengthy apprenticeships. This change had long-term consequences for Jews, removing a large barrier that might have prevented later waves of immigrants from entering the industry en masse. But the restructuring of employment in the ready-made industry did not directly benefit Jews in the short term. Unlike in London, where Jews were already entrenched in the secondhand and slops trades when the garment indus-try underwent its revolution, and therefore were well positioned to enter this new market, in America these changes came when the Jewish popu-lation was still minuscule. There were fewer than three thousand Jews in New York City in 1830; a decade earlier, New York's Jewish population had been smaller than that in Charleston, South Carolina. Because of this accident of timing, Jews in the United States did not follow the more straightforward route into the clothing business that their coreligionists across the Atlantic took. They were not among the pioneers of this new way of stitching and selling clothing in the United States. Instead, as our visitor to Chatham Street and Broadway may have assumed, these innovations in production and marketing looked likely to undermine the tenuous foothold that Jews had established in the secondhand trade by making cheap ready-made clothing ever more competitive with castoffs. As signs of change appeared on Broadway, the rag dealers of Chatham Street seemed stuck in a past that would soon be just a picturesque memory.

New Markets in the South and West

Fortunately for future Jewish clothiers, the dramatic growth in demand for ready-made clothing created far more opportunities than even the best organized of the new breed of New York merchant tailors could exploit. The market for cheap garments grew apace in midcentury, as the size of the American population swelled and the relative cost of clothing declined. Despite the stagnation (and even decline) in the income of people in the clothing industry in the three decades before the Civil War, artisans, laborers, and manufacturing workers in other fields experienced an average increase in real wages of over 1.2 percent a year. These gains, although partially offset by the rise in the cost of living, cumulatively translated into increased purchasing power. As merchant tailors and slop sellers in New York City refined their methods of mass-producing low-cost clothing, they found that their wares were increasingly attractive to cost-conscious customers who might otherwise have preferred to purchase fabric and sew their own apparel or hire a tailor to do so for them. Outside of large cities, the two most important sources of demand came from the South and the Western frontier. In the South plantation owners wanted to outfit their slaves with rough apparel, and townspeople, buoyed by an economy rooted in cotton, filled their wardrobes with imported wares. On the frontier farmers needed stout work clothes such as dungarees as well as finery that could serve as Sunday best.[38] As we will see in the next chapter, these new sources of demand offered opportunity to Jewish immigrants in search of a livelihood, as well as a route into the clothing business.

Far more settlers pushed westward than headed south: in 1790 the Northern and Southern states had roughly equal populations, but by

1860 the Northeast and Midwest were home to 62 percent of the nation's population, and the South to only 35 percent. Nonetheless, the growth of the garment industry in New York City was more closely intertwined with bountiful profits generated by the cotton crop than with money from wheat and corn grown in the Midwest. On the eve of the Civil War the United States earned more from its cotton exports than from all of its other foreign trade combined.[39] This translated into outsized purchasing power for those who profited from the cotton harvest. In 1860 the Mississippi Valley was home to more millionaires than any other region in the United States, and Natchez could boast of more families of great wealth than almost any other town in the South. Agricultural wealth brought an appetite for refinement, as well as the means to afford elegant clothing. The visitor to a market in Lexington, Kentucky, whose listing of the products for sale—"a few cakes of black maple sugar, wrapt up in greasy saddle bags, some cabbage, chewing tobacco, catmint and turnip tops, . . . skinned squirrels cut up into quarters"—probably elicited guffaws from readers of the Eastern newspaper in which it was published in 1810, would have been struck by the wealth and ostentation on display in that city and in others in the South only a handful of decades later. (In response to the howls of outrage that the article generated in Kentucky, the author mischievously replied, "On referring to my notes, taken at the time, I find the word 'halves,' not quarters.")[40] By 1860 Lexington had become an important regional center whose merchants did extensive business with people in Nashville, Knoxville, Chattanooga, Memphis, and Charleston. Bounteous profits from cotton produced store shelves groaning with the finest fabrics from Europe and fashionable clothing fresh from Northern factories. Solicitous New York wholesalers, eager to please their white, Southern customers, now dared not joke of squirrels.

Although the South was outstripped in the size of its population by the Midwest, it grew dramatically in the four decades before the Civil War. Much of this growth occurred along a frontier that galloped westward. Increased cotton yields and lower production costs lured hundreds of thousands of migrants—some willing, many enslaved—to Mississippi, Alabama, Louisiana, and Texas in search of cheap acreage to plant with upland cotton. The population of slave states west of the Appalachians soared from 806,000 in 1810, or 11 percent of the national population, to close to seven million by 1860, or 22 percent of the American total.

Wharves in towns strategically positioned along the Mississippi, Alabama, and Red Rivers sagged under the weight of mountains of cotton awaiting transportation to New Orleans, Mobile, New York, Liverpool, or Le Havre. Memphis grew from a village of forty-six inhabitants in 1820 to more than twenty-two thousand on the eve of the Civil War, making it the seventh-largest city in the South. The same wharves that dispatched bales of cotton to market could be used to unload cloth and clothing bought by farmers flush from the sale of their harvest.[41]

As early as the 1820s, New York merchants were shipping precut apparel southward. Over the next decades, demand for ready-made clothing and cloth consumed a growing share of the city's output. Not all was destined for strutting white Southerners; much of it consisted of presewn outfits and "Negro cottons," often inexpensive calico, denim, twill, fustian, or osnaburg linen that slaves complained was "jus' like needles when it was new." According to one estimate, a typical plantation owner might spend between seven and ten dollars a year to purchase clothing for a field hand, buying one or two suits of cotton clothing for the summer and stockings, jackets, and woolen pants for the winter. Given that the slave population approached four million by 1860, the amount spent on slaves' clothing was not insignificant.[42] In fact, the market was large enough for the Singer Sewing Machine Company to promote a "new, improved sewing machine for the making up of Negro clothing" in the 1850s.[43] The relationships that bound New York's manufacturers and wholesalers together with merchants in the South became increasingly elaborate. Southern retailers and wholesalers began to travel routinely to New York to purchase clothing and dry goods in bulk for the coming season from purveyors in Pearl Street and Broadway. Some stationed or employed agents in the city who placed orders on their behalf. This ensured speedy fulfillment of orders: there could be as little as a two-week delay between the placing of an order and its being dispatched southward. New York's merchants and manufacturers extended credit that was usually good for six months following purchase. This gave Southern storekeepers time to sell the clothing they had ordered and remit their payments before the debt came due.[44]

Once the thrashing paddles of steamboats opened the Mississippi to speedy upriver traffic—the voyage against the current from New Orleans to St. Louis was reduced from three months to roughly two weeks, and the record, set in 1844, was less than four days—a vast hinterland was opened to New York merchants and clothing manufacturers. Many flocked to New Orleans, the gatekeeper of the Mississippi Valley and a city that for a time could claim to be the "commercial emporium of the Midwest." The city sat limpet-like at the end of a steam-navigable waterway roughly seventeen thousand miles long, which funneled trade past the New Orleans levee. On the eve of the Civil War nearly half of the nation's population lived in states that bordered the Mississippi or its tributaries. But New Orleans competed with other commercial centers closer to the Western regions that drew settlers in search of cheap land and fresh opportunity. The combined population of Ohio, Illinois, Indiana, Michigan, Wisconsin, and Iowa reached seven million by 1860, a twenty-eight-fold increase from 1810, "perhaps the highest rate of growth in human history." These Southern and Western customers became ever more important to New York manufacturers as they scrambled to compete with a flood of cheap clothing imported from Europe in exchange for the very cotton, corn, and wheat produced in such abundance in these regions of the United States.[45]

The needs of these new markets created fierce competition among manufacturers and wholesalers of cheap clothing in New York City, relatively few of whom were Jews in the 1830s and 1840s. It was in the West and South, however, that Jews were to establish the initial foothold that enabled them to later conquer the clothing trade in New York. But such a future was barely imaginable at a time when Jewish clothiers were more closely associated with Chatham Street than with Broadway. When Jews did feature in discussions of the clothing trade in the city in the 1830s and 1840s, attention was still focused on their prominence among rag dealers, street sellers, and pawnbrokers. Though their mode of business had largely been left behind by the innovations in the ready-made trade, they remained prominently lodged in the psyches of people who were grappling with dramatic social change. Yet even as the traders of Chatham Street drew the eyes of curious visitors and agitated social commentators, far less conspicuous but far more important seeds were being scattered and taking root along remote roads and byways far from New York City. Fortuitously for the future of American Jewry, dealers in castoff clothing in New York, Baltimore, and Philadelphia who hoped to recruit a corps of collectors encountered another challenge, one that was less familiar to their counterparts in London: competition. Whereas in London the persistence of poverty in the Jewish community ensured that there was no shortage of those who were willing to carry the collector's sack, in America most Jewish immigrants who arrived prior to the Civil War preferred a readily available, alternative source of employment. For Jews in the United States rural peddling, clerking, and country storekeeping provided a surer livelihood than the collection and sale of castoffs. These contrasting routes into the clothing trade had long-term consequences for the unfolding of Jewish involvement in the garment industry on both sides of the Atlantic. The vitality of the secondhand trade pushed Jews in London in one direction, but petty commerce pulled them in another in the United States.

3

Rumpled Foot Soldiers of the Market Revolution

Beneath the drab uniform of shop coat and apron, young John Beauchamp Jones harbored literary ambitions. On days spent shepherding frugal farmers through his store and struggling to extract "hard dollars" from the "well-filled stocking" that served as their purses—"they look at everything, and ask the price of every-thing, at every store in town, before they make up their minds"—he might have dreamed of a life of a writer. If his short career as a storekeeper did not bring him riches, it later repaid him multiple times over. Like many others, his family had moved west, leaving Baltimore for Kentucky in search of opportunity. Failing in business, his father resorted to farming to support his wife and large brood of children. After apprenticing as a law clerk, the younger Jones was lured further west by a brother who had established a store in the "then wilderness of Missouri." He ended up in dull Arrow Rock, a small town in central Missouri that was surrounded by hemp and tobacco fields owned by migrants from Kentucky, Tennessee, and Virginia and tended by their slaves. In 1835, when he was in his midtwenties, he opened one of the first stores in Saline County—named for nearby salt springs—an experience he later mined for several colorful books about frontier life that he published pseudonymously.[1] Wild Western Scenes, published in 1841 was followed eight years later by The Western Merchant, a semiautobiographical narrative framed as a handbook for people seeking advice and direction in an age when it seemed as if all of America was on the move. Jones modestly promised his readers "useful instruction for the Western man of business who makes his purchases in the East," "information for the Eastern man whose customers are in the West," and "hints for those who design emigrating to the West."[2]

The book recounted how a young naïf was toughened by pitfalls and pratfalls into a doughty Western merchant. Such tales often require a villain. In *The Western Merchant*, a nemesis arrived like a "thunder-clap in a clear sky" just as the young merchant, who had secured a monopoly over trade in a small riverine town, was about to purchase a lot to build his store: "There was a stranger among the company at the sale, of whom no one knew anything. He came on foot, but from what place no one knew. He was a young man some-what older than myself, with a prominent nose, high cheek bones, and small sparkling eyes. Before the day was over, I began to suspect he might be one of the venders of 'tender' goods, a cunning Jew, in quest of a location to cheat his neighbors, and spoil the regular trader's business." The merchant's competitor was Moses Tubal, "a *Jew* peddler" and "evil genius" who had peddled his way west from Indiana and now opened a shop beside the merchant's. The new store soon began to draw away business; as the narrator explained, "[Aided by] a very prevalent belief that his goods had cost him less than mine had cost me . . . the very natural inference was that he could afford to undersell me." Jones cursed his competitor for all that was "characteristic of the peddling Jews": "Success is their motto, and they pursue it with indomitable perseverance, and with a total indifference to reputation. They have no credit themselves, and they credit nobody. They trade upon the productions of others (they never create or produce anything), and cheat the Christians with their own wares."[3]

While Jones was wrong in many of his assumptions about Jews, he was right to recognize how transformative the appearance of a Jewish trader could be in a new settlement. The arrival of a Jew often coincided with that of canals, roads, and railways that hitched a town to the regional and national economy. To entrenched commercial rivals who had enjoyed a period protected from competition by the difficulty and expense of transportation, the Jewish peddler or storekeeper was the physical manifestation of the coming of a geographically expansive market that cared little for cozy arrangements between local retailers and producers. Moses Tubal and thousands of others like him who traveled to isolated outposts in the West and South linked remote villages to a larger world of commerce. Individually they struggled to make ends meet in challenging conditions; collectively they created the basis for future Jewish dominance of much of the clothing trade in America.

Peddling in America

The peddling of fancy goods, notions, and clothing to rural customers became a rite of passage for generations of Jewish men in America in the nineteenth century. The first Jewish peddlers were part of a wave of immigration from central Europe that transformed a modest Jewish population in the United States—roughly three thousand strong in 1820 and centered in a handful of cities along the Atlantic seaboard—into a throng of newcomers beckoned westward by the America's glimmering prospects. As historian Hasia Diner has described, peddling acted as an engine of migration and mobility, drawing immigrants across the Atlantic and then westward along the same roads, rivers, and railways that pushed settlers deep into the American interior. By 1850 the United States was home to fifty thousand Jews. A decade later, its Jewish population had more than doubled (and perhaps quadrupled).[4] Some of these immigrants had traveled to America via England, but most only broke their journeys there temporarily. The Jewish community in England, by contrast, grew far more slowly than that in the United States, attracting only a trickle of newcomers. Only a quarter of London's Jews in 1851 had been born abroad. Fewer than ten thousand Jews from the German states settled permanently in Britain during the entire Victorian period, and of those who did, a higher proportion arrived with the resources, education, and experience needed to immediately establish their own businesses.[5] For those immigrants to England who came from urban, middle-class backgrounds, peddling would have been less of a stepping-stone than a considerable step down.

In America peddling offered several inducements to young men with few material resources: independence and self-employment, the prospect of advancement through hard work, and the promise of eventually owning a store. And it was an occupation familiar to many newcomers. Although a large number of Jewish immigrants arrived with training in crafts such as weaving—a consequence of government policies in the German states designed to encourage Jews to forgo trade for what were seen as productive fields—most jettisoned these occupations in favor of commerce. Some had worked as itinerant traders before their departure from Europe; others were born into families in which trading provided a primary source of income. Jews had long traded with gentile farmers in the central European countryside, filling an essential role as purveyors, procurers, and brokers at the fringes of the rural economy. Petty trading in Europe rewarded those who were attuned to the whims of their customers, adept at negotiating social and religious boundaries, and skilled in mediating between local customers and larger markets. Although it would be unfathomable for a peddler in central Europe to encounter a violent Mormon elder enraged by a dispute over chicken eggs, as Louis Jacobs did in San Bernardino, California, in 1856, the basic manner of commerce and need for adroitness was not unfamiliar. (Jacobs knew to resolve the dispute if he wanted to continue to rely on Mormon customers.)[6] Each region of the United States had its own distinct social, legal, and political environment, its own set of racial and ethnic relations, and its own power dynamics that needed to be understood and then carefully navigated.

Familiarity with petty commerce at the margins of the formal economy was only one of the important legacies that many immigrants carried with them to the United States. Jews raised in central Europe shared a second birthright of more recent provenance that proved advantageous on American shores. Central European Jews embraced schooling as a pathway to emancipation at a time when many of their non-Jewish neighbors were ambivalent or indifferent to new modes of public education. Beginning early in the nineteenth century, generations of Jews received at least a basic education in the German states, and sometimes significantly more. The assiduity with which some immigrants later took to creating and joining new social and cultural organizations suggests that many may also have imbibed the German ethos of *bildung*, a philosophy that stressed intellectual self-improvement. Even for those without cultural aspirations, literacy and numeracy proved useful for peddling and essential for more ambitious undertakings such as wholesaling and manufacturing. During the same decades that Jewish immigrants made their way up the economic ladder in America, their kinsmen in central Europe underwent an analogous process of embourgeoisement, supported at least in part by these same factors.[7]

Crucially for Jewish immigrants, peddling was a line of work already well trodden in the United States but seen as an unattractive, dead-end occupation by many native-born workers. Jewish peddlers broadened a trail blazed by young men from New England who had carried mass-produced tinware, clocks, books, and notions to rural customers.[8] Whatever the stigma associated with peddling—the art of selling was regarded with some wariness in Jacksonian America—it provided its practitioners with an immersion course in salesmanship. That was a useful skill to have during a time in which a far broader range of affordable mass-produced items became available. For Jewish immigrants peddling provided a rough schooling in English, an initiation into American customs and preferences, and an introduction to an unfamiliar rural geography and racial order. Perhaps more important, it solidified an ethnic ease with merchandising and mass consumption, an advantageous familiarity with the modern market in an age when some others still viewed it with ingrained suspicion.

Although Jews were not the first to traipse about the American countryside in search of customers, they were prime beneficiaries of the vast expansion of the rural population—in 1850, a miserly 15 percent of Americans lived in communities with twenty-five hundred or more inhabitants—and a dramatic increase in farm productivity in the decades before the Civil War.[9] Many peddlers made their way westward, following in the footsteps of other immigrants who flocked in large numbers to Ohio and other Midwestern states. Nine of ten migrants to this region settled in rural areas during the mid-nineteenth century, precisely the places that were initially poorly served by roads and best suited to peddling.[10] New settlers were soon drawn into the national economy as the centipedal march of railroads, turnpikes, and canals across the country made it possible to carry out commerce at a faster pace, in greater volume, and over longer distances.

Paradoxically, technological change and infrastructural improvement were a boon to people involved in itinerant commerce. Instead of being marginalized by the tentacular growth of railways, turnpikes, and canals, itinerant traders depended on these infrastructural improvements to access inexpensive merchandise. A train or riverboat ticket could extend the reach of a peddler, allowing him or her to use a larger town as a staging area and depositing the traveling trader close to customers who were accessible only by foot or horse. Itinerant traders thrived by bridging the last mile between manufacturers in distant cities and remote customers, carrying packs laden with cheap merchandise from railheads and market towns to frontier and backcountry farmers along poorly maintained rural roads. In the Midwest, where there was no shortage of rutted roadways—one English traveler grumbled in 1851 that "no one can imagine what a bad road is until he has travelled in the Western States of America"—peddlers were aided by a dramatic increase in riverboat traffic. By 1835 the Midwest's waterways were home to more steam vessels by tonnage than plied the Atlantic coast and to almost as many as in the entire British Empire.[11] By and large, fares were relatively inexpensive. One traveler marveled at paying just five dollars for a berth from New Orleans to Cincinnati: "One cannot travel more cheaply anywhere." Joseph Austrian intentionally chose to peddle goods where the roads were bad, calculating that the "difficulty offered people in going to and fro, would be to [his] advantage."[12] Although his customers lived in the outer orbit of the national consumer economy, they were sufficiently attuned to fashion that they chose to buy goods from a passing peddler rather than sew their own. These consumers were kept informed of changing urban tastes by newspapers and by the peddlers themselves. Peddlers relied on many of the features of modern markets—factories to mass-produce cheap fabric, clothing, and notions; wholesalers to supply goods on credit; a legal system to protect their transactions; and customers hungry for consumer goods—but at the same time thrived in the narrow interstices of an incompletely integrated and imperfect economic system. Peddling had a Goldilocks-like relationship with the transportation system. On the one hand, if customers were too remote or the roads impassable, it was difficult for an itinerant trader to earn a reliable income. On the other hand, if customers had easy access to the marketplace, they had little need for a peddler's services. But if customers were both remote and accessible, the conditions were just right for a peddler's progress.

Decennial census returns significantly undercounted the number of itinerant traders. Even so, 10,669 peddlers were listed in 1850 and 16,594 ten years later, two-thirds of whom were based in New York, Pennsylvania, Massachusetts, or Ohio.[13] It is all but impossible to determine how many of these traders were Jewish. Rural peddling encompassed a range of activities and experiences that varied by location, the length of time a peddler had been in the United States, and the resources he (or, less often, she) could muster. Immigrants rarely saw rural peddling as a career, hoping it was the first rung of the ladder of prosperity or at least a source of income when they had few alternative prospects. Many sought to discard the peddler's pack for more sedentary alternatives as quickly as possible. This process often involved several intermediary steps. Over the course of a career, a peddler might swap a basket for a trunk, a trunk for a *pekl* (pack), a *pekl* for a wagon, and a wagon for a store—even then sometimes continuing to peddle. Those who became storekeepers often hired relatives and people from their hometowns to peddle for them, thereby restarting the cycle. This progressive upgrading enabled a peddler to carry a larger quantity of merchandise, to travel further before returning to a depot for resupplying, and to accept heavier items (grain, groceries, and scrap metal) when bartering with customers.[14] Other peddlers defied the stereotype of the weary peddler carrying his pack along lonely rural roads. Instead, they split their time between trading in the countryside and trading in the town. The majority of Jewish peddlers in Columbus, Ohio, appear to have rented stalls at the Central Market, inverting the typical mode of business. Along with using Columbus as a staging point for forays in the city's hinterland, they were also willing to wait for customers to come to them. This may have served as a transitional stage on their journey to owning a store.[15]

Whatever mode of transport peddlers used, they filled their trunks with an assortment of goods that might tickle the fancy of fickle customers. Over a two-month period, one punctilious peddler who visited villages in Ulster County, New York, recorded sales of more than thirty-six items: almanacs, beads, bellows, Bibles, books, breastpins, comforters, gloves, herb oils, painkillers, teaspoons, thimbles, thread, scissors, songbooks, and a variety of other small, mass-produced luxury items.[16] Others added garments and fabric—both of which were relatively light in weight and high in value—or took orders from their customers for ready-made clothing and textiles that would be delivered on a subsequent visit. Simon Halle, a Bavarian-born peddler who kept meticulous records of his travels in Maryland and Pennsylvania between 1848 and 1859, typically marked up the price of the coats, pants, satin, silk, muslin, wool, and linen that he sold by 30–40 percent. Since much of what he and other peddlers carried in their packs were not necessities, their fortunes were tied to the whims and wants of price-sensitive customers. Halle's sales followed a seasonal pattern, rising in the early spring, dropping dramatically in the late summer, and peaking in early winter. During November and December, his busiest period, he averaged a little over $100 profit a month (roughly $3,000 today). As long as the weather remained mild and the roads were not too muddy, this was a good time to peddle. Farmers could be found close to the hearth rather than out in the fields, the winter chill reminded families that their coats were threadbare, and parents made purchases in expectation of Christmas. Given the potential for profits, some storekeepers

The visit of a peddler to a farmstead could conjure excitement among rural customers eager for novelty, company, and the varied wares he toted in his pack or carried in his wagon. This peddler pitched his wares at the women of the household, as did many others. (Collection of the author)

dusted off their packs and temporarily returned to the road in this season. But some years in August—a sweltering month, when Halle must have been grateful for a handful of idle days spent observing Jewish holidays, and his customers worked long hours in the heat bringing in the harvest—he made less than $25 profit. Over the course of a typical year, Halle made around $700 on his sales, a portion of which was expended on food and board.[17]

Peddlers often formed partnerships with other itinerant traders, an arrangement that enabled them to pool their capital, cover more ground, increase their network of business contacts, and raise their trustworthiness in the eyes of the wholesalers on whom they depended for credit. Partnerships were flexible, adding members when expedient and dissolving when they had outlived their usefulness. Some partnerships proved very durable, and many peddlers who did progress to storekeeping, wholesaling, and even manufacturing remained dependent on connections they had formed during their years on the road. Several of the most successful Jewish firms in the wholesaling trade were run by partners who had first formed a bond as peddlers. As a study of another industry in the nineteenth century has demonstrated, firms run by partners who had complementary skills were vastly more likely to succeed than those operated by single proprietors.[18]

Although some peddlers and their partners smoothly followed the four stages identified by a wit—"1st, 'Mit a pack on his back'; 2nd, 'Mit a horse and wagon'; 3rd, 'Mit a store'; 4th, 'Mit a bank or bankrupt'"—more often they experienced missteps, stumbles backward, and long stretches of bone-aching labor and boredom. As the economist Albert Hirschman argued for a different context, such schooling through adversity could be beneficial, particularly when the long-term consequences of temporary setbacks were relatively small. Those who struggled in one location could pick up their packs and try elsewhere. Yet for every plutocrat who began as a plodding peddler, legions more became modest storekeepers.[19]

Southern Byways

The South, home to the Seligman and Lehman brothers when they were still peddlers and country storekeepers, appears to have produced more than its share of peddlers-turned-plutocrats. The region proved particularly fertile for itinerant traders and storekeepers. Given the nature of agriculture across much of the region—islands of intensively cultivated land were surrounded by substantial unimproved tracts—Southern states lagged far behind the Northeast and Midwest in the density of their rural population. Even relatively recently settled states such as Ohio and Illinois enjoyed a nearly two-to-one advantage in rural population density over South Carolina, Georgia, and Virginia. Because productive farms were often dispersed over great distances, the rural roads that linked them attracted less traffic and less infrastructural improvement, raising transportation costs and hindering commercial development. Travelers complained of coaches that ran late, hotels that were "as ill-kept and slovenly as their clientele," and service that was "slipshod and makeshift" in the backcountry.[20] These conditions discouraged farmers from frequently traveling to town to purchase goods and favored those who were willing to carry a small slice of the shop to a farmer's doorstep. Peddlers often did well in areas recently settled by new migrants. In Louisiana and Texas, where a massive wave of newcomers flocked to join in the cotton bonanza, the speed of settlement outpaced the development of a sturdy transportation infrastructure. This was advantageous for those who were able to reach the small farmers whose commodity crop commanded high prices in Mobile and New Orleans. A nimble middleman could benefit twice over, supplying the wants of farmers flush with cotton and then carrying their crop to market and selling it at a profit. Even in such situations, however, conditions were unpredictable. Nineteen-year-old Julius Weis described how, on one expedition in Mississippi, he "happened to strike a very poor piece of country settled mostly by poor white farmers, with very few negroes." His sales were "very small," and he was left "very much discouraged."[21] As Weis's words suggest, peddlers did best where farmers grew commodity crops or generated a marketable surplus. Areas where as much as 30–50 percent of the white population subsisted as hardscrabble farmers, rented out their labor, or lived hand to mouth saw fewer itinerant traders.[22]

Southern consumers possessed an equivocal attitude toward peddlers. On the one hand, a peddler who unpacked his goods before a spellbound audience—a performance that could take an hour, as each item was displayed to best effect—conjured up the excitement of a far-off city. On the other hand, the outsiders with accented English who carried Northern goods across the thresholds of Southern homes exemplified the concerns that generated so much heat and thunder in the South before and after the Civil War. A lone itinerant trader seemingly presented little threat, but together with armies of others, he was seen as the cutting edge of a campaign by Northern manufacturers, merchants, and bankers to drain the South of specie, to undercut local industry, and to render it perpetually dependent. The Yankee peddlers who had preceded Jews as itinerant traders in the region gained a reputation as urban tricksters and dishonest salesmen—for example, selling wooden nutmegs to credulous farmers—tropes easily transferred to Jews.[23] John Beauchamp Jones's slander of Jewish peddlers as dishonest reflected the intermixing of American prejudices against itinerant traders with older ideas about Jewish commercial practices. Partly as a result of this animus toward peddlers, several state legislatures raised licensing fees for peddlers to unaffordable levels in the decades before the Civil War, a measure that was not unpopular with those merchants who feared that peddlers drew away their customers. But new regulations and fees may have been counterproductive, persuading some peddlers to evade paying for permits and others, who were already well established, to expand their operations now that their competition had been thinned for them.[24]

By the Civil War the Jewish peddler was a sufficiently common presence in the South that the eccentric Isachar Zacharie, sent by Abraham Lincoln to New Orleans in 1862 to take the pulse of a restive region, chose to outfit several Jews as itinerant traders and dispatch them to reconnoiter the countryside.[25] These faux peddlers may have had it easier than the transplanted young men who navigated unfamiliar terrain in the 1840s and 1850s. Julius Weis, who joined a cousin in Natchez, Mississippi, in November 1845, was offered the choice of a clerical position or a peddler's pack and chose the latter. Using Natchez as a base, he traveled on horseback, toting a small assortment of goods that he offered first to the wives and daughters of plantation owners and overseers and then, with their consent, to their slaves. (Weis was evidently not disturbed by slavery: during the Civil War he invested some of his savings in the purchase of a "negro man, a fine looking mulatto.")[26] Although the means available to plantation mistresses and their enslaved workers were entirely different, the kinds of articles proffered by a peddler proved popular with both. For white women in the South and elsewhere who sewed and altered their own dresses—but could not afford or had little access to the latest fashionable fabrics—ribbons, lace, buckles, broaches, and other cheap trimmings enabled endless (and relatively inexpensive) refashioning of a wardrobe to reflect changing styles. Stitches could be adjusted and new trimmings added to give a new lease on life to an old dress. Slaves also sought cheap decorative trimmings to enliven the clothing they wore on Sundays. Some wore the castoff clothing of their masters on Sundays, but most who could afford to do so preferred to purchase ready-made or secondhand clothing—some perhaps refurbished on Chatham Street—of their own choosing. Such clothing provided slaves with a rare outlet for public self-expression and contrasted sharply with drab and rough work outfits, compared by one observer to "penitentiary uniforms," imposed by their owners. Garments could act as a form of currency and were a good place to store value in an environment where one could easily be separated from other items.[27] Purchased clothes were a marked improvement on the uncomfortable clothing given to slaves by plantation owners: years after emancipation, Mary Reynolds of Louisiana recalled attending a prayer meeting with other slaves: "We prays for the end of Trib'lation and the end of beatin's and for shoes that fit our feet."[28]

Although Jewish peddlers and storekeepers did sell clothing to slaves, their ubiquity and influence in the South was easily exaggerated. Shrill denunciations by the writer (and later landscape architect) Frederick Law Olmsted and others suggest that the Jewish trader became a convenient foil for expressing a variety of anxieties about slavery and the Southern economy. Olmsted, for example, warned that the "swarm" of Jews that settled across the South—he was not alone in adopting the vocabulary of infestation—engaged in "an unlawful trade with the simple negroes" and encouraged these shackled customers to steal from their masters.[29] This view of Jews as the Judases of slave society who would stop at nothing to earn their shekels may have been reinforced by the prosecution of several Jewish traders for selling goods to slaves on Sunday in direct contravention of Sabbath trading laws.[30] Olmsted's jeremiad echoed contemporary concerns about the corrupting effects of slaves' participation in the consumer economy. Transactions carried on outside the control of planters, some observers feared, would erode the authority of slaveholders.[31] (Although plantation owners were unlikely to have read John Andrew Jackson's narrative of his escape from slavery, the role played by a "Jewish lady" in selling the runaway a cloak would have confirmed their prejudices: she "cheated me," Jackson complained, "and gave me a lady's coat instead of a man's, which however, answered my purposes equally well.")[32] Other observers worried that wily peddlers beguiled purportedly simple-minded slaves with gewgaws; others sneered at slaves for spending their carefully husbanded savings on colorful finery—"strangely cut [and] wonderfully made"—to wear on Sundays.[33] Some of their clothing choices were clearly at odds with the fashion for more sober styles among upper-class Southern whites. Clothing was a marker of class: a white shirt and collar was more difficult to keep clean than was a colored coat, particularly in the sweat-stained South. Plantation records reveal slaves purchasing everything from a "Fine Russian Hat" to silk dresses, oilcloth winter coats, gloves, and other finery, as well as hardier ready-made apparel. Some plantation owners saw signs of rebelliousness in the purchasing habits of slaves, not unlike the missionaries in Australia and South Africa who later divined opposition to white supremacy in the dress of Aborigines and Africans.[34] When plantation owners disapproved of slaves' fashion choices, some slaves were obliged to purchase clothing covertly. Hite, a former slave, recalled later in life, "We sold old clothes to darkies who had mean masters. Dey had to hide 'em though."[35]

Although slaves who lived in urban areas found a variety of ways to generate income, those who lived on small farms or plantations away from towns and cities were further removed from the cash economy. The absence of paper money, however, was a relatively minor obstacle to trade. Betty Brown, born into slavery, recalled of her childhood that her "mamma could hunt good ez any man": "Us'tuh be a coup'la pedluh men come 'round wuth they packs. My mammy'd a'ways have a pile o' hides tuh trade with 'em fer calico prints n' trinkets, n' sech-like, but mos'ly fo' calico prints."[36] Indeed cash transactions presented a variety of challenges to peddlers and purchasers. Paper money was an unreliable store of value; a multitude of notes, issued by banks and private businesses whose stability was uncertain, circulated locally, regionally, and nationally. A peddler willing to accept cash payment would need to negotiate the price of his goods as well as the value attributed to the currency used to purchase them. Paper notes accepted in exchange might prove worthless when the peddler returned to town. Fortunately, many rural and poor urban customers had little access to ready money but plenty of items that an enterprising traveling salesman could resell for profit in another market where such goods were scarcer. Olmsted, traveling in the Mississippi backcountry a few years before the Civil War, met a peddler from Düsseldorf who described this arbitrage in action. "All poor folks," he said,

> dam poor; got no money; oh, no; but I say, dat too bad, I don't like to balk you, my friend; may be so, you got some egg, some fedder, some cheeken, some rag, some sass, or some skin vot you kill. I takes dem dings vot they have, and ven I gets my load I cums to Natchez back and sells dem, always dwo or dree times as much as dey coss me; and den I buys some more goods. Not bad beesnes—no. Oh, dese poor people dey deenk me is von fool ven I buy some dime deir rag vat dey bin vear; dey calls me de ole Dutch [Deutsch, or German] cuss. But dey don't know nottin' vot it is vorth. I deenk dey never see no money; may be so dey geev all de cheeken vot dey been got for a leetle breastpin vot cost me not so much as von beet. Sometime dey all be dam crazy fool; dey know not how do make de count at all. Yees, I makes some money, a heap.[37]

Bernhard Kahn, who peddled laces, ribbons, buttons, and notions from a wagon on the eastern shore of Maryland, accepted furs and feathers as payment. Each week he returned to Baltimore with little money but sacks of pelts and plumes that were sorted and graded by his family in preparation for sale to jobbers.[38] Peddlers were not alone in bartering with their customers; in Springfield, Illinois, dry-goods dealers advertised their willingness to take "all kinds of produce . . . in exchange for goods." An early Jewish retailer in Los Angeles was "virtually forced into the exporting of produce and hides," which he accepted as payment for clothing. A peddler-turned-storekeeper in upstate New York bought from and bartered with peddlers, acquiring snuff, groceries, tin, tea, candlesticks, combs, braid, bread, and cakes to stock his shelves. They formed a regular part of his supply system.[39] In much the same way, Southern storekeepers in the United States and their counterparts in Tasmania exchanged clothing for cotton and wool.[40] Because a clothier who exchanged garments for agricultural commodities would need to convert produce back into cash in order to pay debts owed to suppliers, such transactions carried some risk, but they also held the promise of reselling items at a profit. Money earned from the sale of local produce to Eastern buyers came in handy especially in regions where cash was scarce.

Rather than returning to the depot for resupply with an empty pack or wagon, peddlers carried recyclables that they could trade at a favorable rate of exchange for new stock. Rags formed a central part of the barter economy; demand surged worldwide in the 1850s, outstripping supply and pushing up prices. The collection of rags surpassed that of brass, lead, glass, or any other domestic recyclable. In many households, women collected rags, interacted directly with peddlers, and controlled the spending of "rag money." Rags and old clothing served not only as currency for the peddler and his customers but also as a commodity valued by many of the retailers and wholesalers who supplied the peddler with his merchandise. Linen rags, used by the paper mills of New England, were in particularly high demand. Unable to collect enough domestically, the United States imported ninety-eight million pounds of linen rags in 1850, roughly half from the British Empire. In contrast, the woolen rags collected by peddlers in America were of little value domestically until cotton shortages during the Civil War forced Northern manufacturers to scramble for an alternative fabric to use in mass-producing uniforms and blankets for the Union army. Without a substantial prewar shoddy industry, America exported woolen scraps in bulk to England for reprocessing along with rags from Australia and Europe. There shoddy became a commodity whose price rose and fell like "corn or public securities."[41] In England the shoddy industry grew in tandem with the mass manufacture of menswear; shoddy was mixed with Australian and domestic wool to create cheap cloth that became a staple of the early ready-made clothing industry. At least some of this fabric was exported to the United States for use as blankets and clothing for slaves. Part of the global economy, the shoddy business in Britain was hit hard by the dramatic drop of American demand following the panics of 1837 and 1857.[42] The routine collection of rags and other recyclables ensured that the scrap business too later became part of an emerging Jewish economy.[43]

The Jewish traders who traversed lonely roads in the South and Midwest in search of customers with articles to barter were the rumpled foot soldiers of the market revolution and the vanguard of an expanding ethnic economy. As we will see later, this predilection toward peddling produced a cascade of consequences for Jewish involvement in the garment trade in the United States. Yet even as several historians—most insightfully, Hasia Diner—have rightly recognized the significance of itinerant commerce for Jewish immigrants, a less-well-understood twin occupation provided newcomers to American shores with an equally priceless apprenticeship in the modern ways of doing business. Clerking, no less than peddling, provided Jews with a crucial leg up into the business of selling clothing.

The Clerk's Work

Although the typical male immigrant was more likely to lift a peddler's pack than a ledger book during his first years in America, the early careers of immigrant entrepreneurs often included periods of peddling punctuated by clerking. Stints of clerical work appear in many of the biographies of those who went on to become clothiers and wholesalers. Immigrants often identified peddling as a transformative rite of passage in their memoirs, but time spent behind the counter usually received little more than passing mention.[44] Dreary and routinized bookkeeping and serving customers understandably did not capture the imagination in the same way as pack peddling. Once the aches of peddling were dulled by the curative effects of memory, they could be transformed into marks of pride. Stories of a footsore youth could make economic prosperity later in life seem all the more extraordinary. And toting a pack as part of a stooped fraternity accorded more closely with the American mythology of adventure, self-making, rugged individualism, and pioneering than did totaling figures in a ledger. (Who would voluntarily claim fellowship with Bartleby the scrivener—imagined into being by Herman Melville in 1856—the most famous of America's clerks and perhaps the most dyspeptic?)

Yet memory and popular imagery were at odds with the desirability of clerking prior to the Civil War. Clerical work was highly sought after by many Americans as preparation for a career in business and was financially attractive, especially to younger men. The same was true for Jewish immigrants—what could be better as a stepping-stone to storekeeping?—and particularly so of those who sought to maintain a traditional Jewish lifestyle. Religious observance was far easier for sedentary clerks than for peddlers, whose peregrinations took them far from kosher food and fellow Jews. Abraham Kohn, a recent immigrant from Franconia who arrived in New York in 1842 and failed to find work as a clerk, noted his disappointment in his diary: "Whether I wanted to or not, like all the others I had to pack my bundle on my back and walk out to the countryside."[45]

It was an exciting time to be a clerk. The basic methods of those who peddled in the nineteenth century were little different from the Yankee peddlers of the colonial period, but clerical work underwent dramatic change as the train and the telegraph transformed the way that merchants, manufacturers, and wholesalers conducted business. Railroads and telegraph lines—there were none of the latter in 1844 but twenty-three thousand miles of them by 1852—gave an advantage to businesses able to efficiently access, organize, and respond to information about supply and demand. The historians Michael Zakim and Brian Luskey have presented clerks as the handmaidens of an increasingly sophisticated and specialized economy born in the decades immediately prior to the Civil War.[46] As the scale and speed of commerce increased, those who made and marketed goods came to rely on an ever-growing class of clerks to manage their inventories, balance their books, record their sales, and correspond with suppliers, creditors, and customers. (Isaac Wolfe Bernheim learned when he accepted a job at his uncle's store in Paducah, Kentucky, after a stint of peddling, that a clerk might also be expected to sweep the store

and the pavement outside every day, as well as work long hours as a salesman.)[47] Nationwide there were a little over one hundred thousand clerks
in 1850, making it the sixth-most-common occupation among free men
over fifteen (behind only farmers, laborers, mariners, cordwainers, and
carpenters). The numbers were even more striking in commercial centers:
in Manhattan, clerical work was the third-most-common male occupation,
behind only petty laborers and domestic servants.[48] Ironically, the proliferation of clerical positions in major cities itself generated considerable
new demand for the kinds of inexpensive ready-made clothing offered by
the likes of Elias Moses & Son in London and Brooks Brothers in New
York. A clerk wishing to keep up appearances and emulate the fashions of
urban men of means would be straitjacketed by a meager salary if not for
the cut-price imitations of the latest styles offered by ready-made clothiers. Indeed, the journalist Horace Greeley exulted in 1853 that, because
of declining costs, even the "sober mechanic has his one or two suits of
broadcloth, and, so far as mere clothes go, can make as good a display,
when he chooses, as what are called the upper classes."[49]

Just as the concentration of peddlers varied depending on conditions
in a specific locale, so too did the proportion of the Jewish population
employed as clerks. In Charleston, a port city that had long prospered by
trading cargoes of cotton, rice, and people, just under a third of adult Jewish males identified themselves as merchants in 1850. This category could
include anything from a humble grocer to a shipping tycoon, but in this
case it appears to have most often meant a proprietor of a clothing or dry-
goods store. Collectively these businesses employed a large number of
bookkeepers and salesmen; roughly a quarter of the Jewish men employed
in the city identified themselves as clerks. In contrast, very few Jews supported themselves by peddling, a consequence of the relative prosperity
of the Jewish community, the relatively small percentage of Jews who were
recent immigrants, onerous licensing laws, and brighter prospects for itinerant tradesmen elsewhere. This correlation between mercantile occupations and clerking held true in the Carolinas after the Civil War: 80 percent
of Jewish men whose occupations were recorded on the census during
Reconstruction were either merchants or store clerks.[50] The picture was
reversed in 1850 and 1860 in Boston, a city where Jews, as latecomers and
recent immigrants, struggled to break into a vibrant merchant community.
There a handful of Jewish merchants and clerks were outnumbered many

times over by peddlers. Unsurprisingly, Jewish wholesalers and clothiers in Cincinnati—where the extensive sale of garments to storekeepers and peddlers across the West and South necessitated careful record keeping and voluminous correspondence—employed ink-stained armies of clerical workers. Between 1850 and 1860 Cincinnati's Jewish population grew more than threefold, reaching around ten thousand as the city boomed and becoming for a time the largest Jewish community in the West. Demand for cheap clothing soared in the South, along with cotton prices. As the frontier moved westward and southward, thousands of potential new customers settled in towns and farms accessible to those who distributed clothing sewed in Cincinnati. The brightening horizons of Queen City clothiers were reflected in their need for ever more underlings able to fill orders and tabulate accounts. By 1860 clerks outnumbered peddlers more than two to one, with slightly fewer than one in five Jewish men who worked in the city being employed as clerks and salesmen.[51]

In this age of the account book there was considerable demand for people adept at figuring, filling, and filing orders. Even businesses that were modest in scale employed clerks. But more than offering a stable salary and hope of preferment, clerical work was seen to supply young men—many women also worked behind sales counters, but they rarely enjoyed the status, remuneration, and opportunities for advancement available to their male counterparts—with the kind of practical apprenticeship and connections that might put their feet on the ladder of success. Some clerks may have been willing to put up with low wages in the expectation that their employer would provide encouragement, support, and perhaps even starting capital when the eager employee was ready to strike out on his own. Others may have been reconciled to their work by the fact that their salaries grew faster in real terms than did the wages paid to artisans and common laborers. Even though there was often a substantial gulf between the expectations of clerks and the realities of their dreary work, for many young men who flocked to America's burgeoning cities in the middle decades of the century, clerical work held far more appeal than working on a family farm, laboring in a factory, or carrying a peddler's pack. As with peddling, bookkeepers and salesmen often viewed their occupation as a temporary way station on the path to proprietorship. And for those who were buffeted by financial misfortune, clerical work provided a port of refuge. Ernst Feuchtwanger, described in 1867 by an anonymous agent for a credit-reporting agency in Georgia as the "leading merchant of this part of Macon," resorted to clerking just four years later, to recover from bankruptcy.[52]

Although a period spent peddling undoubtedly supplied immigrants with a rough-and-ready introduction to American capitalism, clerical work offered tutelage in operating a larger and more complex business. The clerk who scribbled and scratched with a quill in an account book became an understudy who learned the successful habits of an entrepreneur (or received an object lesson on how not to run a future business). Repetitive clerical routines trained clerks in fungible skills essential for success in modern commerce—such as record keeping, methodical planning, and the management of inventory, personnel, and credit—and they were doubly important for recent Jewish immigrants. Not only did clerical work provide socialization in the American way of efficiently and effectively conducting business and exposure to compelling role models for entrepreneurial emulation, but it also introduced newcomers to potential future suppliers, distributors, creditors, and partners. Since clerical positions were in great demand, and commercial firms of the first rank typically hired young men of pedigree, young Jewish immigrants with imperfect English (but ample ambition) most often seem to have found employment in firms operated by their kinsmen or coreligionists who came from the same country they did. Those who had already spent time peddling may have had an advantage: because competition for business was intense, firms were eager to hire people who had already formed relationships with potential suppliers and customers elsewhere, hoping that rural storekeepers would prefer to purchase their stock from a familiar source.[53] The willingness of business owners to employ young men who shared their ethnic identity and were often relatives or in-laws reinforced the ethnic character of the dry-goods and clothing trades and ensured that familial ties often overlapped with commercial connections long after former clerks struck out on their own. Given the diversity even within the Jewish immigrant population in the decades before the Civil War—there were Jews from Alsace, Bavaria and other southern German states, Posen, Bohemia, Hungary, and points further east—businesses and the networks that sustained them often took on a subethnic coloration, with Bavarian Jews hiring workers who hailed from their hometowns, and Jews from the Polish provinces of the Russian Empire employing fellow Yiddish speakers. A clerk who demonstrated promise might be asked to join the firm as an agent or partner, or he might be lent money or stock so that he could strike out on his own. The latter option enabled a wholesaler to maintain a continuing commercial relationship with his former clerk and perhaps a financial stake in his success as an investor in his enterprise.

Other clerks consummated their connections with their firms by marrying the daughter or sister of their employer. In this way, lonely and isolated young men created new family networks to replace those they had left behind when they emigrated. Samuel Rosenwald did exactly this in 1857. Rosenwald had been in the United States for three years, about two of which he had spent peddling before he found employment as a clerk in a clothing store owned by the prosperous Hammerslough brothers in Baltimore. His short tenure as a clerk proved more momentous than his time toting a pack: in Baltimore, he met and married his employers' sister Augusta Hammerslough. A month after their wedding, he and his new bride traveled to Peoria, Illinois, to run the brothers' newly opened Baltimore Clothing House. Whether this marriage was arranged or the result of genuine love, it reveals the power of family connections to advance the career of a clerk. After Rosenwald managed outposts in Talladega, Alabama, and Evansville, Indiana, of the growing empire of his brothers-in-law, he settled in Springfield, Illinois. The latter move was made hastily in the early summer of 1861 to seize the opportunities presented by the mustering of soldiers at nearby Camp Butler. The Civil War was good for the Hammersloughs and their brother-in-law: Rosenwald boasted of outfitting at least one locally raised cavalry regiment. In 1868 the Hammersloughs, now involved in manufacturing clothing in New York City, sold their Springfield store to Rosenwald. Samuel Rosenwald's son, Julius, also benefited from working as a clerk for the Hammersloughs. Julius left Springfield at the age of sixteen for a clerical position in his uncles' garment-manufacturing business in New York. After several false starts in the clothing business, he and his brother-in-law purchased Sears, Roebuck & Company in 1895.[54]

Clerking prepared young men for American business in other ways as well. Clerks joined mechanics' institutes, subscribed to library societies, started debating clubs, and purchased manuals, newspapers, and other edifying literature that promised to aid them as they strove toward social and material advancement. Some Jewish clerks participated alongside their non-Jewish counterparts in an array of secular organizations; others created a parallel Jewish world of clubs and societies centered on self-improvement.[55] This enabled members of the Jewish community to participate in the new bourgeois culture, but to do so in a manner that reinforced their Jewish identity and created useful social connections. Yet for the most part, these new social venues included little religious content. The clubs nourished a Jewish secular identity rooted in friendship and fraternity rather than religious tradition. The literary societies provided a space for aspiring members of the bourgeoisie to audition and polish their gentlemanly behavior well away from the critical eye of the Christian public. Substantial numbers of young men were attracted by the opportunity to cultivate the literary tastes and modes of polite behavior regarded as essential for gentlemanly status; perhaps many more were drawn by the camaraderie, fashionable fellowship, and leisure of the clubs. There is some evidence that in larger cities this zeal for joining did not extend to the religious realm. Isaac Mayer Wise complained that in Cincinnati single men—"clerks, bookkeepers, apprentices, [and] journeymen"—remained unaffiliated with the city's synagogues.[56] Peddling could impose limits on the practice of Judaism, as noted earlier. But some of the young Jewish men who found work as clerks also appear to have become more secular, choosing outlets for forming and expressing their identities that were not directly related to religion. Those who clerked in smaller towns seem to have played a more conspicuous role in Jewish life.

The proportion of Jews in commercial occupations, no matter whether they were peddlers, clerks, or proprietors, stood out from the broader American population. Several local studies of Jewish communities in towns and cities across the country between 1850 and 1880 found that anywhere between 70 and 98 percent of Jews in the workforce were engaged in commerce. Significantly smaller numbers earned their living as professionals, artisans, manual laborers, or public officials. This preference for the shop counter, stockroom, and peddler's pack is even more striking when compared with other contemporaneous immigrant streams. Among Irish residents of Savannah, Georgia, in the 1850s, for example, the percentages were reversed: 60 percent had unskilled or semiskilled work, and 16 percent were employed in commerce or professional, managerial, and administrative positions.[57] This, no less than the particular niches in which they clustered, had implications for their future economic trajectory.

Although Jews in England were also well represented in commercial fields, their occupational profile differed from their counterparts in the United States. Clerking and peddling, formative experiences for many Jews in antebellum America, were far-less-common occupations among Jews in England. Many fewer Jewish peddlers marched through the English countryside during the mid-nineteenth century, and, in some measure as a consequence, many fewer established rural stores. Geography was less generous with its favors. A dispersed rural population poorly served by sedentary shopkeepers, as in the United States, was ideal for peddling. But in England a densely settled and comparatively compact countryside speeded the advance of canals, roads, and railways from urban centers and hastened the entrenchment of stores within reach of rural customers. England created an integrated national market well ahead of the United States, where regional differences and the constant tug of westward expansion worked against consolidation and centralization.[58] Perhaps because commercial competition was more intense in England, those Jews who did peddle there were much less likely than their counterparts in America to become storekeepers, and those who did may have operated smaller stores less in need of clerks.[59] The scattering of Jews as peddlers, clerks, and storekeepers across America, and their lighter presence in the English countryside, had long-term economic implications in each setting. In England it limited the penetration by Jews of the clothing retail trade outside of London and a handful of other centers. In America it created an expansive ethnic ecosystem that had momentous implications for their future involvement in the garment industry.

The Ethnic Ecosystem

The ethnic ecosystem was given life by the coursing of money, information, and goods through it. The provision of credit and the promise of mutual benefit fertilized bonds of solidarity, obligation, and reciprocity between Jewish peddlers and the clerks, storekeepers, and wholesalers with whom they did business. For the system to work it had to provide advantages to the wholesalers and manufacturers who sat on top of the food chain as well as the peddlers who grubbed for business at the bottom. Although a peddler might return to the same supplier again and again out of habit and convenience, some storekeepers provided incentives to strengthen these relationships. Those who extended favorable terms to peddlers or supplied goods on credit probably did so in the hope that it would generate repeat business and perhaps even long-term loyalty. A peddler who owed money would need to return to repay his debts and would often replenish his stock when he did so. Some wholesalers recruited and financed peddlers to extend the reach of their businesses and increase the volume of their sales, offering a share of the profit on every article sold. Isaac Bernheim was outfitted at no cost with goods to sell in Wilkes-Barre, Pennsylvania, but he was expected to hand over seven out of every ten cents he earned.[60] Other suppliers fronted goods to recent immigrants on the understanding that the outlay would be recouped with interest; still others paid peddlers a set monthly wage.[61] Storekeepers located in the small towns that served as staging points for peddlers were able to do more than refill a wagon or pack. Their stores were well stocked with a precious cultural currency—gossip, conversation, friendship, and food—dear to lonely peddlers pining for the familiar when far from home. In turn, a peddler who faithfully returned to a supplier regularly could supply reliable information about the shifting preferences of customers and local economic conditions that might, in the aggregate, be beneficial to a storekeeper seeking to judge demand in an otherwise unpredictable market.

The fortunes of Jewish country retailers, almost all of whom had once been peddlers themselves, were intertwined with the agricultural cycle. Storekeepers hoping to stock their shelves with items desirable to farmers and their families needed to order clothing and fabric well in advance. If a harvest was stunted by blight or ruined by rain, a retailer might be stuck with unsold stock that he had ordered months before. Since Jewish traders often sold to customers on credit—despite John Beauchamp Jones's claim to the contrary—with the expectation that debts would be repaid at the end of the season, persistent crop failure could impoverish a farmer and drive a merchant into bankruptcy. Many were doubly vulnerable because of their preference for a business model that was summed up in the advertising motto adopted by a Jewish shopkeeper in Downieville: "A nimble sixpence is better than a slow penny."[62] Traders aimed to turn over their stock quickly, cheaply, and chiefly for cash. Since this approach depended on small profit margins and even smaller margins of error, a forewarning of dark clouds or sunny skies could be crucial. Some sought to reduce their exposure to a single market by opening branch stores elsewhere or occasionally returning to a familiar peddling route to supplement their income.[63]

Retailers enjoyed some financial flexibility in their dealing with their customers because they too could draw on goods supplied on credit. Changes in the American economy worked in their favor. In 1819 an English visitor to Cincinnati was surprised to find that clothing cost about three times as much there as it did in London.[64] Those who bought clothing in the Queen City dressed in garments stitched elsewhere; at the time there was little in the way of local manufacturing. In the first two decades of the nineteenth century storekeepers in towns along the expanding Western frontier bought the latest ready-made fashions from manufacturers in New England, New York, Baltimore, and Philadelphia. From the 1830s onward, however, they could source their stock from suppliers located closer to Midwestern markets. Manufacturers and wholesalers who operated in Cincinnati, Cleveland, St. Louis, Nashville, Pittsburgh, and several other boomtowns were more conveniently positioned to sell to retailers who set up shop in the dust of wagon trains moving westward. Before the extension of rail lines toward the West, clothing sent from Philadelphia to Cincinnati might spend as long as three months in transit and require a payment of a hefty commission to the supplier. In contrast, the paddle steamers that plied the Ohio and Mississippi Rivers could carry merchandise to market more quickly and cheaply. In 1852, at the height of steamboat traffic along the river, eight thousand landings were recorded in Cincinnati; New Orleans was only an eight-day trip downriver. Canals, roads, and railways vastly expanded the hinterland that was accessible to producers and merchants based in the West. This greater relative proximity enabled storekeepers to make more frequent trips to pick out and purchase smaller quantities of stock. Local manufacturers could assess the pulse of the regional market more quickly and adjust their production to match fluctuations in demand. With retailers able to source supplies from either Midwestern factories or their Eastern rivals, competition persuaded some manufacturers and merchants to offer clothing and fabric on more generous terms.[65]

So why, when there were alternative sources of supply available, did Jewish peddlers and retailers often (though certainly not always) do business with Jewish wholesalers? Drawing on an ethnic network for loans bypassed a chaotic banking system that was often reluctant to lend to petty merchants. And, as historian Jeffrey Adler has shown for St. Louis, such connections enabled merchants to tap sources of supply that were often unavailable to their local competitors, and creditors more willing to wait for a return on their investment than firms dealing with strangers. Adler found a direct correlation between the longevity of commercial enterprises and their access to credit and capital. Aside from the benefits derived from accessing willing distributors, those who provided goods on credit to their kinsmen or coreligionists profited from a steady income of interest payments. Since some Jewish businessmen were excluded from alternative sources of credit, they may have felt additional pressure to satisfy their creditors. Contrary to John Beauchamp Jones's claim, Jewish peddlers and storekeepers were sensitive to their reputations, which were the cornerstone of their access to credit.[66]

The risks of informal credit networks were substantial, intertwining the fate of rural shopkeepers with that of their suppliers. Even when market conditions were healthy, a storekeeper still needed to balance sales on credit against the collection of outstanding debts from customers. During times of trouble—for instance, in cases of drought, an investment going sour, or financial panic—the failure of one participant in the lengthy credit chain that connected peddlers, retailers, wholesalers, and manufacturers might create ripples that swamped businesses dependent on the defaulter for repayment of loans or the provision of further credit. The panic of 1857, for example, initiated a wave of bankruptcies in Cincinnati. Jewish-owned firms failed at twice the rate of their competitors as foundering businesses dragged their suppliers and distributors down with them. Jewish merchants in San Francisco, in contrast, who cultivated credit relationships with Eastern cities and Europe, proved more resilient in surviving the fires and jolting downturns of the 1850s. This reflected the unusually labile nature of economic life in that city, the advantages of drawing on distant creditors insulated from localized or regional hazards, and perhaps a greater willingness of absentee partners to bail out a failing business when they had familial ties to its proprietor.[67]

The reliance on ethnic sources of credit also came at a collective cost. Paradoxically, some of the features that made the ethnic ecosystem successful—the overlapping of kinship and commerce, the creation of parallel distribution systems and credit mechanisms, its openness to recent immigrants, and its insularity—simultaneously rendered it suspicious in the eyes of the credit-reporting agencies that emerged in the 1840s and 1850s. These agencies depended on local correspondents to provide subscribers with objective assessments of the creditworthiness of potential customers. They also needed to win over a business culture that was initially skeptical of advancing credit to unknown parties: the *Merchant's Magazine and Review* was not unusual in describing such loans in 1839 as "a species of gambling." At a time when the rates of business failure and transience were high, and enforcement of contracts was challenging, credit reporters offered assurances of trustworthiness to suppliers who advanced goods on credit unsecured by collateral. Often these assessments relied on a subjective evaluation of the character of a businessman, a criterion that worked against groups viewed through the distorting lens of bigotry. When the information available about a business was imperfect, credit reporters relied more heavily on racial and gender stereotypes, and not surprisingly they shared the suspicions and stereotypes of their day. Creoles who operated rural stores in Louisiana, for example, were pegged by some local correspondents as dissolute and dishonest. Historian Rowena Olegario has argued persuasively, however, that the unfavorable language sometimes applied to Jewish businesses in agency reports reflected more than entrenched prejudice.[68] In a nation increasingly marked by movement and change, credit reporters sought evidence of rootedness and stability, judging business owners on their perceived commitment to and integration into the local community. Mobile, young, Jewish newcomers who opened stores in small towns across the country were viewed warily because they had not bought land or because they lived without wives and children. These evaluations, however, were dynamic, changing over time as businesses sunk local roots.

The view that Jews were more transient than most people was not necessarily a sign of hostility, nor was it necessarily inaccurate at a time when many people derived their income from farming. Isaac Leeser, the leading exponent of traditional Judaism in America at the time, also decried footloose Jewish migrants as "roving sojourners, and homeless adventurers" not intent on "making any spot their home"; he was less concerned with credit than with the perceived failure of these newcomers "to contribute a large amount of funds towards erecting suitable houses of worship and engaging ministers."[69] Yet even those whose businesses seemed to thrive were sometimes viewed with distrust by credit reporters. Jewish-owned stores that lined Main Street were highly visible, but the inner workings of the ethnic ecosystem were mystifying to outsiders. Partnerships were usually seen positively by credit agencies because of their potential to pool risk, sustain losses, and incur unlimited liability among all their members. But they were often viewed with suspicion when it came to Jews. Credit reporters struggled to understand the relationships between suppliers and storekeepers, creditors and debtors, partners and employees. They were wary of silent partners who could hide their own history of business failure and legal entanglements behind that of the nominal owner whose name adorned the awning outside the store. The clothing trade, the source of so many Jewish livelihoods, was regarded as a particularly high-risk enterprise. These overlapping suspicions created a self-reinforcing dynamic. When the access of Jewish business owners to alternative sources of money and goods was limited by querulous credit reports, they, whether by choice or necessity, sometimes turned to their coreligionists for assistance. These loans in turn increased outsiders' concerns that Jewish business practices were opaque.[70]

So far from depreciating over time, ethnic ties could gain value as peddlers and storekeepers sought preferential terms with suppliers, wholesalers sought to create a constellation of satellite distributors, and immigrant newcomers sought an entrée into the world of American commerce. As more and more Jews elsewhere moved from peddling and into more sedentary forms of commerce, the ties that bound them together tightened rather than loosened over time. Since bonds between Jewish wholesalers and retailers were mutually beneficial, both parties had an interest in sustaining a sense of solidarity and kinship rooted in a shared origin, cultural affinity, or consanguinity. These connections were useful for trade, and trade was useful for the perpetuation of Jewishness. A storekeeper in rural North Carolina who traveled to Baltimore to purchase his stock would turn to that community when he wanted to find a wife, to recruit a rabbi, or to relocate his business once he had gained a measure of success.[71] Of course, the relationships between peddlers, storekeepers, and wholesalers were not all harmonious or equitable. Ethnic bonds did not guarantee an even distribution of rewards or fair treatment when a peddler's dependence on others made him particularly vulnerable. And ethnic solidarity was complicated. There is some evidence that suggests intraethnic divisions among Jews who peddled and kept shop. In Cincinnati Jews born in the western and southern German states often preferred to lend to other immigrants from those regions rather than to their coreligionists from Posen.[72] The line between competition and cooperation was also easily crossed by a peddler. An itinerant trader could undercut a merchant by stealing away his customers. The storekeepers of Nevada City, for example, could not have been pleased by the temerity of Simon Prager, a peddler who boasted in an advertisement in a local newspaper in 1853 of his ability and willingness to *Sell cheaper Dry and Fancy Goods* than any store keeper"; he explained, "I do not pay any store rent, and I need not put a percentage on my goods, which you . . . have to pay."[73] A shopkeeper in San Francisco was anguished by an effort by his fellow Jewish merchants to raise money to pay officers to arrest unlicensed peddlers: "It cannot be my private interest to favor the trade, as I keep store, and don't like them more than I can help it. . . . [But] if some try to make a living by peddling, is it not better than turning vagrants and thieves?"[74] The editor of a local Jewish newspaper shared this ambivalence: "Our peddlers are no ornaments to our trades, no blessing to our country, but they, after all, are more ornamental to us than our low bar-room, saloon, and dancing cellar keepers; and much more blessing to our country, than our demagogues and politicians."[75]

A New Start in Cincinnati

Jewish peddlers and storekeepers in the Midwest and South drew on credit from Jewish wholesalers for another important reason. Those who chose to stock clothing and dry goods from suppliers in Cincinnati, a city that played an outsized role in Southern and Midwestern commerce in the decades before the Civil War, had little choice but to purchase from Jewish firms. If Jews in New York City struggled to break into the front ranks of a ready-made clothing trade that was dominated by longer-established incumbents in the 1840s and 1850s, their counterparts in Cincinnati encountered an environment far more open to enterprising newcomers. Jews settled in Cincinnati and its hinterland during a propitious period in its development. The city's ascent as a center of trade and industrial production accelerated in the 1830s; by the 1840s, its boosters were proclaiming it, not entirely inaccurately, the "great half-way house from New York and New Orleans." "ENTERPRISE," they announced, "is written on its forehead." The garment trade was only one industry among many in Cincinnati. The city was fattened by the harvest of wheat and hogs raised in the fertile surrounding countryside and profited by producing saddles, plows, engines, carriages, soap, paper, candles, and myriad other articles. The city's foundries, workshops, and factories attracted a population that doubled roughly every decade during its ascendance. And these industrial workers, many of them immigrants, were hungry for the inexpensive fashions sold by local clothiers.[76]

In November and December the streets of Cincinnati were slick with pigs squealing their way to slaughter, earning the city a reputation as "the very Hades of the swinish tribe."[77] Naturally it was not the industry that gave "Porkopolis" its piggish patina that attracted Jews to Cincinnati; rather, it was the city's importance as a distribution center. The city served as a home to Jewish merchants and wholesalers and as a hub for the peddlers and storekeepers they supplied. Many of the former were peddlers and storekeepers made good, men who settled in the city after stints on the road and in the smaller towns in the expansive region that Cincinnati serviced. By 1860 Jewish wholesalers had cornered the clothing trade in Cincinnati; sixty-five of the seventy wholesalers listed in the city directory were owned by Jews. They competed for Midwestern customers with firms operated in the region by New York and Boston merchants, whose entrance into the trade had been very different from their own. Yankee merchants established well-capitalized branches of existing Northeastern firms that sought to colonize Midwestern markets. These were often stocked by clerks and managers who were shuttled in for short stints before returning to Boston and New York. Yankee firms enjoyed superior access to Eastern credit and supplies but had shallower local roots and a sparser distribution network. Both Jewish and Yankee merchants in the Midwest, however, benefited from the weakness of local merchants, who—deprived of steady credit, squeezed for capital, and unable to depend on Eastern connections—failed at a significantly higher rate.[78]

Perhaps to better compete with rivals who shipped clothing to the Midwestern market from the Northeast, several Jewish wholesalers began to experiment with clothing production in the 1840s and 1850s. Much like merchant tailors in New York two decades before, their lack of expertise in needlework was no impediment to manufacturing. Few had acquired a familiarity with the fabrication of garments while peddling in the countryside. Unlike secondhand-clothing dealers in England, who often dabbled in the repair of castoff clothing and the sewing of slops, rural peddlers in America rarely took on this role. Yet as we have seen, changes in way that clothing was made meant that the would-be proprietor of a clothing concern was better served by possessing the strong-arm skills needed to coordinate a workforce than by fingers made dexterous by a long apprenticeship as a tailor. Ironically, if more of them had possessed tailoring skills, their success in Cincinnati may have been less certain. The large numbers of non-Jewish German tailors who settled in Cincinnati and New York were generally reluctant to jettison their craft for a newer mode of clothing production whose methods and wages undercut their own. The new breed of merchant-manufacturers in the Queen City, instead of drawing on their own skilled labor, outsourced production to women—few of whom were Jews—who stitched and sewed from home or in small workshops, or they began to supervise the women directly in small factories.

Jewish merchants in Cincinnati who ventured into manufacturing, moreover, possessed several advantages over other would-be rivals. Those who already dealt in dry goods had fabric at hand and the connections necessary to acquire more. Wholesalers with connections to dry-goods merchants in New York were better able to control one of the largest costs involved in clothing production. Certainly Jewish involvement in the clothing and dry-goods trades grew hand in hand in the city. Several of the leading purveyors of dry goods became manufactures of clothing, and vice versa. This was the case with Jacob Seasongood and Phillip Heidelbach, who invested the savings they had amassed as peddlers in a clothing store at the corner of Front and Sycamore Streets. Two years later they added a dry-goods shop that sold garments at retail rates to passersby and at wholesale prices to peddlers. After adding two siblings to their partnership, they began to manufacture the garments that they sold. They were pioneers of another approach that took hold in Cincinnati in the 1850s. The city's abundant labor and land, inexpensive fuel, and access to substantial markets suited factory production. By 1860 just 6 of the 222 factories and workshops in Cincinnati produced a quarter of the clothing made in the city; Seasongood and Heidelbach's firm generated annual sales of around $1 million (more than $28 million today).[79] Slightly more women still stitched jackets and pants from home than on the production line, but their numbers were in decline.

But by far the most important advantage enjoyed by Jewish wholesalers and manufacturers in Cincinnati with backgrounds in petty commerce came from their ability to efficiently distribute the goods they produced. Given the inadequacies of America's transportation infrastructure and its rudimentary distribution system, one of the largest challenges manufacturers faced was how to get their products into the hands of potential customers. The problem was particularly acute for manufacturers of ready-made clothing, who sought to generate a high volume of sales by putting inexpensive jackets and shirts within the reach of farmers, immigrants, and urban workers. Since competition was intense and margins low, manufacturers able to reliably find buyers for their wares could produce more and thereby generate higher revenues. Manufacturers had a handful of choices when it came to drumming up sales. They could themselves court country storekeepers who traveled to the city to restock for the coming season or employ "drummers" to woo them with "theater tickets, oyster suppers, and entertainment" (the latter sometimes involving chaperoning customers to "places of immoral resort"). They could sell directly to jobbers—middlemen who purchased large consignments that they in turn sold to smaller retailers—avoiding the costly and complicated process of marketing and shipping their own products. Or they could depend on independent wholesalers who took upon themselves the responsibility for marketing and distributing clothing to retailers. Historian Alfred D. Chandler Jr. showed that in the decades before the Civil War, these wholesalers came to play a dominant role in the distribution of goods.[80] It was in this field that Jewish firms enjoyed a competitive advantage. Past experience with itinerant commerce and ties to immigrants who spread like chaff in the wind to establish their own stores and peddling routes in the countryside could be profitably harvested. Jews who graduated from storekeeping to wholesaling had a hard-won familiarity with mass merchandising in rural markets, the challenges of distributing goods over distances, and the importance of credit to traders and their customers. Some who had moved to Cincinnati from the countryside still owned rural stores now run by relatives. Others funneled goods to kinsmen and other immigrants from their hometowns. Those who cultivated their own ethnic distribution networks were rewarded with access to traders who carried their wares to consumers across the Midwest and the South.[81]

Cincinnati's Jewish wholesalers were not alone in seeking to colonize their city's rural hinterland. Merchants in Baltimore, New Orleans, San Francisco, and New York cultivated close commercial connections with peddlers and storekeepers in the towns and villages that orbited these cities. Others in smaller centers such as Rochester and Syracuse in New York, Milwaukee, and Springfield in Illinois did the same on a smaller scale. Some found outlets further afield. Eighty percent of the Jewish merchants in Wilmington, North Carolina, in 1850 were agents of New York and Philadelphia suppliers.[82] But given Cincinnati's importance as a distribution center, and the density of Jewish peddling and storekeeping in the markets served by the city, Jewish wholesalers in the Queen City led the way into manufacturing.

Though Jews had little share in the porcine profits that transformed Cincinnati into a great city, they had little cause for complaint. The early foothold that they established in the distribution of clothing grew apace as the influence of the city and the ambitions of its merchants expanded. And this same foothold provided traction for those who aspired to produce the garments that they sold. These developments in Cincinnati signaled the start of an important transition in Jewish involvement in the clothing trade in America. No longer would Jews be confined to the petty retail of garments in Chatham Street and on rural byways. Now manufacturing and mass distribution were within their reach.

So even as Chatham Street hucksters wowed and repelled writers and tourists in the 1830s and 1840s, the future pattern of the clothing trade was being altered by a scattered army of clerks, peddlers, and petty shopkeepers who labored in obscurity. John Beauchamp Jones, for all his prejudices, was right in recognizing that the Jewish trader was a harbinger of change. From their ranks came the manufacturers and wholesalers of ready-made clothing who later expanded the frontiers of the garment industry. Dusty farm roads and ill-lit back offices were a far better proving ground than antic Chatham Street. This pattern contrasted sharply with that in England, where peddling played a relatively minor role in the Jewish clothing economy during the nineteenth century. Although some peddlers did fill their packs at the clothing exchanges of Houndsditch or carried new fashions into the countryside, they were far less important to the future development of Jewish involvement in the clothing trade in England than were those secondhand dealers who started to experiment with new ways of profiting from the sale of clothing. Some of these dealers began to deploy skills they had learned in repairing, distributing, and selling old garments in the manufacture and retail of new clothing. By the beginning of the 1840s Jews were disproportionately represented among those who sold secondhand clothing in London and who peddled garments, fabric, and other inexpensive wares in the American countryside. In New York City, the leading center of clothing manufacturing in the United States, others had already taken the lead in mass-producing cheap clothing. Outside of Cincinnati, Jews were seemingly stuck in a supporting role in the ready-made trade. In Houndsditch, however, there were already signs of change.

4

Clothing Moses

Ask Londoners in 1843 to name the best known Jew living in their city, and they would probably not answer Moses Montefiore, the much-heralded savior of the Jews of Damascus, but Elias Moses, a clothier whose gas-lit emporiums, parsimonious prices, and aggressive advertising scandalized and delighted the public in equal measure. Elias's renown was not entirely of his own making. In October of that year the *Times* of London recounted the sorry case of the widow Biddell, who, desperate to feed her starving children, pawned a consignment of trousers she had agreed to sew in order to buy "dry bread." Her employer prosecuted her for breach of contract at the Lambeth Street police court. In heart-wrenching detail the *Times* described the misery and meager wages of needleworkers. For each pair of trousers Mrs. Biddell sewed, she was paid seven pence—enough, claimed her employer's foreman, for a "good" living, but in reality barely sufficient to buy a loaf of bread. Saved from prison, she and her children were nonetheless consigned to the poorhouse. The plight of Mrs. Biddell exposed to public view a method of mass-producing menswear that had taken hold in London. The outraged *Times* thought this system transformed a needleworker into "as much a slave as any negro who ever toiled under a cruel taskmaster in the West Indies." During the public outcry stoked by the newspaper, Elias Moses was confused with Henry Moses, a manufacturer of ready-made garments whose firm had employed Mrs. Biddell to sew the trousers. Charles Dickens was guilty of confusing one Moses with the other. He damned Elias—a frequent advertiser in his serialized novels—as the "most impudent dog in the world." The *Times* was not alone in pinning the blame for Mrs. Biddell's plight on Moses and all the children of Israel, "revenging on the poor of a professedly Christian country the

This cartoon, which appeared in *Punch*, accused E. Moses & Son of profiting from the labor of workers paid starvation wages. The accompanying text mockingly suggested that those who bought their clothes from "Moses and Son" would benefit "from frequent changing, for the coats of Moses run very fast to seed, as the flowers of fashion ought to do." (Collection of the author)

wrongs which their fathers sustained at the hands of ours." The episode was kept alive by the publication of the *Song of the Shirt*, a widely reprinted and much-lauded protest poem loosely based on the story of Mrs. Biddell that achieved lasting popularity. Henry Moses wrote to the *Times* to defend the honor of his people (and the rates that he paid his workers), pointing out that only three of the forty wholesale slop sellers and shirt-manufacturing firms in the city were owned by Jews. And Elias Moses, to save his sullied reputation, advertised that he had no commercial connections with Henry Moses, unsurprisingly making no mention of the ties of marriage between the two Moses families.[1]

The two, however, were bound together by much more than their public shaming and a shared surname. In the 1830s, even as many Jews in London continued to earn their keep from the repair and resale of castoff clothing, Elias and Henry Moses and several other secondhand dealers had begun to experiment with the mass manufacturing and retailing of ready-made garments in the hope of profiting from expanding domestic and colonial demand. A variety of factors combined to favor those who had experience in the secondhand trade; Elias and Henry parlayed these advantages into great fortunes, albeit by focusing on different segments of the market. Unlike their counterparts in New York City, they were among the pioneers of mass manufacturing and retailing in England. By the 1840s Elias and Henry enjoyed a position in the ready-made trade in London that no Jew was to enjoy in New York for several decades. Their examples demonstrate two different pathways out of the business of trading in secondhand garments and into that of making and marketing new clothing on a massive scale. How did they, and a handful of others, achieve this feat?

Stitching for Sailors

Elias and Henry Moses were certainly not the first Jews in England to stitch and sell new clothing. Indeed, their enterprises were interlaced with a longer history of making and marketing cheap garments. From the mid-eighteenth century onward small communities of Jewish traders clustered in naval towns, providing the British fleet and its sailors with a variety of services. Dickens remarked snidely that the Portsmouth of his youth was "principally remarkable for mud, Jews and sailors."[2] The services that the traders offered included basic banking—cashing paychecks, distributing money from prizes awarded as bounty to a ship's crew for capturing enemy vessels, and supplying goods on credit to sailors and their wives—as well as stitching and selling slops, the rough apparel worn by seamen.[3] This latter role was important enough for the Jews to eventually enter naval slang. "Jewing" became the naval nickname for tailoring, a "Jewing firm" was a sailor on board ship who stitched for others in his spare time, and a "Jewing bundle" was the bag in which a sailor kept his sewing kit.[4] Jews who sold slops to sailors were at the margins of a much-larger military supply system that played a formative role in the development of the clothing trade. (The navy recognized the need for slops as early as 1623 to "avoyde nasti beastliness by diseases and unwholesome ill smells in every ship.")[5] Business boomed for slop sellers during the first fifteen years of the nineteenth century as the size of the British fleet expanded to frustrate Napoleon's ambitions at sea. In response to surging demand, some slop sellers farmed out production to small workshops that relied heavily on female workers. In doing so, they were little different from the early slop sellers whose premises hugged the wharves along the East River in New York. Naval towns struggled after the Napoleonic Wars as the fleet returned to its smaller peacetime size. Several Jewish slop sellers and navy agents who were left high and dry moved to London, Manchester, and Liverpool. In 1800 there were no Jews among the thirty-five slop sellers listed in London's *Post Office Directory*. But in 1823 *Pigot's London and Provincial New Commercial Directory* listed seventeen Jews, almost all of them doing business near the docks and the "great military clothing depot" in the Tower.[6] Among those who were drawn to the East End to take up slop selling and secondhand dealing was Elias Moses, a trader who had been born in the small market town of Bungay in Suffolk in 1783. By 1831 he was operating a store in Houndsditch in partnership with his eldest son, Isaac.[7]

The knot of slop sellers that formed close to the Thames and the Tower was not unusual in London, a city that still bore the traces of an earlier economic geography. Silk weavers worked their looms in Spitalfields as they had done since the late seventeenth century, and clock makers still strained their eyes in Clerkenwell. Artisans whose workshops were close to one another could share suppliers and distributors, attract skilled workers, develop overlapping areas of expertise, and create economies of scale otherwise unavailable to those who worked alone. The association of a neighborhood with a particular craft and the collective reputation of its artisans drew customers. Dense clusters of craft workers also enabled specialist knowledge to spread, as skills were passed on through apprenticeships and workers quit one business to start a similar one.[8]

Even as some slop sellers continued to service the needs of seamen, others, such as Elias, focused their attention on civilians.[9] In both England and America the market for slops operated parallel to and in tandem with that for castoff clothing. Some clothing dealers, for example, bought surplus uniforms for resale. David Moses, brother of Henry Moses, seems to have begun his career as a member of this modest fraternity, selling clothing and military stores in Petticoat Lane. Jews were particularly active in this market, a role that roused concern during the Crimean War.[10] Other slop sellers in the East End, like their counterparts in Manhattan, made and sold inexpensive socks and underwear, which competed with the "inexpressibles" available in the secondhand market, as well as new shirts that might add a hint of life to a wardrobe filled with the leavings of others. The boundary between old and new was porous. It was not unusual for slop sellers to sell old jackets and coats that they had repaired, nor was it unusual for dealers and storekeepers who specialized in castoffs to hawk new articles of clothing if these were available. And not unlike secondhand dealing, women were well represented in slop selling.[11]

If the lines between slops and secondhand were sometimes murky, the border separating slop sellers from tailors was initially clear and well policed. In London, as in New York, there were few Jews among the tailors and journeymen who dominated the menswear trade in the first two decades of the century. Although they may have resented the methods used by slop sellers to produce inexpensive basic apparel in bulk, tailors in London and New York had a near monopoly on the sale of new suits, jackets, and other items that were hand stitched by masters and journeymen. They resisted the extensive use of cheaper female labor and the subdivision of the production process. Slop selling was seen as unskilled and somewhat disreputable work, particularly since much of the stitching was done by women, and many of the customers could not afford anything better. Tailoring, in contrast, was still the preserve of skilled male artisans who had served lengthy apprenticeships and prided themselves on craftsmanship. Yet familiarity with the methods of mass-production favored by slop sellers proved better suited for the tenor of the times. With the formalization and expansion of state functions, more and more workers required uniforms. The state needed garments to outfit soldiers, policemen, post office workers, hospital patients, civil servants, and convicts aboard hulks anchored in the Thames. Durable and inexpensive slops were also sought after in colonial markets and by plantation owners seeking to cheaply outfit their slaves. A familiarity with standardization and scale positioned slop sellers well for an unexpected shift in the menswear market in the 1830s.[12]

Slops and the City

The same forces that buffeted New York City in the nineteenth century reshaped London's economic geography. With space at a premium and the cost of fuel and rent higher than in towns and cities in the provinces, many of the clusters of craft workers in London—needle makers, weavers, boot makers, and glassblowers, for example—succumbed to competition from factories elsewhere in England that could mass-produce the same items more cheaply. Provincial factories built on a scale unseen in London presented a profound challenge to the capital's primacy. By 1851 there were only seven manufacturing firms in all of London that directly employed over 350 workers. In Manchester parish, in comparison, the *average* cotton factory employed close to that number. Some artisans found that although they could not compete with the industrial assembly line to make their original products, their skills were useful in new industries. Clerkenwell clock makers, for example, turned to making precision scientific instruments.[13] Others remained viable by differentiating their wares from those made by their competitors. Some tailors focused their energies on the bespoke upper end of the market (clustering in Savile Row and Sackville, Maddox, and Conduit Streets, to be close to their clientele in the West End) or introduced innovations in design (vulcanized waterproofs, reversible coats, and other patented features) that kept them one step ahead of the chasing pack. (Who could resist the Hyamonian paletot, an overcoat sold by Hyam Hyam, or the Sternophylon, a heart-shaped chest protector patented by Isaac Moses?)

None of these options proved feasible for the majority of master and journeyman tailors. The ancien régime that underpinned their privileges was already fraying in the 1820s, but it finally succumbed following a series of failed strikes by tailors in the early 1830s that dethroned the powerful London Operative Tailors Union. Instead of patching up their monopoly, the strikers inadvertently further loosened the threads that had ensured their primacy in the menswear trade. Over the next decade, this rent was widened by those who were intent on modernizing the manufacture of clothing. Slop sellers, secondhand dealers, and others who previously had been marginalized by skilled tailors introduced a new mode of production that revolutionized the making of menswear.[14] Within ten years of the strikes, there were at least forty wholesalers in London who manufactured menswear in bulk.[15] A handful of Jewish secondhand dealers—refashioned as manufacturers, merchants, and ready-made retailers—pushed to join the front ranks of the trade. As we have seen, the timing of strikes by tailors and journeymen, and their end results, were almost identical to those in New York.

Even as manufacturers elsewhere moved toward generating efficiencies by directly employing armies of seamstresses who could be put to work in serried ranks, their rivals in London in the 1830s took the same path as those in New York City, dividing the production process into a series of discrete tasks that could be subcontracted to a workforce paid a set rate for each piece that was stitched.[16] The concept of subcontracting was not novel among manufacturers: in the eighteenth century, clock, coach, footwear, and furniture makers in London had delegated parts of the production process to others. But it was new in the making of menswear.[17] Unsurprisingly, it was as unpopular among skilled tailors in London as it was among their peers in New York. After protecting their craft for centuries, these artisans now found their wages and jobs undercut by people they considered to be imposters.

As in New York, manufacturers in London who adopted the system favored by slop sellers—"putting out" shirts, jackets, and pants as "piecework" to a nonunionized and unregulated workforce of needleworkers who stitched from home or labored in small workshops—gained flexibility unavailable to those who employed wage workers and also gained the means to speedily mass-produce garments in a way that created economies of scale. Much as in America, few of these laborers shared the work conditions and rates of pay that unionized tailors had. Rather than interact with workers directly, manufacturers often subcontracted to middlemen, who competed for consignments by a bidding process and were obliged to put up security for the cloth that they received. These middlemen, like their counterparts in New York, were then responsible for recruiting workers and distributing tasks to them, coordinating their work and compensating them for their labor and ensuring that the finished clothing was delivered on time.[18] Some of the early middlemen were bakers, publicans, and coal-shed keepers who took on this role to supplement their regular income. Others provided loans to people at the fringes of the clothing trade to acquire supplies or stood surety. In return for farming work out to needleworkers in their neighborhoods, middlemen and moneylenders might demand exclusive patronage of their bread, beer, or coal.[19] To remain competitive with factories, the putting-out system depended on the abundance of cheap labor. Middlemen in New York City relied heavily on recent immigrants, and their counterparts in London drew on a similar pool of laborers: the wives and daughters of dockworkers who lived in slums close to the Thames, immigrants finding their feet in the metropolis, and others who lived in the densely packed East End neighborhoods of Whitechapel, Spitalfields, Stepney, and Mile End and who needed to find ways to supplement their household income.

Although bespoke tailoring remained a male preserve, women—who would work for less money—came to significantly outnumber men among garment workers in the East End. The labor market in England was much kinder to men than to women, particularly women who were married. Women's range of formal options was narrowed by the withering of handicraft trades and the cultural stigmatization of several categories of work that had previously provided stable employment. For women in London in search of work to supplement their household income, stitching and sewing from home became a popular option or last resort, much as it was for their counterparts in New York. By 1851 roughly a quarter of all employed women in their twenties in London were needleworkers. Yet the scale of migration to cities and the paucity of alternative opportunities for women drove down the wages paid for piecework.

If the gender dynamics of the trade changed quickly, its ethnic composition changed more gradually. From the midcentury onward more and more of those who were recruited to the trade were Jewish. In the 1840s and 1850s Jewish needleworkers were greatly outnumbered by their Christian counterparts, but the Jewish share of the workforce slowly began to rise, in step with the gradual increase in Jewish immigration from eastern Europe. Some Jewish middlemen speeded up this process by delegating work to their more recently arrived relatives and coreligionists.[20] Ultimately this transformed the needle trade into a staple industry of the Jewish working class in England. Whereas once many of the poor and recent immigrants had found employment in the various branches of the used-clothing business, now they became the poorly paid cutters and sewers who underpinned the piecework system. Some immigrants arrived with experience working in artisanal trades, including practical tailoring. Given the deskilling of the garment industry and most immigrants' lack of familiarity with mechanized production, it is unclear, however, whether this background gave them any significant advantage. Jews and others who took in piecework did so out of economic necessity. The work offered people who were floundering a way to keep their heads above water. According to one estimate, at least half of London's Jews—who by 1850 numbered somewhere between twenty and twenty-five thousand and were overwhelmingly native-born—were struggling to eke out a living. Some already worked in marginal occupations such as rag collecting and hawking that were associated with the clothing trade; others were artisans cast adrift in an economic environment where old ways of work had been unmoored by the waves of industrial change.[21]

Resented by master tailors, sweating was hardly more popular among the journalists, novelists, and social reformers on both sides of the Atlantic who believed that piecework replaced the honest labor of tailors with an unregulated and exploitative system that consigned those who stitched from home to desperate poverty. The *Times* exposé of the plight of the widow Biddell was typical of this vein of criticism. Similar articles sometimes took on an openly antisemitic coloration.[22] There is little evidence that Henry Moses's defense of the sweating system in the wake of the scandal earned him any public sympathy. Claiming that low wages were a product of intense competition in the trade (and arguing that he paid better than most), he pointed to his profit margins—5–8 percent and "very frequently" short of even that—as proof of the difficulties in making an honest return from the garment industry.[23] His plea for understanding was drowned out by those whose pleas of poverty were more convincing. It was not difficult for journalists who went looking for evidence of the effects of sweating to find misery in the East End or, for that matter, in the lower wards of Manhattan. Since the profit margins of the middlemen who recruited and paid workers were directly related to the rate they agreed to pay for piecework, they had an incentive to squeeze (or to "sweat," in the parlance of the time) as much labor out of workers for as little money as possible. This compelled needleworkers, who were paid per article rather than per day, to labor for long and grinding hours. Given that there was an abundant supply of men and women in search of work, laborers had very little leverage to negotiate better wages. They also knew that steady work was ephemeral: demand fluctuated with the seasons. An informal poll conducted by London's *Jewish Chronicle* of a hundred families in Bishopsgate and Spitalfields in January 1859 found that only four or five could count on a reliable weekly wage year-round. During the slow season the rest could not secure work "even to make trousers at a penny a pair," a ruinous rate of pay. In the hard months when demand was slack, some workers collected and sold old clothing or made frequent trips to the pawnbroker in order to stave off the icy grip of hunger. Some critics complained that sweating created an insidious cycle that was very difficult to escape. Because the drudgery of repetition trained needleworkers in only a handful of tasks, it was difficult to acquire the proficiency necessary to move upward into other skilled occupations in the production process.[24]

In both London and New York sweating predated the introduction of the kinds of machinery that made factories competitive. The band knife, which cut multiple pieces of cloth at once, and the sewing machine, whose stitching outpaced even the fastest tailor sewing by hand, added speed, scale, and efficiency to the production process. Early versions of these machines were linked to steam-driven shafts. Because manufacturers generated the largest gains in efficiency by running banks of sewing machines simultaneously, steam-driven models were ill suited to London and New York, where space and fuel were more expensive than elsewhere. Hyam "Henry" Hyam, who began as a pawnbroker and secondhand dealer, was one of the first to advertise the availability of machine-made clothing at his Oxford Street store. Presumably sewed at his factory in Colchester, the clothing was produced, Hyam boasted, "at a considerable reduction in price." Other manufacturers opened modern factories in Manchester, Bristol, and Leeds, cities that were closer to the mills that churned out cheap fabric and the coalfields that provided inexpensive fuel. Until the cost of hand- and foot-powered sewing machines began to decline steeply in the 1860s, they remained out of reach of needleworkers who worked from home. This did not, however, spell an early end to clothing manufacturing in London. Even as other cities nipped at its heels, the capital continued to produce more clothes than any other city in the country. The 1861 census counted 34,678 tailoring workers in London—fifteen times more than in Manchester, the city with the next-largest number of needleworkers in England at the time. Over the preceding decade, more men and women had joined the tailoring trade in London than the entire number of tailors and seamstresses who worked in Manchester.[25] How was this possible?

Changes in the East End

Early versions of the sewing machine could stitch the straight seams found in trousers and waistcoats at high speed, but the machines were less proficient at fabricating more complicated garments. Machine-made coats acquired an early reputation for fitting poorly. Factory production was most efficient when orders were large and relatively uncomplicated. Given the capital required to install steam-powered sewing machines, the need to run these as continuously as possible to recoup the initial investment, and the limited skills of much of the workforce, factory owners favored large contracts of the kind placed by state agencies for uniforms. These contracts promised predictability to manufacturers, involved little variation in style, and used fabrics that could be purchased in bulk. Sweatshops, in contrast, were better equipped to satisfy retailers whose profits depended on being responsive to shifting fashions. By placing more frequent smaller orders with manufacturers who were close at hand, clothiers in London and New York could better modulate production to meet their needs and were less likely to be stuck with unwanted stock. Piecework given out in the afternoon could be finished and returned the next day. The utility of the sweatshop in the age of the factory is demonstrated by decisions made by men such as Hyam, who was involved in manufacturing and retailing, to use both methods of production. In addition to the wage workers who labored in his factory, Hyam employed more than a thousand outworkers in London. He and other manufacturers might assign work to the factory or to a sweatshop depending on the season, the scale of the order, and the nature and quality of work required.[26]

Unsurprisingly, in London the sweating system took root most tenaciously in the East End. In 1860 the *Post Office Directory* listed forty-eight clothing-manufacturing firms, the majority of which were in Whitechapel and Spitalfields. Many smaller firms and sweatshops in these neighborhoods went unlisted. Although on the surface East London was an unlikely incubator of innovation, it possessed several advantageous features. East of the Tower, the Thames was flanked by a dense cluster of docks, wharves, and warehouses from which merchandise could be dispatched, cargoes unloaded and distributed, and news received of market conditions abroad. St. Katharine's Docks, immediately below the Tower, were an embarkation point for ships carrying emigrants overseas and a debarkation point for immigrants entering the city. The East End's notorious slums and densely packed courts housed a large, economically marginal population that could be set to work sewing and stitching. The Minories, Spitalfields, and Whitechapel were well served by the new train termini that linked London to the provinces. The stations at Fenchurch Street, London Bridge, and Bishopsgate brought heavy weekday traffic to the area. With no railway yet crossing the City, many passengers planning to continue a journey north or south were forced to travel between stations by foot or carriage. Steady, slow-moving street traffic was good for retailers but also a bonanza for petty criminals plying their quick-fingered trade among travelers who were slowed and distracted by luggage. During 1851 more than three million passengers arrived at or departed from Fenchurch Street station; London Bridge station had over five million passengers. Railways linked London's manufacturers to the provinces, and provincial manufacturers to England's largest market. The already-impressive retailing and manufacturing enterprise established by Hyam expanded dramatically because of his early appreciation of the potential of the railway to carry cloth from London to his warehouse in Colchester, as well as the need for uniforms to outfit railway men. Hyam's retailing empire had grown to eleven establishments by the early 1850s.[27]

Most important, the East End was already home to markets in Rosemary Lane and Houndsditch. The Jewish dealers in used clothing and slop sellers who traded in the streets and alleys of Spitalfields, Whitechapel, and Aldgate competed with one another, but they also formed a mutually beneficial cluster of expertise in clobbering and cheap retailing. These neighborhoods were home to more than half of London's Jews, including pockets of newcomers, with immigrants from Poland clustered in Aldgate and those from Holland in Spitalfields.[28] The practices of putting out and piecework were already employed by slop sellers who stitched shirts and waistcoats and by used-clothing dealers who found it profitable to subcontract to others the cleaning and repairing of worn or damaged clothing for resale. Such methods were transferable to the sewing of more elaborate menswear, particularly since early manufacturers could draw on a pool of local contractors and workers familiar with this system. Given that the stitching was performed by a temporary workforce that paid for its own heat and rent, it required relatively little capital to set oneself up as a manufacturing wholesaler.[29]

Crucially for the likes of Elias Moses, large numbers of Londoners associated these neighborhoods with cheap clothing and were already in the habit of making the trip to Houndsditch to purchase inexpensive outfits. Those who trawled the Clothes Exchange for bargains already encountered an assortment of inexpensive new clothing in the marketplace. Given the sophistication of the exchange as a site of sale and distribution, some manufacturers and retailers of new clothing used it as an outlet to sell slops and other inexpensive new garments that were flawed or remained unsold at the end of the season. Those who sold new clothing at the Exchange competed with a growing number of stores in the area that hoped to siphon shoppers away from the secondhand markets. There was more and more competition for customers. During the first half of the century shops mushroomed in London at a considerably faster pace than the rate of population growth in the city. For many of the same reasons a quarter of New York's clothiers, particularly those who specialized in inexpensive ready-made garments, clustered around Chatham Street and the Bowery during the 1840s.[30] Several observers in London claimed not only that there were more shops but that they were better appointed than before. Stores appealed to shoppers by attractively displaying the goods for sale, adding decorations, and improving their lighting. Dickens described an "epidemic" among dry-goods merchants and clothiers, the primary symptoms of which were "an inordinate love of plate-glass, and a passion for gas-lights and gilding. The disease gradually progressed, and at last attained a fearful height. Quiet, dusty old shops in different parts of town were pulled down: spacious premises with stuccoed fronts and gold letters were erected instead; floors were covered with Turkey carpets; roofs, supported by massive pillars; doors, knocked into windows; a dozen squares of glass into one; one shopman into a dozen." Although there is considerable debate among scholars about whether this constituted a retailing revolution or merely reflected the continuation of preexisting trends, the variety and quantity of goods available to the average Londoner increased. Innovations in production, distribution, and retailing brought items hitherto regarded as unattainable luxuries by much of the population, such as new clothing, into the reach of a broader segment of society. Despite rising wages and the falling cost of clothing, the average working man in London spent more rather than less of his income on clothing as the century wore on. In the 1840s clothing consumed 6 percent of his income; five decades later, the percentage had doubled. This offered a boon to clothiers.[31]

Many of the new stores that sprung up in close proximity to the clothing markets of Houndsditch were opened by those who had worked in the secondhand trade. Rarely were these "slop shops," which sold ready-made clothes, and "show shops," which sold made-to-measure garments that were produced using mass-manufacturing techniques, on the scale of the grand new emporia that lined New Oxford Street. Yet some of these clothiers were careful to differentiate their mode of retailing from the rowdiness of street sellers. Visitors to the market expected to haggle for clothing that varied in quality, but in some of the new stores prices and quality were fixed. Stall holders engaged in effusive patter, but in the stores a customer might encounter more genteel coaxing. (Storekeepers were less reticent when it came to advertising.) The presentation was designed to give consumers confidence in the quality of the jackets, shirts, and pants for sale: mirrors and display cases promised a kind of transparency unavailable in the used-clothing markets, where sellers routinely bluffed and buffed their wares. Over time, retailers of inexpensive ready-mades won an increasing share of the market. Several of the most successful retailers stocked their shelves with coats, jackets, and pants sewn by workers directly in their employ. Instead of placing orders with others, they opened factories and hired outworkers in order to control the entire production process. One hostile observer estimated that these manufacturing retailers had already cornered more than a third of the clothing trade in London by 1850.[32]

Moses of the Minories

Although the birth of the mass ready-made trade proceeded in a roughly similar fashion on both sides of the Atlantic, the role played by Jews in midwifing these changes was very different in each setting. Unlike in New York, a handful of Jews with backgrounds in the trade in castoff clothing and slops were at the cutting edge of this transformation in London. Among the most prominent of these was Elias Moses (Hyam was another; his eldest daughter, Rachel, was married to Isaac Moses, Elias's son). Both Elias and Isaac Moses were early adopters of the sweating system, but their greatest innovations were in retailing. Their ascent was swift. As late as 1831 they were described on insurance policies as modest slop sellers and dealers in clothing with premises in Houndsditch. Within a decade, however, father and son were overseeing a sprawling concern that introduced innovations in production and marketing. Never short of braggadocio, they claimed to be among the first to adopt the piecework and subcontracting system. Relying on rapid turnover to make their low margins profitable, they produced large quantities of cheap clothing that they then sold quickly at their retail store to price-conscious shoppers.[33] They also became masters of salesmanship and self-promotion. Their emporium in the Minories prefigured the architecturally ornate department stores of Paris and New York. The store required the conversion of seven houses into a single large establishment with separate departments

The opulent interior of E. Moses & Son's showroom in the East End, sketched in 1847. Among the first in London to use gas lighting and large plate-glass display windows, the store was mahogany paneled and lit by chandeliers. (Courtesy of the London Metropolitan Archives)

for different kinds of garments. Customers were encouraged to try clothing on.[34] This flagship store was soon followed by several others. By 1849 E. Moses & Son had eight branches in total, including stores in the industrial cities of Bradford and Sheffield. Twelve years later, the company had three stores in London, including one on the upscale New Oxford Street, all of which closed at sunset on the Jewish festivals and Sabbath (reopening Saturday evening and not closing again until midnight).[35] Famous in London—not least because of aggressive advertising—Elias and Isaac Moses gained access to the eyes and purses of the public in a way that that no single Jewish clothing retailer did in the United States until well after the Civil War.

Despite having imposing storefronts on major thoroughfares, Elias and Isaac relied predominantly on the sale of aspirational clothing to consumers from the working class and lower middle class. London's population more than doubled over the first four decades of the nineteenth century, adding close to a million residents to a city that had already been one of the two largest in the world in 1800. The majority of this growth was the result of migration: in 1851 close to half of all Londoners had been born elsewhere.[36] Even as the boundaries of the city pushed outward to accommodate newcomers, tightly packed tenements in older neighborhoods were torn down to make way for railway lines and other urban improvements. The influx of migrants and zealous urban works projects created "incessant internal movement within the metropolitan antheap." It was not just London that was straining at its seams. In 1801 there were five other cities in England had more than fifty thousand residents; half a century later, there were twenty-four.[37]

Unlike in the United States, where the market — abetted by new canals, railways, and turnpikes — expanded fastest by incorporating farmers and new settlers into the nation of consumers, in England demand was primarily driven by a growing industrial and urban workforce. The average male worker in England who could find employment — not always easy for laborers whose prospects might rise and fall with changing seasonal demand and for craftsmen whose trades were undercut by factory production — saw a near doubling of his wages in real terms between 1820 and 1850. Although rents remained high in London and other cities, as already-overcrowded neighborhoods split at the seams for want of space, the declining cost of food — an expense that ate a large share of household budgets among the urban poor and working classes — meant that families on average had more disposable income.[38] In London industrial workers, skilled artisans, commercial clerks, household servants, and shop assistants made up the bulk of the city's working population. By 1851 three hundred thousand Londoners — one-third of the city's workforce — labored in manufacturing, a number greater than the entire population of Manchester. For some of these people purchasing and wearing new clothing provided the means to signal their social aspirations and respectability. For others it was a tangible reward for the fruits of hard labor or a reliable store of value against future misfortune.[39] The mill workers, miners, and factory hands who labored in the soot-stained cities that mushroomed in the Midlands, Lancashire, and the West Riding of Yorkshire were also potential customers for the clothing, furniture, and other goods that were mass-produced in workshops and manufactories whose clattering gears and gyrating wheels became the metronomic chorus of industrialization.

More of these workers could afford to purchase new clothing because of a windfall from far-away fields unscarred by mills and mines. As we saw in chapter 2, large tracts of fertile land in Mississippi, Alabama, and Louisiana were opened to cotton planting in the 1820s and 1830s.[40] Bales of cotton loaded by sweating stevedores in New Orleans and Mobile and bound for the increasingly efficient mills of Lancashire pushed down the price of cotton goods by as much as two-thirds between 1820 and 1845. Abundant cheap fabric persuaded some manufacturers of inexpensive clothing to shift from wool and linen to cotton, savings they could pass on to price-sensitive customers who might otherwise not be able to afford ready-made clothing.[41] Clothiers such as Elias Moses who courted this market were assisted not only by a decline in the cost of cloth but also by a change in cut. For much of the eighteenth century the wardrobes of men who kept abreast of the latest styles were dominated by clothing whose ornamentation and palette would make a peacock proud. But nineteenth-century fashions tended to be more sober in color and simpler in cut, and these styles were considerably easier to reproduce in bulk.[42]

E. Moses & Son boasted in its advertising of its ability to mass-produce knockoffs of the latest tailored styles at rock-bottom prices. Unlike the master tailors who promised style-setting sartorial elegance hand stitched to fit their aristocratic customers, Elias and Isaac Moses promised to reproduce these fashions at a fraction of the price. The capital's dandies might not willingly be caught dead in cheap ready-made fashions of the kind hawked by Elias Moses, but if contemporary advertisements are to be believed, they were happy to outfit their servants in mass-produced livery. The firm was careful, however, to suggest in its advertisements that it attracted a clientele that included members of London's upper crust. Although it is unclear how many doeskin shooting coats and riding habits of superfine quality it really sold, by including these items in its brochures, the firm implied that there was nothing déclassé about purchasing ready-made clothing or being measured for a suit that would be made to order in a sweatshop. In fact, by invoking the patronage of the elite, Elias and Isaac may have flattered commercial clerks, mechanics, and artisans into thinking that their suits and coats would elevate their social standing or at least enable them to emulate the fashions of their supposed superiors. (Not to be outdone, Samuel Hyam boasted of the "Scottish, Italian, British, Neapolitan, Swedish, Austrian, Parisian, Aquatic, American, Hibernian, Spanish, Hungarian, Polish, Canadian, Tyrolese, Hanoverian, Bohemian, Grecian, School and Cricketing Clothes . . . of great cheapness" for sale in his stores.)[43] For customers with unlimited aspirations but limited means, Elias and Isaac provided additional encouragement to shop at their stores. Suits could be bought on an annual contract, obliging the customer to exchange the original suit for a new outfit a year after purchase. This particular stratagem, a forerunner of the lease system, allowed the firm to profit both from the sale of the new garment and from the resale of the worn suit on the secondhand market, as well as ensuring repeat custom. Although E. Moses & Son left the public trappings of the old-clothing trade behind, at least a portion of the business remained in a symbiotic relationship with it.[44]

Father and son also grasped the potential of mass marketing, particularly the new advertising techniques facilitated by inexpensive printing. Although fashion advertisements already featured prominently in journals in the late eighteenth century, the steam-powered press put inexpensive serials, newspapers, and books into the hands of a much-larger reading public.[45] According to one (almost certainly inflated) contemporary estimate, the firm spent £10,000 a year on advertising, making it the second-largest advertiser in England, behind only Holloway's patent medicines.[46] The firm was far from bashful, printing a barrage of brochures, most featuring the direst doggerel, which may have been written by Isaac: for example, "A dress coat, if it fit too tight / Will make the wearer look a fright. / And if the garment fit too loose, / It scarcely is of any use" and "In order to provide a vest, / At once the cheapest and the best, / We (heedless of expense) have sent, / An agent to the Continent." Not all of the firm's brochures were filled with frippery and fun (and prices). Several contained lengthy disquisitions on weighty subjects relating to the history of garments, presumably intended to bolster its brand by suggesting that being well dressed (preferably in its clothing) was in step with Victorian notions of seriousness and self-improvement. So well known were these advertisements that imitators in Melbourne who advertised in verse were described as emulating the "Moses style."[47]

Elias and Isaac were also masterful opportunists. Their rhyming advertisements in the *Times* frequently improvised on current events.[48] When
news reached London in 1842 that Britain had signed the Treaty of Nan-
king, which forced China to open five of its ports to foreign trade, they
advertised in the *Illustrated London News* to solicit custom from "naval
and military men, merchants, captains, and emigrants" bound for the Far
East.[49] Father and son were quick to appreciate the benefits of advertising to a nation on the move. Several observers complained in the 1850s
and 1860s that "advertising now overflow[s] into our omnibuses, our
cabs, our railway carriages, our steamboats. . . . The emissaries of Moses
shower perfect libraries through the windows of carriages which ply from
the railway stations." Railway bridges were daubed with "Buy your clothes
of Moses and Son"; on the Thames, "there is not an arch in London but
has its advertisements painted on it."[50] The firm placed its advertisements
prominently in Dickens's serialized novels (supplementing the text with
such poetic gems as "The Proper Field for Copperfield").[51] During the
Australian gold rush the firm advertised extensively in the shipping col-
umns of the Liverpool press.[52] *Punch*, the satirical magazine, singled out
the firm's flagrant self-promotion for heaps of scorn.[53] And its avid self-
promotion meant that the name of Moses was well enough known for a
parliamentary inquiry on Sunday trading to ask specifically about the practices of the firm.[54]

Visitors to London in the middle decades of the century were struck
by the ubiquity of advertising in the city, where posters, billboards, pamphlets, and men toting sandwich boards made it seem "as if the world were
on sale for a penny a bit." To survive, a retailer "must either advertise or
perish."[55] By the 1840s competition between retailers had become intense.
The journalist Henry Mayhew, who counted eighty stores selling ready-
made clothing and inexpensive bespoke outfits in the East End alone,
disapproved of the scramble for customers. Retailers resorted to sale techniques associated with the secondhand dealers of Houndsditch:

> Every art and trick that scheming can devise or avarice suggest, is displayed
> to attract the notice of the passer-by, and filch the customer from another.
> The quiet, unobtrusive place of business of the old-fashioned tailor is trans-
> formed into the flashy palace of the grasping tradesman. Every article in the
> window is ticketed—the price cut down to the quick—books of crude,

bold verses are thrust into your hands, or thrown into your carriage win-
dow—the panels of every omnibus are plastered with showy placards, telling you how Messrs —— defy competition.[56]

Mayhew was far from alone in griping about the "puffery" produced by
"moonlight rag gatherers and dealers in *shoddy* cloth." This unease with
"puffing" reflected a discomfort with a set of very real changes in how
goods were sold.[57]

The gas lighting that illuminated Elias and Isaac's Holborn store
included "many thousands of gas-flames, forming branches, foliage, and
arabesques, and sending forth so dazzling a blaze, that this fiery column
of Moses is visible to Jews and Gentiles at the distance of half a mile."
Seen by some people as gaudy and ostentatious (if not another way to
dupe customers, who felt more likely to get an honest deal in daylight),
the eye-catching spectacle served its purpose in overshadowing rival
businesses and spotlighting the Moses name.[58] Elias and Isaac were innovative in seeking to create a widely recognized brand. As the historian
Giorgio Riello has argued, brands played a particularly important role in
cities that grew dramatically in scale; in such urban environments, it was
increasingly difficult for consumers to assess the quality and durability of
the items they bought.[59] Once a customer might have returned a faulty
purchase to the artisan who made it, but now production was farmed out
to pieceworkers or made by anonymous factory hands. In vast and fluid
markets such as London, where a consumer might be left in the lurch if a
new suit bought from a fly-by-night salesman split its seams, retailers such
as E. Moses & Son sought to build reputations based on the quality of
the goods they sold. Such reputations were particularly important in the
clothing trade, since many customers were unaccustomed to purchasing
ready-made garments and the used-clothing dealers of Houndsditch were
regarded as untrustworthy.

The firm's puffery and self-aggrandizement expanded along with its
empire. With typical immodesty E. Moses & Son described itself as "Mon-
archs of Trade" in the 1840s. In 1850 it boasted of its renown "all over the
world." Not to be outdone, Samuel Hyam claimed in 1851 that his was the
largest clothing establishment in the world. Perhaps to trump this claim,
in the following year, the Moses firm proclaimed itself the "greatest Merchant Tailors in the Universe."[60] Although the firm trumpeted that it sent

clothing "all over the world"—and by the 1870s it had engaged agents in Australia, New Zealand, the Cape Colony, India, China, the West Indies, Japan, and the Americas—in reality its success was rooted in the domestic market.[61] As this listing suggests, however, Elias and Isaac were not blind to opportunities presented by Britain's expanding ambitions abroad. In the late 1830s they identified a largely untapped and growing segment of the clothing market. Paradoxically, the vast increase in the number of people—both foreign- and native-born—leaving Britain's shores for the colonies and the United States from the 1830s onward created a new source of domestic demand. In recognizing this market, Elias and Isaac were not unlike the clothiers in New York who catered to the growing number of migrants heading west and south. In England an industry developed to serve the needs of travelers, including handbooks offering basic advice to emigrants. As early as 1823 *Godwin's Emigrant's Guide to Van Diemen's Land* suggested that travelers buy slops for the voyage to the Antipodes and directed them to slop sellers in the Minories.[62] As the numbers of emigrants increased, these travelers proved to be a boon for clothiers. The travelers typically bought what were known as "emigrant outfits" before departure, consisting of an assortment of clothing, bedding, and toiletries needed by a new migrant to distant shores.[63] Some government-sponsored settlement schemes required emigrants to bring set quantities of clothing with them.[64] Elias and Isaac sold several collections aimed at emigrants, ranging from a basic wardrobe of work clothes and suits for more impecunious travelers to elaborate attire intended for gentlemen who foresaw the need for clothing for shooting, fox hunting, and banqueting.[65] So important was this market to Elias and Isaac that they claimed that the emigrant outfitting department at their emporium in Aldgate was the "the root from whence sprung all those other branches [of their business] to which so many vast establishments are now devoted."[66] They were certainly not the only Jewish entrepreneurs to sense opportunity in the empire's expansion. If Elias and Isaac Moses moved from the slops and secondhand trade to a position of fame and fortune by supplying a domestic market eager for inexpensive wares as well as emigrants leaving England, Henry Moses— whose firm, H. E. & M. Moses, had hired Mrs. Biddell—did so by pursuing customers much further afield.

5

The Empire's New Clothes

Joseph Lyons must have cursed his bad luck. Called to testify as a witness in an assault case in Sydney, Australia, in 1841, he appeared at the Supreme Court "in very handsome dress, sporting a couple of gold rings on his fingers," which, the *Sydney Monitor and Commercial Advertiser* noted scornfully, "he appeared very anxious should attract the notice of the audience." To observers Lyons looked the part of a colonial dandy. Alas, under questioning this cloak of respectability was exposed as threadbare. Not only did he admit to masquerading as a "medical man"— he had performed surgery and treated patients despite limited training— but with "great reluctance" he revealed that he was a convict who had been "transported for felony" for stealing a purse in London. He had reason to lament the exposure of his bogus credentials: his gold rings were evidence of the profitability of a phony practice that presumably withered once exposed to the harsh Australian sunlight.[1] As this sorry tale suggests, dress was a crucial marker of respectability and status in the fluid frontier setting of Australia. Middle-class consumers sought to underline their social status (and to separate themselves from less savory settlers) through their choice of attire. In a society of newcomers, where traditional symbols of worth and position were unavailable or unreliable, habiliment played an outsized role.[2] Clothing, however, could conceal as well as reveal. Scoundrels arriving from abroad were sometimes able to outpace the law, leaving distressed creditors in every port. The correct combination of clothing and confidence could mask malevolent intent, allowing the predatory Lyons to look as meek as a lamb.[3] For many settlers more honest than Lyons who also sought a fresh start, the colonies provided opportunity for reinvention. As Lady Duff Gordon, visiting

Cape Town in 1861, wryly remarked, "a change in hemisphere will reverse reputations."[4] Some who left Albion impecunious (or in shackles) were able to replace a tattered reputation with one gilded by success. But colonial opportunity was not limited to those who ventured to distant shores. Economic life in England was dynamically interrelated with that in the colonies. Ripples in distant markets created new eddies of opportunity in England. In London demand from abroad hastened the transition from a domestic market dominated by castoff clothing to one increasingly centered on ready-made apparel, and it opened new outlets for retailers, wholesalers, and manufacturers willing to enter the risky business of shipping new garments overseas.

At midcentury Jews in London, led by the likes of Elias Moses, were already well ahead of their counterparts in New York City in entering the business of manufacturing and selling ready-made menswear, and the dramatic growth of colonial markets appeared to make it impossible for American Jews to overtake them. The livelihoods of several leading Jewish clothiers in London became interstitched with the fortunes of the British Empire. Some of these clothiers were particularly well positioned to identify and exploit colonial demand. In several cases their willingness to embrace the risks of colonial commerce and their ability to do so had propelled them from the underside of the clothing trade to the forefront of the ready-made industry. The most successful were those who leveraged their colonial contacts to facilitate this transition. They benefited from networks of relatives and trading partners that were well suited to the challenges of doing business with people on a distant commercial frontier. Conditions in these new markets accentuated the advantages that their distribution and credit networks gave them. On the surface no one exploited these new colonial opportunities better than Elias and Isaac Moses, whose emigration outfits adorned streams of emigrants departing Britain's shores. But Henry Moses, their lesser-known competitor and relative by marriage, proved far more adroit at selling clothing to immigrants. Unlike Elias, who preferred to clothe emigrants before their departure, Henry sold clothing to consumers in the colonies, perfecting a new mode of colonial commerce centered on mass consumption. In transforming himself into a major manufacturer and colonial merchant, Henry embodied a potential second route for Jews out of the trade in castoff clothing and into the ready-made manufacturing.

Clothing the Colonies

Henry's success was rooted in several larger processes. At a time when the share of the American market held by British manufacturers was shrinking because of tariffs that made imports less competitive, they found a ready replacement in the expanding settlement colonies of the British Empire. Australia, New Zealand, Canada, and South Africa became their fastest growing export markets. The value of clothing exports rose in the 1830s and 1840s and then tripled in the 1850s. Between 1875 and 1914 three-quarters of all British clothing exports were consumed in the empire's colonies.[5] This growing dependence on exports was aided by declining shipping costs and expanding shipping routes. These same two factors also facilitated a significant outflow of emigrants from Britain.[6] Emigrants carried invisible cultural cargo with them that shaped their preferences and attachments even after they had left Britain's shores. Many settlers were wedded to imported products that reminded them of home. Moreover, their "tastes, expectations and values were readily familiar, communicable and comprehensible to manufacturers back in Britain." Some metropolitan manufacturers played off settlers' psychological attachment to Britain to boost their profits, emphasizing the "Britishness" of their products to increase consumption in colonial markets. But consumers in Melbourne and Montreal did not march perfectly in step with their counterparts in Marylebone and Manchester, even though colonial tastes were often similar to those in Britain. Since colonial clothiers relied heavily on imported goods, this privileged those with connections to manufacturers and exporters in Britain. A British manufacturer with knowledge of market conditions and local fashion preferences could better modulate production to fit foreign wants; the colonial storekeeper could more quickly and reliably stock his or her shelves with attire that was in demand.[7] As we have seen, this same interdependence worked, on a more limited geographic scale, to the advantage of peddlers, rural storekeepers, and their suppliers in the United States.

Jews were far from the only religious and ethnic group to benefit by doing business with colonial markets in the British Empire. As historians Gary B. Magee and Andrew S. Thompson have argued, ethnic business networks played a prime role in trade between Britain and its colonies. Britain's imperial identity was relatively porous, enabling Jews and others to identify with (and profit from) the imperial project. Doing business with far-off markets was relatively risky because lengthier sailing times slowed returns on investment, demand was difficult to gauge, and the business environment overseas was unfamiliar. But businessmen in the metropole could potentially reduce the "psychic distance"—the uncertainty of doing business abroad—by cooperating with relatives, coreligionists, and settlers who had originally come from the same part of the world as they had.[8] As we will see later, such arrangements promised a variety of advantages, particularly the supply of reliable information at a time when travel between London and colonial port cities could take months, the provision of credit in places where local sources of capital were relatively scarce, and access to distribution systems in markets where such facilities were still primitive. The dependence of colonial businesses on goods and credit supplied by their metropolitan partners also encouraged self-policing. Because of the shortcomings of alternative mechanisms for evaluating the reliability of potential and existing business partners from a distance, maintaining a positive public image became particularly important. So significant was credit to colonial businessmen that many were quick to resort to the courts to protect their integrity, lest damage to their reputations harm their access to money at home and abroad.[9] Business networks could also draw strength from a shared sense of group loyalty, intermarriage between members, and a hierarchical structure that vested authority with a senior partner. But as the historian Francesca Trivellato has argued convincingly for an earlier time period, having shared ethnic origins was no guarantee of trustworthiness, nor did it preclude productive commercial relationships between members of different religious and ethnic groups. Given that ethnic networks were self-limiting—restricting their membership by drawing on only people with a shared background—they also narrowed the field of talent available.[10]

Long before the Moses clan began to send clothing to the colonies, English Jews had been involved in overseas trade. For members of the Sephardic and Ashkenazi elite with capital and connections, international commerce served as a vehicle to make and bolster fortunes. Jewish firms traded with Europe, India, North Africa, the Levant, and the Caribbean. Even Jewish hawkers in London were at the bottom end of an international distribution chain that in a number of instances included Jewish intermediaries. Among the baubles sold by Jewish peddlers in the street trade were sponges from the Levant and Adriatic; ostrich feathers from North Africa; and oranges and lemons, fruits of Mediterranean commerce. As we saw in chapter 1, Jewish secondhand-clothing dealers sent castoff clothing in the opposite direction. In some colonial markets these garments were sold by Jews. A visiting naval chaplain recalled his "horror and disgust" on first passing the bustling "Negro Market" in Port Royal on a Sunday in August 1819. He noted with displeasure the presence of "Jews with shops and standings as at a fair, selling old and new clothes, trinkets and small wares at cent. per cent. to adorn the Negro person." Other evidence confirms that some Jews in Surinam and Barbados specialized in the sale of clothing, both old and new.[11] Later in the century, eastern European Jewish peddlers and storekeepers in South Africa catered to migrant black mineworkers eager to demonstrate their worldliness through their choice of clothing when they returned home to their villages.[12]

But by far the largest colonial market for clothing old and new in mid-century was Australia. In the early decades of the century Jewish old-clothes traders bought and sold garments on the hulks—superannuated warships converted into prison ships and moored in English ports—that housed convicts awaiting chained migration to Australia. A portion of their Jewish convict customers were intimately familiar with the clothing business.[13] Jews transported to the Antipodes as convicts were soon outnumbered by their unfettered coreligionists. Despite the taint of criminality, Australia attracted scores of free settlers, and its economy was remarkably open to enterprising immigrants. Although the rate of failure there was high and recessions were not infrequent, settlers benefited from growing international demand for colonial produce and an expanding domestic market driven by immigration. The Antipodean colonies provided a fluid economic and social environment, relatively free of entrenched competition and barriers to entry, that enabled legions of settlers to transcend their humble antecedents. By 1841, 856 Jews lived in New South Wales, most of them clustered near Sydney. Jewish economic life centered not on the wharves, shipyards, mills, distilleries, and breweries that lined the waterfront but on the storefronts of George Street. The conspicuous presence of Jewish clothiers and dry-goods dealers who sold slops and secondhand clothing along this major commercial thoroughfare was remarked on by visitors to the city. Stores were flanked by "screens of coats, waistcoats and inexpressibles hung up invitingly," and garrulous proprietors were eager to extol the wonders of their wares.[14]

The same was true in Melbourne, a town that grew rapidly from little more than a village of "huts embowered in the forest foliage" in the late 1830s into the modest capital of the Colony of Victoria. In 1841 it had 4,479 residents; ten years later its population had grown to 23,000, many of whom directly or indirectly earned their livelihoods from the export of wool produced by pastoralists who tended vast runs that were home to six million sheep.[15] Into the early 1840s, the streets and byways of the town were frequently rendered impassable by the weather and the ceaseless traffic of bullock-drawn drays. Travelers less successful in navigating around the puddles left behind after a rainstorm would find their choices much limited if they preferred to avoid the Jewish-owned stores that lined Collins Street when seeking to replace a mud-bespattered outfit. In 1845 twenty-five out of forty-seven dry-goods and clothing stores in the town were owned by Jews.[16] Smaller colonies of Jewish traders were visible in Auckland, Launceston, and Hobart, often connected by kinship ties to relatives in New South Wales and Victoria. Their stores typically sold cheap imported garments—some manufactured specially for the colonial market, others from bankrupt businesses or dealers hoping to dispense with surplus stock—and fabric from England. Some slops imported in the 1840s were altered to give the impression that they had been locally produced or came with labels falsely proclaiming "Warranted Colonial Made" in order used to circumvent popular campaigns to encourage manufacturing in New South Wales.[17] The success of imported clothing was sufficient to produce handwringing among social commentators in England who were eager to encourage the apprenticeship of poor children into trades: "If he is to be sent abroad, where is the use in teaching him the trade of a tailor? Let him go to any of the colonies, he will find that the slop-seller . . . is there before him. There is not a market they do not supply."[18]

Well into the 1850s imported clothing was often first sold by auctioneers. The auction system grew out of necessity. Metropolitan exporters were unable to perfectly assess the demand for their goods at their destination, particularly when cargo spent months in transit. Colonial fashion was fickle. Auctions ensured that prices were determined by people with knowledge of the local market. The use of an auction house also overcame some of the limitations of a primitive colonial distribution system, dividing large consignments up among multiple wholesalers and retailers. Even in New York, auctions were widely used by importers into the 1840s.[19] In Sydney and Melbourne a striking number of auctioneers were Jewish—as, unsurprisingly, were many of their customers, who bought garments to stock their shelves.[20] The apparent affinity between the Jew and the gavel did not escape public notice in the Antipodes and elsewhere. Jewish auctioneers were frequently accused of rigging sales, tricking the innocent, and substituting bad for good once a sale was complete. Some probably did engage in unscrupulous tactics.[21] Then again, Jewish bidders from Jamaica to Australia were thought to be little better, accused of forming cartels to suppress prices and create monopolies. William Kelly, visiting Victoria in 1853 after a stint in the gold fields in California, reflected these suspicions in his vivid description of an auction mart in Melbourne:

> To an uninitiated person, [the mart] might have been mistaken for a Jewish synagogue; for, during the loud excitement in the street, the Hebrew family congregated in a dense mass about the pulpit, perching themselves, too, on every elevated point or prominent position. . . . Whatever feelings of persecuted brotherism bind them together on other occasions, they seem to ignore creed, country, and relationship when running the scent of wearing apparel, and, like a pack of ravening wolves, they growl and tear each other into metaphorical pieces over a valueless lot of damaged baragon jackets put up for sale "for the benefit of whom it may concern." . . . In sales of merchandise, especially that appertaining to the external comfort of adornment of both sexes in the lower grades of fashion, they fairly outstrip and distance all competition. Most, if not all, of the Melbourne Jewish clothiers have direct connexion with the great Houndsditch and other East London outfitters, and if any foreign importation comes upon the market, they buy it over the heads of all Christian competitors, at prices far beyond the limits of remuneration, so as to retain exclusive possession of the trade.[22]

Kelly's conspiracy-minded jeremiad was correct in only a single respect: connections to Houndsditch helped.[23] Such connections, moreover, worked to the advantage of more than just the colonial retailers, transforming a handful of modest metropolitan enterprises into firms with international reach.

Henry Moses of Tower Hill—and Sydney

Nowhere is the advantage of intercontinental connections better illustrated than in the business network established by Henry Moses and his London firm, H. E. & M. Moses. Over two decades, Henry created a sophisticated distribution system that linked his factories in London and Colchester with retailers in Australia, New Zealand, and eventually Canada. He began his career in much-humbler circumstances. He was born in 1791 in Upper East Smithfield, very close to the used-clothing market in Rosemary Lane, where his father worked intermittently as a hardware man; dealer in sticks, sponges, and slippers; stick maker; toy man; silversmith; and slop seller. Henry followed in his footsteps, becoming a jack-of-all-trades: a silversmith, hardware man, speculator in sponges, used-clothing dealer, clothes salesman, and slop seller.[24] If his varied early career was not unlike that of numerous other Jews in London who got their start in the underside of the clothing trade, why did it diverge from that of his contemporaries? And why were so few of his peers able to follow his path from the margins of the trade to its center?

Henry's move during the 1830s to Tower Hill reflected a fortuitous set of developments in far-off Australia, as well as events closer to home. Until the failure of the massive strike of 1834, the London Operative Tailors Union and the workers it represented had stoutly resisted the use of unskilled workers and female laborers. As we have seen, the breach of this bulwark enabled manufacturers to adopt the sweating system, using cheaper labor in place of skilled craftsmen. Slop sellers such as Henry Moses, whose profits had long depended on stitching rough garments efficiently and cheaply by farming out piecework, now began to apply these same methods to produce a better quality of clothing. Turf that had once been the preserve of skilled tailors was now open to anyone who could operate efficiently in this new environment. As prices of shirts, suits, and pants fell, the number of consumers who could afford these items increased. To the contemporary observer Henry Moses's experimentation with mass-producing ready-made clothing would have seemed much like that of other slop sellers. What set him apart was found not in London but in Sydney.

An earlier misfortune, the transportation in 1827 of a ne'er-do-well nephew of Henry Moses to New South Wales for stealing jewelry from

The trade card of Benjamin & Moses, a retail and wholesaling firm in Sydney, Windsor, and Goulburn part owned by Elias Moses, one of Henry Moses's nephews. (Courtesy of the Australian Jewish Historical Society)

a peddler, redounded to the benefit of his extended family. After Moses Joseph brought his family shame, he propelled it to fortune. His reports of Antipodean opportunity persuaded four of his siblings and at least ten of his cousins to leave England for Australia and New Zealand. The first of a stream of relatives arrived in May 1833. Within months, the general store that Joseph had opened in Sydney was advertising "trousers and other clothing" for sale, perhaps supplied by his uncle in London.[25] Henry Moses was clearly impressed by the rapid success of a nephew whose reputation had been bleached clean under the glare of the Antipodean sun (and the watchful eye of the penal authorities). Henry also sniffed opportunity. Before two of his sons and several of his nephews departed for the Antipodes, he gave them commercial training and one hundred pounds of stock as start-up capital. This was a wise investment. The flotilla of relatives who sailed south created a beachhead for the family firm, establishing stores in Wellington, Auckland, Sydney, Adelaide, Melbourne, Hobart, and Launceston.[26] Henry Moses was not the only such opportunist. Moses Benjamin, the scion of a rival clothing family, arrived in Melbourne in 1843 with two thousand pairs of trousers and eighty-four hundred shirts to stock his new store.[27]

This colonial distribution chain appears to have given H. E. & M. Moses a significant boost, permanently pushing Henry Moses out of dealing in secondhand clothes and slops and into the mass production of new clothing. Although he also supplied clothiers and the military in England, the overseas market quickly became an important component of his tailoring business.[28] Here was an opportunity of a kind unavailable and unimaginable to Jewish wholesalers and manufacturers in the United States at the time. What Jewish firms in New York City could scarcely dream of clothing customers continents away? It was challenging enough for them to get their wares into the hands of rural customers, let alone to break into large markets such as that in the South that were dominated by better-entrenched rivals. In contrast, by the middle of the 1850s Henry Moses had at least two manufacturing premises in London and another in Colchester, fifty miles away, producing clothing wholesale.[29] His firm employed the putting out and piecework systems, along with factory production. Like several other manufacturers, it hired female inmates at the Brixton and Millbank prisons to stitch large orders of shirts and military uniforms. Moses and other "Houndsditch Jews," however, were singled out for undercutting honest free workers.[30] Though Moses's manufacturing operation was little different from that of others who experimented with mass-production, he proved particularly adroit in profiting from the price advantage enjoyed by British clothing exporters. Higher labor costs in the United States and the colonies made British exports more competitive. According to one estimate, clothing purchased in America, Australia, and at the Cape was 25 percent more expensive than that bought in England, leaving a fat margin for British manufacturers and exporters to exploit.[31] Labor shortages in the settlement colonies, the uncertainty of local demand, and distance from raw materials made mass manufacturing challenging. The most successful merchants who ventured into this market were those who, like Henry Moses, were able to achieve vertical integration, controlling production, distribution, and retail.

An immigrant parading down the dusty high street of an Antipodean town in a new outfit bought from a retailer in London might be aghast to discover identical fashions on display in store windows, sometimes at cheaper prices. The family stores in the colonies were supplied with lenient credit and ample stock from the warehouses in London. In turn, they shipped wheat, wool, tallow, hides, old clothing, canned meat, and kauri gum to London as return cargo to be reprocessed or sold. In 1851 H. E. & M. Moses described itself as "agents for the sale of colonial produce."[32] This ancillary business enabled the London firm to profit twice over from its Australia connections. In colonial markets serviced by a new and still-primitive banking system, and desperately short of currency and capital, such seamless arrangements between kin benefited both parties. Colonial markets were often starved for credit, but those in London had access to cheap long-term loans. This put businesses in the colonies that could draw on metropolitan partners at a distinct advantage.[33] Through reliable agents British suppliers gained access to colonial consumers, who were particularly profligate during boom times. Additional sales supported the model of high turnover and low margin that underpinned the business of the British manufacturers and wholesalers. These colonial branches — three other nephews established a large retail store in Montreal — provided Henry Moses with greater economies of scale for manufacture, access to more consumers, and the means to dispose of stock that was not selling well in England. Retailers in the colonies gained a competitive advantage over their rivals: easy credit and access to new fashions at wholesale rates and with low transaction costs. As we have seen, this reliance on ethnic capital to supply credit needs, bypassing credit agencies suspicious of Jewish newcomers, was also a hallmark of Jewish business networks in the United States.

Jewish clothiers in the colonies imported not only garments to stock their shelves but also the kind of sales techniques familiar to visitors to Petticoat Lane and Chatham Street. In several Antipodean towns clothing spilled from small storefronts onto the pavement outside. In Melbourne this practice earned the disapproval of the municipality, which imposed fines for "causing an obstacle to passers-by."[34] A visitor to George Street in 1841 complained that Jewish proprietors had adopted a "regular system of entreating, stopping and pulling over passersby into their cribs." Echoing complaints made in New York, he noted that the sellers focused their efforts on "strangers of all classes, but chiefly those with sailors' toggery."[35] As in America, wily salesmen favored sailors in port who had wages in their pockets after a long voyage. A visitor to Auckland grumbled that "any one standing a moment or two" before Mr. Levi's secondhand shop "was sure to be accosted, and business matters introduced in the course of conversation."[36] Those who owned larger stores advertised aggressively. In Melbourne Michael Cashmore, the proprietor of Victoria House as well as of the London and Manchester Warehouse, specialized in versifying in dreadful doggerel in the pages of the local press about the wonders of his stock. One of his competitors pioneered the never-ending going-out-of-business sale.[37] Clothiers did more than just introduce modern sales techniques. Firms that imported stock from abroad aided the diffusion of consumer culture throughout the colonies and promoted "shared habits of consumption" and norms of desirability between Britain and its settler outposts.[38]

Cashmore and his competitors chose for their stores grand titles that were intended to suggest the sophisticated styles of the far-off metropolis. These titles suggested the "proximity, and even romance of Britain" to immigrants pining for home. By buying clothing at the London and Manchester Warehouse, a colonial consumer may have subconsciously demonstrated his desire to maintain cultural ties with the home country.[39] In 1841 Victoria House competed with the patriotic Waterloo and Albert Houses, as well as the more prosaic Liverpool and London Marts. Solomon and David Benjamin's Cheapside House not only reminded patrons of the bustling London neighborhood but beckoned shoppers with the promise of bargains within. In Brisbane the California Store, which may have been opened by one of the thousands of migrants who left San Francisco to try their luck on Antipodean shores, took advantage of the aura of the Golden State. (Similarly, Jewish-owned stores in the American South and West often had names that conjured up the style and sophistication of New York City.)[40] Miners from California brought a distinctive style with them to the Antipodes: cabbage-palm hats.[41]

An Australian Gold Mine

Jewish clothing firms based in England that made early investments in the Australian market struck pay dirt in the 1850s. The nebulous fortunes of the colony during the previous decade, which had been beset by recurrent economic crises, were transformed by the discovery of gold in 1851. Within months, New South Wales and then Victoria became magnets for fortune-seeking immigrants. Word of the discoveries initiated what some people later described as "the Australian madness" in Britain, a mania that crossed class lines. Such was the intoxication in 1852 that more English, Scottish, and Welsh immigrants left their homeland for Victoria than for anywhere else, Australia briefly outstripping the United States as the preferred destination. By 1860 the Australian population had grown to 1.25 million, an astounding hundredfold increase from fifty years before. This boom was aided by improvements in transportation that made the lengthy voyage from Britain to Port Phillip or Sydney shorter, safer, and cheaper. Once the initial rush to the gold fields slowed, the scale of immigration did not return to pre-gold-rush levels. Although travel to the Antipodes remained relatively expensive, some immigrants benefited from subsidized fares and the soothing promises of recruiting agents.[42] The Australian Jewish population more than doubled in size during the 1850s.[43] George Washington Peck, an American traveler who was elected to Congress soon after returning from a voyage to Australia, provided a Seussian listing of the "Chatham street" Jews he encountered in Melbourne in 1853: "English Jews, German Jews, French Jews, *Jew* Jews—Israelites of the Israelites. . . . [G]reat Jews, little Jews, rich Jews, poor Jews, fat Jews, lean Jews, dark Jews, light Jews, hooky-nosed Jews, and Jews with reddish hair. I saw American Jews, Irish Jews, even—all but Scotch or Yankee Jews."[44]

After an initial exodus of townspeople to the gold fields, Sydney and Melbourne boomed as immigrants arrived by the shipload, miners stocked up on supplies, and the fortunate celebrated their bonanzas. Within a decade, Victoria had been transformed from a bucolic backwater with a population of fewer than eighty thousand and an economy sensitive to the well-being of the local sheep into a thriving colony that was home to more than half a million people. In the early stages of the gold rush, shops struggled to keep up with surging demand, and prices rose accordingly. (A *Sydney Morning Herald* correspondent claimed that it would be impossible to find a "worse regulated, worse governed, worse drained, worse lighted, worse watered town" than Melbourne in 1852; he felt certain that "a population more thoroughly disposed, in every grade to cheating and to robbery, open and covert, does not exist.")[45] Merchants as far away as Boston sought to ship clothing and fabric to Australia to meet the need. Inflation and short supply worked to the advantage of clothiers who relied on imported stock. Not only could they sell to a ballooning population— just short of ninety-five thousand migrants arrived in Victoria in 1852

alone—but their profit margins soared as the cheap ready-made clothing they imported commanded a premium price. Ironically, their customers included new immigrants eager to shed the manners and dress that
marked them as inexperienced recent arrivals. Importers faced little local
competition. Local clothing manufacturing was constricted by an acute
labor shortage precipitated by the lure of the gold fields. To meet burgeoning demand, the volume of clothing imported to New South Wales from
Britain quadrupled between 1848 and 1853.[46] This spike created ripples as
far away as Montreal. There, Henry Moses's nephews cottoned on early
to the need for work clothing for miners and began to ship much of the
output of the large factory they opened to Australia, taking advantage of a
tariff structure favorable to intercolonial commerce.[47]

In Melbourne and Sydney shopkeepers made prosperous by a sprinkling of gold dust abandoned makeshift wooden stores for elegant new
storefronts. Successful businessmen swapped their workaday wardrobes
for black frock coats, trousers, and top hats more appropriate for dank
London than the unforgiving southern sun. Several metropolitan Jewish clothing moguls entered the market during the gold rush, including
the Moseses' major Manchester rival, Benjamin Hyam.[48] Even Elias and
Isaac Moses established a grand edifice in Melbourne in 1852, initially an
imported corrugated-iron store eighty-eight feet by twenty-two feet with
plate-glass windows, in anticipation of "immense business." Despite rep-
licating some of their London sales techniques—including advertising
on wagons, carriages, and stagecoaches and prolifically in newspapers
as far away as Hobart—the firm's Australian branch went belly-up when
the gold-rush bubble burst.[49] The feverish economy swooned in 1854 and
again in 1857, bankrupting many of those who had been infected by the
gold bug. Henry Moses's Antipodean operation seems to have survived
the crash, suggesting that its resilient network of family-owned stores
made the firm better attuned to local fashions and market conditions.
Some of its London rivals whose connections with Australia were shallower may have been slower to receive word of economic difficulties down
under, delayed reducing their shipments to Melbourne and Sydney, and
been less inclined to prop up a failing Antipodean enterprise until the market improved.[50]

The effects of the gold rush were also felt in the secondhand-clothing market in London. The runaway demand for the hardy, inexpensive

clothing preferred by many miners in Australia was a boon for dealers in used clothing. Advertisements for "left-off clothes for Australia" became sufficiently common in the capital for the satirical magazine *Punch* to speculate that "Australia would seem to be in want of a sort of Rag Fair, at which worn-out wearing apparel may be obtainable." Antipodean demand for the "left-off liveries" of courtiers and the "regimentals" of soldiers, the magazine jested, did "not say much for the cause of progress in Australia."[51] By the 1870s some London used-clothing dealers were advertising their international reach, boasting of demand from Australia, New Zealand, South Africa, and the United States.[52] These advertisements, coupled with the advice of emigrants' guidebooks that reported a healthy demand in the colonies for "clothing of antiquated pattern, shape, and material" and other articles of "an exploded construction or which are unsaleable in the mother country," may have persuaded some immigrants to fill their trunks with surplus garments in expectation of a quick return on their investment once they reached their destination. Part of a growing industry that had sprouted to serve the needs of emigrants, the guidebooks also offered advice on the purchase of emigration outfits.[53] Immigrants who arrived in Melbourne during the gold rush hoping to turn a profit by disposing of their surplus clothing were probably disappointed. The market for immigrants' castoffs was quickly glutted. Rag Fair, an "impromptu bazaar," sprung up near the wharf with about fifty traders hawking heaps of clothing and supplies from trunks and boxes. Some were impecunious immigrants hoping to sell their wardrobes to earn passage to the gold fields. Others were speculators hoping to turn their investment in clothing into cash. Although Jewish clothiers were accused of erecting stalls in Rag Fair and masquerading as impoverished immigrants in order to shoulder in on this trade, it seems much more likely that they were among the shopkeepers who lobbied the town corporation to close this market, fearing that the unlicensed hawkers would suppress demand for their wares. There is some evidence that Jewish dealers were among the buyers at this Antipodean Rag Fair, probably purchasing garments that could be resold elsewhere for a profit.[54]

After the closure of Melbourne's Rag Fair in 1855, its "Jewish traders took to trekking into the bush with their bundles of wares."[55] Although the itinerant trade in Australia was not the rite of passage that it was for many recent arrivals in the United States, some Jewish immigrants did peddle fabric, clothing, and haberdashery between isolated upcountry settlements. As in rural America, peddlers were sometimes obliged to barter with their customers, receiving payment in wheat, skins, and other produce. There was more money to be made at the diggings, where some miners preferred older, durable garments more likely to stand up to the rigors of backbreaking labor.[56] Some complained that there were "swarms" of Jews among the storekeepers and publicans in Bendigo and other mining boomtowns.[57] More Jews seem to have made their fortunes in supplying the miners than in prospecting for elusive nuggets. Given the geography of the gold fields—in Victoria, the chief gold deposits stretched in a broad band north and west of Melbourne, some as far as 150 miles from the city—and the opportunities for opening stores in small towns in the interior, a significant portion of the immigrants ultimately settled in rural outposts. By 1861 a full 40 percent of Australian Jews lived in the hinterland, a trend that was in line with a broader shift in the Australian population.[58]

The dispersal of Jews into the Australian countryside as storekeepers and petty traders probably benefited H. E. & M. Moses and other London exporters by indirectly broadening their access to rural customers. The firm continued to generate handsome returns by shipping inexpensive garments to Australia. Although the scandalous wages paid to Mrs. Biddell did not help the firm's public image, its renown grew alongside its Antipodean sales. Those in London seeking to celebrate Jewish involvement in colonial enterprise, which was a source of pride for some, would find few better homegrown champions than the firm's founder. His fortune was not on the same scale as that of the Rothschilds, but Henry Moses's humble origins and the nature of his business would have been easier to relate to than the silver-spoon privilege and financial speculations of Anglo-Jewish grandees. That remained the case even after he moved to a house adjacent to Regent's Park, his sons became communal worthies and changed their names to Beddington (a cruel wit rhymed that the Beddingtons "could change their names but not their noses"), and one married a Montefiore. (Elias Moses's children also relinquished a name that clearly marked them as members of the Mosaic persuasion for the gentrified Marsden.)[59]

False Prophets of the Ready-Made Trade

Elias and Henry Moses, who both refashioned themselves in later life, presented contrasting paths out of the business of dealing in castoff clothing and into that of making and marketing menswear. The former made his fortune as a new kind of retailer, the latter as a manufacturer focused on the export market. Yet those who watched the clothing trade closely would have noted that their trajectories were far from representative. If few secondhand salesmen emulated the scale of Elias Moses's successes as a retailer, even fewer followed Henry Moses's example as an exporter. It was not for a want of trying. Many sought to follow their lead, but few achieved more than modest success; and many more became mired in an unforgiving production system. Henry Moses's observation during the Biddell scandal that Jewish-owned firms were a small minority among the largest wholesaling houses in London was not far wrong. This less flattering reality was very consequential for future Jewish involvement in the garment industry in England well after Henry, Elias, and their contemporaries had left the scene. So why were the benefits of rapidly growing demand for clothing at home and in the colonies not shared more widely by metropolitan Jews? And why, given the dominance of Jewish dealers in the secondhand trade in London and their prominence among slop sellers, did relatively few—Henry, Elias, and a handful of others aside—become leading wholesalers, manufacturers, and retailers before the 1880s?

The successes of Henry, Elias, and their ilk in making menswear more affordable and accessible placed pressure on those who lingered longer in the secondhand trade. Ironically, dealers of used apparel who were squeezed by a gradual decline in prices may have found it more difficult to muster the resources to venture into a new market. Certainly two of Henry's brothers who tarried as traders in Rag Fair enjoyed little of his vaulting success. One was supported in his dotage by his children, who joined the family exodus to the Antipodes.[60] Emigration, which had bolstered demand for mass-produced cheap clothing, provided a potential escape for ragmen whose source of livelihood withered. Most of the secondhand dealers who sought to emulate Henry Moses's example by setting themselves up as manufacturers, or Elias Moses's by opening retail stores, may soon have wished that they had chosen a new beginning abroad instead. Their prospects for economic mobility were almost certainly better in Australia than in the garment industry in London.

Several substantial headaches awaited those who followed Elias Moses into mass retailing. For one, the market quickly became significantly more competitive, in no small measure due to innovations introduced by Elias Moses and his rivals. The arms race between storekeepers who turned their show windows into spectacles, emblazoned their names in large letters above their stores, and advertised to the masses tilted the playing field against smaller retailers and newcomers to the field. Extensive advertising branded the suits Elias sold as fashionable, affordable, and hard wearing, substantial advantages at a time when the wares of the typical East End purveyor of inexpensive clothing were viewed with a measure of distrust. Not only was this extravagant approach to courting customers out of reach for those who started with little capital, but it also, paradoxically, made it more challenging for them to compete on cost. Stores such as those operated by Elias Moses profited by selling large quantities of stock on low margins, a model that depended on luring throngs of customer through their doors. Because of the scale of the sales in the stores of Elias Moses, he could also drive hard bargains with his suppliers, demanding suits and shirts for sums that made it more challenging for smaller storekeepers, and particularly newcomers to the business, to compete because it crimped their margins.

Elias's approach also did few favors for most of those who sought to set themselves up as manufacturers. Paradoxically, as the scale of the ready-made market grew, competition among small producers became more intense and less remunerative. Since the barriers to starting sweatshop production were low and wholesalers' primary loyalty was to price when distributing contracts, workshops proliferated. With so many people jostling for work, and with few ways to differentiate one's work from that of rivals, it became harder to ascend the production chain from sweatshop producer to large-scale manufacturer and wholesaler. Those who labored in workshops or at home found their wages under pressure as contractors pared their pay in order to compete on cost. This dynamic, ironically, benefited businessmen such as Henry Moses who were well entrenched in the manufacturing trade and were already, as the case of Mrs. Biddell demonstrates, outsourcing production to others. Rather than present a realistic career trajectory for a hardworking entrepreneur to emulate, Henry

Moses's success as a manufacturer may therefore have appeared a cruel tease to those who were unable to extract themselves from a manufacturing system that must have seemed less a ladder to prosperity than a cousin to the shredding machine whose blades were used to produce shoddy. In America the particular circumstances of Jewish entry into the garment industry opened somewhat-broader avenues for the economic ascent of Jews caught up in the sweatshop economy. Although sweatshop labor was no less exhausting and downward pressures on wages no less acute there than in England, a series of unexpected developments threw open new opportunities for those who wished to remain in the clothing trade, as well as those who sought to leave it behind.

Henry also profited from a head start that gave him early access to the Australian market; those who followed him into the export business even a handful of years later found themselves entering a crowded and cutthroat field. Few had the connections and resources—particularly the network of nephews in Australia and Canada—that enabled Henry to enter the colonial market at such advantage. Given that the costs of doing business over great distances were considerable and that some of the risks associated with exporting goods to Australia increased as that market became more competitive, few others benefited from the mutually reinforcing dynamic of colonial trade as much as the Moses clan. Demand from Australia underpinned their system of efficiently producing clothing in bulk in England, and readily available supplies from London solidified the early advantage that their distributors had in Australia.

Legacies of the Secondhand Trade

The secondhand business also bequeathed several legacies—not all advantageous—to those who moved on to the ready-made trade. Earlier modes of doing business, existing organizational structures, and well-practiced patterns of trade proved hard to shake. Those who were schooled in the secondhand markets of Houndsditch, for example, developed a mode of doing business particular to their environment. Native-born clothing dealers in London had little need to forge expansive connections outside of their immediate marketplace, to cultivate customers and creditors, and to develop a distribution chain when throngs arrived of their own accord to shop and haggle in Houndsditch. Nor did they need to create a supply system of their own when anonymous rag collectors delivered garments to the clothing exchanges.

Another inheritance was a preponderance of family firms. This was no less true at the upper reaches of the clothing business than it was at its lower end. John Mills, who published a book in 1853 about Judaism and Jewish life in Britain, correctly identified E. Moses & Son, H. E. & M. Moses of Tower Hill, and Moses, Son & Davis of Aldgate as among the most noteworthy Jewish businesses in the city.[61] Interrelated via marriage, the families behind these clothing firms were also interconnected by marital ties with the Hyam, Hart, and Levy clans, other pioneering manufacturers and retailers. Family enterprises worked well in the second-hand trade and often persisted once their members moved on to making or selling menswear. Since very little capital—but lots of motivation— was required to make a living from castoffs, bonds between brothers or between fathers and sons formed the basis of many small Jewish ventures. If a firm was successful, nephews and other relatives could be drafted to provide additional help. A consanguineal model of enterprise did not stop some firms from succeeding spectacularly—the firms created by Elias and Henry being prime examples—but family businesses faced potential challenges over time when it came to expansion, adaptation, and continuity. The success of H. E. & M. Moses and E. Moses & Son, for example, reveals the inherent limitations of a mode of enterprise that depended on the continued commitment of family members. Henry and Elias Moses built fortunes with the aid of their sons (and, in the case of Henry, of energetic and adventurous nephews). But their grandchildren, wealthy members of the gentry, had less interest in retaining a connection to the line of work that had brought them prosperity.

The potential implications of these legacies become clearer when contrasted with patterns seen among Jewish peddlers and storekeepers in America. Although it was not unusual for Jewish enterprises in the United States to build on blood ties, many future clothing firms started as partnerships between peddlers who were far from home and family and who first met each other in small country towns. These partnerships, rooted in happenstance and congruent economic needs between unattached newcomers, were more easily dissolved than bonds of blood. Small firms that drew on relatives and landsmen also typically displayed an openness to outsiders that was less often seen in businesses where a founding family clung to control. Clerks who proved their worth, for example, often became partners, as did those who provided capital and useful connections that would enable a business to expand. As we have seen, moreover, the nature of peddling and country storekeeping compelled Jewish immigrants in the United States to develop a wide network of contacts in order to secure access to creditors, suppliers, distributors, and customers.

These structural differences—inheritances of the contrasting ways that Jews entered the business of making and marketing menswear in England and America—had long-term consequences. Would-be Jewish retailing and manufacturing moguls in England had little equivalent to the nascent network of peddlers and petty shopkeepers emerging in America for distributing and selling goods on a national scale. Partly as a result, they found it more difficult to escape the crushing calculus that faced smaller operators. Some, such as Elias Moses and Hyam Hyam, created their own distribution systems by establishing branch stores. But this route—which required considerable amounts of capital—became more and more challenging as the marketplace became crowded. And, as we will see in chapters 6 and 8, the more flexible and expansive model of enterprise that predominated among Jews in the clothing trade in the United States was better suited to the dramatic growth in demand for ready-made clothing in the second half of the nineteenth century, as well as the growth of America itself as it pushed westward, than were the family businesses that dominated in England.

Such concerns with the limitations of a family partnership and the legacies of the secondhand trade, however, would have seemed ridiculous in the 1840s and 1850s, when the renown of E. Moses & Son far outstripped that of any Jewish clothier in America. A casual observer in 1850, beguiled by the advertising of Elias Moses and awed by the wealth of Henry Moses, would probably not have noticed the far-less-appealing reality that faced most Jews who swapped the trade in castoffs for work with ready-made clothing. Henry and Elias Moses seemingly provided firm proof that Jews in England had achieved a level of success in the clothing trade that appeared unimaginable for Jews in America. Whereas modest peddlers and petty shopkeepers there contented themselves with rural customers on country byways, the Moses name adorned flashy shop fronts in England's capital, and the family's reach extended as far as Canada and the Antipodes. How, then, did Jews in America catch and then surpass their counterparts in England? We will see that even as Jews in England encountered headwinds in the ready-made trade in the 1850s and 1860s, a sequence of unexpected events filled the sails of their contemporaries in America. Several of these developments were analogous to those encountered by Jews in England, but in the United States they benefited a far broader swath of Jews in the clothing trade.

6

A New Dawn in the West

Jewish New Yorkers who surveyed the scene in their city in 1850 might have looked wistfully at London. There were sixteen thousand Jews in New York City, more than double the number of a decade earlier but still significantly fewer than in the British capital. The gap was more telling in the industry most closely associated with Jews in both places: clothing. Demand from home and abroad had pushed the likes of Hyam Hyam and Elias Moses to prominence as clothiers in England a decade earlier, and it would be easy to assume that Jews in America would forever trail behind their counterparts across the Atlantic. After all, the history of Jewish involvement in the clothing trade in New York—the largest center of production in the United States—was still somewhat threadbare. Compared with their coreligionists in London, Jews in New York were relative latecomers to the business of making and marketing ready-made clothing. As we have seen, they were not among the pioneers who created new methods of manufacturing and selling garments in the city in the first half of the century, and they had long remained on the periphery of a business dominated by a motley mix of native-born and newcomers. A mere eight Jewish heads of household had described themselves as involved in the clothing trade in New York in the census of 1830, barely worthy of notice amid the hurly-burly of an urban industry growing at breakneck speed.[1] Two decades later, there was nary a Jew among the most prominent clothiers and dry-goods merchants in the city, no New World equivalent of Hyam and Moses among the proprietors of the marble palaces on Broadway and other imposing thoroughfares built by James Beck & Company, Hearn Brothers, Daniel Devlin, Lewis & Hanford, and the Brooks brothers.

For those who had a competitive streak, there was additional cause for pessimism. Although by 1850 peddling and clerking had given Jews an entrée into the wholesaling of clothing and dry goods in New York, Jewish firms still struggled to catch the coattails of local rivals in the dash to win new customers in the city and countryside. More important, they were late entrants into the market that provided New York firms with their most reliable source of profits and that looked likely to grow even more quickly in the 1850s. By the time Jewish wholesalers and manufacturers became active in the lucrative Southern trade, its juiciest portions had already been claimed by others. Although some Jewish firms were fattened by Southern consumers whose appetite for clothing grew along with cotton prices, more scrapped for the leavings of those who were better positioned to glut themselves on the demand from the South.

Jewish New Yorkers, however, soon had reason to crow. Several unexpected events conspired to propel Jewish economic life in New York forward at a dramatic pace. Within fifteen years, many Jewish firms in New York, Baltimore, and Cincinnati not only had overtaken their counterparts in London but had left them in the dust. Indeed, the early lead established by Jews in London and Manchester turned out to be chimerical, a case of the tortoise and the hare. The secondhand and slops businesses in England ultimately channeled far fewer Jews into the ranks of wholesalers than peddling and clerking did in America. And by a stroke of good fortune, the relatively sluggish start of Jews in the clothing business in the United States turned out to be an advantage rather than an impediment. With many of the prime pickings already taken in the South by the time Jewish firms were able to compete with longer-established competitors, Jewish wholesalers and manufacturers were hungrier than their rivals, who were preoccupied by surging profits from the Southern market, when word reached New York of potentially rich but risky offerings in California. In San Francisco and Sacramento at the time of the gold rush, Jewish firms did not need to content themselves with the leavings of others but could claim the head seat at the table. For several reasons that we will explore, California presented opportunities to many more Jews in America than Australia did to Jews in London and had a greater impact on the development of Jewish involvement in the clothing trade. And the early foothold established by Jews in California and their shallower footprint in the South proved to be less a liability than a source of salvation at the beginning of the next decade.

The Southern Market in the 1850s

The foregoing set of outcomes did not seem likely during a decade in which rising cotton prices produced a boom in the South and a tightening of economic ties between that region and New York City. According to one estimate, roughly half of all clothing manufactured in the city during the 1850s was sold to Southern consumers; the New York Chamber of Commerce pegged the percentage even higher when it estimated that an astonishing two-thirds of garments were shipped to the South in 1858.[2] Those who profited in the 1850s might have done well to remember that the conjugal knot that tied the city's clothing and dry-goods firms to merchants in the South worked both in good times and in bad. Demand for clothing was contingent on the availability of cotton and healthy cotton prices. The financial panic of 1837, for example, had blighted the cotton market for more than a decade, diminished the buying power of Southern consumers, and driven many garment manufacturers and wholesalers into bankruptcy when Southern storekeepers were unable to repay their debts. (The lawyer George Templeton Strong compared the string of failures in his diary to the "explosion of a pack of [fire] crackers—pop, pop, pop—one after another they go off, and all their substance vanishes in fumes.")[3] When ruinous cotton prices were finally replaced by healthy ones in the 1850s, farmers reaped bountiful profits, and many white Southerners enjoyed a sustained period of prosperity. Those who owned slaves benefited twice over, as the value of their chattels soared. In 1850 a male slave in his prime sold for an average of $877; six years later, he would earn his owner an average of $1,243 on the auction block. Not even the financial panic of 1857 could undo these years of plenty: cotton prices remained stable even as Northern banks failed and many merchants were left penniless.[4] This dependence on the Southern market undoubtedly played a role in shaping the political views of merchants, manufacturers, and workers in New York and other cities such as Cincinnati and Chicago that sold their wares down the river. Of course, not everyone was as mercenary as one writer in the *Chicago Times* who exclaimed shortly before the outbreak of the Civil War, "Let the South have her negroes to her heart's content, and in her own way—and let us go on getting rich and powerful feeding and clothing them. Let the negroes *alone!*—let them ALONE!"[5] But many Northerners understood that workshops and factories in the North were kept humming because of demand generated by slave-picked cotton.

The knot that bound New York City to the South may have been almost matrimonial in nature, but the relationship certainly involved plenty of bickering. Before the Civil War, New Orleans and New York were locked in a contentious relationship that was made up of equal parts cooperation and competition. The cities were rivals for the affections of King Cotton and reluctant bedmates in his harem. Even though half of the South's cotton made its way through New Orleans in the decades before the Civil War, much of this cotton was transshipped to Europe through New York. Cotton was one of the city's chief exports. To the chagrin of people in the Crescent City many of the bankers who provided loans to plantation owners, factors who bought cotton and sold supplies to planters, and exporters who shipped bales across the Atlantic conducted their business from New York. According to some contemporary estimates, this supporting cast received "forty cents of every dollar spent in the cotton market."[6] The two cities competed as export hubs—New Orleans briefly surpassed New York in the value of exports in the 1830s—and as ports of entry for immigrants (more than one in three of New Orleans's white residents in 1860 was foreign-born). Cincinnati, a younger, landlocked upstart, initially had little choice but to float boatloads of its wares to New Orleans, a journey that took two months before the coming of steamboats. When rail routes across the Alleghenies and a canal system via the Great Lakes connected Cincinnati directly to Eastern markets, its merchants, manufacturers, and farmers could play coy mistress to two suitors.[7]

New York dry-goods merchants and clothing manufacturers established stores and offices on Canal and Magazine Streets in New Orleans; by one estimate "seven-eighths of the commercial houses in the city were agents of New York firms" in the 1830s. Because of the city's position at the gateway of a natural riverine highway, its proximity to cotton and sugar plantations in the rich alluvial soils of the delta, and its role as linchpin in the supply of slaves and financing of slavery, New Orleans developed into a major importing and retailing hub and became one of the wealthiest cities in the nation. The trade that flowed up and down the Mississippi River was the city's lifeblood. New Orleans's population grew close to tenfold in the five decades before the Civil War. By 1861 the city ranked second in size only to Baltimore in the South, ahead of St. Louis, Louisville, and

Richmond. New Orleans's large population ebbed and flowed as migratory merchants left town for the vaporous summer months, planters and their retinues settled in for the fall and winter social seasons, immigrants disembarked before making their way westward, and a constant tide of upriver storekeepers, farmers, and salesmen arrived by steamboat in the seething city. Largely thanks to merchandising in New Orleans, Louisiana became home to the second-highest proportion of stores per thousand residents of all the states in the Union in 1840.[8] New York clothing wholesalers who set up shop in New Orleans faced significant competition from locally produced garments, particularly at the lower end of the trade. In 1860 menswear was the largest manufacturing industry in the city and, in Louisiana, producing more revenue than meat packing in Chicago and more garments than Pittsburgh. Much of this was "Negro clothing," garments sold to plantation owners to inexpensively outfit their slaves, rather than fashionable clothing of the kind sewed in New York. Soaring revenues from the sale of cotton and falling prices for clothing persuaded many planters to purchase ready-made garments rather than fabric for slaves to use in sewing their own clothes. Local manufacturers competed for this lucrative market with clothing imported from Cincinnati, New York, and England.

Although a significant portion of the Jews in of New Orleans were involved in selling clothing and fabric, their experience illustrates the limited Jewish success in penetrating the front ranks of the garment industry in the South before the Civil War. There were no more than sixty Jews in the city in 1820 and only about a hundred more a decade later, when New Orleans was the fifth-largest city in the United States. Alsatian Jews were disproportionately represented among the early settlers, and they gravitated toward the dry-goods trade. Despite devastating epidemics of yellow fever, the white population of the city had swelled to over 144,000 by 1860, of whom between four and five thousand were Jews. Roughly 40 percent of Jewish heads of household were involved in the clothing and textile trades as retailers and wholesalers of garments and shoes, tailors and cobblers, and dry-goods merchants; according to credit-agency records, Jewish firms constituted almost a quarter of the clothing and dry-goods businesses in the city.[9] Yet only a handful of Jews became manufacturers on a substantial scale. Instead, the majority were shopkeepers who purchased their stock at auction, dealt with jobbers who bought in bulk for resale, or made annual buying trips to New York. (One New Orleans newspaper warned merchants against Chatham Street: "You can expect nothing less than being eventually regularly sewed up.") Others relied on partnerships with wholesalers and manufacturers in Cincinnati or New York, sometimes cemented by family ties. Larger merchants stationed resident buyers close to their suppliers, enabling them to adjust their orders to meet shifts in style and demand. An ambitious and successful minority opened their own factories in the North. Leon Godchaux, who moved to New York in 1858 to begin manufacturing directly for his stores in New Orleans, reportedly employed two hundred workers. He was one of at least ten Jewish clothiers to do so. These manufacturing clothiers were able to extend their trade well beyond Louisiana, selling garments in Texas, Arkansas, and California.[10]

It was not just manufacturers who were buoyed by the spring tide of cotton that flowed through New Orleans in the 1850s. Yet in spite of the growing presence of Jewish-owned businesses in the marketplace, relatively few appear to have consistently purveyed large quantities of garments to the plantations that flanked the Mississippi. Commerce in the antebellum plantation economy was dominated by cotton factors, merchants who marketed cotton for planters and performed a variety of other commercial and banking functions for them. These merchants preferred to bypass smaller suppliers in order to purchase in bulk, earning profits on every transaction. With a few exceptions Jewish clothiers and dry-goods merchants in New Orleans derived much of their business from rural storekeepers and peddlers, whose numbers swelled in the 1840s and 1850s. By 1860 nearly a third of all Jews in the South lived in Louisiana, many along the Mississippi and its tributaries. Here they were helped by the vast expansion of cotton cultivation in new areas of settlement. Cotton factors were accustomed to serving the needs of larger plantations, but many of the new settlers farmed on a small scale, far from railways and macadamized roads. Peddlers and petty storekeepers depended on people at the margins of an economy geared toward cotton planters—including yeoman farmers, fur trappers, townspeople, river men, and slaves—for the majority of their business. The German traveler Friedrich Gerstäcker, who lived for a time in Louisiana, reported that in Bayou Sara, and presumably in other small towns that clung to the muddy banks of the Mississippi, "nothing . . . is more common than to find a Jewish dandy decked out in the most tasteless fashion. He strolls around grandly with a lorgnette or, coming from one of the little country towns to buy wares from the Bayou Sara merchants, lies back casually in his one-horse buggy, legs sticking out to one side, and smokes a cigar. They do very well, and I have found similar types only among Berlin firms at the Leipzig fair." For all his snobbery, Gerstäcker was delighted to purchase a "quite decent lightweight suit" from one of these merchants, who "competed with one another in selling the clothes as cheaply as possible."[11] Gerstäcker was a direct beneficiary of a mercantile network that had adapted to riverine commerce. Jewish wholesalers in New Orleans and other regional centers, many of whom had begun as peddlers, were familiar with the challenges of selling goods in areas poorly served by transportation infrastructure. In a pattern similar to that in the Midwest, Jewish storekeepers and peddlers along the Mississippi formed partnerships with these urban merchants, acted as the agents of larger concerns, or relied on loans from wholesalers in New Orleans, New York, Philadelphia, Baltimore, and Cincinnati. This gave them a good preparation for the new economic reality produced by the splintering of the plantation system and the emergence of a new system of cotton cultivation after the Civil War, but it relegated them to a position of secondary importance in the plantation economy before 1861.[12]

Jewish firms in New York that relied on these storekeepers and peddlers for custom were carried higher by the tide of cotton profits that flowed northward, but it raised few of them into the upper reaches of the garment industry. By the early 1850s Jews had a significantly broader and deeper presence in the clothing and dry-goods businesses than they had had just a decade before. New York City's Jewish population had grown substantially, reaching almost forty thousand by 1860. Many proprietors of retail stores, wholesale outlets, and small manufacturing operations had begun their careers carrying a peddler's pack or tending a rural store. Like their counterparts in Cincinnati, they continued to rely on a network of itinerant traders and petty merchants to act as their distributors. They were aided by the expanding footprint of peddlers and storekeepers in the West and the South and by the dominant position of Jews in the wholesale trade in Cincinnati. But they were by and large bypassed by plantation factors who directed their business to those who had established relationships and reputations in the South. Although some Jewish firms created subsidiaries in the cotton belt, in most cases these were outside of the major cities and operated on a much smaller scale than did the largest New York merchant houses. For a time it must have seemed that Jewish firms in New York would be permanently consigned to a middling rank in the garment industry, profiting from access to a dynamic distribution system in the Midwest but outmuscled by rivals who could turn Southern cotton into gold. Few, if any, of those who looked on as envious spectators to the marriage between Northern manufacturing and Southern money realized that within a handful of years this conjugal knot was to tighten into a noose that choked the same manufacturers and wholesalers who had been its largest beneficiaries. By the end of the decade fate had upended well-worn patterns in the clothing trade.

The Good Word from the West

In the late 1840s and early 1850s, however, a future in which a dependence on Southern sales was a recipe for ruination was barely conceivable. Manufacturers and wholesalers were preoccupied with white-hot prices for cotton that made for late nights in their countinghouses. Paradoxically, the ready rewards of the Southern trade may have made the largest firms more timid when it came to new ventures. When word began to filter eastward of the discovery of gold in far-off California, and then of the boom that transformed the sleepy village of Yerba Buena into San Francisco—already a makeshift city of thirty-five thousand by 1852—those firms preoccupied with Southern profits appear to have weighed the substantial risks of this new market more heavily in their calculations than did those with less to lose. Jewish merchants who operated small and middle-size firms, clerks and shop assistants who had learned the clothing business behind the counter, and peddlers who had done so in the countryside proved more responsive to the news from the Pacific Coast. Over the next fifteen years, gold propelled Jews into a commanding position in the menswear trade, while cotton hobbled many of their competitors. But for this unexpected sequence of events, Jewish firms might have long remained on the margins of the garment industry in New York and never achieved the dominance of some sectors of the business that they had after the Civil War.

President James K. Polk confirmed the intoxicating rumors that gold had been discovered in California in an address to Congress in December 1848, describing an "abundance . . . of such an extraordinary character as would scarcely command belief." The news set hearts aflutter and legs, carriages, wagon trains, and ships into motion. California became a magnet for fortune-seeking migrants. The floodwaters did not soon recede. In the early months of 1850 Jewish newspapers breathlessly reported on the exodus of "large numbers of Israelites" from New York and New Orleans bound for the "Eldorado on the shores of the Pacific." (In the same pages, New York dry-goods merchants opportunistically advertised their readiness to secure orders on clothing they had had sewn up from their stockpile of imported fabric "expressly for the CALIFORNIA TRADE.")[13] "Not a vessel" departed without "a large proportion of the enterprising sons of Israel" aboard; cargo holds were crammed with "a vast quantity of old style manufactured goods of every description." A less charitable passenger observed that such was the concentration of "traders and speculators" aboard his vessel that the place amidships where they clustered acquired the nickname " 'Chatham Street,' or the 'Jewry.' "[14] Much like Melbourne, San Francisco was transformed from a sleepy town of a little over eight hundred people (many of whom deserted their homes and businesses in the spring of 1848 to try their luck prospecting with metal pans and sluice boxes along the American River) into an exuberant city of newcomers. Enough migrants came from Australia that the city was soon home to a tent village known as Sydney Town (its reputation for lawlessness and licentiousness was little diminished when it was renamed Barbary Coast). A state census in 1852 recorded that 43 percent of people in San Francisco who identified as having British origins were Australian; along with Germans, immigrants from the British Empire were the most numerous among the city's residents. Their numbers remained high despite the substantial reverse flow of migrants across the Pacific when word reached California of the discovery of gold in Australia. Early settlers were conscious of the ethnic and geographical origins of neighbors and newcomers, and Jewish settlers were generally held in higher regard than Antipodean migrants, who dragged convict reputations with them across the Pacific, as well as those whose skin color marked them as different.[15] By 1850 California's population had swollen to over ninety-two thousand. Men outnumbered women twelve to one, and more than half of the male residents were in their twenties. Within a decade, the state's population more than tripled in size again, growing at a rate roughly equivalent to that of Victoria in Australia (in 1861, Victoria still had a larger population than California, and Melbourne had more than double the number of residents that San Francisco had).[16]

On the surface California offered poor soil for the rooting of Jewish commercial networks, thinner even than that in Australia. Before the influx of gold seekers, a scattering of isolated Jews had been scratching out a living on the Pacific coast of America. Within a handful of years, thousands of Jews—peddlers, clerks, storekeepers, new immigrants, and a host of others—had joined the exodus westward, staking out new Jewish communities in inland ports, mining camps, mountain towns, and trading posts. By 1855 there were about six thousand Jews in California—more than the number in Australia. Five years later, there were ten thousand. And there were sixteen thousand by the mid-1870s, when San Francisco was briefly home to the second-largest Jewish population in the United States, only surpassed by New York City. For a time Jews made up a significant portion of San Francisco's residents. In fact, one possibly elevated estimate was that they made up as much as 9 percent of the city's population of fifty-seven thousand in 1860.[17] Many of those who flocked to California from points east had experience in the retail trade. Julius Weis, who had peddled around Natchez, Mississippi, for several years before hearing of the gold discovery was tempted to join their number. He "decided to quit peddling" to join "several of the young men of [his] acquaintance" who had been bitten by the gold bug, but he was dissuaded by his parents.[18] Other Jewish pioneers left for California from as far away as Europe with the encouragement of relatives, who loaned them money. Several Jews crossed the Pacific from Australia and New Zealand.

As in Australia, the vast majority of Jewish migrants to California chose to enter commercial occupations rather than prospect for gold. They were certainly not alone in doing so; many others with backgrounds in merchandising similarly sought to profit from the miners rather than from the mines. The potential windfall from prospecting was greatest during the earliest phase of the rush, when pickings were best—a miner with a Midas touch might pan as much as $8,000 in alluvial gold in a day— while the profits of those who could provision the miners became steadily more dependable. This was certainly the case once the costs of supplying the gold fields rose, the easiest gold to find had been panned, and capital-intensive industrial methods of mining began to predominate.[19] The rewards were particularly rich for those who could muster quantities of clothing, tools, and liquor and march them into San Francisco in the heady first year of the gold rush. Jesse Seligman left his dry-goods store in Watertown, New York, in the hands of one of his brothers and made his way westward via Panama with a large stock of goods. Jesse was purportedly instructed by his oldest brother, Joseph, not to dabble at the diggings: "If you go, it is to be a merchant, and not as a gambler hoping to make a strike." His initial winnings would have satisfied many a habitué of San Francisco's gambling halls, since tin utensils, blankets, and whiskey commanded inflated prices. Twelve years later the firm he established was reported to be worth $900,000.[20] Seligman's success was exceptional, but many more Jews followed a pattern similar to that of newcomers to Australia during its gold rush, opening modest stores in mining camps and, if fortune smiled on them, returning to settle in a larger town—perhaps San Francisco itself—as a proprietor of a wholesale operation with branch stores in the gold fields. As the historian Ava Kahn has noted, relatively few Jews peddled in California because of the tax imposed on those who did and the comparative ease of setting up shop in a mining camp.[21] Not all of them began as storekeepers; there were enough Jewish clerks in San Francisco to organize a mutual-aid society of their own. There was ample need for clerks, as successful merchants in San Francisco came to fill much the same role as their counterparts in Cincinnati and New York, distributing goods on credit to a dispersed web of peddlers and storekeepers. Although it certainly helped to arrive in San Francisco as an agent of an East Coast concern, there were ample opportunities for those who set up shop without such formal connections. Many more Jews started their Californian careers by opening small stores with limited funds and larger risks than those who arrived with the kinds of advantages enjoyed by the likes of Jesse Seligman. But once they had established a reputation for reliability, they could tap into a rich vein of credit offered by San Francisco distributors and Eastern wholesalers eager to expand their presence in the Californian market. For those who were successful, San Francisco provided a high degree of social mobility. In 1852 more than a third of the city's merchants were men who had started in California as manual workers and clerks.[22]

Cosmopolitan, polyglot, and commercially minded, San Francisco was dubbed the "New York of the Pacific" as early as 1858 because of its dominance of trade on the West Coast and its expanding hinterland. (A nearby town, not short of braggadocio, briefly took the name "New York of the Pacific" but later retreated to the humbler Pittsburg.) San Francisco's Jewish pioneers also got in on the act, naming their first two synagogues after the leading congregations in New York City.[23] But if the vibrant trade in San Francisco reminded visitors of New York, those who looked closely might have noticed that in the clothing trade, Jews occupied a position undreamed of in the Northeast. A visitor who observed that "dealing in ready-made clothing" was the "peculiar forte" of Jews in San Francisco was not far wrong.[24] Jewish clothiers formed a conspicuous part of the German merchant community, one of San Francisco's largest and most commercially active minorities. According to one estimate, Jewish firms constituted 94 percent of German-owned clothing-related enterprises in the 1850s. A little under half of all Jews in the city whose occupations were recorded were clothing and dry-goods dealers, clerks, salesmen, bookkeepers, and merchants.[25] Travelers also noted with wonderment the presence of Jews hawking "red and blue flannel, thick boots, and other articles suited to the wants of the miners" from "rattletrap erections about the size of a bathing-machine" in even the most remote mining camps. Whenever "twenty or thirty miners collected in any out-of-the-way place, ... the inevitable Jew slop-shop also made his appearance, to play his allotted part in the newly-formed community."[26]

On the gold fields Jews typically wore the suits favored by men of commerce rather than the "uniform" of "a broad-brimmed slouched hat, a red or blue flannel shirt, a patterned kerchief, blue denim pants, a thick belt to which was attached at least one bowie knife and a pistol, and leather boots" that was preferred by European and American miners. Merchants and traders were outnumbered by miners many times over. In Nevada City, one of the largest mining towns in the early stages of the rush, there were ten miners to every trader and merchant; in nearby Rough and Ready, a mining camp of 672 residents originally established by prospectors from Wisconsin, the ratio was a little more than three to one. (But for the intervention of neighbors in a violent altercation between two Jewish clothiers—one may have drawn a knife; the other attacked him with a pair of boots—about a charitable gift, the town's complement of merchants might have been reduced by at least one.)[27] Conditions in the hamlets that sprang up wherever miners gathered were primitive. In an environment dominated by bespattered miners, the cleanly attired trader hawking unmuddied clothing attracted attention. Jewish merchants, however, drew notice in larger centers too. As in New York, London, and Melbourne, in San Francisco visitors were fascinated by the cluster of stores on Commercial, Sacramento, Clay, and Washington Streets that were "presided over," as one observer put it, "by those . . . elastic and persistent tradesmen, the Jews." Thomas Massie, a visitor from Virginia, spent his last night in the city wandering through the ethnic enclaves of the commercial district. After goggling the "dense crowds of moving celestials" in Dupont Street, he and a friend made their way "from China through Jerusalem" on their way back to their hotel. Mesmerized by the accented banter of an auctioneer—"a sharp and noisy fellow with a rabble crowd about him"— selling shirts, handkerchiefs, and cigars, their resolve to remain spectators was overcome by the bargains that were available.[28] Others were less enamored of the exotic scene. Another traveler was indignant that Jews had "presumptuously usurped" the sidewalk by erecting "little wooden racks and projections" from their "miserable little shops." Rent was high and space at a premium; these jerry-rigged displays were intended to catch the eye of passersby. "In any other place than California," the traveler sniffed, "such unjust appropriations of the streets of a city would not be tolerated; but here, where usurpation, illegality and confusion reign supreme, no attention is paid to it."[29] He clearly had not visited London and Sydney, where others shared his battered sense of decorum.

It is important to remember that the commanding position enjoyed by Jewish clothiers in San Francisco and Sacramento was not the inevitable outgrowth of Jewish involvement in the clothing business in New York and Cincinnati. Indeed, in New York, the largest portion of manufacturing and marketing of clothing was still in the hands of non-Jewish firms. A credit agency reported in January 1861 that fewer than one in five of the 1,676 businesses in clothing, dry goods, and related fields located in New York was Jewish owned. Yet it was Jewish firms in New York that took the lead in seizing the opportunities presented by the California gold rush, not their better-financed competitors who had been established longer. According to the same credit-agency data, Jewish firms were only slightly more likely to do extensive business outside New York than were their rivals. Approximately 12 percent of Jewish firms had branch stores or agents in other states. The orientation of these differed, however, from that of their competitors. Although both Jewish and non-Jewish firms based in New York had operations in New Orleans and Mobile, Jews were more likely to have a presence in small towns in the South—a reflection of the roots of these firms in peddling and rural storekeeping—and much less likely to do business with partners in Boston. Where Jewish merchants stood out was in their involvement in the Californian trade. Compared to their non-Jewish rivals, significantly more Jewish firms had branches or agents in California than in the South. New York Jewish firms were strikingly overrepresented in the Golden State: of the forty-seven firms identified by the credit agency that had permanent representatives there, more than one in three was Jewish-owned.[30] The conspicuous examples of success achieved by some Jewish entrepreneurs may have encouraged others to try their hand at the California trade.

California's market seemed to have been magically created by a sprinkling of gold dust. Those who arrived first had an unusual opportunity to lay claim to virgin territory, establishing an early presence that made it more challenging for those who came later to stake their own claims. The historian Peter Decker has demonstrated that the earliest wave of merchants and traders who made their way to San Francisco were more likely than those who followed to move up the economic ladder. This was particularly true for those who began as petty shopkeepers, clerks, and peddlers and for many Jews—whose economic mobility "far surpassed" other native- and foreign-born merchants.[31] In the South Jewish traders were obliged to adapt to patterns of trade established by others—not so in California. Business with plantation owners in the South followed a well-practiced formula involving familiar intermediaries and reliable mechanisms. Business with California was much less certain. Who would distribute and sell the goods that Easterners shipped westward? Who could be trusted? How would profits be returned to the East? Nimble immigrant entrepreneurs had more to gain and less to lose by venturing onto this new and uncertain terrain than some of their more storied and staid competitors did.

Trade with California carried considerable risks for New York firms no matter what their size. The gold price was labile and market conditions manic. The price of merchandise rose and fell with as little predictability as "fancy stocks" on the " 'Changes of New York, London or Paris." More goods entered California in the two years following the gold rush than gold was exported. The market moved from scarcity to saturation as competing shipments arrived from the East, only to return to shortage once cargoes were sold and stocks depleted.[32] To visitors to San Francisco in the 1850s and 1860s the rambling and shambling presence of Joshua Abraham Norton provided an object lesson in the risks of the Californian market. Galvanized by news of the discovery of gold, Norton left the Cape Colony for San Francisco in 1849. There he initially prospered as a wholesale grocer and speculator, but, in keeping with a past history of persistent failure, he was badly burned in 1853 when the rice market boiled over. Bankruptcy appears to have tipped Norton into lunacy. Until his death in 1880, he proclaimed himself to be "Emperor of the United States, Protector of Mexico, and Sovereign Lord of the Guano Islands" (he eventually added the title "Emperor of the Jews"), and he paraded through the streets of San Francisco in a regal costume (composed of a tatty uniform, cavalry sword, and feathered hat), issuing scrip and proclamations to the subjects of his imaginary kingdom. (His suggestion that a bridge be built linking the city to Oakland was ahead of its time.) Another case was even less fortunate. Selig Ritzwoller, a merchant in Sonora, along with his debts left this pathetic plea after hanging himself: "Dear God pardon and forgive me—my poor wife and poor children, pardon and forgive me—my heart is broken—the Hebrew Benevolent Society in San Francisco take pity on my poor wife and children—do not let them starve—to my kind brothers in law Rosner I owe a great deal of money—Dear God in thy hands I recommend my soul amen—Joel Levy and Kaufman take care of my wife and children."[33]

Norton's picaresque presence did not scare off others who sought riches in San Francisco. If his "ascent to an imaginary throne was atypical," the challenges that precipitated his descent were more commonplace.[34] David and Philip Bush, immigrants from eastern Europe, built up a clothing business in New York City with a branch in Charleston. They were considered to be "good businessmen" and "fair in their dealings." To expand their sales, one brother moved to California to open a store. On July 1, 1851, the brothers were described as creditworthy: they were "honest and always paid promptly." A little over two weeks later, the credit agency's ledger clerk revised his assessment. His laconic entry—"failed, were in the California trade"—suggests that commerce with the West Coast had become shorthand for risky enterprise. This is confirmed in the assessment of Jacob and Leopold Lithauer, who manufactured clothing in Hartford and New York. Although they were considered "good for moderate" loans, they were seen to have "lost credit by going into California trade and have injured their business very much." Bach Barnett & Company, clothiers in New Orleans, were "said to be largely in the California trade" but would "not admit they are doing much at it." The firm later lost heavily in one of the calamitous fires that turned the combustible canvas and flimsy wooden structures of San Francisco into an inferno in 1851 (eight large fires left the city smoldering over the course of the decade, four of them before 1852); one of the partners "perished in the flames." Jesse Seligman's store was one of the few to survive the conflagration; he disposed of his entire stock within the week at a large markup because of sudden shortages caused by the fire. Joel Mintz and his family were less fortunate. When a subsequent fire roused them from their beds and burned down their home, the *San Francisco Gleaner* commiserated that it "is easy enough for dealers to resume business; but a poor man with a family comprising five souls, for such to be obliged to leave the house actually naked is hard." They were lucky to get out alive. The storekeeper Alexander Mayer reported that in a fire in June 1851 "tow jehudem Burned to deaths again they stoot in their Store to save their goods." According to one estimate, as many as three-quarters of all merchants were "burned out" by fire before 1852. In addition to fires (a traumatized Mayer lamented that "a Fire may come to night and Loose every thing and not have enough to pay a Breackfast withe") and other unexpected mishaps, the unpredictability of the market, and the uncertainty of returns, creditors worried about being fleeced by truant partners. It was difficult and costly to recoup losses from businesses that defaulted or failed in far-off California. Samuel Bachrach—a partner in a New York firm that was "well spoken of by their Jewish brethren" who was nevertheless dismissed by a credit reporter as "not a first rate businessman"—was able to recover after fire in San Francisco left him with losses. Within a year, further losses in California brought down his business. He was far from alone; credit-agency ledgers are filled with such business failures. According to one estimate, between half and two-thirds of all merchants failed in San Francisco in the 1850s.[35]

Much like the situation in Australia when gold was discovered there, the perils of doing business in California in the 1850s simultaneously discouraged some people and magnified the advantages of others, particularly those who could draw on ethnic networks. Many of the larger New York and Boston merchant houses eyed the Californian trade gingerly, wary of

waiting six months to a year for their investments to yield an uncertain
payoff. Since Eastern banks were reluctant to extend loans to businesses
in San Francisco and local banks were wary of shopkeepers, merchants
without means of their own relied on money or stock borrowed from
friends and family or acted as agents for firms that fronted them capital.
Flexible credit and forgiving creditors were invaluable in a market where
supply and demand were so often out of sync. When Mayer arrived in
San Francisco with trunk loads of supplies at the beginning of 1851, after
an arduous crossing of Panama, he reported on conditions to his uncle in
Philadelphia. Mayer was shocked to discover that there was "No use to
Offer any Goods at Presents": "I really belive there are More Cassi[mere,
or cashmere] pants here than in the hole [whole] of Phila[delphia]."
There were "a great many Ratts every wheres" but fewer customers willing to pay prices equivalent to what Mayer had paid when purchasing his
stock before his departure. He found "plenty on the market" of many of
the items he had lugged with him at great cost and effort; he hoped that
his uncle had "not Sent any More Goods. at present" and advised him to
avoid advancing credit to people planning to enter the Californian trade.
Mayer complained a month later that business remained "very Dull . . .
Why it cant be otherwise, There are So many Jehudem Here in Buisness
and Every One Want to Sell." A shopkeeper or wholesaler who was not
obliged to jettison his stock in order to satisfy clamorous creditors at a
time when the market was flooded could reap handsome returns when the
market swung to the opposite extreme. Mayer, for example, hoped that his
uncle would have "patience about Money" so that he would not need to
"sacrofice Goods" but "rather let them lay a while Yet."[36] Business partners
on the East Coast who were also kinsmen may have been more willing
to carry or cover losses and even offer fresh credit after failure.[37] But, as
Mayer discovered, they could also be a liability. In March 1851 he rebuked
his uncle, "I where very much disapointed that You have send me Over
Coats. . . . There is no hopes there are to many here." The arrival of the
new stock made matters worse at a time when business was already bad:
"peable here they sad [sat] down in Day time and play Cards. You must
think how brisck Business is."[38] After a "dreatfull" fire destroyed much of
Mayer's remaining stock and killed four of his friends in May 1851, he wrote
to a relative that he hoped his uncle had sent "no Goods," so that he would
"be home again next Fall."[39]

Mayer spent many weeks waiting for word from his relatives in Philadelphia, and when letters or stock arrived by ship, he had to respond to decisions made weeks and even months before. As in Australia, in California distance initially exerted an inescapable tyranny. Travelers had the choice of an arduous overland journey (the Butterfield Stage ran only seasonally, and even then a passenger could expect to spend more than twenty days cooped up in a stagecoach on a bone-jarring journey from a railhead to distant San Francisco), a risky voyage around the Horn that took upward of seven months (in 1854, the clipper *Flying Cloud* sailed from New York to San Francisco in a record eighty-nine days), or the quickest option, which was still slow as well as expensive and unhealthy: crossing Mexico, Nicaragua, or the isthmus of Panama. In the early 1850s the passenger who embarked in New York might pay more than $500 for a passage to San Francisco. Trunks of clothing dispatched from New York did not, of course, suffer the torments of seasickness and mosquitoes, but they too spent months in transit. Freightage fees might gobble as much as 50 percent of the value of the cargo.

But the challenges of doing business in distant California were mitigated in ways that were impossible in the case of Australia. A continental divide was easier to bridge than an ocean. The circuitous voyage to Australia from England covered sixteen thousand miles of sometimes-placid but often-rough ocean. A slow-sailing ship might take up to two hundred days to reach Australia. Clippers could cover the distance in a little more than sixty days if winds blew favorably but take up to forty days longer if becalmed. People in search of the quickest passage from New York to San Francisco also developed sound sea legs. Travel via Panama remained the most efficient method of crossing the continent from New York to San Francisco until the completion of the transcontinental railroad in 1869. But even during the 1850s the expense of transit declined, and the relay of information became speedier. In 1851 a merchant in San Francisco could expect to wait from three to four months for delivery after first dispatching an order to a supplier in New York; by 1876 the *Transcontinental Express*, aiming to set a new record, covered the distance in a blistering eighty-three hours. As a result of the increasing ease of doing business across a continent, the opportunities presented by California had far broader and deeper consequences for Jewish clothiers in New York City than the possibilities in Australia had for Jews in

London. Many more Jews migrated to the Golden State during the gold rush than to the Antipodes. And even though California was distant, enterprises there could be wired more quickly and tightly into an existing ethnic economy.[40]

Clothing unloaded in San Francisco was only at the beginning of a journey that might take it from the wharf to a wholesaler or auction house, on to a storekeeper, and finally into the hands of a distant customer. Manufacturers and wholesalers in New York who were able to rely on dependable distributors in California reduced the considerable risks of shipping goods westward. Trustworthiness was worth its weight in gold in a place where banks and other institutions were often not. Alexander Mayer, for example, would not extend credit to Mr. Rheinstrom, who he knew had failed before arriving in San Francisco, and indeed Rheinstrom soon failed again.[41] The influx of migrants and the inevitable delay in the verification of the bona fides of newcomers meant that it was very difficult to reliably assess the reputations of potential partners, creditors, and debtors. San Francisco became a city of refuge for people eager to leave a sullied past behind. According to one estimate, just under a third of all merchants who set up shop in the city during the gold rush arrived after their businesses elsewhere had failed. Among their number were several disgraced Jewish clothiers from England and the East Coast who had fled creditors and the law. This was not unusual in frontier settings. For example, Texas in the 1840s has been described by one historian, perhaps with a little exaggeration, as a " 'default frontier,' populated by bankrupts and defaulters fleeing from busts further north."[42]

As we have seen, familial and ethnic networks were particularly beneficial in markets, like those of California and Australia, where there was a prolonged "information float." As the historian Peter Decker has described, many merchants in San Francisco and many wholesalers and manufacturers in New York and Boston flailed blindly because of a paucity of reliable information. This increased not only the volatility of the market but also the benefit of even a momentary advantage. Unlike other fields where demand was somewhat more predictable, the fickleness of fashion ensured that early access to information about market conditions was priceless. A shopkeeper in close contact with suppliers could profit if his merchandise was unloaded at a wharf in San Francisco days ahead of the stock of his rivals. Mayer sent detailed lists to Philadelphia of the items that were in demand, goods that "will sell well if they come in the rite time": "If you do sent any, sent them by Quick Vessels from New York." Although Jewish merchants in San Francisco communicated with business partners and suppliers who were often friends, family members, or coreligionists, this was no guarantee of success given the risks inherent in attempting to judge supply and demand months in advance. Misjudgment could lead to business failure. Goods that arrived when the market was flooded languished until disposed of at knock-down prices at auction. Mayer complained to his uncle in Philadelphia: "You Know How it is with the Jewis at Auction is every think cheap." By June 1851 he had sold multiple items at auction for lower prices than he had paid for them in Philadelphia.[43] Ethnic bonds, however, may have provided a slight edge when reliable information was at a premium. Once the initially explosive rate of migration slowed, and the population of San Francisco became more settled, the advantage of doing business with members of the same ethnic group declined. But until that point there was value in preferring to do business with someone who was not completely unknown. These momentary advantages could be parlayed into long-term dominance.[44]

The merchants of the 1850s were well positioned to transition to manufacturing in the 1860s. Given that Jews predominated among German-speaking dry-goods and clothing merchants in San Francisco in the 1850s, it was no accident that they became overrepresented among the city's clothing manufacturers. Levi Strauss was the most famous of those who followed this trajectory. Born in Bavaria and the son of a dry-goods peddler, Strauss briefly joined two brothers in New York before spending a period peddling. He arrived in San Francisco in 1853; opened a business near the waterfront that sold hats, fabric, clothing, and other articles supplied in part by his siblings in New York; and occasionally left the city to peddle hardy work pants—originally canvas and later denim—on the gold fields. He and other would-be manufacturers benefited from being early innovators in an open market. By the 1860s his denim "waist overalls" were being manufactured under the supervision of Strauss Brothers in New York and shipped to San Francisco. Two decades after arriving in California, Strauss had established a thriving wholesale business in grand, gas-lit premises. Then he received a letter from a tailor in Nevada, containing a fateful suggestion: add metal rivets to the seams, so the trousers could better withstand the pressures of a miner's life. Although the

Two trade cards produced by Levi Strauss & Company to advertise its hardy merchandise.
(Courtesy of the Arnold and Deanne Kaplan Collection of Early American Judaica
at the Library at the Herbert D. Katz Center for Advanced Judaic Studies, University
of Pennsylvania)

patented addition made Strauss and his partner a fortune, they were far
from alone in moving from selling clothing on the gold fields to manufacturing clothing on a larger scale. More than half of those who were manufacturers in San Francisco in 1880 had started their careers in clerical or
blue-collar occupations.[45]

The Californian market also delivered a bonanza to East Coast firms
that weathered the crises of the 1850s. In aggregate, early entry into
the Californian trade redounded to their benefit. Since local production
could not keep up with demand—less than 3 percent of all San Francisco residents were involved in manufacturing trades in 1860, compared
with close to 19 percent in Cincinnati—and wages were significantly
higher than on the East Coast, those who sent clothing and fabric westward when demand was strong could sell these at a premium. New York
firms also gained access to gold shipped in payment for orders. Later

this proved an extraordinary asset, providing a source of windfall profits and a vital hedge against inflation.

The Impact on New York

No matter whether clothing firms in New York City derived their profits from California, New Orleans, or closer to home, they typically did well in the first seven years of the 1850s. One Jewish newspaper calculated that the fifty leading Jewish manufacturing firms in the metropolis in 1857—most, but not all, of whom were in the clothing and dry-goods line—employed nearly 14,000 workers, or an average of 278 employees each. Of these manufacturers, Bachrach & Praslor (with 150 employees), J. Straus (275), and Seligman & Company (480) did extensive business directly with California; while Morrison & Haber (550) did business with New Orleans, Isaac Elkins & Company (100) with Memphis, and I. & G. Lichtenheim (300) with Indiana. Other manufacturers were contracted by wholesalers and merchants to produce garments for these markets. The figures, however, are somewhat misleading. Even if the numbers are accurate—they were presumably estimates or reported by the manufacturers and not verified—almost all these workers probably labored at home or in independent workshops that were contracted to fulfill seasonal orders placed by these firms. The numbers do not account for seasonal variability or the way in which firms increased and decreased their workforce depending on demand. And the largest firms on the list—the clothing manufacturer Laisch, Stubblefield & Barnett (with 1,500 employees) and the shirtmakers Einstein & Jacobs (1,000), P. H. & L. Lewis (880), and Stettheimer & Rosenbaum (800)—were outliers that pushed the average upward. More than a quarter of the largest Jewish manufacturing firms employed no more than a hundred workers.[46]

The 1850s were not an entire decade of smooth sailing in New York. Those who depended on profits from California discovered, as did their counterparts in London who relied on growing demand in Australia, that their initial rate of return was unsustainable. And when crisis struck New York, it was much more acute than the one that hit London. Not even carefully husbanded profits generated in California could save many firms in 1857, when financial panic caused overextended merchants to fail en masse. Their defaults created a systemic crisis that toppled wholesalers, manufacturers, importers, and banks like a row of dominos. The gains made by Jewish firms in the clothing trade seemed to have been undone almost overnight. A month after the crisis began, a Jewish newspaper in New York noted with trepidation "the tumult of falling houses and suspending banks." "Hard times" had become the "staple fare of New Yorkers." New York City and the Midwest were particularly hard hit, and soon there were forty thousand unemployed workers in the metropolis. The "unvarying tale is told by our merchant friends," warned the editor of the same newspaper, *they can get no money from the interior.* "Pay up, pay up, no matter at what cost," he implored rural storekeepers.[47] More than a third of all businesses in San Francisco were bankrupted. By January 1858 Arnold Fischel, a minister at one of the leading synagogues in New York, bemoaned the "misery and distress, with which we are surrounded." Optimism was replaced by "gloom and apprehension for the future." Thousands had "been hurled down into the vortex of indigence." The "universal cry is 'Hard Times.' "[48] Of the fifty firms listed in 1857 as the largest Jewish manufacturers in New York City, only nineteen appear to still have been in business under the same name a little over three years later.[49] Worse was soon to come: just as merchants began to find their footing again, financial panic gave way to political crisis.

Signs of looming trouble had long been evident; discord over slavery had left the bonds of the Union brittle. Clothiers and dry-goods merchants in New York watched the escalating political crisis with trepidation. They received a foretaste of what the future might hold when the stock exchange teetered in the weeks before the 1860 election. Much of the city's merchant class prayed for a Democratic victory, fearing that the election of Abraham Lincoln as president would be the death knell of the Union. The exchange's perilous gyrations continued to follow the mood swings of the public, which at one moment exulted at the prospect of a political compromise and at the next resigned itself to the worst. As the national mood soured, manufacturers began to lay off workers, retailers cut back on their purchases of new stock, and customers prepared for a season of thrift. The sense of crisis deepened in the first months of 1861. Banks failed across the North, after revealing that they had issued notes backed by Southern states' bonds. In Illinois only 17 of the state's 104 banks survived the summer. Barring an unexpected turn of events, New York City appeared all but certain to be one of the largest losers if the South was to secede, robbing the metropolis of its largest market. The *Daily Tribune* foresaw the end of New York's prosperity: beneath its ruins "ten thousand fortunes are buried. . . . Last Fall, the merchant was a capitalist, today he is a bankrupt."[50] The city's politicians cast about for solutions, some vainly proposing that it too should push for independence. Clothing firms that had struggled to resurrect their fortunes after the panic of 1857 now faced the prospect of slow strangulation. Businesses that depended on the Southern market shed workers. Rumors that Southern merchants might renege on their debts added to the dismal atmosphere. In some instances these whispers proved accurate, and close to a hundred dry-goods businesses were driven into insolvency. Many clothing firms that had barely survived the panic of 1857 now toppled into oblivion. Hotels reported higher-than-usual vacancy rates as Southern merchants who normally flocked to the city in the spring for the first of their semiannual purchasing trips stayed away. Lazarus Straus, one of the few merchants who did make the trip, found dry-goods houses "surprised at his presence." Some retailers, hoping to profit from these fears and the growing stockpiles of unsold surplus goods, advertised that they were dumping their orphaned stock. Their advertisements brought a poisonous word back to the air in America's commercial capital: panic.[51]

Yet less than two years later, a reporter for a Jewish newspaper in New York wrote triumphantly of what he saw in Broadway, the heart of the clothing trade:

> A walk up Broadway will satisfy any one that the influence of Israelites is daily making itself felt in the commercial world. Broadway, from Bowling Green to Canal Street, presents a formidable array of Jewish firms. What a grand effect would be produced by a general closing of these places of business on the Sabbath day! . . . Let us take a look at this magnificent street on a "working day" and read the "signs" as we proceed. Here we find a block of massive buildings, tenanted almost exclusively by Israelites. Between Beaver and Wall Streets, on either side, are the extensive wholesale establishments of L.J. & I. Phillips, M.I. & J.A. Joseph, the Kings, Samuels, Wolffs, and many others.—Further up, the double marble store occupied by C.E. Bresler; still further, on the corner of Warren Street, Lehmaier's collosal establishment; further on, Brunner's, Solomon & Hart's—another block, between Franklin and White streets fully representing Jewish firms; then

the Seligman's commodious building, at the corner of White Street. The Bernheimers have likewise joined in the general movement up town, and are located at the spot once the site of the Broadway Theater—at the junction of Pearl Street and Broadway. Contiguous to them, we notice the advent of a Cleveland House, Davis & Co. Not to particularise further, a walk up Broadway will satisfy any reasonable being that the Israelites of New York are among the most enterprising of her citizens.[52]

Jewish New Yorkers who read this article would have had reason to gloat. A decade before, the absence of Jewish names atop marble palaces along America's most important commercial thoroughfare might have seemed lamentable, compared to the situation in London, but now their coreligionists across the Atlantic might envy New York Jews. But how, instead of succumbing to the commercial cataclysm predicted in the early months of 1861, had these firms risen to commanding heights, exchanging the taint of Chatham Street for glorious Broadway?

The source of this newfound prosperity was not to be found among the migrants and settlers who paraded about San Francisco in fashionable clothing but among the armies of new customers that had been mustered in the spring and summer of 1861. These men had little choice as to their wardrobe. Their Prussian- and sky-blue outfits had a transformative impact on the fortunes of Jewish clothiers, a development scarcely anticipated in the early months of 1861, when the US Army was only sixteen thousand strong. Instead of heralding disaster for Jewish firms, the drumbeat of war unexpectedly pushed them into the front ranks of clothing manufacturing in America. With less exposure to the Southern market than many of their rivals—some of whom were swept away by unpaid debts—and with access to customers in California whose appetite for clothing was not diminished by the disruptions in the East, Jewish clothing businesses were well positioned to respond to the changes wrought by war.

The impact of the conflict was not confined to the United States, however. An English firm established in 1852 to compete for contracts to outfit the British Empire's soldiers and sailors also got into the act. Even though English clothiers had long since been supplanted in the American market by domestic manufacturers, this firm derived its largest profits from reversing this trend. In the process Samuel and Saul Isaac become unrivaled outfitters of the Confederacy.

7

Clothing the Blue and Gray

At dawn on Friday, May 10, 1861, sailing ships and steamers from across the world waited to dock in Liverpool's harbor. The bustling English port had once been a center of the slave trade, its merchants made rich by dispatching their vessels to rendezvous with slave traders at forts that dotted the West African coastline. Now it prospered by importing cotton—picked by slaves on plantations in the American South—to be transformed into cloth in the factories of Lancashire. More than 85 percent of the US cotton crop made its way to Liverpool, where it was sold by the city's cotton brokers. Weeks after the fall of Fort Sumter in Charleston harbor had signaled the beginning of the Civil War, many people in Liverpool, where pro-Southern sentiment ran high, expected that they would soon be doing business with the Confederate States of America. If they had known who was aboard one of the ships that arrived that May day, the stevedores might have given one of the inconspicuous passengers who hurried ashore a hero's welcome. After disembarking, Caleb Huse was in no mood to tarry after his circuitous voyage of three weeks. The thirty-year-old West Point graduate, freshly commissioned as a captain in the newly established Confederate army, was on his way to London, well aware that the task before him might determine the fate of the Confederacy.

Although Southerners continued to exult in the weeks that followed their victory at Fort Sumter, away from the parades and celebrations the hastily convened Confederate government was confronted with a stark reality. In its rush to war the Confederacy had had little time to create the stockpiles and systems needed to sustain armies in the field. Once it began to muster enthusiastic men into regiments—the Confederate Congress authorized an army of one hundred thousand volunteers in March

1861—it quickly found itself at a massive disadvantage. On the eve of the war only a fraction of US factories were based in the South. The Confederacy could barely shoe its soldiers: the North produced more than 90 percent of the nation's boots. Each regiment was initially charged with supplying its own uniforms. This policy was quickly reversed when it became clear that the volunteers were unable or unwilling to supply outfits that approximated the cadet gray standard. Instead, the unenviable task of outfitting the Confederate armies fell to a Quartermaster Department hurriedly cobbled together under the command of Abraham C. Myers. But for the decision of Alfred Mordecai, a senior officer in the Ordnance Department of the US Army, to reject the overtures of Jefferson Davis in March 1861, two of the most senior supply offices of the Confederacy would have been filled by Jews. By June 1861 Myers was placing orders for fifteen hundred uniforms a week with manufacturers in New Orleans, a quantity that soon proved insufficient to satisfy demand. Myers's challenges were compounded by the blockading of Confederate ports, which kept profitable cotton moldering in warehouses and imported supplies from landing.[1]

Barring divine intervention, the Confederate government realized that it would need to rely on imported weapons and uniforms if it were to have any chance of victory—hence the dispatch of Caleb Huse to London to begin purchasing the vast quantities of military supplies needed to surmount the Confederacy's shortfall. Huse arrived without detailed instructions and with considerable discretionary powers to buy and ship goods to Southern ports. He found stiff competition for rifles and other equipment from representatives of the Union, vendors who demanded exorbitant cash payments and were reluctant to supply the Confederacy at a time when its longevity and credit were uncertain, and overwhelming demands on his time as a one-man supply bureau. For help he turned to two firms experienced in filling military contracts. So began a fateful partnership that paired Huse with S. Isaac, Campbell & Company. Huse worked without underlings of his own and under considerable pressure to forward supplies as quickly as possible, and he came to rely on the firm to satisfy the new nation's gluttonous appetites for war materiel. Samuel and Saul Isaac, the firm's two partners, were not only willing to extend large amounts of credit at critical moments, but they also offered their expertise in navigating the landscape of the British arms industry, negotiating contracts with potential suppliers, inspecting purchased articles for defects, and organizing shipping to bypass the Northern blockade.[2]

Who Were S. Isaac, Campbell & Company?

The rise of S. Isaac, Campbell & Company was rooted in a longer history of the kind we have already encountered of Jews who sold slops to the sailors of the Royal Navy. Samuel Isaac was born at the end of the Napoleonic Wars in Chatham—a town with a strategic naval dockyard and army barracks—to a family whose income almost certainly depended on renting housewares to the transient population of military officers who came and went with the tides. Two of his uncles were slop sellers, and his family was related to that of Lewis Isaacs, one of the owners of the Clothes Exchange in London. By 1838 Samuel had set himself up as clothier, selling outfits to soldiers and sailors; soon he opened a grand store in the center of Chatham. He moved to London in the early 1850s and established S. Isaac, Campbell & Company, a decision that reflected his broadened ambitions.[3] No longer would Samuel focus on satisfying the persnickety whims of single soldiers and sailors. Henceforth he sought to outfit entire armies. Samuel was soon joined by Saul, his younger brother, and a formidable partnership was born.

As in many matters relating to business, Samuel's timing was portentous. The size and needs of the British military were expanding as the empire's reach circled the globe. In 1856 London's *Jewish Chronicle* crowed that Samuel and Saul's firm had won the contract to outfit the entire British Army in the East. Closer to home, the firm also won contracts to supply boots to the army depot at Weedon—a venture that persuaded Samuel to purchase a factory in Northampton, the town that supplied Britain with much of its cheap footwear.[4] Although S. Isaac, Campbell & Company appears to have entered the boot business too late to have its footwear dispatched to British soldiers campaigning in the mud of the Crimean peninsula and to have played only a relatively small role as a supplier during the Crimean War of 1854–1856, it became entangled in the reformist zeal galvanized by that war. Eerily foreshadowing events in America, in the Crimea a hastily mustered volunteer army went to war underprepared and ill equipped. Confident of a quick victory, the troops were outfitted in parade uniforms that were hopelessly inadequate when the war dragged on into the winter. Much of the replacement clothing sent to the shivering troops proved deficient. There were suspicions that some suppliers had won contracts fraudulently and that some contractors had increased their margins by using shoddy cloth to manufacture uniforms.

As a conspicuous beneficiary of a new centralized system for supplying the military, S. Isaac, Campbell & Company quickly attracted unwanted attention. An inquiry into army contracts in 1858 found evidence that the firm had provided articles of an "inferior description, and not worth the sum paid for them by the government." Even more damningly, the commission aired accusations of corruption. Despite Samuel Isaac's vigorous protestations of innocence, the firm was struck off the list of contractors permitted to compete for military orders from the War Department.[5] Isaac was right to worry about the stain left on his reputation. In future years foes of the firm returned to this episode, working a dark seam of innuendo and calumny that undermined S. Isaac, Campbell & Company at what should have been its finest hour. The firm scrounged for new business at home and abroad, showing its willingness to support quixotic causes when it outfitted a volunteer British Legion that supported Giuseppe Garibaldi in Italy in 1860 and when it later aided Chile in its war with Spain.[6] Political ructions across the Atlantic proved more promising. The arrival of Caleb Huse must have been greeted with excitement. If the Confederate cause appealed to Samuel and Saul Isaac's romanticism, its cotton promised to resurrect their fortunes.

Jewish Suppliers to the Union

There was little such enthusiasm among clothiers in New York City in March and early April 1861. As we have already seen, the outlook appeared ominous for merchants and manufacturers in the months before the outbreak of war. At best, they would encounter new tariffs imposed by an independent Confederacy and greater competition from Southern ports. At worst, they would be separated by war from the customers in their largest market. And then came unexpected salvation. On April 15, 1861, the day after the surrender of Fort Sumter, President Lincoln called seventy-five thousand militiamen into service to crush the rebellion. In mid-July, as it became clear that the conflict would not be resolved quickly, Congress authorized a volunteer army of five hundred thousand troops. By

1865 more than two million people had worn the Union uniform. Their outfits were of material interest to the garment manufacturers who had despaired in the months before the first artillery shells were lobbed at Fort Sumter. The rapid mobilization overwhelmed the regular army, which was unprepared for the avalanche of enlistees. In theory, each one was entitled to an annual allowance of at least one cap and hat, two jackets, three flannel shirts, trousers and drawers, and four pairs of stockings and shoes. By the end of the war most were wearing uniforms of the distinctive Prussian and sky blue. But in the heady summer of 1861 many regiments, such as the dashing Fire Zouaves—composed of rowdy New York firefighters—drew from a brighter palette. Whatever the eager enlistees wore in the spring and summer of 1861 needed to be produced in great haste and great quantity. The rush to outfit the volunteers set federal money coursing through a parched garment industry. Drought was replaced by deluge, shortage by surfeit.

Since the Union Quartermaster Department had no existing plans for mass mobilization, its overworked officers struggled with the herculean task of coordinating a military-supply system that expanded apace in the first months of the war. Given the urgency of the times, orders needed to be placed in great haste with manufacturers who had little or no experience in supplying the US Army. Charged with creating what became, in the words of the historian James McPherson, the "most lavishly supplied army that had ever existed," they were responsible for a gusher of dollars that could easily be misdirected.[7] Exigency often overrode concerns about cost. One potential option—importing uniforms from abroad—was foreclosed after an initial order placed with a French firm elicited protests from domestic producers.[8] Republican congressmen, freed of their constraining Southern counterparts, soon after introduced protective tariffs that raised much-needed revenue and made imported goods more expensive. With demand far exceeding supply from established firms, and with the clothing industry still struggling to regain its footing after the double blows of financial panic in 1857 and political ructions in 1860 and 1861, there was opportunity in crisis for those who had previously been at the margins of the garment business.

During the first year of the war the federal and state governments operated parallel procurement processes. The federal government delegated to the states authority to purchase and requisition the supplies needed to equip locally raised regiments. Governors had little time to establish efficient supply bureaus. Speedily assembled procurement boards, stocked with political appointees, operated with little oversight and an overriding sense of urgency. A significant portion of their outlay was devoted to purchasing uniforms and blankets. Soldiers were relatively expensive to clothe, with the cost of one man's annual clothing allowance double that of a rifle, and their uniforms stood up poorly to the rigors of campaigning, requiring replacement once in tatters, lost, or discarded. This pattern was replicated on the national level. According to the historian Mark Wilson, clothing contractors were "easily the greatest of the North's military suppliers" in terms of volume of business over the course of the war. He estimates that the Quartermaster Department spent twice as much on clothing and equipment as it did on weapons. By the end of the war it had purchased and produced astronomical quantities of clothing: over four million forage caps, six million pairs of trousers, eleven million shirts, and twenty million pairs of stockings.[9]

The worst prewar predictions of Cassandras in New York quickly came to pass: trade between New York and the South all but ceased, and Southern merchants suspended payments. Nonetheless, war provided an unexpected windfall. Within weeks after the war began, once-idle workshops begun to hum with activity. For many local manufacturers the bonanza reached its apogee in the first year of the war. The *New York Times* reported that factories on Broadway were splitting at the seams for want of space; tables "groan[ing] beneath piles and stacks of uniforms" were spilling out into the streets.[10] Jewish dry-goods merchants, clothing dealers, wholesalers, and clothiers—some of whom had only relinquished their heavy peddlers' pack a handful of years before—found themselves fortuitously positioned.[11] They were in the right industry with the right skills at the right moment, a phalanx of foot soldiers mustered into service by the Union's wartime economy. Many of their entrenched competitors had succumbed in 1857 and in the months before the firing on Fort Sumter. A nation pulled asunder by civil war, disastrous for so many of their competitors in the clothing trade, transformed their fortunes.

In New York the period of plenty began inauspiciously. In the weeks after Fort Sumter fell to the Confederacy, several Jewish firms sent agents laden with samples of overcoats, drawers, caps, and cloaks to Albany to compete for the lucrative contracts to be awarded by the hastily convened

The uniforms of the Union army. The United States Quartermaster Department spent twice as much on clothing and equipment as it did on weapons during the Civil War. By the end of the conflict it had purchased and produced astronomical quantities of clothing: over four million forage caps, six million pairs of trousers, eleven million shirts, and twenty million pairs of stockings. (Collection of the author)

State Military Board. Those who were unfamiliar with the workings of the state capital quickly discovered that business was often conducted with a wink and a nod. On occasion the tender process was merely theater played out for the sake of appearances: a preferred contractor had already secured the bid. As elsewhere, corruption flourished in an opaque system awash with money but short on oversight. Thomas Murphy, the Irish-born partner in a firm of jobbers that specialized in hats, straw goods, and furs, recalled several months later that he had encountered "all the Jews in town up there."[12] Although Murphy's claim that there were a "great number" of Jewish merchants and clothiers competing with other firms for business in Albany has a ring of truth, he made the statement as part of an attempt to divert attention from his own avarice. Good political connections and a well-placed bribe landed the firm of Murphy & Childs a contract to manufacture fifteen thousand blue army fatigue caps at the inflated price of ninety-five cents each, beating out several lower bids — including that of L. J. & I Phillips, an established Jewish-owned firm of shirt and cap manufacturers in New York City.[13] Once Lewis Phillips, who had traveled to Albany to solicit orders, "saw and heard that the contract was not to be given out fairly," he prudently decided to return home.[14] Murphy & Childs did not intend to manufacture the caps themselves. Instead they profited in a way not atypical of the times: once Murphy had a contract in hand, he encouraged the very firms he had defeated in the bidding process to compete with each other to supply him with the hats he had promised to the state. Phillips, who had originally bid to manufacture these same caps for fifty-eight cents each for the state, was now paid sixty cents per cap to do so for Murphy (who made a profit of thirty-five cents on each of the fifteen thousand caps).[15]

Flipping contracts in this way and shopping orders to subcontractors were practices that were widespread among prime contractors.[16] In Wisconsin E. B. Crawford and his Jewish partner, Michael Friend, won approval from the assistant quartermaster to manufacture twenty-five hundred infantry overcoats and, as Crawford related, promptly "made an arrangement with Bernheimer & Bros. [of New York City] that they furnish the capital and cloth, and do all the work," with Crawford and Friend receiving "one-third of the clear profits on the contract."[17] It is likely that Bernheimer & Brothers, itself a substantial firm that had focused primarily on dry goods rather than clothing before the war, passed on the actual work of manufacturing these overcoats to others. Large orders were cut into smaller pieces and passed from hand to hand down a chain of contractors, until they reached small firms and workshops far removed from the bidding process. Jewish firms in Cincinnati and New York that won contracts often relied on Jewish subcontractors—men who, in many cases, had only recently swapped peddling, clerking, or petty shopkeeping for a chance to profit from the rush to produce uniforms. Given the changes to the production process, discussed in chapter 3, that removed many of the barriers that would have otherwise kept out people without extensive experience in manufacturing, the familiarity these men had with sourcing supplies of fabric and their connections to their coreligionists were more valuable during wartime than was a background in tailoring. In this way wartime subcontracting ultimately led to a vast expansion of Jewish involvement in clothing manufacturing. Ethnic connections and bonds of solidarity and reciprocity that were established during years of peddling and shopkeeping were called on when prime contractors sought out sub-contractors and suppliers, and subcontractors turned to yet more subcon-tractors to complete the actual work of sewing uniforms. Although the profit margins of subcontractors were smaller, they sidestepped many of the risks assumed by prime contractors. The outsourcing of orders created several problems. Some prime contractors squeezed their subcontractors so hard that they were compelled to cut corners. Other vendors prom-ised too much in order to win contracts and then failed to deliver goods according to specifications. In other instances the lengthy chain of respon-sible parties involved in any one contract bred irresponsibility.

Subcontracting became a standard practice in the industry, as well as a savvy way of soothing jealous competitors. Nonetheless, Lewis Phillips was irked when Murphy and Childs won two substantial no-bid contracts for fifty thousand more caps. Phillips denounced the Irishman to a state committee of inquiry into corruption in the contracting process.[18] Mur-phy tried hard to discredit his accuser. When the committee interviewed him, he sought to play on stereotypes of Jewish disloyalty and dishon-esty, bombastically charging that New York's Jewish merchants were guilty not only of manufacturing caps for the Confederacy—an act tantamount to treason—but also of seeking to "monopolize all the caps made at the North."[19] Marshaling all of his righteous indignation, Murphy unctuously told the committee that the "contract ought to be given and was given" to him "in preference to awarding it to Jews," because he was "a more respon-sible party." The committee chairman saw through this self-serving bluster, witheringly ending the interview by reminding the mendacious Murphy that despite his assertion that Jews could not be trusted to make "an hon-est cap," he had relied on "a Jew, Mr. Fox, [who] made the sample, and the firm of L.&J. Phillips, [that] made the caps" for him.[20] Although Murphy escaped censure (and later became a state senator), his competitor had little reason and even less time to mope. By early 1862 L. J. & I. Phillips estimated that it had manufactured "in the neighborhood of a million of caps" for the Union army.[21]

Shenanigans of this kind were not unusual in the first months of the war, nor were they particular to wartime. A discreet gift could pay quick dividends. Jesse Seligman conceded that his brother Joseph, who was sta-tioned in Albany to win contracts for the family firm, had given the wife of Philip Dorsheimer, the state's treasurer at the time, a silk dress. Jesse explained the gift as a reflection of the "very friendly terms" Joseph had been on with Dorsheimer, a prominent Republican politician, since before the war. Joseph Seligman was following the lead of others. The payoff was even greater for Brooks Brothers, which not only gave Mrs. Dorsheimer a dress but also expensively outfitted Philip, his son, and the state's attorney general.[22] These sartorial schemes proved fruitful. Dorsheimer was instrumental in allocating contracts for military supplies. In the weeks following the fall of Fort Sumter, the Seligmans and several other leading New York clothing firms were awarded contracts to manufacture thousands of uniforms. Over the summer, the Seligmans bid on contracts for shirts, caps, jackets, overcoats, pants, and blankets, eventually employing twenty-five hundred workers to fulfill its obligations—which included producing one thousand uniforms for the Zouaves.[23] By the end of the year the firm was the eleventh-largest military supplier to the state. (Brooks Brothers earned even larger profits, becoming the second-largest private contractor to the state during the first year of the war.) The Seligman firm replicated this success on the national stage. Between August 1861 and the end of July 1862 it secured orders for a little under $1.5 million, equivalent to tens of millions of dollars today. Joseph Seligman soon left for Europe to mind his family's growing fortune and to hawk Union bonds, experience that stood the family firm in good stead after Appomattox.[24]

Joseph Seligman was certainly not alone in seeking to cultivate relationships with those who had a controlling hand on a state's financial spigot. Samuel Sykes—a Jewish clothier based in Detroit, who became the single largest military contractor to the state of Michigan in 1861—was accused by a rival Jewish firm of having presented the wife of the quartermaster with a sewing machine and paying bribes directly to state officials.[25] There were suspicions of a tainted tender process in Wisconsin as well. The largest supplier to the state was Marcus Kohner, a German-born Jew who had settled in Madison in the 1850s and opened his own tailoring business in the year before war broke out. It was no accident that Kohner and the two other major Jewish suppliers had strong local ties to people in the state capital.[26] Connections in Madison, not Milwaukee, mattered, even if the latter had been a regional manufacturing center before the war. Soon after the surrender of Fort Sumter, Kohner began to aggressively court the quartermaster, visiting the supply office "two or three times every day" during the summer of 1861. During the first year of the war Kohner received the largest share of the state's contracts—several of which were not competitive—most of which were supplied by his brother Joseph, who was based in New York City. Such contracts were not without risks, particularly given the galloping inflation that could quickly raise the cost of textiles and labor.[27]

Then, in the waning months of 1861, the federal government consolidated control over contracting in a handful of US Army depots. Hardnosed and incorruptible Edwin Stanton, the new secretary of war, was determined to clean the Augean stables.[28] State officials were relieved of all responsibilities for procurement, overnight losing a notable source of patronage. Although the supply depots in Philadelphia, New York, and Cincinnati continued to place vast orders—by the summer of 1862, each was instructed to stockpile enough supplies to outfit one hundred thousand new troops and maintain another two hundred thousand in the field—the scale and complexity of the contracts put them out of direct reach of many who had been gorging at the brimful state trough.[29] There were still, however, rich pickings to be found at the margins for those who were willing to subcontract work from the prime contractors, as well as those able to form consortia to bid on federal contracts.

Military Supply and Wartime Antisemitism

Although Joseph Seligman and Marcus Kohner were far from alone in seeking tactical advantage over their competitors by cozying up to quartermasters, Jewish contractors were singled out for special opprobrium. The conspicuous presence of Jews among the contractors did not escape the notice of people prone to antisemitism, and the atmosphere at the time was not short on nativism and suspicion. People who pointed to a supposed shortage of Cohens in the ranks claimed that Jews put their energies not only into evading the recruiting sergeant but also into profiting from the blood sacrifices of their Christian countrymen. This canard built on a long history of Jewish military suppliers' outfitting and financing the armies of central Europe. It did not help Jews that all contractors soon became pariahs in the eyes of the public. In the first months of the war, as the Union armies struggled on the battlefield, the press cast around for culprits. Loath to admit that poor leadership and inexperienced troops were responsible for the military failures, newspapers placed much of the blame on those who supplied the vast new volunteer armies. This was not difficult to do. Some contractors proved eager to line their own pockets at the expense of the public purse, and others adopted slipshod practices that later proved embarrassing.

In the rush to outfit the troops, private contractors who were inclined to be unscrupulous had ample opportunity to earn quick profits. Nowhere were there more serious scandals than in the outfitting of enlisted men with uniforms. The scarcity of heavy woolen cloth persuaded several firms to innovate in the early weeks of the war, not always for the better. Blazing a dishonorable trail, Brooks Brothers scrimped by adulterating more expensive new wool with a material that became synonymous with substandard wartime supplies: shoddy. The war provided a substantial boost for the shoddy industry, which recycled scraps of wool. Less expensive—but also less resilient—than new fabric, shoddy had been used before the war in a variety of ways, such as lining for jackets. The cotton shortage precipitated by secession and the demand for durable fabric for uniforms and blankets for the Union army forced Northern manufacturers to scramble for alternatives.[30] Shoddy offered several benefits to parsimonious contractors. It was easily and cheaply available—shoddy mills and the ragmen who supplied them thrived during the war (bulk rag prices rose twentyfold in 1861)—and it was difficult to detect when mixed with new wool. In the early months of the war, contractors, expecting a rapid end to the hostilities, may have rationalized such economies. Why would soldiers need the finest fabrics if the war was to be over well before winter? Such arguments were more difficult to justify once the realities of the conflict became apparent. Nonetheless, some contractors continued to leaven their wares with shoddy through 1864.[31]

Sensational reports of substandard uniforms—clothing "dropping to pieces after a few days' wear" that left soldiers "almost naked"—soon scandalized the public.[32] Some members of the officer corps expressed their outrage more soberly. Ulysses S. Grant, the commanding officer at Cairo, Illinois, at the end of 1861, complained that his troops had been clothed with uniforms "almost universally of an inferior quality and deficient in quantity."[33] Shoddy captured the public imagination, and the word rapidly evolved from a narrow technical term to one applied first to other substandard military supplies and the contractors who made them and then to all manner of inferior goods. Several Northern newspapers hostile

SHODDY PATRIOTISM.

Recruiting Sergeant—Come, Moses, rub up your patriot‑ism, and join the Union forces.

Jew—Mine cot, no! I have as mooch as I can do to supply de army mit coot uniforms, upon vich I makes noting at all, s'elp me got!

During the Civil War military suppliers were lambasted in cartoons and satirical verse as "shoddy contractors" and "shoddy vampires." Here a Jewish contractor is accused of "shoddy patriotism" as he evades enlistment and profits by supplying slipshod merchandise to the army. (Collection of the author)

to the Republican Party led the charge. Contractors whose profits and ostentation were deemed dishonest and immoral were derided as crass and ill-mannered nouveaux riches: the "shoddy aristocracy." Given the different moments at which shoddy entered the popular consciousness in England and America, the term assumed subtly different meanings in each context. In the United States it came to mean second-rate goods, as a result of the slipshod manufacturing of wartime contractors; in London it denoted cheap imitations, of the sort conspicuously advertised by the likes of Elias Moses, which masqueraded as high fashion. As several historians have shown, however, the scourge of profiteering parvenus was largely imaginary.[34]

Although Jews were not exclusively blamed for shoddy manufacturing—Brooks Brothers and New York's profiteering mayor came in for their fair share of flak—the term not infrequently assumed an antisemitic tinge.[35] Wartime increased existing fears about the corrupting influence of the market on the nation's morals, and these fears were easily extended to Jews. New concerns were grafted onto older ideas about Jews and commerce. The motif of the disreputable Chatham Street old clo' dealer proved particularly popular. In a Southern variation on this theme, Confederate Secretary of War Judah P. Benjamin was jeered as a "King Street Jew, cheap, very cheap," almost certainly a reference to the cluster of Jewish clothing dealers in Charleston, the city where he had spent part of his childhood. (He had it better than the English politician, and later prime minister, Benjamin Disraeli, who while campaigning in 1837 was met by crowds yelling "old clothes" and waving sticks spiked with bacon.)[36] A variety of cartoonists delighted in identifying Jews as the archetypal cunning contractor, not only refusing to enlist but actively undermining the war effort in order to turn a quick buck. In the first year of the conflict several Northern newspapers used the terms "Jew" and "contractor" interchangeably.[37] The fact that many of the leading contractors were merchant capitalists who outsourced manufacturing to others did not help matters. The complaints of a Cincinnati seamstress who wrote President Lincoln to protest the diversion of orders from public factories to private contractors—claiming that "a class of *wealthy men*, mostly *Jews*," benefited from the "starvation prices" paid by subcontractors—reflected the fusing of all these strands.[38]

Wartime Manufacturing in the Midwest

Whatever the suspicions of the public and the press, most Jewish firms won contracts not through underhanded means but because they were well positioned to do so. This is seen most clearly not in New York but in the Midwest, the region where Jewish peddlers, storekeepers, and whole-salers had established the firmest foothold in the clothing trade before the war. Non-Jewish rivals noted the particular success of Jewish firms. The Indianapolis dry-goods merchant William Glenn, for example, reflect-ing on his firm's disappointing fortunes during the first year of the war, lamented that he had often been bested by "some Jews in Cincinnati."[39] Glenn's plaint, tinged with a frustration at opportunities lost, was more faithful to reality than Thomas Murphy's crude innuendos. Five of the twenty leading contractors to the state of Indiana were Jewish firms based not within the borders of that state but in the Queen City. (A sixth, which was the private contractor that supplied the state with by far the most goods, operated in both Indianapolis and Cincinnati.)

By 1860 Cincinnati had become the commercial hub of the region and the third-largest industrial center in the nation; its factories and wholesal-ers dominated trade up and down the Ohio and Mississippi Rivers. The city's garment workers produced more than $6 million worth of clothing in that year (approximately $167 million today), and the industry was the single largest employer in Ohio. Much of this clothing was made in facto-ries: Cincinnati had begun to shift toward a consolidated system of factory production in the 1850s, when the arrival of sewing machines increased the scale of manufacturing. Unlike New York, the cost of space and fuel did not crimp this mode of production. By 1860 tailors and seamstresses were operating more than one thousand of the machines in Cincinnati. The city parlayed its natural advantages and proximity to its markets into manufacturing and distribution profits, more than tripling in size in the two decades before the war. The 1860 census counted an urban population of more than 160,000, of which fewer than 10,000 were Jews. As we have seen, they had already cornered parts of the clothing trade and dry-goods trades in the city and distributed garments to customers in the South and Midwest.[40] Now wartime provided opportunity to extend their reach even further.

Most Jewish businessmen in Cincinnati, like their counterparts in New York City, initially expected that war would mean economic disruption and the disastrous loss of Southern markets. But spirits were soon lifted by an unexpected influx of dollars into the city. As Ohio mobilized for war, sending three hundred thousand men to the Union's armies, Cincin-nati's Jewish wholesalers found themselves at an advantage, able to draw on considerable manufacturing capacity, much of it in factories well suited to fulfilling large orders of standardized products; having well-established relationships with Eastern textile suppliers; and having extensive connections across the region. Erstwhile rivals banded together to form temporary alliances, a pattern also seen among a handful of the largest New York merchants but nowhere on the same scale as in Cincinnati. These consortiums enabled the partners to pool their capital, purchase raw materials in bulk, and bid more effectively for contracts on the national level, which demanded large-scale production and a heavy financial commitment. They were aided by the presence of a major depot in the city that was given significant responsibility for requisitioning supplies. By cooperating, these firms appear to have bypassed the bidding wars that otherwise drove costs higher and profits lower. As a result, the largest mercantile houses in Cincinnati avoided much of the rancor and recrimination that resulted from hot-blooded competition elsewhere.

Crucially, such arrangements mitigated risk. Although these firms had experience operating in challenging times—they had weathered the panic of 1857—wartime presented additional uncertainties. After the federal government had paid for many of its initial orders in gold, it began instead to issue certificates and vouchers whose value was unstable. And it was often slow to pay its bills. Joseph Seligman, for example, was forced to resort to pleading at the end of January 1862 after the federal government suspended payments due to a severe financial crisis. Owed a million dollars, he warned that the firm risked "dreadful catastrophe" that would "drag down 20 other houses" if not paid soon. Such costs ate into margins that were already pressured by a rise in the expense of labor and fabric. And quartermasters were unpredictable, showering favored firms with contracts one year only to turn their affections elsewhere the next.[41]

In some instances these temporary alliances brought together firms of dramatically different size. Jacob Seasongood and Philip Heidelbach, formerly peddlers but now partners in a large clothing and dry-goods business, collaborated with two smaller clothiers during the war.[42] Their closest rivals were a coalition made up several sets of siblings, each the owner of a leading clothing or dry-goods business that had a history of past cooperation: the four Mack brothers, a quartet of Glasers, and three Stadlers. The constituent firms in this coalition competed against one another when bidding on state contracts but banded together when pursuing the gargantuan orders placed by the Union Quartermaster Department. This strategy of pooling capacity proved prescient. In 1861 Mack, Stadler & Glaser became the second-largest supplier of uniforms to the entire Union army. In one frenetic four-month period, from August to December 1861, the firm manufactured 191,548 articles of clothing for the infantry and cavalry: pantaloons, blouses, overcoats, blankets, shirts, drawers, and socks. The *Israelite* crowed that the Union was marching off to war with the mark of Mack.[43] (The Macks are better remembered for their ill-fated partnership with Jesse Grant, father of the commanding general of the Army of the Tennessee at the time, to smuggle Southern cotton northward, a speculative scheme intended to turn filial loyalties to best advantage. Historian Jonathan D. Sarna has postulated that this venture was the proximate cause of Ulysses S. Grant's General Orders No. 11 expelling Jews from the vast territory under his command.)[44] These orders were dwarfed the next year, when the firm's contracts with the Union more than tripled in value, elevating it to one of the largest partnerships in the country. Despite a dramatic decline in orders after 1862, when the supply depot in Cincinnati shifted its ordering to Eastern firms, both Mack, Stadler & Glaser and the consortium led by Seasongood and Heidelbach ended the war among the twenty largest suppliers of clothing to the Quartermaster Department, the only two businesses in this group that were not on the East Coast.[45]

Cincinnati's Jewish manufacturers were remarkably successful not only in Ohio and at the national level but also in plucking plum contracts in neighboring states. Here they were aided by their ability to tap into a geographically dispersed network; several Cincinnati firms mobilized regional relationships during the war to pursue contracts in Indiana, Wisconsin, and Michigan.[46] More than 40 percent of the Union's soldiers came from the Midwest, a considerably larger share than any other region. All needed the accouterments of war. So large were the orders from neighboring states during the fall of 1861 that demand outstripped the capacity of Cincinnati's manufacturers. In October Ohio's quartermaster "had great difficulty in obtaining clothing at all. The soldiers suffered for want of clothing; colonels came in and complained."[47] Despite overwhelming demand, Cincinnati manufacturers were very well positioned to profit from the region's needs for materiel. Wilson argues that the weightiest challenge faced by firms was not the manufacturing process itself but finding supplies of textiles for uniforms and distributing the finished goods.

This fact put leading clothiers and wholesale merchants such as the Macks, Seasongood, and Heidelbach at an advantage because they could draw on prewar systems for purchasing textiles, supplying credit, coordinating the labor of thousands of outworkers, and channeling goods to retailers. The firms producing the largest quantities of ready-made clothing in antebellum Cincinnati and New York had already adopted a flexible and scalable system that employed an underpaid army of seamstresses as outworkers who were hired and fired to meet variable seasonal demand. These same seamstresses—women and teenage girls who could be paid less than men and who were available at a time when male labor was scarce due to enlistment—were soon set to sewing uniforms as the firms ramped up production for the military.[48]

The picture was different elsewhere. In Illinois, for example, Jewish firms were conspicuously absent from the ranks of the leading suppliers (Henry Mack complained of the "great rascality" in the contracting process there.)[49] Although several Jewish-owned businesses won substantial orders for uniforms in Pennsylvania and New York, they never attained the preeminence that Jewish contractors achieved in some Midwestern states. In the Northeast newer Jewish firms were obliged to compete with older, entrenched rivals for prime contracts. Many more profited less conspicuously during the war by filling orders on behalf of others. In the Midwest, in contrast, the clothing industry had shallower roots. Jewish immigrants who began their careers as humble peddlers in the two decades before the war had risen far enough to command attention and favorable treatment when quartermasters in Cincinnati, Madison, Detroit, and Indianapolis disbursed orders for uniforms in the first months of the war.

Even though access to orders varied from state to state and from year to year, the cumulative impact of contracting was immense. When larger Jewish firms made hay, a multitude of smaller Jewish businesses also profited from the harvest. An expanding number of Jewish firms competed for scraps of business thrown their way. This dramatic broadening of Jewish participation in manufacturing, as well as the expertise and experience gained by contractors large and small during the war, paid large dividends later. With a handful of exceptions their kinsmen and compatriots in the South were rarely at the cutting edge of clothing the Confederacy.[50] There Jews came to play a central role in the clothing trade after the war by a different means.

It was not, however, only Jewish clothing manufacturers in the North who benefited from the burgeoning military market. Closer to the front lines, the war provided an unexpected boon for people involved in the retail trade. Some clothiers in Northern towns and cities sold uniforms and accouterments to soldiers wanting to supplement or replace the kit issued by the quartermaster.[51] But arguably the war had a larger impact on itinerant traders. For many recent Jewish immigrants enlistment provided a tempting alternative to the tedium of peddling. The Union army promised (although it rarely delivered) a reliable income and—before casualty counts revealed the ferocious attrition caused by musket and canister shot—the prospect of adventure.[52] Certainly not all peddlers chose to swap their own packs for those proffered by Uncle Sam, and the army itself provided a moving market for traders hoping to hawk their goods. Peddlers had good reason to flock to camps on payday: soldiers were spendthrifts when they had money in their pockets. As one dyspeptic soldier put it, "every trash and bauble found ready and contending purchasers at any price."[53]

Peddlers had limited access to army encampments, but sutlers faced fewer restrictions. Each regiment was entitled to its own sutler, a civilian trader licensed to sell supplies to soldiers in the field. The sutler carried his store with him in a wagon, setting up shop in a canvas tent when the regiment bivouacked. The interior was an Aladdin's cave of articles chosen to appeal to the wants of the infantryman bored with his monotonous diet and drab camp life. A soldier could replace worn-out or lost clothing, hear news from home, and purchase items not supplied by the quartermaster.[54] Fragmentary evidence suggests that Jews were well represented in the ranks of sutlers in both the Union and the Confederacy. Unsurprisingly, many seem to have been peddlers and shopkeepers who were familiar with the challenges of itinerant commerce.[55] What were wagon-borne sutlers but glorified peddlers, with monopolies to sell goods to soldiers in the field? Jewish sutlers probably drew on a familiar supply system, stocking their wagons with goods purchased on credit from wholesalers and in turn extending credit to their customers. The position was not without risks unfamiliar to peddlers. Sutlers could easily lose their investments and sometimes even their lives. When the army marched into enemy territory, the slow-moving sutler's wagon was a juicy plum to guerrillas and raiding cavalrymen. During a pell-mell retreat the wagon and its stock was an unwanted encumbrance. Given these dangers, many sutlers preferred to base themselves well to the rear of the army. When regiments were campaigning, sutlers could be absent for months, almost invariably timing their return to coincide with the equally infrequent visits of the paymaster.[56] (One soldier in the New York State Volunteers observed, "Before the poor and much disrespected representative of money made its appearance, it was as hard to see a sutler as a swallow in winter; but it no sooner came than they flocked as thick as a cloud of hungry and devouring locusts.")[57] Even when safely ensconced in camp, the sutler's stock was vulnerable to the weather, spoilage (soldiers complained of rancid butter and dysentery brought on by dubious pies), and theft.[58] Whatever the risks sutlers encountered, some turned their wartime experience to good advantage once the Confederacy capitulated.

Supplying the Confederacy—from London

And what was the fate of Samuel and Saul Isaac, the brothers who supplied the Confederacy from London? This was not a story that ended well for the Isaac brothers or for the Confederacy. Even as Caleb Huse came to depend on S. Isaac, Campbell & Company, so too did Samuel Isaac stake the future of his firm on the Confederacy. Both he and his brother had begun their careers humbly as slop sellers and shopkeepers who sold cheap clothing. Now they were bit players in international affairs, seemingly holding the fate of the Confederacy in their hands. Operating as commission merchants—connecting Huse with suppliers, arranging financing, and extracting a commission fee from both parties—S. Isaac, Campbell & Company quickly became the conduit for vast quantities of munitions and ordnance, as well as cloth, leather, and uniforms.[59] When others demurred, the firm extended credit even as the Confederacy's creditworthiness fluctuated wildly with the ebb and flow of its fortunes on the battlefield. By June 1863 the Confederacy owed the firm the astronomical sum of £515,000. Despite the scale of the orders—millions of yards of fabric and hundreds of thousands of boots and blankets—the Confederate purchasing agents could not come close to slaking the South's charnel appetite for war materiel.[60]

Default by the firm's largest debtor was only one of the risks that S. Isaac, Campbell & Company confronted. The firm also took a leading role in shipping goods through the tightening noose of the Union blockade. Clothing was designated by the Confederacy as second only in priority to arms and ammunition as cargo on blockade runners.[61] Along with greatcoats, socks, trousers, shirts, blankets, and boots, ships also carried garments and fabric for sale to those who could afford it. As the war progressed, Southerners clamored for clothing to replace their tattered and frayed finery. Cloth and clothing was in such demand that it held special value when bartered. John de Bree, head of the Confederate navy's Office of Provision and Clothing, explained that in the countryside, "the people have a little more provisions than they absolutely need, but are short of tea, coffee, sugar, molasses, and especially of osnaburgs, yarns, and shirtings. . . . Not a pound of bacon or wheat can be bought at any price, for money [but] the sight of a pound of yarn, or a yard of cloth will produce an effect almost magical."[62] In Richmond John Beauchamp Jones—the same man who had written unfavorably about Jewish merchants in the Midwest—lamented in November 1863 that his family's clothing was "as shabby as Italian lazzaronis—with no prospect whatever of replenished wardrobes."[63] Southern Jewish storekeepers and merchants were accused not only of hoarding supplies to artificially raise prices but also of conspiring to buy up the cargoes of ships running the blockade. One bigoted British merchant who visited Charleston during the war complained that the city's auction houses were "crammed" with his "Hebrew friends." He was astonished by the "number of Jewish-looking faces" that he "had met on the stairs, in the halls and parlours of the hotel, and at breakfast": "Fully one-half of the large number of guests of the house seemed as if they had just stepped out of Houndsditch, and reminded me what a friend in Mobile said, that, 'I should meet more Jews in Charleston than I could see in Jerusalem.' They also seemed absorbed in the study of the auctioneers' pamphlets, and the long advertisements of sales which half filled the papers."[64] Such fantasies, alas, tell us more about the writer than about historical reality.

As cargo and cotton crossed the Atlantic despite the best efforts of the Union navy, Britain became by far the largest European supplier to the Confederacy, Caleb Huse by far the South's most important purchasing agent, and Samuel Isaac his preferred partner. What went wrong? Huse was quickly joined in London by other Confederate purchasing agents representing a variety of military bureaucracies, state governments, and private interests.[65] Several of them came to resent his primacy, believing his schemes were thwarting their own ambitious plans, and some of his competitors impugned his motives and patriotism.[66] They did so on the basis of both his birth—he hailed from Massachusetts—and his close relationship with S. Isaac, Campbell & Company. What began as murmuring about extravagant contracts signed in the desperate first months of the war turned into a full-scale campaign waged by Huse's rivals to discredit him on the basis of alleged financial impropriety.

Several of Huse's detractors fingered S. Isaac, Campbell & Company either as the conjurer befuddling a naïve quarry with accounting tricks and misdirection or as a scheming confederate conniving with Huse to profit at the expense of their Southern paymasters. It was no secret that Samuel and Saul Isaac were Jews; John Beauchamp Jones, who had swapped his fledgling career as a writer for a position as a clerk in the Confederate War Department, noted this fact with displeasure in his diary.[67] One of Huse's fiercest antagonists pointedly reminded the Confederate secretary of war about Samuel Isaac's sullied reputation from the contracting scandal of 1858. There was enough damning proof of kickbacks to convince the War Department that there might be truth to the larger accusations. The drama entered a protracted final act with a prolonged investigation that uncovered evidence of systematic overcharging, deceptive bookkeeping, double billing, and breach of trust. Although S. Isaac, Campbell & Company was unusual in having its deceptions so thoroughly exposed, and noteworthy because of its central role in supplying the South, it was certainly not alone in extracting rich returns from its dealings with the Confederacy.[68] The payment of kickbacks and bribes was reputed to be standard practice among military commission houses in England; Confederate purchasing agent Edward Anderson described this as "the English way of doing business."[69]

While Samuel and Saul Isaac profited in the short term, they soon received their comeuppance. Paradoxically, their financial affairs were undermined by the Confederacy's payment of its debts. The bonds that the South used to compensate S. Isaac, Campbell & Company proved very volatile. After the surrender of Vicksburg in July 1863 cut the Confederacy off from the Mississippi River and the cotton plantations along it, the value of cotton securities plummeted. Saul Isaac whimpered that the blow had crippled his firm, imperiling its credit and capital, and made its ability to transact business uncertain. Now the bonds could only be sold at a "disastrous" loss; Grant's victory had wiped out 30 percent of their value overnight. Although the firm struggled on for a few years after the war, it never fully recovered from its losses and was forced to declare bankruptcy.[70]

For the Isaac brothers the Civil War provided a springboard from the clothing and boot business to unlikely careers as arms brokers. Much like Henry and Elias Moses, who, as we saw, seized opportunities offered by the expansion of domestic and colonial markets, Samuel Isaac transformed a modest enterprise into a leading firm in response to a new source of demand. All took advantage of a familial familiarity with selling clothing, a (sometimes disastrous) penchant for risk taking, and a willingness to venture into new markets in order to create ambitious businesses with international reach that did not exist—indeed, could not have existed—when they began their careers a handful of decades earlier. And much like Henry and Elias Moses, the experience of Samuel Isaac was atypical of his peers. By 1862 he and his brother were less focused on boot making than on blockade running, in the process becoming a British bête noire of the US government. The demands of the Confederacy perforce drew them away from shirts and trousers and toward rifles and ordnance. For all the notoriety that the brothers earned, their exploits should not obscure the limited impact of the war on Jewish involvement in the clothing trade in England—not so, as we have seen, in the United States.

Unsurprisingly the consequences of the Civil War on the clothing trade were more dramatic across the Atlantic, where they left a critical legacy for American Jews. Although the war affected Jews in a variety of other ways, its most durable impact was in the commercial realm. Before the war began, even the most optimistic Americans agreed that violent gusts of discord risked unraveling not only America's political fabric but also the nation's economic prosperity. Yet in the 1850s, few anticipated the ferocity of the storm and the extent of the changes that it was to bring. People in the clothing business—a truly national enterprise that had created bonds of commercial interdependence between the South, Northeast, West, and Midwest—had particular reason to fear that the nation would be blown asunder. In that sector of the economy the winds of change loosed by the Civil War uprooted much that had seemed perpetual in American society. Although at the fringes of the whirlwind, the clothing trade, an enterprise unrelated to the purpose of the conflict, was violently upended. At its lowest reaches, the plodding peddler was blown temporarily off his familiar path; in the upper branches, the existing pattern was sent aflutter.

Unexpectedly for people familiar with the garment industry, Jews—better represented among the plodding peddlers than in the sturdy upper branches—were propelled by a wartime tailwind to the forefront of the clothing trade. Instead of the calamity predicted in the months before the war, the clothing business and the position of Jewish clothiers in it experienced a revolution. The war provided an extraordinary boost for the minority of Jews such as the Seligmans, Macks, Glasers, and Stadlers who had been wholesalers and manufacturers on a substantial scale before the conflict started. And, as we will see in the next chapter, it expanded the horizons of the Jewish sutlers who followed the army on the march. But the most significant legacy of the war for Jews was in the dramatic broadening of Jewish participation in the production of ready-made clothing. Wartime subcontracting enabled Jews with limited financial means but ample social capital to enter the lower ranks of manufacturing. Connections with relatives and immigrants from the same region, as well as social contacts, proved useful in winning subcontracts from the larger Jewish consortiums in Cincinnati and from prime contractors elsewhere. The opportunities presented to sew uniforms for the Union army launched a flotilla of small and midsize enterprises, most little more than workshops in which Jewish proprietors directed the labor of German and Irish tailors. Even those who did not become wartime contractors benefited from having their competitors distracted by war work, leaving space for new entrants into the industry. Whereas before the war most Jewish firms were clustered on the margins of the ready-made trade, soon after the war Jews found themselves in a commanding position in several key sectors of the garment industry. Without the Civil War, the ready-made clothing industry might have remained the preserve of non-Jewish firms. This was a development of great and lasting consequence for the future of American Jewry. It is to this legacy, felt for decades after the last musket was fired, that we now turn.

8

A Ready-Made Paradise

Joseph, the oldest of eleven Seligman siblings and the first to make his way to America, was in a glum mood in the spring of 1863. He had returned to Europe after close to twenty-five years in the United States, no longer the callow seventeen-year-old who had left Baiersdorf, in Bavaria, but now an earnest man of business. He read grimly of the war in America, distrusting what he took to be the patriotic "bluster of American newspapers." When his brothers requested that he purchase stock to supply their sprawling family enterprise, which manufactured clothing, sold dry goods, and out-fitted the Union army with uniforms, Joseph demurred. He replied that he foresaw only impending "ruin and disaster to our beloved country." Instead of investing anything further in a nation that was foundering, he counseled his brothers to quickly dispose of their homes and furniture "without making too much noise," as "it is well to prepare for the worst." Should the Union falter, they would then be ready to join him in Europe "until the storm is passed." (His brother Isaac, Joseph suggested, should sail soonest, to avoid being drafted into an army profligate with the lives of its soldiers.) Seligman was not foolish to worry about the future of his family and his firm in the darkest days of the Civil War. Yet even as he despondently forecast calamity for his American-built fortune and his adopted homeland, his presence in Europe and his postwar prosperity was in significant measure a consequence of a wartime dividend that his firm reaped along with other clothing and dry-goods enterprises that had invested heavily in San Francisco in the decade before the conflict.[1]

The Seligmans were unusually successful before and during the Civil War, the result of their business savvy, a durable partnership among eight brothers and a handful of brothers-in-law who pooled their capital and complementary skills, and an adroit cultivation of their connections in the Republican Party. Nonetheless, their pathway to prosperity was not atypical of Jewish migrants who sought opportunity in the South and West. Joseph first landed in New York City in the late summer of 1837; presumably he left Baiersdorf before word arrived of the economic panic into which America had slumped months before. Realizing that the money he had been given by his mother would not last long in a place where his prospects for work were slim, he joined a relative in the coal town of Mauch Chunk, Pennsylvania. After a brief period working first as a cashier and store clerk for the town's leading merchant and then as a peddler, he was joined by his younger brothers William and James in 1839. James had served a truncated apprenticeship as a weaver with an uncle in Floss before his departure for America, and he did not care for the position his brother found for him with a carpenter in Bethlehem, Pennsylvania. Perhaps fearing that nothing good could come of a reluctant Jewish woodworker in Bethlehem, Joseph purchased a supply of goods for James to peddle in Pennsylvania. Commerce came more naturally to James than carpentry. After a profitable year on the road, he moved to the South to try his luck. Such were his profits as a self-described "itinerant knight of commerce" that he persuaded Joseph, William, and the newly arrived Jesse to join him in rural Alabama.[2] Like so many other peddlers, the brothers invested their earnings in a small store. Joseph managed the store, and James bought goods for it in New York on credit. Within a handful of years, the brothers were operating stores in Selma, Greensboro, Eutaw, and Clinton, towns that stretched in an arc across less than eighty miles of rich plantation country in southern Alabama, where slaves outnumbered the white population more than two to one. Fifteen-year-old Jesse ran one of these stores and oversaw its clerks.

By the end of the decade the brothers had wound up their affairs in Alabama and scattered to pursue opportunities elsewhere. James and Joseph established a firm in New York City to import dry goods; William, a clothing store in St. Louis with a brother-in-law who had previously sold garments in Natchez; and Jesse, the New York City Dry Goods Store in Watertown, New York, where he befriended Ulysses S. Grant, a lieutenant stationed nearby at Sackett's Harbor. Jesse's stay in Watertown was temporary; as we have seen, in 1850 he transported "a large quantity of merchandise" to California, which he sold at great profit. The glittering prospects presented by the Golden State persuaded William in 1852 to return to New York, where he started a manufacturing concern that sent clothing westward to stock Jesse's shelves in San Francisco.[3]

Like many other Jewish entrepreneurs who established an early presence in California, the Seligmans soon found themselves dealing in the gold that made California so enticing. Many merchants and wholesalers in San Francisco expected their bills to be paid in gold. This specie was sent eastward to satisfy creditors or as profits remitted to partners and investors. (The Moses clan in Australia and London dabbled in gold for much the same reason.) Those wholesalers in New York who could depend on a steady stream of bullion from the West Coast could use this hard currency to import fabric at an advantage from European suppliers. Dry-goods wholesalers and clothing manufacturers such as the Seligmans began the cycle anew by shipping imported cloth, as well clothing stitched from workshops in New York, westward. This created a triangular trade that transformed clothing produced in New York into Californian gold, gold into imported fabric, and fabric back into clothing destined for California. By the late 1850s the Seligmans' firm in San Francisco was among the largest shippers of gold to New York; others included an agent for the London Rothschilds and Levi Strauss & Company.

It was during wartime, however, that this vein yielded its most priceless ore. In the nervous months when the threat and then the reality of war terminated trade with the Confederacy, those same New York firms that had once rued their inability to compete with rivals entrenched in the South must have celebrated their lucky reprieve. Not only were they on aggregate less dependent on Southern customers than their rivals were, but they could still sell their wares in the West. The Californian market, which had been risky during the gold rush, became a lifeline in desperate times when other commerce was disrupted. San Francisco boomed as it experienced a massive inflow of newcomers and captured trade from Eastern cities.

Commerce with California was made doubly profitable by a quirk of wartime. When the US Congress passed the Legal Tender Act in February 1862 in order to be able to pay its soldiers—for the first time authorizing the Treasury to print paper money not backed by gold or silver—banks and merchants in California repudiated the government's greenback dollars and instead maintained a quasi-gold standard. During the war greenbacks, untethered from gold, depreciated substantially against the gold dollar, which remained the preferred tender in California. (People who sought to pay with the new currency there were dismissed as "greenback-ers.") One gold dollar, at the peak of its purchasing power in 1864, was worth $2.85 in greenbacks, a rate of exchange that made it possible to purchase $100 worth of goods in New York for $35 in gold-backed cur-rency. This divergence benefited those businesses in the East that paid for labor in greenbacks but sold clothing in California for gold. Wholesal-ers and merchants with access to gold could earn substantial profits on currency transactions, since greenbacks could be purchased at a discount in exchange for specie. One merchant claimed about currency exchange during the war, "we made more in selling our gold when buying eastern exchange than we did in our goods."[4] Profits from California that were returned to New York in gold increased in value rather than suffering from the corrosive effects of wartime inflation, which caused prices to rise an average of 69 percent in the Union over the course of the war. Access to gold was helpful in other ways, too. European firms that supplied fabric often demanded payment in specie, as did the US government for the payment of import duties. Rampant inflation was not necessarily a bad thing for those who controlled production in the clothing trade. Except for those firms that produced clothing according to fixed contracts, manu-facturers benefited from the decline in value of greenbacks because the prices they charged rose much more quickly than the wages they paid. Clothing retailers benefited because the debts they owed wholesalers declined in real terms, even as the prices they could charge for the stock on their shelves increased.[5]

Although Joseph Seligman complained that profits from California were barely enough to sustain eight households, particularly once the threat of Confederate navy raiders raised insurance rates on cargo, his carping belies a substantial rise in the net worth of the family firm dur-ing the war. The depth of the Seligmans' involvement in California and the extent of their contracts with the Quartermaster Department set them apart from other Jews, but they were far from alone in finding themselves in a very different economic place in 1865 than they had occupied four years before. As we have seen, many who had begun the war already firmly entrenched in the foothills of the clothing trade were carried upward at a speedy double march by wartime contracting. The war, however, did more for the position of Jews in the clothing trade than provide opportunity for profit from contracts and currency transactions. The conflict leveled a playing field that had been tilted in some places against Jews, and in others it created conditions that played to their strengths once the war was over. Quirks of circumstance and context presented fresh opportunities after Appomattox that were unavailable to Jews across the Atlantic. In the wake of the war the clothing trade and its ancillary industries pushed Jews in America onto an economic path that increasingly diverged from that of their counterparts in England.

The Postwar Economy

The United States was a nation transformed in April 1865, its industries, financial system, and government remade by war. Yet the excitement that manufacturers must have experienced as patriotic citizens when they heard of Robert E. Lee's surrender at Appomattox may not have long masked the dread they felt as businessmen. An economy that had suckled on wartime contracts was in short order to be weaned off government money. An army a million strong was rapidly demobilized: by the end of 1866, only sixty thousand soldiers remained in the ranks. To make matters worse for those who had grown accustomed to doing business with the Quartermaster Department, the military flooded the market with a massive stockpile of surplus uniforms. In 1866 alone gear sold at auction exceeded 10 percent of the government's domestic revenue. By 1871 the War Department had cleared its warehouses of nearly 1.3 million coats and jackets, more than 350,000 pairs of trousers, and over 400,000 shirts.[6] Those who depended on surplus profits generated by the sale of gold also suffered, as its value plummeted to a fraction of its wartime worth. When the United States returned to the gold standard in 1879, this supplemental source of revenue disappeared.

The distress felt by manufacturers may have been lightened by the promise of a peace dividend. Veterans who were mustered out of the service in the summer of 1865 came home with wallets stuffed with back pay. Fred Lazarus, who worked in his father's store in Columbus, Ohio, recalled that "they were buying clothes and doing away with their army blue and the clothing business was good. The soldiers had money and were willing to spend it. Soldiers would go into the basement of the new store and change their army togs for the store clothes."[7] Clothing manufacturers who quickly transitioned from war work to producing for the civilian market were cushioned by a postbellum retail boom, which Lazarus described in miniature, as well as a dramatic decline "almost without a parallel in violence and generality" in wholesale prices for commodities such as fabric that had ballooned in cost during the conflict. Such was the speed and impact of deflation in 1865 that, according to one estimate, the average real value of wages paid to workers, which began the year at two-thirds of what they had been worth in July 1860, almost reached parity with this prewar level by the middle of the year. This vastly increased the purchasing power of consumers. Clothing manufacturers had it better than other military suppliers, who struggled to find new markets to compensate for the drop in demand for rifles, tents, and artillery pieces. But it was difficult to sustain wartime levels of employment and production in an industry that might have doubled the size of its workforce in New York City alone to keep up with wartime orders.[8]

The health of the garment industry in the immediate postwar period varied considerably by location. In Philadelphia, a city second in size only to New York, there were soon signs of malaise. In 1860 clothing manufacturing had been the single largest source of industrial employment in the city. By the end of the decade the industry had shed more than three thousand workers, a 19 percent decline, even as rival industries caught and then surpassed it in size and value of output. The contagion was even more acute in allied fields such as cap, hat, shirt, and collar making, in which employment shrank by as much as 74 percent. Manufacturers in New York City experienced temporary discomfort after the war, but it was hardly equivalent to the swoon seen in Philadelphia. By 1870 close to twenty-three thousand men and women labored in New York's garment factories and workshops, a healthy increase of eight thousand from ten years before. Just over a third of those employed in the city's major industries sewed menswear, slightly more than before the war, even as several rival industries declined or stagnated.[9]

Significantly, there were almost twice as many clothing firms in New York City in 1870 as there had been two decades before. As we have seen, many of the newcomers to manufacturing were Jews who had accumulated skills and capital during wartime that they now deployed in producing fashionable suits and sturdy dungarees in small workshops in New York and in factories elsewhere. Jews operated an increasing percentage of small tailoring enterprises in New York and owned half of the firms that were exclusively in the wholesaling business.[10] As was the case before the conflict, the majority of the stitching and sewing was still done by non-Jews—German and Irish immigrants—in the 1860s and 1870s. Jewish enterprises also rose in importance in other urban centers such as Baltimore, Chicago, Milwaukee, and Rochester that had grown during the war. But the structure of manufacturing in New York City made it easier for people there to become proprietors, even if only of modest enterprises, if they lacked the capital needed to open a factory. New York remained less dependent on factory production than did other centers, where land and space was less expensive.

Manufacturing in New York, however, was forced to adapt to the coming of the sewing machine. The *New York Tribune* expressed almost messianic expectation about the future of the new technology:

> The needle will soon be consigned to oblivion, like the wheel and the loom, and the knitting-needles. The working woman will now work fewer hours, and receive greater remuneration. People will have more work done, will dress better, change oftener, and altogether grow better looking, as well as nicer looking. The more work can be done, the cheaper it can be done by means of machines—*the greater will be the demand*. Men and women will disdain the soupcon of a nice worn garment, and gradually we shall become a nation without spot or blemish.[11]

The technology was transformative but not entirely in the ways that the newspaper predicted. The Singer Sewing Machine Company and its rivals sold sixty-five thousand machines in America in 1865 and close to twelve times that number in 1872. Brooks Brothers boasted that a skilled sewing-machine operator could produce a frock coat in three hours instead of the sixteen it would require if the work were done by hand.[12] Since it was more costly in Manhattan than elsewhere to concentrate a mass of workers together under a single roof, most manufacturers in the city instead adapted their existing flexible system of production to meet this new mechanical challenge. Once wholesalers had relied on middlemen to farm piecework out to needleworkers to stitch at home. Now they (or their foremen) came to do business directly with contractors who operated small workshops centered around the sewing machine and the presser's table.

This image, dating from around 1879, depicts one of the large, modern factories built after the Civil War to mass-produce clothing for the burgeoning civilian market. The trend toward consolidation accelerated outside of New York over the following decades as menswear lines that had been the preserve of the city's sweatshops were cornered by factories in other cities. (Collection of the author)

A typical workshop, often no more than a suite of rooms in a tenement converted for the day into a miniature factory, performed many of the tasks required to transform precut cloth into a salable garment, before passing the all-but-complete item to a home worker for finishing. Workshops varied in size and composition depending on what they produced, much as the pattern of manufacturing in each line (pants, outerwear, underwear, shirts, suits, and cloaks) followed a configuration of its own. Some manufacturers in New York did consolidate production in order to achieve economies of scale: the infamous Triangle Shirtwaist Company factory near Washington Square was a modern factory that employed up to five hundred people, not a tenement sweatshop. But in 1913 three-quarters of all firms involved in the production of menswear in the city employed five or fewer workers. Nationally, however, the average clothing factory hummed with the activity of thirty-six men and women, and more than half of the dress and shirtwaist workers labored in factories that employed more than seventy-five workers.[13]

The predominance of workshop production in New York and the increasing prominence of Jewish firms in that city and other urban centers had unexpected but far-reaching implications over the next half century. It is all but impossible, however, to accurately quantify the relative importance of Jewish firms in the garment industry on the cusp of the 1880s. This has not stopped several historians from offering estimates. The claim that Jewish firms accounted for 75 percent of all clothing businesses—retailers, wholesalers, and manufacturers—nationwide and controlled 90 percent of the total trade in 1880 has been repeated by several scholars, but it is none the more reliable for all the frequency of its repetition.[14] Evidence from commercial directories indicates that even in New York City, Jewish firms came well short of having a monopoly of tailoring, retailing, and wholesaling.

Whatever the proportion of the national trade accounted for by Jews, they were carried higher by a rising tide. Several trends worked to the advantage of clothiers and their suppliers after the Civil War, and some of these affected a broad swath of the economy. Almost all farmers and manufacturers, for example, benefited from new tariffs that dramatically raised duties on imports. Retailing gathered steam in cities and smaller centers, fueled by a postwar economic boom and the growth of urban occupations relative to farming that further speeded the wheels of industry. Despite galloping wartime inflation, recurrent economic contractions, prolonged recessions between 1873 and 1879 and between 1882 and 1885, and a financial panic in 1893, real wages paid to nonfarm workers increased an average of 1.1 percent per year between 1860 and 1900. Workers who groused over their pay in 1900 earned 270–330 percent more in real terms for a day's work than their great-grandparents had at the beginning of the previous century. Workers in manufacturing industries, who made up more than a third of the national workforce after 1860, had not only more money in their pockets but also more time to spend it. The average workweek for such workers was ten hours shorter in 1900 than in the early 1830s, although it was still a taxing fifty-nine hours long.

Other changes were particular to the clothing trade. Persistent complaints of ill-fitting and mismatched uniforms during the war yielded improvements in the sizing and fit of garments. Although some scholars have incorrectly claimed that the outfitting of soldiers led to the introduction of standardized sizes for the first time—in fact, a numerical system was used in London in the 1740s and had become commonplace in slops shops by the 1780s—manufacturers and retailers moved toward greater consistency and uniformity after the Civil War, aided by physiological measurements collected during wartime conscription. This aided the spread of chain and department stores, whose appeal to customers was in part rooted in the reliability of merchandise and the replicability of the shopping and purchasing experience. By the end of the nineteenth century Jewish firms—many of them initially led by men with roots in peddling and petty retailing or by sons who built on their parents' enterprise in those fields—were among the leading exponents of these new types of mass merchandising. It certainly helped that department stores often sprouted from wholesale enterprises. Soon a constellation of local and regional Jewish-owned stores were orbiting what, in the twentieth century, became bright stars in the firmament of American retailing: Rich's in Atlanta, Filene's in Boston, Macy's in New York, Gimbels in Philadelphia, Kaufmann's in Pittsburgh, and Neiman-Marcus in Dallas.[15]

More and more newly prosperous Americans, encouraged by the insistent entreaties of advertisers and retailers and emboldened by the clink of coins in their pockets, were replacing their utilitarian wardrobes with ones that took fashion into account. Demand for ready-made outfits, especially suits, grew apace. By 1900 the market for ready-mades was twice that for custom-made clothing. Within two decades, bespoke garments accounted for less than 10 percent of the menswear produced in America. The striking increase in demand for clothing from working men and women was reflected in the ballooning size of the workforce employed in the garment industry. In 1860 sixty thousand men and women were producing clothing. An additional one hundred workers had joined the garment industry by 1880 and two hundred thousand more by 1900. The industry's hunger for inexpensive labor grew voraciously in the decades after the Civil War, and it was none too particular about the ethnic identity of the sewing machinists, basters, and sewers whom it added to its ranks.[16] The same processes were evident across the Atlantic, but America's economy grew at a much faster rate than Britain's after the Civil War. In 1870 the gross domestic products of the United States and Britain were roughly equivalent, meaning that America's population, which was eight million larger, lagged considerably behind in per capita production. By 1913 America's population was forty-one million larger than Britain's, its gross domestic product was more than twice that of Britain, and its per capita production was substantially larger too.[17]

Not all US workers could afford to participate in this consumer economy, however. As we have seen, work in the clothing trade did not guarantee a living wage. According to one estimate, 40 percent of industrial workers in America lived below the poverty line in the 1880s, and 45 percent were just barely above it. Nonetheless, this broadening of consumer culture accelerated the fashion cycle, as manufacturers and retailers were increasingly forced to compete on the cut as well as the cost of the clothing they produced and sold. As the dictates of fashion grew more important and the longevity of fashion cycles shorter, predicting future preferences for particular styles of clothing became more difficult. This played to the strength of the sweating system, which could scale up production to meet sudden spikes in demand. However, the particular challenges of doing business with the Californian market temporarily lengthened the production season. For a period after the war the growing significance of Californian consumers reshaped the timetable that determined when garments were to be ready for spring and fall. Given the inevitable wait between dispatching a trunk in New York and its unloading in San Francisco, manufacturers needed to begin production earlier than had previously been the case in order to ensure that seasonable clothes arrived on time on the West Coast. This reduced the period between seasons when work was slack for seamstresses. But once the transcontinental railroad speeded distribution and reduced transportation costs, production timetables contracted again. The staggering rate of railway construction did seamstresses few favors, but it worked to the advantage of retailers, wholesalers, and manufacturers as distant regions were knitted into the national economy.

Once the Civil War ended, a fresh supply of migrants and settlers arrived in the West, propelled forward by steam locomotives, impatience, ambition, and the catnip of promises dangled in front of future farmers by the Homestead Act. Peddlers also returned to the roads in large numbers after Appomattox. During the war the pool of peddlers appears to have been drained by a drop in the replenishing flow of immigrants from Europe and the siphoning of men into the military and other wartime work. Half as many peddlers used Syracuse, New York, as a base in 1865 as in 1860. But in 1870, 143 peddlers were recorded in the town, twice as many as ever before. This surge, however, proved short-lived. The decline was precipitate over the next decade—in 1880, there were only 18 Jewish peddlers in Syracuse—a consequence of the slowing of immigration of

Jews from central Europe and a change in their economic profile. Given the economic mobility of Jews in Germany, more of those who crossed the Atlantic after the Civil War were likely to have arrived with resources and connections that enabled them to find work that did not entail carrying a pack.[18] The decline also reflected a resumption of the upward march of Jews from peddling, clerking, and petty storekeeping in towns and villages across the country.

Although clerking remained popular, the profile of clerks shifted subtly as storekeepers aged and expanded their businesses. In the 1840s and 1850s clerkships in Jewish stores were filled by new immigrants who often did not differ much in age from their employers. But by the 1870s the position had become a stepping-stone for the native-born sons of local merchants. Clerking introduced sons to their parents' line of work and established the basis for future partnerships and succession. In the past clerks might have taken to the road to accumulate capital so they could open their own stores; now many young men followed a career path that bypassed peddling. The advantages of this alternative route into commerce are amply demonstrated in Savannah. Two-thirds of Jews who were clerical workers or salesmen in the city in 1870 and remained a decade later had become merchants. As sons followed fathers into the business of selling garments, they reinforced and embellished an existing ethnic niche. By 1880 Jews owned nearly 80 percent of all clothing stores in Savannah and dominated the wholesaling trade as well. In Columbus, Ohio, where "every Jewish family entered the clothing business" with the exception of a single contrarian, all eighteen of the clothiers listed in a commercial directory in 1872 were Jews of central European origin. In the space of two decades they had moved from clerical work and petty commerce to the status of "large proprietor." A local newspaper noted that they appeared to "take to the clothing business as a duck does to water."[19] This pattern was repeated in towns across the Midwest and West. In cities such as Chicago and New York that grew quickly after the Civil War, the economic status of Jews was more diverse. The sprinkling of those atop the clothing trade sat above a larger cohort of middling wholesalers and shopkeepers, with clerks, peddlers, and laborers trailing far below. But the general trend was upward.

For people eager to strike out on their own, the West continued to exert a strong pull in the postwar years. Those drawn westward included settlers

enticed by the promise of fertile farmland and feverish fortune seekers attracted by word of new discoveries of gold and silver. Not all were
impressed by the lure of gold. The Scottish philosopher Thomas Carlyle
considered digging for gold in California and Australia the "maddest and
stupidest" of "all the mad pursuits any people ever took up," asserting that
all the gold dug up was not "worth a mealy potato to mankind."[20] It is
unlikely he thought any more favorably of Northerners whose eyes shone
with excitement and expectation at the renewal of the cotton trade after
Appomattox. Yet Jewish merchants who prospected for opportunity after
the Civil War paradoxically found some of the most promising terrain in
the ravaged region where they had been relegated to a secondary status
before the conflict.

New Opportunities in the South

Jews had good reason to reenter the Southern market tentatively. In the
South major cities lay in ruin, and roads and railways had been wrecked
by intention and four years of neglect. The South's white population was
dramatically reduced in both circumstance and number: two-fifths of
the region's prewar property had been sacrificed in vain to Moloch, and
a quarter of those who enlisted never returned from the battlefield.[21] The
path out of this morass was unclear. Within a handful of years, the bed-
rock that undergirded the Southern economy had been swept away. Gone
were most of the cotton factors, who had been the unrivaled masters of
prewar commerce. Gone too were plantations, at least in the form found
before Fort Sumter. Formerly imperious planters were brought low by
the war and the loss of slaves, who now demanded wages for work and
a modicum of respect. The market was "flooded . . . with plantations for
rent or lease." In South Carolina the owner of a rice plantation valued at
$500,000 in 1860 would have been lucky to find a buyer willing to pay half
that amount in 1865, and the property was sold for $6,000 a decade later.
All the sugar plantations of Louisiana were worth $200 million in 1861 but
only $7 million in 1865.[22] Many planters who staved off bankruptcy hoped
that commodity crops would be their salvation. With cotton prices seemingly holding steady by the end of 1865, planters who went deep into hock
may have deluded themselves that the prewar economy would soon be
resuscitated. Then began a series of plagues that tormented farmers and

factors: drought, flooding, invasion (this time by army worms rather than Yankees), and a catastrophic decline in crop prices. Cotton that sold for upward of a dollar per pound in New York in 1864 could be bought for forty-nine cents in December 1865, thirty-three cents at the end of 1866, and fifteen cents in December 1867. The recovery from this low was slow and uneven—not quick enough to save struggling cotton factors and those planters who relied on them for credit.[23]

But the dramatic reconfiguration caused by the purging fires of war opened new vistas for people searching for opportunity. With many leading merchants ruined alongside their planter customers, second-rank traders and merchants could step forward to fill the breach. Some of these were newcomers lured south by the prospect of profits; others were prewar merchants seeking to resurrect their fortunes or invest capital they had managed to cloister during the conflict. Northern manufacturers, eager to regain access to the Southern market, aided this process by offering goods on generous terms. Storekeepers accustomed to playing second fiddle to cotton factors now found themselves setting the tune in the plantation economy. Despite the drop in the value of cotton, it remained America's leading export, presenting opportunities for those who were able to market it on behalf of its producers in place of factors. In turn, the new agricultural system that replaced prewar plantations created a large crop of small-scale tenant farmers in need of the very goods that these storekeepers sold and receptive to the credit they offered.

As several historians have described, a striking proportion of those who formed the new core of commercial life in the Mississippi Delta, itself the center of the cotton economy, were members of immigrant minorities that could access Northern credit networks in a region that was starved for ready money. Their position may have been strengthened by a reluctance of larger New York firms to directly venture into a region that was still in the midst of political and social turmoil. Such was the need for newcomers that the *Daily Democrat Natchez Steam Press* was even willing to woo commercially minded Northerners with headlines such as the one that proclaimed "WE ARE ALL YANKEES NOW."[24] The percentage of foreign-born merchants was particularly high in and around Natchez and Greenville. In 1870 close to half of the storekeepers in Greenville, the town that dominated commerce in the lower delta, were Jews; ten years later, Jews made up two-thirds of the town's merchants (a significant portion of the remainder were Chinese). Hostility directed at Jews and other migrants was only one of the challenges that the postwar South presented. In a region that depended on fickle harvests, the rate of failure was high. A credit reporter's evaluation of Moses Dreyfus, who kept a modest store in Tensas Parish, near Natchez, suggests the vulnerability of marginal merchants: "He does not own anything more than the stock of goods say 15c$ [$1,500] in his store. If the crop turns up well, of wh[ich] there is every prospect, he will do well—if there be disasters in the Cotton Crop he as well as most of the mrchts [merchants] in the South w[ould] be almost ruined." In some locales nearly one in two Jewish firms failed during the postwar period. Others used their profits to leave merchandising behind as quickly as possible.[25]

Some of the newcomers to Natchez were familiar with the town because they had been stationed there during the Civil War. Henry Frank and Isaac Lowenburg were not the only Jewish sutlers who opened clothing and dry-goods stores in Southern towns after the end of hostilities (still others used carefully husbanded wartime profits to establish enterprises in the North or West), but they were among the most successful. They began the war in St. Joseph, Missouri, and reached Natchez with Grant's army in the summer of 1863. The sutlers ingratiated themselves with members of the local Jewish community by intervening on behalf of twenty-year-old Ophelia Mayer, the daughter of a prominent shopkeeper, who had fallen afoul of government officials when she was discovered to have written letters expressing anti-Union sentiments. (Her parents were sufficiently committed to the Confederate cause to name a son Joseph Eggleston Johnston Mayer, after the Confederate general whose forces defended Vicksburg.) Isaac married Ophelia in 1865, and Henry married her sister three years later. It might have helped Lowenburg's courtship that his loyalties were somewhat scrambled; his brother had served in the Confederate army, as had Ophelia's. Their future brother-in-law was Julius Weis, who had boarded in the Mayer home when he first arrived in Natchez as a peddler. Within a handful of decades, the three owned, respectively, the largest dry-goods store in Natchez, the largest plantation supply and commission house in the town, and a cotton brokerage that one historian claims wielded "unequalled economic influence in the cotton areas of the lower Mississippi" and that another speculates may have been the most successful in the entire region.[26]

The rise of Jews—even some who had been associated with the Union army—into the merchant class in Natchez and elsewhere in the South may have been made somewhat more palatable in the eyes of their neighbors because several had served in Confederate ranks. Yet the conspicuous patriotism of the Mayer family did not save it from the dismissive sneers of one young planter. "They are now just looking over the front steps of the crem de la crem," he complained in January 1866, "they themselves having but recently become of the consolidated milk of this society."[27] To offset such hostility, some Jewish storekeepers deliberately drew on the powerful bonds of camaraderie forged during wartime. Isaac Wolfe Bernheim, who had peddled around Wilkes-Barre, Pennsylvania, before accepting an uncle's offer of a clerkship at his store in Paducah, Kentucky, recalled that one of his duties was to serve as second-string salesman behind Joe Ullman: "[His] services were particularly valuable because he had served as a soldier in the Confederate army throughout the war. He knew most of the farmers for miles around Paducah by their given names. In the spring and summer, when leaf tobacco was brought in from the surrounding counties, . . . Joe sold them their dry goods and clothing, swapped yarns with them about their experiences in the army, and sent them home rejoicing."[28] Such sensitivity to Southern norms was crucial to the success of the substantial number of Jewish migrants, like Bernheim, who made their way southward during Reconstruction.

Those merchants who settled in the South hoped to profit from the demand for consumer goods that had dammed by four long years of shortages and blockades. As in the North, returning veterans, long deprived of decent clothes, were eager (if somewhat less able) to swap their discolored uniforms for new garments. To their number were added four million former slaves, who were even more impatient to exchange the tattered clothes of bondage for garments that displayed their new status. Even during the war, those slaves who escaped Confederate control had demonstrated a desire to reclothe themselves as free men and women. In August 1863 a Union soldier described contraband slaves at Camp Westman in Williamsburg, Virginia, as willing to do "anything to get money of which they seem to be as craving as a Chatham street 'old clo' man' ": "Speaking of old clothes the wenches appear to have laid violent hands on mistresses wardrobes. The other day, there was a darkey funeral near here, and you should have seen the darkeys, how they spread themselves—their trails extending as consequentally as that of a Fifth Avenue belle."[29] When the war was over, freed slaves became a potentially lucrative market for those who were willing to solicit their trade. Such commerce was still viewed askance by the prewar mercantile and planter elite in the years immediately after the war; one credit reporter noted of a firm in the Natchez area that it traded a "g[ood] deal with Negroes which prejudices people vs them."[30] Similarly, Stephen Powers, a visitor to Charleston ("a city . . . of idle ragged negroes") in 1872, complained that "Jews and Massachusetts merchants [were] doing well on the semi-loyal and negro custom." His observation reflected more than mere prejudice; contemporaneous credit reports describe a substantial number of Jewish-owned dry-goods and clothing stores that served a black clientele.[31]

The kind of prewar familiarity that Jewish peddlers and storekeepers had acquired in trading with slaves and smallholders came in handy when courting those, such as former slaves, who were maneuvered into tenant farming in the late 1860s and 1870s. Jewish merchants become "prime purveyors" of supplies and credit to white and black sharecroppers, providing goods for cash (or, more often, credit) in advance of the harvest. This was a much-maligned economic niche. Accusations of exploitation were made during the war and only became shriller over time.[32] There were significant risks to doing business with tenant farmers and their landlords. By 1867 merchants were already beginning to demand that landowners provide mortgages on their cotton harvest and real estate as surety for loans; tenant farmers who bought clothing, seed, and tools on credit had to use instead their tools and draft animals, as well as a share of the crop.[33]

Just as dealing in gold yielded unexpected outcomes for clothiers in California, this arrangement produced unanticipated consequences for those petty merchants whom fate favored. A handful who began their careers hawking clothing to people on the margins of antebellum economic life became, through the defaults of their customers and savvy purchases at a time when acreage was being sold at bargain prices, owners of sizable amounts of land. In Natchez, where this phenomenon was most striking, five Jewish merchants (including Lowenburg) came to own fifty thousand acres across at least twenty-five plantations. Julius Weis sold his vast Natchez plantation for $42,000—equivalent to roughly a million

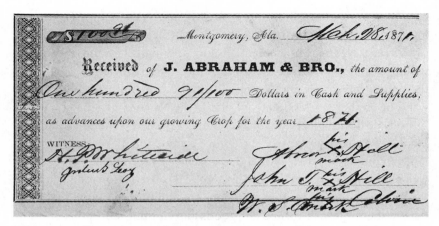

This note, issued in 1871 by a Jewish merchant in Montgomery, Alabama, recorded a transaction typical of the crop-lien system that emerged after the Civil War. Merchants advanced goods on credit before the growing season; sharecroppers and other farmers who borrowed against their future harvest were obliged to repay the full amount after the growing season ended. This economic niche carried considerable risk for merchants but transformed some into substantial landowners. (Courtesy of The Arnold and Deanne Kaplan Collection of Early American Judaica, Library at the Herbert D. Katz Center for Advanced Judaic Studies, University of Pennsylvania)

dollars today—in 1884. More common was for storekeepers to be drawn into the business of marketing commodity crops, a function that had been performed by cotton factors before the war. Since crop liens required a farmer to provide his or her cotton to a merchant as soon as it was ginned, storekeepers who accumulated bales of cotton as payment for debts were obliged to sell or otherwise dispose of the cotton to pay their own creditors. Some reinvested their profits from these transactions in the retail trade, expanding their stores and courting a broader range of customers. Others shifted away from the retail trade, becoming buyers, brokers, shippers, and speculators in cotton. This was a risky and stressful alternative. Adolph Brandeis, father of the future Supreme Court justice, failed as a cotton broker in Louisville in the mid-1870s. Weis, who made a fortune as a cotton broker, recalled, "my nerves were strained by the tension, my general health became impaired."[34] The most famous Jewish merchants to make this transition, already well advanced before the Civil War, were the Lehman brothers, who, like the Seligmans, had peddled in rural Alabama and become dry-goods merchants in Montgomery.[35]

Branching Out into New Businesses

Leaving the clothing and dry-goods trades, as the Lehmans and the Selig-mans did, was not unusual among those who had earned large profits from gold, cotton, and military contracting. For the Seligmans the move from clothing to banking was relatively rapid. The brothers formally entered the banking business at the beginning of May 1864 and sold their mer-chandising operation in San Francisco—then valued at half a million dollars—three years later. A bank branch in New Orleans, opened soon after Appomattox, was run by a brother-in-law and his sibling, who had started as an errand boy in a Seligman store and rose to become a partner in the firm. Conservative by instinct—Joseph admonished two of his sib-lings to trust no one: "The main thing in a banker is safety"—the family was slower to end its involvement in importing dry goods and cautious when investing. The banking firm became a conduit for European capital into the American market.[36] A striking number of other American Jew-ish banking dynasties also had their roots in the clothing and dry-goods trades. Quite a few of those who opened or underwrote private banks after the Civil War—Isaac and Simon Bernheimer, Philip Heidelbach, Jacob Seasongood, Abraham Kuhn, Solomon Loeb, Julius Weis, and others—not only had earned substantial financial rewards from filling wartime contracts but had also learned a variety of sophisticated financial skills in doing business with a government that was often slow to pay its bills. As elsewhere in the ethnic economy, these firms and their principals were interwoven by marriages, business and religious ties, and shared ties to a common homeland.[37] Some had realized immense wartime gains: the value of the Macks' firm, for example, increased more than fivefold during the war, and the Bernheimers were among the wealthiest residents of New York City. These assets served as a springboard into a variety of other high-status occupations. Marcus Kohner, who had earned dubious profits from his relationship with the quartermaster in Wisconsin, wisely bought prime New York real estate, as did Lewis Phillips. Real estate was also the pre-ferred investment of Henry Moses and several other clothing merchants in London, who—as landlords in the East End—profited from an acute housing shortage that drove up rents.[38]

A clothier did not need immense wartime profits to refashion himself as a financier. There are many examples of storekeepers in the Southwest,

West, and South who—after playing part-time banker, broker, and agent for rural customers ill served by existing lenders—sought to swap a frayed store coat for a banker's suit. The banks they built were often modest affairs, initially little more than a sideline to an existing enterprise.[39] Henry Vere Huntley's evocative description of his visit to the California gold fields to meet with his local agent suggests how unglamorous such beginnings in banking could be. Huntley recalled his experience after reaching Placerville in the late afternoon: "My Hebrew put me up in his shop; he got dinner ready, beefsteak and coffee, our plates were laid on the counter, amongst woollen frocks, shirts, stockings, boots, trousers, jewelry, &c.; we afterwards slept in the shop. I had a comfortable corner, my Hebrew opposite to me. Breakfasted next morning at the counter again."[40] Since far fewer Jews were scattered about England as rural storekeepers and there were far fewer country banks than in America, this pattern was largely absent across the Atlantic.

Rural retailers who gained a measure of prosperity in the United States, as many did in the decades after the war, were well positioned to become leading boosters of local economic and civic life. As immigrants and entrepreneurs who relied on goods supplied from larger centers, they often possessed a measure of cosmopolitanism that set them apart in rural settings, where parochialism and localism was more typical. Access to distant contacts and credit networks were invaluable when establishing a local bank or another large enterprise. By investing time and money in improving the infrastructure that boosted the prospects of local businesses—lobbying, for example, for the extension of a railway to connect a town to a trunk line or joining others in establishing a chamber of commerce—they advanced their own long-term economic interests. In many small towns, particularly those where there was only a modest merchant and professional class, their rising economic position translated into an elevated social status. In Greenville, Mississippi, for example, three Jews served as mayor in the 1870s (the last by virtue of being the sole member of the town council to survive a yellow-fever epidemic).[41]

Not all changes introduced by the Civil War redounded to the benefit of Jewish merchants, however. The taint attached to Jews by the shoddy scandals of 1861 and 1862 was not instantly washed clean after the war was over. Although hostility toward Jews seems to have abated somewhat in the years immediately after the conflict, antisemitism revived in the 1870s and drew on several themes seen during the war years. The humiliating exclusion of Joseph Seligman, a man who had conspicuously benefited from military contracting, from the Grand Union Hotel in Saratoga, New York, in 1877 was the most notorious reflection of this new mood. Although the episode, which related to an existing dispute between Seligman and the hotel's proprietor, attracted considerable public attention, it was only the most prominent manifestation of the spread of a racialized form of antisemitism during and after the war. When fused with anxieties about increasing levels of immigration, new thinking about race, and nativist political pressure, this increase in intolerance had very significant consequences for American Jewry in the first decades of the twentieth century.[42]

The Clothing Trade in England in the 1860s and 1870s

The Civil War unleashed a host of dynamic forces in the United States that brightened the prospects of Jews in the clothing trade. In contrast, many of their counterparts in England remained mired in a rut that offered far fewer opportunities for rapid advancement. No deus ex machina appeared in London, Leeds, or Manchester to upend the clothing trade and speed the path of Jewish entrepreneurs. Instead, the clothing industry developed in the 1860s and 1870s along lines established in earlier decades. Most Jewish firms continued to struggle to break into the first ranks of manufacturing, wholesaling, and retailing. Few of those who abandoned the secondhand trade for ready-mades achieved more than middling success. The Australian market created an important new source of opportunity, but as we have seen, its richest spoils were claimed by a handful of those, such as Henry Moses, who could draw on family connections in Sydney and Melbourne. Although colonial exports became ever more important to the overall health of the garment industry in England over the following decades, they did not provide the means for the majority of Jewish firms to leapfrog over their competitors.[43] The wants of miners and farmers in distant colonies may have kept legions of sewers busy in London, but this did not produce a substantial crop of new Jewish wholesale manufacturers or a radical remaking of the production process.

There was, however, change afoot at the cutting edge of the trade in London. As in New York, the sewing machine refashioned the basic organization of production. Among Jews involved in manufacturing, the impact was greatest for those in coat making, a section of the trade that Jews had cornered by the 1880s. The two or three sewing machinists in the typical coat-making workshop in that decade kept six to seven other workers busy with basting, pressing, and buttonholing garments. (Although the men in these workshops were typically Jewish, not all of the women were.) This system took advantage of the efficiencies of a machine that could stitch straight seams at ten times the speed of work done by hand. The shift toward small workshops did nothing to alleviate the pressures created by the intensity of competition in the industry. The contractor who made coats intended for clerks and shopkeepers in London and the colonies could produce an average of fifteen to twenty-five a day in the 1880s but would often need to rely on the labor of his wife and the savings accrued by using his home as a work space in order to generate a modest profit.[44] A similar pattern prevailed among Jews in Leeds, a city that had come to dominate suit making in England by the 1880s. Factories in Leeds coexisted and cooperated with scores of smaller independent workshops that offered spare capacity at times of peak demand and provided specialist skills to manufacturers. Jews were less often found on the factory floor than in the workshops that acted in concert with larger manufacturers.[45]

It was difficult for workers in these cramped workshops in England to rally the resources to move beyond manual production. The tailoring trades, which provided the largest single source of employment for the roughly sixty thousand Jews in Britain in 1880, became a treadmill for many workers and petty entrepreneurs, with contractors and workers in constant motion to sustain the level of production required to turn a profit. Unlike their counterparts in America, who typically entered clothing production after careers in petty commerce and who were more likely to organize production than to baste and sew, Jews in England more often entered the industry as sewing machinists, pressers, and basters and continued to labor in clothing workshops. Given the persistence of poverty in Anglo-Jewry, there was no shortage of Jews in need of this work, and they had fewer attractive alternatives. Once recruited to the tailoring trades, their potential paths out of this occupation were much more limited than those of Jews in America. With no access to anything equivalent to the geographically dispersed ethnic networks and traditions of entrepreneurship created by peddlers, storekeepers, and wholesalers in the United States, they typically lacked the resources, connections, and inspiration that such structures provided. These differences, which predated the beginnings of mass eastern European Jewish migration, played a role in shaping the opportunities available to future generations of Jewish garment workers.

Prospective Jewish immigrants were well aware of this divergence by 1881. The emergence of Jewish investment bankers, the rapid success of Jewish merchants in the South and Midwest, and the climb of Jewish wholesalers and manufacturers to the top of the clothing trade contributed to the perception that America was a land of unlimited opportunity for Jews. Despite the disruption caused by the Civil War, the Jewish population of New York City doubled between 1860 and 1880 to eighty thousand, about twenty thousand more Jews than in the entire British Isles. With demand growing apace for ready-made clothing, Jews who had become wholesalers and manufacturers in New York and other cities were soon in need of ever more workers to feed the seemingly unquenchable demand of American consumers for cheap jackets, suits, and pants. The flood of Jews fleeing eastern Europe that began in the 1880s more than satisfied their needs. These newcomers were recruited to the clothing trade, slotting into and dramatically expanding an existing ethnic niche. Jewish wholesalers, who divvied up orders among subcontractors and supplied them with pre-cut cloth, were the midwives of this process. Their margins depended on the difference between the prices paid by the retailers who placed orders with them and the workshops that they paid to produce garments on their behalf. Thus, they had an incentive—increased profits—to rely on inexpensive immigrant labor. Although in the 1860s and 1870s Jewish wholesalers and contractors relied primarily on the labor of Italian and German workers, in the 1880s they increasingly turned to eastern European Jews. Jewish needleworkers now sewed clothing in workshops operated by Jewish contractors, who competed for orders placed by Jewish wholesalers for goods that would be sold, in many instances, by Jewish retailers. An earlier generation of Jewish immigrants thus came to facilitate the entry of new immigrants into the field.[46] Not only did central European Jews, ethnic incumbents within a crucial section of the trade, channel many of the immigrants into their workshops and factories, but they provided an object lesson in how to succeed and ceded their position on the industry's lower rungs as the newcomers began their rise.

In England, where the footprint of Jewish firms in the clothing trade was narrower and shallower, the penetration of this new wave of immigrants into the garment industry was much more limited. In part this was also a consequence of a difference in the scale of immigration to England and America, a factor that had several other important economic implications over the long term. Jewish immigrants clustered in New York City, and within its garment industry and other allied fields, with a density not found in London or Leeds. In menswear Jews in England specialized in coats and waistcoats but had less to do with trousers, shirts, and vests. It was not, however, only the difference in the depth and breadth of Jewish participation in the clothing trade in England and America that influenced the future trajectories of these new immigrants. For reasons that will soon become clear, the clothing trade itself proved to be a particularly supple springboard for eastern European Jews in the United States, as it had been for immigrants from central Europe before them. In England, in contrast, the typical immigrants who flocked to the sweatshops of London and the workshops of Leeds had fewer advantages when they entered the trade and fewer advantages when they later left it behind.

Conclusion

We have established that the early experience of Jews in the ready-made trade in England and the United States—their pathways into the business and their trajectories within it over time—diverged in material ways before 1881 in large measure because of the dynamics of the industry in each setting and the weight of wider events. But did it matter over the long term that Jews in America had stepped to the front of the menswear business, and Jews in England lagged behind, when the great age of eastern European Jewish mass migration dawned in 1881? And how might this fact help us answer the questions about the origins of Jewish prosperity with which we started? What role, if any, in other words, did the clothing trade itself play in the rise of Jews in the United States?

The Jews who were ensconced in the clothing trade in 1880 were rapidly outnumbered by newcomers who flooded into the industry. The scale of eastern European immigration, and the proportion of those immigrants that clustered in the clothing trade, was astonishing. According to one more conservative estimate, Jews accounted for 39 percent of the total workforce in the garment industry in New York City—and a quarter nationwide—by 1910 but cut out an even larger share of the cloak, coat, suit, and shirtwaist lines. In that same year garment work was by far the most popular occupation among Jews, both immigrant and native-born, in the city: more than 50 percent of immigrant Jewish men born in Russia were employed in the production, retail, or wholesale of clothing, as were 44 percent of Jewish men born in America. Jewish women typically worked from adolescence until marriage or the birth of their first child, after which they withdrew from full-time labor in the industry.[1]

In Britain the participation rate was even greater. But because many fewer Jewish immigrants settled there permanently between 1881 and 1914—around 150,000 compared with the approximately two million who made their way to America—they made up a significantly smaller portion of the total workforce in the garment industry, only about 5 percent in 1911. As we will see, Jews who settled in New York City—a metropolis where a far higher percentage of residents were foreign-born—benefited economically from their numbers in ways not seen in London, where they constituted a smaller community. Nonetheless, Anglo-Jewry was transformed by the influx of newcomers. Immigrant enclaves sprouted in Manchester, Leeds, Glasgow, Dublin, Liverpool, and dozens of other urban areas. The vast majority, however, settled in the capital. By 1914 a third of all Jews in Britain lived in the East End.

Did the newcomers arrive primed for success in the garment industry? If so, this might serve as an alternative explanation for their rapid rise through its ranks, as well as for broader patterns of economic mobility within the immigrant community. Since there is ample evidence that a large share of Jews, particularly those who chose to emigrate, worked in the tailoring trades in eastern Europe, several historians have concluded that Jewish immigrants were unusually well prepared for the work they found in New York and London. Yet the evidence that supports this supposition has been challenged by several scholars who dispute the reliability of Russian census data, shipping and immigration records, and surveys that otherwise seem to indicate that a preponderance of immigrants arrived after having earned an income by stitching and sewing in the Old World. Undoubtedly at least some of the newcomers were "Columbus tailors" whose claim to existing tailoring skills was more a product of imagination than prior experience. Others have questioned how transferable skills acquired before emigrating were to a New World setting. Those who arrived with a familiarity with an artisanal mode of tailoring would have discovered that this was out of step with the way that clothing was produced in American garment workshops.[2]

Although a familiarity with garment production undoubtedly provided a bridge between the Old and New World for some immigrants, this was certainly not the only reason why Jews clustered within this particular industry. As we have already seen, the entry of eastern European Jews into the business was smoothed by Jewish contractors and wholesalers eager for inexpensive labor. And a person did not need to be especially nimble with a thimble to find work in a garment workshop where many of the roles in the production process were easily learned and required little more than rote repetition. Recent immigrants were attractive to potential employers less for their existing skills—Irish and German tailors could perform the same tasks as efficiently—than for their abundant availability and willingness to accept low wages. Once the first wave of immigrant Jews established a foothold in the trade, those who followed them to America were recruited into the field along pathways typical in the formation of ethnic niches. Their employers were culturally and linguistically familiar and similar to them, and the work environment was unthreatening and located in the immigrant neighborhood. A job in the garment industry could also offer "niche protection" by supplying on-the-job training to *griners* (greenhorns) and offsetting the inadequacies of skills, language, education, and experience that might otherwise make immigrants poor candidates for alternative occupations. The seasonality and flexibility of garment work appealed to some immigrants, particularly mothers who could care for children while working from home. Employers gained access to a workforce that they knew how to mobilize and motivate. The needs of the immigrants for work and the economic niche for tractable workers became mutually reinforcing. As the historian Nancy Green has noted, however, hiring practices shifted over time: workshops became more cosmopolitan as employers turned to other immigrant groups for labor.[3]

What seems to have set Jews apart from other immigrant groups who were recruited to stitch in the early twentieth century, however, was not the speed with which they sewed but the rapidity with which the typical worker sought to strike out on his or her own. Here the possession of hard-won tailoring skills may have discouraged rather than encouraged innovation and entrepreneurship among immigrants who found work as tailors and seamstresses. We have seen evidence that an earlier generation of skilled tailors in New York and London were reluctant to jettison their craft when faced with a new mode of making clothing and were slow to innovate since doing so would dilute the value of their skills. Jews who acquired training before emigration may have, paradoxically, been less willing to abandon tailoring than those who were unskilled in this line of work. So how else might we account for immigrant entrepreneurship within the clothing trade?

Immigrant Entrepreneurship in London and New York

The social investigator Beatrice Webb's overdrawn sketches of the ascent of nameless newcomers in the East End could easily have been penned by an observer of the Lower East Side. After an apprenticeship "toiling day and night for a small labor-contractor in return for a shake-down, a cup of black coffee, and a hunch of brown bread," the newly arrived *griner* became a self-reliant wage earner. Not content to work for wages, however, he transformed himself into his own master, from a sweated laborer to one who sweated others:

> His living-room becomes his workshop, his landlord or his butcher his security; round the corner he finds a brother Israelite whose trade is to supply pattern garments to take as samples of work to the wholesale house; with a small deposit he secures on the hire system both sewing machine and presser's table. Altogether it is estimated that with 1L. in his pocket any man may rise to the dignity of a sweater. At first the new master will live on "green" labour, will, with the help of his wife or some other relative, do all the skilled work that is needed. Presently, if the quantity of his work increases, or if the quality improves, he will engage a machinist, then a presser.[4]

Although no admirer of the gumption of immigrant tailors-turned-petty-capitalists—and certainly disdainful of the garments they manufactured—Webb did recognize that their preference for self-employment over wage labor produced a pronounced pattern of upward mobility among Jews.[5] The path Webb sketched out for the Jewish immigrant revealed her own prejudices but also reflected the aspirations of many an immigrant:

> He has moved out of the back court in which his fellow countrymen are herded together like animals, and is comfortably installed in a model dwelling; the walls of his parlour are decked with prints of Hebrew worthies, or with portraits of prize-fighters and race-horses; his wife wears jewelry and furs on the Sabbath; for their Sunday dinner they eat poultry. He treats his wife with courtesy and tenderness, and they discuss constantly the future

of the children. He is never to be seen at the public-house round the corner; but he enjoys a quiet glass of "rum and shrub" and a game of cards with a few friends on the Saturday or Sunday evening; and he thinks seriously of season tickets for the People's Palace. He remembers the starvation fare and the long hours of his first place: he remembers too the name and address of the wholesale house served by his first master; and presently he appears at the counter and offers to take the work at a lower figure, or secures it through a tip to the foreman. But he no longer kisses the hand of Singer's agent and begs with fawning words for another sewing machine; nor does he flit to other lodgings in the dead of night at the first threat of the broker. In short, he has become a law-abiding and self-respecting citizen of our great metropolis, and feels himself the equal of a Montefiore or Rothschild.[6]

What impelled this imagined immigrant, and so many of his real-life counterparts, to pursue the path of petty entrepreneurship?

Since, as we saw in chapter 8, much of the clothing produced in New York and London was still made in humble workshops rather than in large factories, immigrants who arrived with little capital could scrimp and save enough to start a small enterprise of their own relatively quickly. In 1900 a would-be entrepreneur needed a relatively small sum, less than a hundred dollars, to purchase fabric and lease two sewing machines and a presser's table in order to set up shop on his or her own, particularly if he or she could depend on the labor of unpaid family members and was willing to convert a tenement apartment into workspace during the day in order to save on rent. Loans were available from several sources, including free loan societies, to cover this cost. Working conditions in the trade were unpleasant, with workers crowded together in makeshift spaces heady with glue vapors, fabric particles, steam, and smoke and overheated by the press of bodies and the hissing of irons. Together with the marginal wages paid to workers and the prevalence of strife between bosses and laborers, these conditions provided little incentive to tarry in entry-level jobs in the trade. Nor did the erratic nature of employment in sweatshops build the kind of deep loyalties that might have discouraged a sewing machinist or a baster from leaving a stable workplace and setting himself up in competition with a former employer. And given that the vast majority of Jewish immigrants intended to settle permanently in America, they were strongly motivated to improve their working conditions as quickly as possible. In the clothing trade the logical route upward was through self-employment.

The volatility and competitiveness of the menswear trade ensured that many small workshops established by immigrants lasted only briefly, vacuuming up excess demand during peak periods before folding during the slack season. According to one estimate, a third of all contractors went out of business every year. Some immigrants cycled back and forth between being employed by someone else and employing others. A machinist who worked as an employee one year might open an operation of his own the next and, if necessary, revert to paid employment if his venture failed. Entrepreneurial skills were sharpened by the whetstone of failure; lessons learned could be applied in a future enterprise. And there were plenty of entrepreneurial role models—employers, fellow workers, and neighbors—nearby for those who labored in small workshops to observe and emulate. By working in close proximity to employers who were fellow Jews, newcomers saw firsthand that aspiration to betterment was culturally and socially appropriate.

The seasonal nature of production also encouraged entrepreneurship. During the enforced idleness of slack periods that might last for more than four months a year, workers engaged in the entrepreneurship of survival, scrambling for money by engaging in petty commerce. As in the nineteenth century, there was still money to be made in lean times by collecting and selling scraps of waste fabric, as well as damaged but salable garments. Hoping for employment, laborers lined up in open-air hiring markets; both the one in Whitechapel Road in London and the one on the corner of Hester and Essex Streets in New York were called the *hazer mark* (pig market). Observers noted that the streets were as busy as they had been in the mid-nineteenth century, alive with peddlers and hawkers and choked with stalls.[7]

The preference for self-employment identified by Beatrice Webb would appear to bolster the case of the scholars who argue that Jewish immigrants arrived with an innate proclivity for entrepreneurship. Yet the picture was more complicated than it might at first seem. As the historian Andrew Godley has shown, the rate of self-employment among Jews was consistently and significantly lower in England than in America, albeit still higher than that of other groups in English society. According to his calculation, more than one in three Jewish immigrant men were entrepreneurs in New York in 1914, but fewer than one in five were in London.[8] Over time, this variation in rates of entrepreneurship translated into very real differences in status and attainment. Despite the clustering of Jews in London in the same industry as their kinsmen across the Atlantic, in aggregate they moved more haltingly out of the working class than did their coreligionists in New York. If all Jewish immigrants shared a proclivity toward entrepreneurship, why were Jews in the British capital on aggregate less entrepreneurially inclined than those in New York City? And what might this difference tell us about the role that an ethnic niche might play in shaping economic outcomes?

Since those who laid down their immigrants' sacks after crossing the English Channel do not seem to have been appreciably different from those who lugged their trunks across the Atlantic, this variation is unlikely to have been caused by differences between the cultural baggage of those who chose to settle in England and those who went to America. What else might have accounted for this divergence? One leading scholar, working from the assumption that immigrant Jews encountered a garment industry in England that was little different from that in the United States, proposed that newcomers to Albion rapidly assimilated their host culture's tepid enthusiasm for entrepreneurial activity, while those who landed in America embraced its ethos of economic individualism.[9] It is unclear, however, how and why Yiddish-speaking immigrants would have absorbed these influences so quickly and broadly, particularly when economic advancement was no less a motive for immigration among those who settled in England than among immigrants to America. Moreover, the preceding chapters have shown that the ethnic niche that eastern European immigrant Jews entered and enlarged in England was distinct in important ways from that of their coreligionists in America. These existing differences mattered, influencing the opportunities and conditions that Jews encountered in the clothing trade in each setting after 1880. For reasons that will soon become clear, the garment industry encouraged Jewish entrepreneurship in both England and America, but with a differing degree of urgency. This emphasis on the importance of the niche itself does not discount the role of other factors—the density of Jewish settlement, the prevalence of antisemitism, and other historical contingencies—in shaping Jewish economic behaviors. Instead, it recognizes that these factors acted on and in concert with developments in the clothing trade to shape the opportunities open to Jews.

Why Were Rates of Entrepreneurship Lower in London?

There are several reasons intrinsic to the clothing trade that may at least partly explain the lower rate of entrepreneurship among garment workers in England than in the United States. Jews in London appear to have been more willing to see a future for themselves in the tailoring trade. Andrew Godley identified a striking rise in the number of Jewish men in London who described themselves as skilled craftsmen in the decade before the First World War, which may suggest that they had chosen to work their way upward into better-paying positions in the field, such as sewing machinists and cutters, rather than seeking work in alternative trades. A significant proportion of children born to eastern European Jewish immigrants in England before 1914 followed their parents into this line of work, indicating that it was viewed as an acceptable and viable career path. Although antipathy toward Jews — particularly in sectors that were heavily unionized, such as construction and the dockyards — and the belief that they were unsuited for certain kinds of work limited the options available to them, such prejudices also acted on Jews in the United States. The relative dynamism of the US economy may have persuaded more Jews in America that their future lay outside the clothing trade. Certainly children born in America to Russian Jewish immigrants were only half as likely as their parents to work in garment manufacturing in 1910.[10] But discrimination and a paucity of alternatives does not preclude the possibility that marginally more Jews in England preferred work in the clothing trade to other options than did their counterparts in the United States.

Why might Jews in London have been more likely to feel this way than their coreligionists in New York? Although many observers viewed sweating before the First World War as much the same whether it occurred in the East End or on the Lower East Side, the industry was subject to greater government regulation in England than in America. Legislation passed in 1867 and 1871, however imperfect it was in practice, sought to regulate working hours in workshops and introduced inspections of working conditions. Perhaps as a result, the average workday for English garment workers was slightly shorter than that for their American counterparts.

Beginning in 1909, wages in England were fixed by trade boards. And even though some labor unions were leery of Jews, at the beginning of the twentieth century unions in England exerted a stronger influence over working conditions in the industry than US unions did. The frequency of strikes among immigrant garment workers in New York is somewhat misleading in this regard, since unions became effective at systematically enlisting and mobilizing garment workers only after 1909. Protections for workers in the garment industry were patchier in America—where oversight was not driven by the federal government—than in England. New York State passed legislation in 1892 that introduced licensing requirements for those who produced goods in tenements, but there was little momentum for significant new legislation until after the tragic Triangle Shirtwaist Company factory fire in 1911. There is also evidence that the wages paid to workers in London rose substantially in the first decade of the twentieth century—recovering from their fall in the 1880s and 1890s—although they remained depressed in New York until collective bargaining was introduced in 1910.[11]

The garment workshops in the East End and on Lower East Side, however, could serve as a nutritive growth medium for entrepreneurship only as long as London and New York remained competitive in the clothing trade. In the 1880s ominous signs may have begun to trouble the sleep of contractors who depended on the menswear business for their livelihoods. A Southern storekeeper in need of light summer suits might prefer the shorter trip to Baltimore than the longer journey to New York, and a wholesaler in search of bulk quantities of pants would do better in Boston than on Broadway. Department stores that placed rolling orders for suits now logically looked to Leeds rather than London, and Chicago instead of New York, for their supplies. By the end of the decade a little over a quarter of ready-made menswear sold nationwide was sewn in New York City. As the national market for menswear expanded, department and chain stores played a more important role in driving demand in the industry, and factories became more adept at producing apparel to their specifications at a speed and a cost that was difficult to match. Unlike in London and New York, where proliferating workshops cut up the market among themselves, large factories in other cities cornered a growing share of production. By 1911 just nineteen firms in Chicago produced half the city's output of clothing. Leading Chicago suit makers adopted scientific management techniques in their factories and reached accommodations with unions, increasing the scale and efficiency of manufacturing and avoiding disruptive strikes.

The trend toward consolidation accelerated outside of New York over the next decades, led in some cases by Jewish firms, including Hart Schaffner & Marx in Chicago, Henry Sonneborn & Company and L. Greif & Brother in Baltimore, and A. B. Kirschbaum & Company and N. Snellenburg & Company in Philadelphia. Since it was many times more expensive to establish a factory than a workshop, it was far more challenging for eastern European newcomers to join the ranks of leading manufacturers in cities where this mode of production predominated. As these manufacturers developed national brands and reputations that differentiated their products from those of their rivals in the minds of consumers, and as they achieved vertical integration and efficiencies of scale in production, distribution, and marketing, they undercut the mode of manufacturing menswear in New York City that depended on intense competition between subcontractors. On the surface New York still appeared to be holding its own against a bevy of upstarts. In 1911, for example, it produced 38 percent of all the clothing manufactured in the United States, more than the output of a chasing pack that included Chicago, Baltimore, Philadelphia, Rochester, Cincinnati, Boston, St. Louis, and Louisville. This percentage, however, concealed a significant shift within the industry. New York's rivals had already sewn up lines that had once been the preserve of its tailors. Such was the speed of the change that by the 1920s Rochester and Chicago had usurped New York's position at the center of the menswear industry.[12] If workshops in New York and London had fallen behind factories in the making of menswear, how did they remain vital engines of mobility for Jews?

The Wonders, and Vicissitudes, of Womenswear

If not for a fortuitous development, historians of modern Jewry might have cursed the garment industry in the East End and on the Lower East Side as a stultifying ethnic trap instead of celebrating the dynamism of the sweatshop economy. For even as factories came to master menswear, a vast new market emerged that played to the strengths of small-scale producers. The workshop was saved by womenswear. Aside from cloaks, coats, mantillas, hoop skirts, and caps, before the 1860s women's clothing had proved difficult to mass-produce because of the complexity of styles, the importance of a close fit, and the absence of standardized sizing. Instead, women sewed their own dresses, bought outerwear imported from Germany and France, or relied on dressmakers. Beginning in the 1860s and accelerating dramatically in the 1880s and 1890s, workshops in London and New York began to sew fashionable women's clothing for the mass market. In the ten years after 1899 the quantity of ready-made womenswear produced in the United States and the number of tailors and seamstresses employed to stitch it more than doubled. Fin de siècle fashion, dominated by shirtwaist blouses and skirts, proved particularly amenable to mass-production, as did new fabrics such as rayon and, later, nylon. The market for ready-made womenswear was boosted by innovative marketing and the proliferation of stores eager to court female customers. In 1899 a survey of working-class women in New York City found that they spent more on their clothing than men did. This was music to the ears of New York's clothing manufacturers and essential to the health of their industry. In that same year the city produced nearly two-thirds of all ready-made women's clothing sold in the United States. At the peak of its prowess in the 1920s, it claimed more than three-quarters of a national market that had overtaken menswear in the value of its output and the size of its workforce. Because of the sensitivity to style, the brevity of fashion cycles, and the emphasis on modest prices, mass-produced womenswear was initially better suited to the nimble mode of production perfected by workshops in the East End and on the Lower East Side—and adopted by manufacturers who decamped to the new Garment District on the West Side of Manhattan.[13] Jewish contractors were ideally placed to benefit from this surge in demand. Central European Jews had hitched their fortunes to the boom in menswear, but the eastern European men and women who labored in sweatshops in London and New York pulled themselves out of poverty thanks to women's clothing.

But timing was everything. Work in clothing workshops sewing womenswear remained far more attractive to Jewish immigrants in the East End for far longer than it did for their counterparts on the Lower East Side. In the 1930s the garment industry was still the largest employer of Jews in England, providing work for approximately a quarter of all employed

Before the 1860s, women's clothing had proved difficult to mass-produce. But once sweatshops and workshops became adept at making corsets and other items of womenswear, this trade became a lifeline for petty manufacturers on the Lower East Side and in the East End. (Collection of the author)

Jewish men in London and half of employed Jewish women. Even though the percentage of children who followed their parents into the trade declined, it remained high. Compared to American Jews, far fewer English Jews left garment workshops for the retail sector in the 1920s and 1930s, although some did so with great success. Tellingly, there is evidence of Jewish workers in Leeds swapping jobs in unpredictable workshops for the more reliable wages offered in modern factories, rather than leaving the industry altogether. This is not to suggest that Jews were economically immobile in England but instead that a larger proportion of them rose in status and income by assuming skilled roles in the clothing trade than was the case in America.

Jews in the United States, in contrast, proved on average less committed to tailoring and, as we have seen, more inclined to entrepreneurship. The longer the typical immigrant lived in America, the less likely he or she was to work in the garment industry. The same was true in England, but the change occurred more slowly. According to one estimate, 40 percent of Russian Jewish immigrant men in New York had become white-collar workers by 1905, and 50 percent had by 1925. The vast majority of these were owners of small businesses, many of which were related in one way or another to the production, distribution, or sale of garments and related items. Yet in the 1920s and 1930s, the garment industry itself still provided a vital backstop in America for the children of immigrants whose ambitions were stymied by antisemitism, as well as for people who entered it from other sectors of the economy during the Great Depression. Irving Howe's parents, for example, became garment workers after their store went bankrupt in 1930. Nonetheless, the general trend out of the trade was already well advanced. So common was it for Jews to exit the sweatshops that New York manufacturers worried about replenishing this workforce with others when immigration restrictions were imposed in 1924. And by the middle of the 1930s, Italians outnumbered Jews among garment workers.[14]

While working conditions in New York may have goaded Jewish immigrants to forsake sweatshop labor at a faster rate than was the case in London, some of the potential alternatives were also more readily apparent and accessible to Jews in America than in England. The history of Jewish involvement in the clothing trade prior to 1880 played an important part in this divergence, as did differences in the scale of immigrant settlement in each city. The density of the community in New York, as well as its distribution into a broader variety of occupations, undoubtedly widened the options available to those who sought to escape the garment industry and eased their entry into new fields. Pathways into petty retailing and wholesaling, moreover, had already been well furrowed by the feet of those who came before them. Not only did the earlier generation of Jews who had made their mark as wholesalers, clothiers, and department-store owners present an enticing entrepreneurial model, but in practical terms the members of that generation were still participants in what had become a vastly larger ethnic economy. They were now responsible for distributing and marketing much of the clothing that eastern European Jewish contractors and their laborers sewed. Given that the scale of production and demand continued to grow apace, and the industry itself was becoming more segmented and sophisticated, there was plenty of opportunity for newcomers to carve out spaces for themselves. And as earlier immigrants moved upward and outward in the clothing business, they created vacancies in the chain that were filled by their fellow Jews.

Although Jewish immigrants in London were also drawn into the broader clothing business—marketing as well as making garments—they had a much-smaller base on which to build than did Jews in America. As we have seen, by 1880 US Jews had established an elaborate distribution system that carried their wares to customers in the South, West, and Midwest. In contrast, English Jews, with a handful of exceptions, were not among the leading innovators in the mass marketing of clothing before 1880. Partly as a result of this fact, fewer than 3 percent of Jewish men in England who recorded their occupation in the 1901 census were shopkeepers and traders, a full twenty years after mass immigration had begun. This was not because the retail trade was drying up: according to one estimate, the number of clothiers in Britain increased tenfold in a little over three decades before the First World War.[15] Instead, Jewish immigrants in England were grafted onto a stump that had produced only spindly shoots; those who came to America added greenery to a solid trunk that already had deep roots in American soil.

The difference in the speed with which Jews in London and New York left garment workshops for alternative sources of employment had far-reaching consequences. Within a matter of decades, womenswear too turned into a mobility trap for its workers. Several forces worked against the long-term interests of laborers. First, competition among workshops increased in the years between the two world wars, as the jobbing system took hold. Because jobbers—intermediaries between subcontractors and store owners—in effect acted as the agents of retailers by farming out orders to workshops that competed for contracts, this system accentuated a dynamic of undercutting in the industry. Second, some new lines, particularly dressmaking, required less skilled tailoring, which meant that employers were less beholden to experienced workers and could hire more newcomers.

Third, the lead established by small workshops specializing in wom-enswear was eaten away by larger workshops and factories, as well as by clusters of seamstresses in rival geographic centers. In 1909 more than 60 percent of all the people in this line of work in America were employed in New York City, but by 1941 the figure had fallen below 40 percent. The slide reflected higher production costs in the city—partly because of suc-cessful pressure from unions for better pay—and the concomitant rise in the appeal of sending stitching to seamstresses in New England, Penn-sylvania, and Southern states who could be paid less for the same work. In general, lines that lent themselves to standardization were the first to leave. The number of needleworkers hired in the city continued to rise, but wages in the garment trade in New York stagnated and then fell relative to other industries in the metropolis, as manufacturers sought to save on labor so they could remain competitive. These trends accelerated after the Second World War.

Finally, a process of consolidating production into factories and larger workshops, akin to that seen in menswear, stripped away many of the mechanisms that had encouraged and enabled men and women who labored in workshops to get ahead. Larger units replaced small workshops as the engines of much of the womenswear trade, and it became increas-ingly difficult for workers to raise the money needed to start competi-tive enterprises of their own. By the 1920s the start-up costs for a typical workshop had risen to $2,000 to $3,000, twenty times what it had been at the beginning of the century. Similar pressures eroded the position of garment workers in London.[16] By dint of good fortune a larger proportion of Jews in New York had already fled the field or made their way into its more secure upper reaches, leaving its most competitive sections open for other groups less fortunate in their timing and its more desirable positions already claimed. A far larger share of their counterparts in London, by con-trast, were caught in the industry once it began its long decline.

Not only was the exodus of Jews from garment manufacturing in New York timely; so too was their entry into a variety of other fields in the first decades of the twentieth century, when mass consumption was bal-looning in the United States. Some continued to orbit the clothing trade. Because of its scale and complexity, the industry supported a variety of niches that served its needs and depended on its bounty. The increased complexity of the clothing trade created demands for clerks, accountants, lawyers, managers, and advertisers, often the university-educated children of immigrants. And there was work aplenty in a variety of roles in department, chain, and local stores that proliferated in the early twentieth century. Others took flight from the platform that their past experience in retailing and distribution provided. Since several other sectors were averse to hiring Jews, closing off a variety of alternative economic pathways, many flocked instead to new consumer-oriented industries where there were fewer entrenched competitors. These fields—the film and music industries being the best known examples—tended to benefit those who created dense networks that interconnected producers, distributors, and purveyors. A sensitivity to fashion and a hardheadedness in matters of business came in handy, much as it had for earlier peddlers and petty shopkeepers, when Jews were persuading skeptical Americans of the value of aspirational products that they sold from their storefronts, suitcases, and car trunks. Persuasion and persistence paid off as much in the furniture business as it did for clothiers. It was perhaps no accident that several Hollywood moguls and sheet-music publishers started as salesmen in the clothing trade. (Morris Brill is better remembered for the music produced in the building in New York that bore his name than for the clothing store he ran on the ground floor.) In turn, several of these new fields became Jewish ethnic niches. With the exception of the entertainment industry, the speedy process of economic diversification already seen among Jews in America in the interwar years proceeded more slowly in England.[17]

Legacies of an Ethnic Niche

This brief account, focused more on broad patterns than on specific examples, has smoothed out the wrinkles and trimmed the loose threads that in reality complicated and sometimes confounded the economic lives of first- and second-generation eastern European Jews in New York. Few followed a seamless and unruffled transition from the sweatshop to the store counter and beyond, particularly when the Great Depression and a surge of antisemitism unraveled even the best laid plans. But paradoxically, economic turmoil and prejudice may for a time have bolstered entrepreneurial tendencies within the ethnic economy. Many Jews who graduated from college during the interwar years encountered sufficient prejudice in hiring practices within several professions and white-collar industries to instead choose to strike out on their own or turn to commercial fields where antisemitism was less acute. This trend also points to a variety of factors that acted in concert with the internal dynamics of the consumer industries in which Jews clustered to boost the prospects of Jews, despite an increasingly inhospitable environment for them in society at large during the 1920s and 1930s. Jews, for example, invested heavily in educating their children—Jews attended college at more than double the rate of the American population overall in the interwar period, despite restrictive quotas at many of the most prestigious schools—a decision that paid large dividends over the long term. But in the short term Thomas Kessner's conclusion, drawn from a statistical overview of Jewish immigrants, is convincing: "It was not medicine, law or even their vaunted thirst for education that carried them forward. It was business."[18]

Yet even as the broader Jewish community moved upward, there were plenty of Jews in New York and other cities and towns who remained lodged in the lower reaches of the American economy. It is easy to lose sight of poor Jews when we focus on the general economic uplift of American Jewry. Secondhand-clothing collectors who mimicked their nineteenth-century forebears by calling out their trade in urban centers— "I buy! Cash clothes!"—still walked the streets of American cities and towns within living memory. Working-class Jewish communities long continued to thrive in Queens, the Bronx, and parts of Manhattan.[19] This was even more the case in London. Although few statistical data are available, several studies have described the persistence of a substantial Jewish working-class in London in the decades immediately after the Second World War. Some English Jews had left immigrant neighborhoods and the garment industry behind; but many remained in working-class and lower-middle-class occupations, and relatively few became professionals. Although on average, English Jews born after the First World War were better educated and more socially mobile than their parents were, they still lagged behind their American peers. Other factors undoubtedly weighed on the advance of Jews in England in the 1950s and 1960s: the deadening hand of discrimination, slow economic growth, the rigidity of the class system, the effects of the flattening of neighborhoods in the East End during the Blitz, the limitations of the state educational system, low rates of university attendance compared to their peers in the United States, and a

A dense Sunday crowd in Petticoat Lane in 1930. (Collection of the author)

regulatory environment that made it more challenging than in America for small businesses to consolidate and grow.[20]

If the interwar years provided a comparatively modest bounce for Jews in England, in America they served as a springboard for many Jews. By the end of the Second World War, with the United States on the brink of one of the longest periods of sustained growth in its history, Jews were ideally positioned in consumer industries, an area of the economy that grew most rapidly in the next decades. Unsurprisingly, earlier patterns pushed Jews in certain directions, but they were also influenced by a decline in employment discrimination and rising rates of college education. In 1950 first- and second-generation Russian Jewish immigrants were already earning slightly more on average than native-born whites were; in 1970 the second generation was exceeding the average earnings of native-born whites by 50 percent. And while a larger slice of the Jewish population moved into the professions, and others pursued work in parts of the economy that had previously been closed to them, those who opted for careers in commerce often did so in mercantile fields in which Jews had made earlier inroads. Those who remained in the clothing trade—a declining share of the Jewish workforce—typically did so in ownership or management positions. In 1950 second-generation Russian immigrant Jews who persisted in this field were earning significantly more on average than were the members of their broader immigrant Jewish cohort, indicating that this pattern of working in higher positions was already pronounced. To some extent these occupational trends still hold true. Among the wealthiest Americans today, for example, Jews remain overrepresented in the apparel, cosmetics, and finance industries but underrepresented in heavy manufacturing, transportation, and utilities, all of which are capital-intensive areas that were historically less welcoming to Jews.[21]

The legacy of Jewish involvement in the clothing industry becomes even clearer when the trajectory of Jews is compared to that of other groups of immigrants who settled in urban areas in the United States at roughly the same time. Some immigrant groups dominated industries that suited their intention to return to their homelands, tolerated work that those who planned to stay permanently were quicker to abandon, and invested few of their resources in attaining the skills and capital needed to start their own businesses. For other groups of immigrants who intended to stay but clustered in large bureaucratic and hierarchical organizations—city government, for example—the "logical next step [was] not to go out and set up one's own business" but to pursue advancement by acquiring training, patronage, or seniority. An immigrant who became familiar with the skills needed to advance within the public sector, construction, or any number of other fields would be little prepared for starting a small business. Those future immigrants who followed him or her into an expanding ethnic niche would have few entrepreneurial role models to emulate.[22] Several influential studies have compared the rapid advance of Jews with the more leisurely pace of Italian and Irish immigrants.[23] Although Italians also clustered in the garment industry in New York, they came to the field in large numbers only in the early 1900s, entering at a time when eastern European Jews were already entrenched in it and factory production cut out a growing share of the market. Garment work was more closely associated with Italian women, who often worked from home as finishers, than with men. A patriarchal family culture, higher rates of illiteracy, and a common understanding that immigration was a temporary sojourn rather than a permanent relocation also crimped entrepreneurship among Italians. Evidence from Dallas, Houston, and Galveston, however, suggests that in the right environment, Italian migrants embraced independent enterprise at rates equivalent to, and at times exceeding, those of Jews. But in New

York the occupations preferred by Italian men—most often unskilled seasonal work—did them fewer favors over the long term than the garment trade did Jews.[24]

The experience of other ethnic groups highlights again how early economic choices could have intergenerational consequences. The preceding chapters have also demonstrated that there was nothing inevitable about the speed with which Jews rose within the American economy. All the advantages that a better education and a sense of ethnic solidarity conferred on Jewish peddlers, clerks, and petty shopkeepers might have been diminished or even negated if their occupations had diverted them into the sluggish backwaters of the economy instead of carrying them swiftly into its main currents. Petty trading might have remained a marginal activity but for the explosive expansion of America and its markets. Jews were fortunate in the field in which they clustered; few of the humble traders who toted heavy packs in the Midwest and South or the bored clerks who totaled figures in Cincinnati and New York could have foreseen that these pursuits would provide a degree of privileged access to a core modern industry when garment production took off in unexpected ways. And even when Jews had established a firm footing in the retail and wholesale trades in the Midwest, the elaborate networks that interconnected peddlers, shopkeepers, and wholesalers through credit and common purpose could carry them only so far. For a time in the 1840s and 1850s most Jewish firms in New York seemed to be stymied by their late start in the Southern market. The discovery of gold in California, followed in quick succession by economic crisis and the Civil War, did what they otherwise could not have managed, propelling them to the front of the clothing industry nationwide. They also benefited from a postwar environment that was alive with potential. Lean peddlers and petty traders grew stout as sedentary shopkeepers. Ambitious store owners, covetously eyeing the bounty of the period, expanded their enterprises or experimented with retail banking and brokering. A handful whose appetite for profit was no longer sated by the bland business of selling clothing found richer rewards in finance. The Jewish immigrants who followed them to America built on their successes. Eastern European Jews too were fortunate in their timing, entering the garment trade when womenswear offered a new lease on life to workshops and departing before their decline became irreversible. The sweatshop economy proved an unexpected gateway to a more prosperous future, encouraging Jews to seek opportunity as petty capitalists and facilitating their entry into new fields.

The experience of American Jews' kin in England provides an important reminder that things need not have turned out this way. To an objective observer in the 1830s the Jewish secondhand dealers of London would have looked more likely to be the midwives of future Jewish dominance of the clothing trade than would the scattering of peddlers in the Midwest. The early success of Henry and Elias Moses suggested that such a future might have been possible. But unlike in America, the transition to mass manufacturing and retailing of inexpensive ready-made garments produced only a handful of Jewish prodigies. For all the seeming promise of the secondhand business, it was an imperfect platform for entry into the ready-made trade. Focused on the collection of clothing and its sale in marts and on the streets, the English secondhand trade did not create the elaborate and geographically dispersed distribution chain that peddlers at the outer reaches of an ethnic economy established in America. The centripetal nature of this ethnic niche in England was not as beneficial in the long term as the centrifugal structure of the one in the United States was. When Jewish secondhand dealers began to shift into manufacturing in England, they could not tap into a prefabricated distribution system of the kind that assisted their coreligionists in Cincinnati and New York, unless they could call on a network of well-placed family members of the kind that aided Henry Moses in Australia. Those who remained in the secondhand trade in London soon found that the abundance of used garments discarded by consumers hungry for fresh fashions provided them with a reprieve but not a pardon. As ready-mades became ever cheaper, the allure of castoffs shrank.

Nor did the stars align for Jews in London in as helpful a fashion as they did for Jews in New York. In England there was no calamity like the Civil War to scramble the hierarchy of the ready-made trade and to open fresh fields of endeavor. When eastern European Jews began to arrive in England en masse, the ethnic niche they found was far more modest than was its counterpart in America. There were few Jews among the leading manufacturers and wholesalers who could help shepherd them forward but plenty of Jewish contractors and petty clothiers whose own ambitions had been frustrated by the intense competition of sweatshop manufacturing and mass retailing. Although the garment industry encouraged entrepreneurship among the newcomers, Jews in England had somewhat less incentive to leave tailoring, fewer role models to emulate, and a shallower presence in other fields, and thus they were slower to exit the sweatshop. This had important consequences, slowing their ascent and narrowing the range of new fields that they entered. Although the upward mobility of eastern European Jews in England compared favorably with that of other groups in their host society, their passage was belabored when compared to their American counterparts.

The prosperity of Jews in the United States was not wrought by magic and genius. Nor was it solely a product of eastern European immigrants and their children. Much had occurred before their arrival in America to make their progress possible. To be properly understood, the economic experience of Jews in twentieth-century America must be seen in the context of a much-longer history. The culture that immigrants carried with them undoubtedly aided their ascent. There was nothing inevitable, however, in the rise of Jews from Chatham Street; theirs is a history larded with a dose of good fortune. But for the confluence of structural forces in the American market, the fortunate positioning of Jewish immigrants on the edges and then at the center of the unfolding industry, and considerable individual effort aided by ethnic cooperation, the outcome would have been subtly or substantially different. In short, the clothing trade proved a good fit for generations of Jewish immigrants. Although Jews may have been responsible for making parts of the modern clothing industry, without question the clothing industry—to at least some extent—made the Jews in America.

ACKNOWLEDGMENTS

It is fitting to conclude a book that deals with credit, debt, and supportive networks by reflecting on the centrality of these same factors to my own work. My obligations may not be of the material kind, but they are no less important than those incurred by the dealers, peddlers, and merchants whom I have studied. Nor have I been any less reliant on good fortune than were the luckiest of my subjects. For at every turn I have been aided by friends and colleagues generous with their time and patient of my requests.

This project was born in spite of good advice that went unheeded. As a freshly minted PhD I spent a year at the Herbert D. Katz Center for Advanced Judaic Studies in Philadelphia. Instead of speedily transforming my dissertation into a book, as wiser heads counseled, the allure of the new (or in this case, the secondhand) proved powerful. *Shmattes* became my siren song. Setting aside an existing manuscript that devoted only a handful of pages to the clothing trade, I began a full-time pursuit of elusive ragmen and secondhand dealers. I am very pleased that I did so. There was no better place to begin this project than the Center for Advanced Judaic Studies. Without the time to read and think that this fellowship afforded, the intellectual energy that the center provided, and my conversations with colleagues there, this book would not exist.

I was no less fortunate to move from Philadelphia to Charleston. My colleagues in the Jewish Studies Program at the College of Charleston— Larry Krasnoff, Joshua Shanes, and Dale and Ted Rosengarten—were supportive and encouraging from the first and have all become good friends. Marty Perlmutter, whose energy, enthusiasm, and warmth is infectious, has been a wonderful mentor and role model in Charleston. Enid Idelsohn, an organizational dynamo, helped in many ways large and small.

The college supported my research on this project, as have several other organizations. I received generous grant and fellowship funding from the American Jewish Historical Society and the Southern Jewish Historical Society. I am also indebted to the archivists and librarians who brought the raw materials of history within reach, no matter whether I was in Charleston, Philadelphia, New York, London, Melbourne, or Sydney. I owe particular credit to Kevin Proffitt and his team at the American Jewish Archives and to Arthur Kiron and the staff of the Library at the Herbert D. Katz Center for Advanced Judaic Studies. Judith Leifer, a stalwart at the Katz Center has always been a wonder (and pleasure) to work with. Her counterparts in the Interlibrary Loan Department of the College of Charleston Library—Chris Nelson, Brandon Lewter, and several others—have also performed yeoman work on my behalf. My thanks to Harlan Greene and Dale Rosengarten of the Special Collections Department of the College of Charleston Library and to Sam Stewart, who so kindly scanned most of the images used as illustrations in this book. George Rigal generously shared his research into the Moses family, and Bastien Gomperts supplied invaluable information about Samuel and Saul Isaac.

I owe a large intellectual debt to friends and colleagues whose input and feedback sharpened my thinking and strengthened my arguments. Mark K. Bauman, Mike Cohen, Marni Davis, Ava F. Kahn, Rebecca Kobrin, Jörg-Ole Münch, and Dale Rosengarten read and commented on sections of the manuscript, as did participants in the Working Group on Jews and the Modern Economy at the Center for Jewish History, the Tauber Institute Jewish Studies Colloquium at Brandeis University, and several other conference sessions and seminars. Hasia Diner, Jonathan Karp, Stuart Rockoff, Jonathan D. Sarna, and two anonymous readers supplied thoughtful feedback on the entire text. Jeanne Ferris and Andrew Katz saved me from many stylistic infelicities. Jennifer Hammer, my editor at New York University Press, expertly shepherded this project from the start.

Even though far from Cape Town, Boston, and Philadelphia, I have continued to draw on support from friends in these and other places. Matt Kaliner, Simon Rabinovitch, and Mike Cohen have remained firm friends despite hearing far more about *shmattes* than any reasonable person can bear. Howard Phillips, Milton Shain, and Jonathan D. Sarna, teachers who taught me their trade, have continued to offer cherished counsel and care long after I left their classrooms.

Most of all, I am grateful to my own personal Anglophone Jewish diaspora, which has branches in Cape Town and Kennett Square and many places in between. A far-flung family has made research trips that much easier and more pleasurable. David and Jeanne Katz have always been wonderful hosts in London, as have Debra and Leon Feigenbaum and Evan and Ruth Katz in New York. Jessica and Gerald Aronstan in Sydney and Sandra and Arthur Baigel in Melbourne provided a warm welcome in Australia. My parents have always provided a perfect balance of support and encouragement. To them I am deeply indebted. Alongside interest and friendship, my brothers supplied occasional assistance with photocopying and scanning. Although I have yet to test the photocopying skills of Ellen and Richard Finkelman, they have been supportive in every other way.

Even though part of my heart remains in Cape Town, the rest now belongs to my wife, Andrea, and my son, Sam. Andrea has been a constant companion and contributor throughout the research and writing of this book. She has made this process smoother and more pleasurable in innumerable ways. And Sam, who still prefers books that can float in the bath and will not be able to read this himself for a while, has made life that much more fun.

NOTES

NOTES TO THE INTRODUCTION

1. For claims of exceptional upward mobility, see John Higham, *Send These to Me: Immigrants in Urban America* (Baltimore: Johns Hopkins University Press, 1984), 123; Barry R. Chiswick, "The Occupational Attainment of American Jewry: 1990–2000," *Contemporary Jewry* 27, 1 (2007): 80–111; Chiswick, "The Economic Progress of American Jewry: From Eighteenth-Century Merchants to Twenty-First-Century Professionals," in *The Oxford Handbook of Judaism and Economics*, ed. Aaron Levine (New York: Oxford University Press, 2010), 625; David A. Hollinger, "Rich, Powerful, and Smart: Jewish Overrepresentation Should Be Explained Instead of Avoided or Mystified," *Jewish Quarterly Review* 94, 4 (Fall 2004): 595–602; Yuri Slezkine, *The Jewish Century* (Princeton: Princeton University Press, 2004), 1–39; Jerry Z. Muller, *Capitalism and the Jews* (Princeton: Princeton University Press, 2010), 101–102; Peter Temin, "An Elite Minority: Jews among the Richest 400 Americans," in *Human Capital and Institutions: A Long-Run View*, ed. David Eltis, Frank D. Lewis, and Kenneth L. Sokoloff (New York: Cambridge University Press, 2009), 248–249; Lisa J. Neidert and Reynolds Farley, "Assimilation in the United States: An Analysis of Ethnic and Generation Differences in Status and Achievement," *American Sociological Review* 50, 6 (Dec. 1980): 844–847.

2. The most significant of these earlier studies was Werner Sombart's *Die Juden und das Wirtschaftsleben* (Leipzig: Duncker and Humblot, 1911), published in abridged form in 1913 as *The Jews and Modern Capitalism* (New York: E. P. Dutton, 1913). Max Weber's interpretation of Jewish economic behavior in terms of "pariah capitalism" had a smaller impact than Sombart's tendentious treatise. On "pariah capitalism," see Max Weber, *General Economic History* (New York: Collier Books, 1927), 196, 358–360. For an overview of Jewish understandings of their economic distinctiveness, see Derek Penslar, *Shylock's Children: Economics and Jewish Identity in Modern Europe* (Berkeley: University of California Press, 2001), 134–173. For a masterful discussion of how Europe thought about Jews and commerce during the Enlightenment and the period of emancipation, see Jonathan Karp, *The Politics of Jewish Commerce: Economic Thought and Emancipation in Europe, 1638–1848* (New York: Cambridge University Press, 2008).

3. For examples of this approach, see Werner Mosse, "Judaism, Jews and Capitalism: Weber, Sombart and Beyond," *Leo Baeck Institute Yearbook* 24, 1 (1979): 6–13; Temin, "Elite Minority," 248–264; Slezkine, *Jewish Century*; Muller, *Capitalism and the Jews*, 82–132; Moses Kligsberg, "Jewish Immigrants in Business: A Sociological Study," *American*

Jewish Historical Quarterly 56, 3 (1967): 283–318; Bernard Sarachek, "Jewish American Entrepreneurs," *Journal of Economic History* 40, 2 (June 1980): 359–372; Simon Kuznets, "Immigration of Russian Jews to the United States: Background and Structure," in *Jewish Economies: Development and Migration in America and Beyond*, vol. 2, *Comparative Perspectives on Jewish Migration*, ed. Stephanie Lo and E. Glen Weyl (New Brunswick, NJ: Transaction, 2012), 143–232; Arcadius Kahan, "Economic Opportunities and Some Pilgrim's Progress: Jewish Immigrants from Eastern Europe in the United States, 1890–1914," in *Essays in Jewish Social and Economic History* (Chicago: University of Chicago Press, 1986), 101–117; Reuven Brenner and Nicholas M. Kiefer, "The Economics of the Diaspora: Discrimination and Occupational Structure," *Economic Development and Cultural Change* 29, 3 (1981): 517–534; Eliezer B. Ayal and Barry R. Chiswick, "The Economics of the Diaspora Revisited," *Economic Development and Cultural Change* 31, 4 (1983): 861–875; Carmel U. Chiswick, "The Economics of Jewish Continuity," *Contemporary Jewry* 20 (1999): 30–56.

4. Several scholars have disputed this explanation. See, for example, Simon Kuznets, "Economic Structure and Life of the Jews," in *The Jews: Their History, Culture, and Religion*, ed. Louis Finkelstein (Philadelphia: Jewish Publication Society of America, 1960), 1597–1666; Eli Berman, "Sect, Subsidy, and Sacrifice: An Economist's View of Ultra-Orthodox Jews," *Quarterly Journal of Economics* 115, 3 (2000): 905–953; Maristella Botticini and Zvi Eckstein, "Jewish Occupational Selection: Education, Restrictions, or Minorities?," *Journal of Economic History* 65, 4 (Dec. 2005): 922–948; Maristella Botticini and Zvi Eckstein, "From Farmers to Merchants, Conversions and Diaspora: Human Capital and Jewish History," *Journal of the European Economic Association* 5, 5 (Sept. 2007): 885–926.

5. For the Jewish embrace of public education, see Simone Lässig, *Jüdische Wege ins Bürgertum: Kulturelles Kapital und sozialer Aufstieg im 19. Jahrhundert* (Göttingen, Germany: Vandenhoek and Ruprecht, 2004). For the educational background of Jewish immigrants, see Tobias Brinkmann, *Sundays at Sinai: A Jewish Congregation in Chicago* (Chicago: University of Chicago Press, 2012), 26–30.

6. See Eli Lederhendler, *Jewish Immigrants and American Capitalism, 1880–1920: From Caste to Class* (New York: Cambridge University Press, 2009). For an essay that suggests that Jewish culture may have been as much an advantage as an impediment when it came to participation in a modern capitalist economy, see Joel Mokyr, "The Economics of Being Jewish," *Critical Review* 23, 1–2 (2011): 202–204.

7. For a forceful critique of studies that rely on cultural values as an explanation of economic success, see Howard E. Aldrich and Roger Waldinger, "Ethnicity and Entrepreneurship," *Annual Review of Sociology* 16 (1990): 125–126. For work that stresses the unpredictability of the relationship between culture and economic outcomes, see Deirdre N. McCloskey, *Bourgeois Dignity: Why Economics Can't Explain the Modern World* (Chicago: University of Chicago Press, 2010), 273–285, 374–376. For a study that suggests that distinct values dissipated among third-generation American Jews, see Fred L. Strodtbeck, "Family Interaction, Values and Achievement," in *The Jews: Social Patterns of an American Group*, ed. Marshall Sklare (Glencoe, IL: Greenwood, 1960), 147–165.

8. Sociologists have produced a voluminous literature on ethnic (and particularly immigrant) economic activity that seeks to account for differences in their economic performance. This study relies heavily on work on ethnic economic niches, particularly that of Roger Waldinger, who has tied economic mobility to particular opportunity structures that favor ethnic enterprise, ethnic succession within the workplace, and the "fit" between immigrant groups and particular niches.

9. For examples, see Penslar, *Shylock's Children*, 124–133; Nancy L. Green, *Ready-to-Wear and Ready-to-Work: A Century of Industry and Immigrants in Paris and New York* (Durham: Duke University Press, 1997); Marni Davis, *Jews and Booze: Becoming American in the Age of Prohibition* (New York: NYU Press, 2012); Sarah Abravaya Stein, *Plumes: Ostrich Feathers, Jews, and a Lost World of Global Commerce* (New Haven: Yale University Press, 2008); Adam Teller, *Money, Power, and Influence: The Jews on the Radziwill Estates in 18th Century Lithuania* (Hebrew) (Jerusalem: Merkaz Zalman Shazar, 2005); Ewa Morawska, *Insecure Prosperity: Small-Town Jews in Industrial America, 1890–1940* (Princeton: Princeton University Press, 1996). An entire section of *Chosen Capital: The Jewish Encounter with American Capitalism*, ed. Rebecca Kobrin (New Brunswick: Rutgers University Press, 2012), is devoted to ethnic niches occupied by Jews.

10. In using the term *clothing*, this book refers both to apparel (dresses, coats, suits, trousers, hats, and caps) and to underwear (shirts, socks, and stockings) but does not, for the most part, consider accessories (gloves, handbags, umbrellas, and scarves) and shoes.

11. This study is indebted to comparative work on the clothing trade conducted by Andrew Godley and Nancy L. Green. See, in particular, Godley, *Jewish Immigrant Entrepreneurship in New York and London, 1880–1914: Enterprise and Culture* (Basingstoke, UK: Palgrave, 2001); Green, *Ready-to-Wear and Ready-to-Work*.

12. On rates of entrepreneurship, see Thomas Kessner, *The Golden Door: Italian and Jewish Immigrant Mobility in New York City, 1880–1915* (New York: Oxford University Press, 1977), 52, 60, 110. For comparative data, see Suzanne Model, "The Ethnic Niche and the Structure of Opportunity: Immigrants and Minorities in New York City," in *The Underclass Debate: Views From History*, ed. Michael B. Katz (Princeton: Princeton University Press, 1993), 172–187.

13. For ethnic succession within the trade, see Roger Waldinger, *Through the Eye of the Needle: Immigrants and Enterprise in New York's Garment Trades* (New York: NYU Press, 1986); for an international perspective, see Jan Rath, ed., *Unravelling the Rag Trade: Immigrant Entrepreneurship in Seven World Cities* (Oxford, UK: Berg, 2002).

14. See Beverly Lemire, *Dress, Culture and Commerce: The English Clothing Trade before the Factory, 1660–1800* (New York: Palgrave Macmillan, 1997), 75–77.

15. Claude Lévi-Strauss, *Totemism* (Boston: Beacon, 1963), 89.

16. Robert Ross discusses how fashions crossed borders and pays close attention to the role of different national and ethnic groups in speeding (and sometimes resisting) these exchanges but pays little attention to Jews. See Ross, *Clothing: A Global History* (Cambridge, UK: Polity, 2008).

17. For examples of Jewish involvement in the clothing trade in the medieval and early modern periods, see Lemire, *Dress, Culture and Commerce*, 172n12; Patricia Anne

Allerston, "The Market in Second-Hand Clothes and Furnishings in Venice, c. 1500–c. 1650" (PhD diss., European University Institute, 1996), 7–9, 37–62, 119–165; Todd Endelman, *The Jews of Georgian England, 1714–1830* (Ann Arbor: University of Michigan Press, 1999), 178; Michael Miller, *Rabbis and Revolution: The Jews of Moravia in the Age of Emancipation* (Stanford: Stanford University Press, 2010), 19, 90; Salo W. Baron, Arcadius Kahan, et al., *Economic History of the Jews* (New York: Schocken Books, 1975), 191, 266–278; Mark Wischnitzer, *A History of Jewish Crafts and Guilds* (New York: Jonathan David, 1965); Joachim Eibach, "Stigma und Betrug: Delinquenz und Ökonomie im jüdischen Ghetto," in *Kriminalität und abweichendes Verhalten: Deutschland im 18. und 19. Jahrhundert*, ed. Helmut Berding, Diehelm Klippel, and Günther Lottes (Göttingen, Germany: Vandenhoek and Ruprecht, 1999), 15–38; Jonathan Israel, *European Jews in the Age of Mercantilism* (London: Littman Library of Jewish Civilization, 1998), 141–142; Raphael Mahler, *A History of Modern Jewry, 1780–1815* (New York: Schocken Books, 1971), 108–109; Cecil Roth, *The History of the Jews of Italy* (Philadelphia: Jewish Publication Society of America, 1946), 372–375; Bernardino Ramazzini, *Diseases of Workers* (New York: Hafner, 1964), 287–289, 385–386; Steven M. Lowenstein, *The Berlin Jewish Community: Enlightenment, Family, and Crisis, 1770–1830* (New York: Oxford University Press, 1994), 59–60, 217n17; Marion A. Kaplan, *Jewish Daily Life in Germany, 1618–1945* (New York: Oxford University Press, 2005), 58, 131; *Encyclopedia Judaica* (New York: Macmillan, 1971), 705–712.

18. For examples of the persistence of peddling in Europe, see Paula Hyman, *The Emancipation of the Jews of Alsace: Acculturation and Tradition in the Nineteenth Century* (New Haven: Yale University Press, 1991), 32–39; J. C. H. Blom, R. G. Fuks-Mansfeld, and I. Schöffer, *The History of the Jews in the Netherlands* (Portland, OR: Littman Library of Jewish Civilization, 2002), 114, 167–168, 174, 215, 227; documents in Monika Richarz, ed., *Jüdisches Leben in Deutschland: Selbstzeugnisse zur Sozialgeschichte 1780–1871* (Stuttgart, Germany: Veröffentlichung des Leo Baeck Instituts, 1976), 70–136; Kaplan, *Jewish Daily Life in Germany*, 58, 132–133, 135, 140. For contemporary descriptions, see Louis Simond, *A Tour in Italy and Sicily* (London: Longman, Rees, Orme, Brown and Green, 1828), 257; Moses Jacob Ezekiel, *Memoirs from the Bath of Diocletian* (Detroit: Wayne State University Press, 1975), 457; Augustus J. C. Hare, *Walks in Rome* (London: George Allen, 1871), 174.

19. Historians of Anglo-Jewry have paid some attention to Jews and old clothing in the eighteenth century. See, for example, Harold Pollins, *Economic History of the Jews in England* (Rutherford, NJ: Farleigh Dickinson University Press, 1982), 66–69; Endelman, *Jews of Georgian England*, 179–183.

20. For work on America, see Seth Rockman, *Scraping By: Wage Labor, Slavery, and Survival in Early Baltimore* (Baltimore: Johns Hopkins University Press, 2009); Wendy A. Woloson, *In Hock: Pawning in America from Independence through the Great Depression* (Chicago: University of Chicago Press, 2009). Woloson's book also pays careful attention to the role of Jews (both imagined and real) in pawnbroking. The scholarship on second-hand markets in Europe is much more expansive. See Laurence Fontaine, ed., *Alternative Exchanges: Second-Hand Circulations from the Sixteenth Century to the Present* (New

York: Berghahn, 2008); B. Blondé, ed., *Fashioning Old and New: Changing Consumer Preferences in Europe (Seventeenth–Nineteenth Centuries)* (Turnhout, Belgium: Brepols, 2009); Jon Stobart and Ilja Van Damme, eds., *Modernity and the Second-Hand Trade* (New York: Palgrave Macmillan, 2011). For studies that focus on the clothing trade specifically, see Madeleine Ginsburg, "Rags to Riches: The Second-Hand Clothes Trade 1700–1978," *Costume* 14 (1980): 121–135; Beverly Lemire, "Consumerism in Preindustrial and Early Industrial England: The Trade in Secondhand Clothes," *Journal of British Studies* 27 (1988): 1–24; Lemire, "Shifting Currency: The Culture and Economy of the Second Hand Trade in England, c. 1600–1850," in *Old Clothes, New Looks: Second-Hand Fashion*, ed. Alexandra Palmer and Hazel Clark (New York: Bloomsbury Academic, 2005), 29–48; Manuel Charpy, "The Scope and Structure of the Nineteenth-Century Second-Hand Trade in the Parisian Clothes Market," in Fontaine, *Alternative Exchanges*, 127–155; John Styles, *The Dress of the People* (New Haven: Yale University Press, 2008), 321–323. In contrast with Jan de Vries, who emphasizes the decline of the secondhand trade after the eighteenth century, this book highlights its continued dynamism. See de Vries, *The Industrious Revolution: Consumer Behavior and the Household Economy, 1650 to the Present* (New York: Cambridge University Press, 2008), 144.

21. For theories as to why this subject has not received sustained attention, see Muller, *Capitalism and the Jews*, 1–3; Gideon Reuveni, "Prolegomena to an 'Economic Turn' in Jewish History," in *The Economy in Jewish History*, ed. Gideon Reuveni and Sarah Wobick-Segev (New York: Berghahn, 2011), 8–9; Ira Katznelson, "Two Exceptionalisms: Points of Departure for Studies of Capitalism and Jews in the United States," in Kobrin, *Chosen Capital*, 19.

22. An important exception is the now-somewhat-dated work of Egal Feldman. See Feldman, *Fit for Men: A Study of New York's Clothing Trade* (Washington, DC: Public Affairs, 1960); and Feldman, "Jews in the Early Growth of New York City's Men's Clothing Trade," *American Jewish Archives* 12, 1 (1960): 3–14. Jews qua Jews are strikingly absent from Michael Zakim's *Ready-Made Democracy: A History of Men's Dress in the American Republic, 1760–1860* (Chicago: University of Chicago Press, 2003), the best recent study on the birth of the American clothing trade. Steven Fraser briefly references the role of central and eastern European Jews in his study "Combined and Uneven Development in the Men's Clothing Industry," *Business History Review* 57 (1983): 522–547.

23. For an overview of the production of women's clothing, see Joan M. Jensen, "Needlework as Art, Craft, and Livelihood before 1900," in *A Needle, a Bobbin, a Strike: Women Needleworkers in America*, ed. Joan M. Jensen and Sue Davidson (Philadelphia: Temple University Press, 1984), 3–19. According to one estimate, the average household in middle and late nineteenth-century Europe spent 12 to 15 percent more on outfitting the male household head than it did on outfitting his wife. See Richard Wall, "Some Implications of the Earnings, Income and Expenditure Patterns of Married Women in Populations in the Past," in *Poor Women and Children in the European Past*, ed. John Henderson and Richard Wall (London: Routledge, 1994), 328–330.

24. See John Lauritz Larson, *The Market Revolution in America* (New York: Cambridge University Press, 2010), 57–58, 88–89; and Gary B. Magee and Andrew S. Thompson,

Empire and Globalisation (Cambridge: Cambridge University Press, 2010), 6 (quote), 59–60.

25. Magee and Thompson, *Empire and Globalisation*, 12, 44, 85.

26. Peter Cunningham, *A Handbook for London*, vol. 2 (London: John Murray, 1849), 561.

NOTES TO CHAPTER 1

1. John Hassard, *A Pickwickian Pilgrimage* (Boston: James R. Osgood, 1881), 118. For evocative accounts of trading in Houndsditch, see *Builder*, July 3, 1858, 453; George Sala, *Dutch Pictures* (London: Tinsley Brothers, 1861), 330–336; *Chamber's Edinburgh Journal* 1 (1844): 334–335; *Newcastle Journal*, July 29, 1842, 4; *Northampton Mercury*, May 2, 1856, 4; George Augustus Sala, "The Streets of the World," *Temple Bar* 10 (1864): 335–337. By 1864 London's *Times* felt confident that the mart "has been so often described in popular works that people are now pretty familiar with it, by name at least." *Times*, Nov. 3, 1864, 6.

2. James Greenwood, "The City Rag Shop," *Saint Pauls Magazine* 12 (1873): 658. See the surveyor's plan of the mart, "City of London: Streets," COL/SUD/PL/02/A/128, London Metropolitan Archives (hereafter cited as LMA). For the "positively overpowering" stench, see Henry Mayhew, *London Labour and the London Poor*, vol. 1 (London: George Woodfall, 1851), 368.

3. Ben Jonson referred to the old-clothes trade in Houndsditch in *Every Man in His Humor* (first performed in 1598).

4. Jewish traders also clustered in Holywell Street into the 1840s but were displaced to Houndsditch and the Minories by an influx of booksellers. For an evocative description, see Lynda Nead, *Victorian Babylon: People, Streets, and Images in Nineteenth-Century London* (New Haven: Yale University Press, 2000), 174.

5. *Times*, July 28, 1828, 3; *Parliamentary Papers, Great Britain, Parliament, House of Commons*, 1847, vol. 9 (reports, vol. 5), cmd. 666, 1847, "Reports from the Select Committee on Sunday Trading," q. 1587 (hereafter cited as PP 1847). For an early account of a visit to Rag Fair, see Benjamin Silliman, *Journal of Travels in England, Holland and Scotland*, vol. 1 (New York: D. & G. Bruce, 1810), 208–209. For markets in England in the first half of the nineteenth century, see Ian Mitchell, "Retailing Innovation and Urban Markets c. 1800–1850," *Journal of Historical Research in Marketing* 2, 3 (2010): 287–299.

6. PP 1847, q. 1570.

7. *Times*, July 28, 1828, 3.

8. On Dutch traders in London, see Gedalia Yogev, *Diamonds and Coral: Anglo-Dutch Jews and Eighteenth-Century Trade* (New York: Holmes and Meier, 1978), 17, 73–77, 260 (quote on 74); Bianca du Mortier, "Introduction into the Used-Clothing Market in the Netherlands," in *Per una storia della moda pronta* (Florence, Italy: Edizione Firenze, 1991), 123. On the East India Company warehouses, see Margaret Makepeace, *The East India Company's London Workers* (Woodbridge, UK: Boydell, 2010), 5, 17, 20–21. On the role of the East India Company as an importer of fabric, see Maxine Berg, "French Fancy and Cool Britannia: The Fashion Markets of Early Modern Europe," in *Fiere e*

mercati nella integrazione delle economie europee, secc. xiii–xviii (Prato, Italy: Le Monnier, 2001), 539.

9. Sala, *Dutch Pictures*, 322; Mayhew, *London Labour*, 1:368; Lemire, *Dress, Culture and Commerce*, 75–77, 79–85; Lemire, "Consumerism in Preindustrial and Early Industrial England," 14–17. On the role played by women in the trade, see Henry Mayhew, *London Labour and the London Poor*, vol. 2 (London: Griffin, Bohn, 1861), 125; John Brown, *Sixty Years' Gleanings from Life's Harvest* (New York: D. Appleton, 1859), 153–154; Miles Lambert, " 'Cast-Off Wearing Apparell': The Consumption and Distribution of Second-Hand Clothing in Northern England during the Long Eighteenth Century," *Textile History* 35, 1 (2004): 13–14. On Jewish women, see Lemire, *Dress, Culture and Commerce*, 79–86. A similar gender division was evident within the secondhand trade in Paris. See Charpy, "Scope and Structure," 128. For the routes followed by collectors, see Brown, *Sixty Years' Gleanings*, 161; Betty Naggar, "Old Clothes-Men: 18th and 19th Centuries," *Jewish Historical Studies* 31 (1990): 172. On the role of servants in selling clothing, see Ben Fine and Ellen Leopold, "Consumerism and the Industrial Revolution," *Social History* 15, 2 (May 1990): 169–170.

10. Lemire, *Dress, Culture and Commerce*, 75–77, 79–85; Lemire, "Consumerism in Pre-industrial and Early Industrial England," 14–17. On female old-clothes peddlers, see Mayhew, *London Labour*, 2:125. For examples of the clothing dealer in English fiction, see Maria Edgeworth's *Harrington* (1817), Thomas Carlyle's *Sartor Resartus* (1833–1834), Dickens's *Sketches by Boz* (1836) and *Oliver Twist* (1838), Thackeray's *Catherine* (1839), and Eliot's *Daniel Deronda* (1876). For visual representations of Jewish old-clothes men, see Frank Felsenstein and Sharon Liberman Mintz, *The Jew as Other: A Century of English Caricature, 1730–1830* (New York: Jewish Theological Seminary, 1995), 21–23, 25, 30–31.

11. George Augustus Sala, "Old Clothes!," *Household Words*, Apr. 17, 1852, 95.

12. *Jewish Chronicle*, Dec. 7, 14, 21, 1849; Endelman, *Jews of Georgian England*, 182–185; Anne Cowen and Roger Cowen, *Victorian Jews through British Eyes* (Oxford, UK: Littman Library of Jewish Civilization, 1998), 4–8; *A View of London* (London: B. Crosby, 1804), 107. For early modern fears that street hawkers and peddlers were engaged in criminality, see Linda Woodbridge, "The Peddler and the Pawn," in *Rogues and Early Modern English Culture*, ed. Craig Dionne and Steve Mentz (Ann Arbor: University of Michigan Press, 2004), 149–151; Georg Stöger, "Disorderly Practices in the Early Modern Urban Second-Hand Trade (Sixteen to Early Nineteenth Centuries)," in *Shadow Economies and Irregular Work in Urban Europe: 16th to Early 20th Centuries*, ed. Thomas Buchner and Philip R. Hoffmann-Rehnitz (Münster, Germany: LIT Verlag, 2011), 160–162.

13. B. A. Shepherd, "Popular Attitudes to Jews in France and England, 1750–1870" (PhD diss., University of Oxford, 1983), 241.

14. See Ginsburg, "Rags to Riches," 122–123, 127; Lemire, "Consumerism in Preindustrial and Early Industrial England," 1–6.

15. For clerks shopping in the clothing markets, see *Times*, Nov. 3, 1864, 6. For evidence that some middle-class consumers also relied on secondhand and recycled clothing and

housewares, see Stana Nenadic, "Middle-Rank Consumers and Domestic Culture in Edinburgh and Glasgow 1720–1840," *Past & Present* 145 (1994): 125–135.

16. Lemire, "Shifting Currency," 34–40; *Times*, Mar. 27, 1833, 7; Mar. 14, 1837.

17. Melanie Tebbutt, *Making Ends Meet: Pawnbroking and Working-Class Credit* (New York: Methuen, 1983), 6–7, 16–17, 123.

18. Heber Hart, *The Law Relating to Auctioneers, House Agents, and Valuers, and Commission* (London: Stevens and Sons, 1903), 436; Pamela Sharpe, " 'Cheapness and Economy': Manufacturing and Retailing Ready-Made Clothing in London and Essex 1830–50," *Textile History* 26, 2 (1995): 203–204; Lemire, "Shifting Currency," 37–40.

19. Tebbutt, *Making Ends Meet*, 8–9, 18, 22–23; Ginsburg, "Rags to Riches," 127.

20. Margaret Spufford, *The Great Reclothing of Rural England: Petty Chapmen and Their Wares in the Seventeenth Century* (London: Hambledon, 1984), 16; Lemire, "Shifting Currency," 32; Naggar, "Old Clothes-Men," 177.

21. The original letter states 1700, while the catalogue entry claims 1701. "Inhabitants of Rosemary Lane, Whitechapel Ask That the Rag Fair Be Suppressed," MJ/SP/1701/01/001, LMA. On earlier complaints about vendors of old clothes, see James Davis, "Marketing Secondhand Goods in Late Medieval England," *Journal of Historical Research in Marketing* 2, 3 (2010): 274–275. On efforts to contain and curtail street markets elsewhere, see Mitchell, "Retailing Innovation," 291–292.

22. MJ/SP/1701/01/002, LMA.

23. At least one trader was committed to New Prison for placing "severall stalls hampers benches and forms" in Cable Street; see "Commitment of Gregory Sherredon to New Prison, October 26, 1733," MJ/SP/1733/12/053, LMA.

24. For later complaints along these lines, see PP 1847, q. 718, 721, 727, 733, 775, 780, 935, 940, 941, 944, 1149–1150.

25. "Orders of the Court of Aldermen to Suppress the Market or Fair for the Buying or Selling of Old Rags and Cloths," CLA/048/PS/01/064, LMA; "Further Order of the Execution of the Orders to Support the Market at Little Tower Hill," CLA/048/PS/01/065, LMA. All spellings in quotations are original.

26. *Times*, July 28, 1828, 3.

27. Pearson quote from PP 1847, q. 1570–1571. On the tactics used by hawkers to evade the police, see *Parliamentary Papers, Great Britain, Parliament, House of Commons*, 1850, vol. 19 (reports, vol. 11), cmd. 441, 1850, "Select Committee on the Sunday Trading Prevention Bill," q. 347 (hereafter cited as PP 1850). For a detailed summary of the laws regulating peddlers and hawkers, see *The Law of Hawkers and Pedlars: with the Adjudged Cases and Numerous Precedents* (London: J. Butterworth and Son, 1822).

28. *Builder*, July 3, 1858, 453.

29. Jerry White, *London in the Nineteenth Century* (London: Cape, 2007), 38; H. J. Dyos, "Railways and Housing in Victorian London," *Journal of Transport History* 2, 6 (1955): 15.

30. H. J. Dyos, "Some Social Costs of Railway Building in London," *Journal of Transport History* 3, 1 (1957): 25; Dyos, "Railways and Housing," 90–91.

31. Dyos, "Some Social Costs," 29n2; Mayhew, *London Labour*, 1:109–111, 2:45–46. For Irish migration and settlement in London, see White, *London in the Nineteenth Century*,

130–131, 133–134; Lynn Hollen Lees, *Exiles of Erin: Irish Migrants in Victorian London* (Ithaca: Cornell University Press, 1979), 44–50, 56–60, 67–68, 80; *Times*, Aug. 30, 1843, 3; June 19, 1834, 6; *Jewish Chronicle*, Mar. 16, 1855; PP 1847, q. 990. For the image of Irish migrants, see Roger Swift, "Heroes or Villains? The Irish, Crime, and Disorder in Victorian England," *Albion* 29, 3 (1997): 399–421.

32. This impression is reinforced by a sample of court records. On Irish employment patterns, see Lees, *Exiles of Erin*, 92–100.

33. Patrick Colquhoun estimated that there were fifteen hundred itinerant Jewish collectors of old clothes and scrap metal in the city in the late eighteenth century. Colquhoun, *A Treatise on the Police of the Metropolis* (London: J. Mawman, 1800), 119–121, 219–322. If Colquhoun's evaluation of Jewish criminality is any guide, his estimate of rag collectors is scarcely more reliable. For Mayhew's estimates, see *London Labour*, 1:106, 2:135.

34. Sala, *"Old Clothes!,"* 94 (reprinted in Sala, *Dutch Pictures*, 326). There is some evidence of tensions between Jews involved in the rag trade and newer Jewish immigrants who also sought to enter the trade. See *Times*, Dec. 1, 1821, 2.

35. These estimates are collated in V. D. Lipman, *Social History of the Jews in England, 1850–1950* (London: Watts, 1954), 31. Mayhew suggests that Jewish street sellers had left for America. See *London Labour*, 2:117.

36. *Times*, June 28, 1839, 7.

37. On the "near-riot" in Cutler Street, see Robert Wechsler, "The Jewish Garment Trade in East London 1875–1914: A Study in Conditions and Responses" (PhD diss., Columbia University, 1979), 24; *Jewish Chronicle*, Dec. 10, 1841; PP 1847, q. 1115, 1478, 1177. On tensions between Irish and Jews, see Shepherd, "Popular Attitudes to Jews in France and England," 247–249; *Times*, Jan. 5, 1832, 4.

38. For further efforts to close the markets, see PP 1847, q. 1126, 1146, 1570. For other early examples of activism by clothing dealers, see *Jewish Chronicle*, Apr. 13, 1855, 132–133; *Standard* (London), May 10, 1866, 3. On efforts to regulate the secondhand trade in Europe, see Stöger, "Disorderly Practices," 144–155.

39. On Still Alley as a "haunt of infamy," see *Times*, May 28, 1822, 3; Oct. 23, 1822, 3. On the "notorious and abominable" brothel kept by a Mrs. Nathan in the alleyway, see *Times*, May 3, 1823, 3. On market halls, see Mitchell, "Retailing Innovation," 292–296.

40. PP 1847, q. 1121–1123, 1155. By 1850 Henry was no longer connected with the Exchange. PP 1850, q. 360.

41. *Times*, Sept. 5, 1842, 7; Oct. 27, 1843; *Jewish Chronicle*, Dec. 10, 1841; July 22, 1859; Oct. 27, 1911; PP 1847, q. 1130, 1177, 1187. On Simmonds (elsewhere spelled Symonds), see *Daily News* (London), Oct. 9, 1849, 6.

42. PP 1847, q. 1438.

43. PP 1847, q. 1124. There is some persuasive evidence, however, that they saw themselves and their mart as primarily in the old-clothes trade. See *Jewish Chronicle*, Apr. 13, 1855, 132.

44. PP 1850, q. 359.

45. PP 1847, q. 1129.

46. PP 1847, q. 1180.

47. PP 1847, q. 1125, 1177, 1182; PP 1850, q. 309, 342.

48. PP 1847, q. 1135–1136, 1142.

49. PP 1847, q. 1129, 1152, 1157; PP 1850, q. 243, 245, 314; *Jewish Chronicle,* Mar. 16, 1855. For striking descriptions of "renovating," see *Jewish Chronicle,* May 10, 1872; Greenwood, "City Rag Shop," 655–658.

50. PP 1847, q. 1136, 1147. Quote from James Ewing Ritchie, *Here and There in London* (London: W. Tweedie, 1859), 119.

51. PP 1850, q. 318; Ritchie, *Here and There,* 122.

52. PP 1850, q. 241.

53. The Isaacs brothers attempted to charge a toll on Sundays, "but the public would not submit to it, and they broke down the barriers." PP 1847, q. 1148. PP 1850, q. 337.

54. Tim Hitchcock, Robert Shoemaker, Clive Emsley, Sharon Howard and Jamie McLaughlin, et al., *The Old Bailey Proceedings Online, 1674–1913,* Jan. 27, 1868, 17–22, http://www.oldbaileyonline.org (accessed Mar. 24, 2012).

55. Ibid., Oct. 27, 1851, 783–784.

56. Ibid., Jan. 27, 1868, 17–22.

57. *First Report of the Commissioners Appointed to Inquire as to the Best Means of Establishing an Efficient Constabulary Force in the Counties of England and Wales* (London: HMSO, 1839), 33. On theft, see Alison Toplis, "The Illicit Trade in Clothing, Worcestershire and Herefordshire, 1800–1850," *Journal of Historical Research in Marketing* 2, 3 (2010): 314–323.

58. On the association of clothing—and clothing markets—with crime, see Kellow Chesney, *The Victorian Underworld* (New York: Penguin, 1991), 107, 132–133, 160; Shelley Tickell, "The Prevention of Shoplifting in Eighteenth-Century London," *Journal of Historical Research in Marketing* 2, 3 (2010): 300–313; Lemire, *Dress, Culture and Commerce,* 212–146; *Report of the Constabulary Force Commissioners,* 33. For examples from the medieval period, see Allerston, "Market in Second-Hand Clothes and Furnishings in Venice," 76–92, 105–113. On pawnbroking and crime, see George Rudé, *Criminal and Victim: Crime and Society in Early Nineteenth-Century England* (New York: Oxford University Press, 1985), 92–93. On similar ideas in Paris, see Charpy, "Scope and Structure," 129.

59. *Jewish Chronicle,* Mar. 16, 1855; Endelman, *Jews of Georgian England,* 195–197. As late as 1891 visitors to the clothing markets in Houndsditch were warned "to leave their watches and valuables at home, and not take offence at a little 'Bishopsgate Banter.'" Henry Benjamin Wheatley, *London Past and Present,* vol. 2 (London: John Murray, 1891), 238.

60. PP 1847, q. 1186.

61. PP 1847, q. 1176.

62. PP 1847, q. 1174.

63. PP 1847, q. 1184.

64. PP 1850, q. 297.

65. PP 1847, q. 1451.

66. My thanks to Jörg-Ole Münch for this latter suggestion. See PP 1847, q. 1169.

67. For Lewis Isaacs's change of heart about street sellers, see PP 1850, q. 252.

68. PP 1847, q. 1153, 1173.

69. PP 1847, q. 1570.

70. PP 1847, q. 1148.

71. PP 1847, q. 633. On middle-class disapproval of disorder in the streets, see Clive Emsley, *Crime and Society in England, 1750–1900* (London: Longman, 1987), 187–189, 193; Gareth Stedman Jones, *Outcast London: A Study in the Relationship between Classes in Victorian London* (London: Penguin, 1984). On the process by which the boundaries between "regular" and "irregular" economic practices were demarcated in the nineteenth century, see Thomas Buchner and Philip R. Hoffmann-Rehnitz, "Introduction: Irregular Economic Practices as a Topic of Modern (Urban) History—Problems and Possibilities," in Buchner and Hoffmann-Rehnitz, *Shadow Economies*, 22–24, 28–29; Charpy, "Scope and Structure," 144. For similar complaints about Jewish street vendors in Europe, see Kaplan, *Jewish Daily Life in Germany*, 132–133.

72. PP 1847, q. 1570.

73. PP 1847, q. 1169.

74. PP 1847, q. 1439–1443.

75. PP 1847, q. 1187.

76. John Hotten, *The Slang Dictionary* (London: Chatto and Windus, 1874), 268, 335; *Times*, Nov. 3, 1864, 6. For similar methods used by Jewish dealers in Rome to revive threadbare clothes, see Simond, *Tour in Italy and Sicily*, 257.

77. The *Times* recounted an almost certainly apocryphal encounter with a Jewish clobberer who boasted that after training a female apprentice for two years, she "could mislead the sharpest eye; it didn't signify how threadbare a coat or breeches was, she was quite at home in them." *Times*, July 12, 1830, 5.

78. *Jewish Chronicle*, Mar. 16, 1855.

79. PP 1847, q. 1175, 1554.

80. For the practicalities of this trip, see Peter Cunningham, *Hand-Book of London: Past and Present* (London: John Murray, 1850). Isaacs quoted in PP 1850, q. 250. See also PP 1847, q. 1151.

81. Quote from PP 1850, q. 248; see also q. 246. Sabbath-observant Jewish owners of businesses in Houndsditch that employed women to sew shirts, furs, and shoes reportedly did not pay their workers until late on Saturday evening. See PP 1847, q. 1913–1914.

82. PP 1847, q. 697, 1164.

83. PP 1850, q. 251.

84. For discussion of the shoppers, see PP 1850, q. 287.

85. Ritchie, *Here and There*, 120.

86. PP 1850, q. 356.

87. PP 1847, q. 1129, 1166; PP 1850, q. 245.

88. On demand for secondhand clothing in the north, see Lambert, "'Cast-Off Wearing Apparell,'" 3–9; Alison Toplis, "A Stolen Garment or a Reasonable Purchase? The Male Consumer and the Illicit Second-Hand Clothing Market in the First Half of the Nineteenth Century," in Stobart and Van Damme, *Modernity and the Second-Hand Trade*, 62.

89. *Jewish Chronicle*, Oct. 27, 1911, 33; Sala, *Dutch Pictures*, 332–337; *Chamber's Edinburgh*

Journal 1 (1844): 334–335; John Mills, *The British Jews* (London: Houlston and Stone-man, 1853), 264–270; Mayhew, *London Labour*, 1:104–105, 1:368–369, 2:26–29, 2:38–39; Watts Phillips, *The Wild Tribes of London* (London: Ward and Lock, 1855), 60, 63; Andrew Wynter, *Peeps into the Human Hive*, vol. 2 (London: Chapman and Hall, 1874), 277–286; George Sala, "Layard in London," *Illustrated London Magazine* 1 (1853): 228; Ritchie, *Here and There*, 120–122; *Hansard's Parliamentary Debates* (London: Cornelius Buck, 1858), 3rd. ser., vol. 151, June 25, 1858, 418–421; Diana De Marly, *Working Dress: A History of Occupational Clothing* (New York: Holmes and Meier, 1986), 97; Lipman, *Social History*, 33; Lemire, "Consumerism in Preindustrial and Early Industrial England," 17–18; Ginsburg, "Rags to Riches," 124–125.

90. *Harper's New Monthly Magazine* 35 (Sept. 1867): 517; *Times*, Nov. 3, 1864, 6. Quote from John Timbs, *Curiosities of London* (London: Longmans, Green, Reader, and Dyer, 1868), 484.

91. *Old Bailey Proceedings*, Oct. 27, 1851, 785; Jan. 27, 1868, 17–22, 193; Betty Naggar, *Jewish Pedlars and Hawkers, 1740–1940* (Camberley, UK: Porphyrogenitus, 1992), 14–15.

92. Edward Hyams, ed., *Taine's Notes on England* (London: Thames and Hudson, 1957).

93. Sala, *Dutch Pictures*, 337–338. On the recycling of secondhand goods, see Stöger, "Disorderly Practices," 141–144.

94. *Old Bailey Proceedings*, Oct. 27, 1851, 784–785.

95. Walter Harrison, *A New and Universal History, Description and Survey of the Cities of London and Westminster* (London: J. Cooke, 1775), 549; Joseph Nightingale, *London and Middlesex*, vol. 3 (London: Longman, 1815), 134; John Wallis, *Wallis's Guide to London* (London: Sherwood, Neely, and Jones, 1814), 347; *Times*, Nov. 3, 1864, 6; Naggar, "Old Clothes-Men," 181; Endelman, *Jews of Georgian England*, 179.

96. The preference of some Dutch consumers for secondhand over new clothing is less surprising than it might first seem. New clothing—often poorly fitting and shoddily made—was regarded as inferior to used garments that had already proven their durability and were often available in greater variety. For similar biases in London, see Styles, *Dress of the People*, 176. On the secondhand trade in the Netherlands, see B. W. de Vries, *From Pedlars to Textile Barons: The Economic Development of a Jewish Minority Group in the Netherlands* (Amsterdam: North-Holland, 1989), 36–38, 44, 48, 280, 282, 285–290; Blom, Fuks-Mansfeld, and Schöffer, *History of the Jews in the Netherlands*, 114, 117, 167, 227; Mortier, "Introduction into the Used-Clothing Market," 120–121; Stephen Raes, *Migrating Enterprise and Migrant Entrepreneurship* (Amsterdam: Het Spinhuis, 2000), 57–59; Chesney, *Victorian Underworld*, 195.

97. PP 1847, q. 1165.

98. See *Times*, June 28, 1839, 7; Lemire, "Shifting Currency," 43.

99. *Old Bailey Proceedings*, Jan. 27, 1868, 193.

100. Ritchie, *Here and There*, 120. This was not the only example of observers fantasizing about the afterlives of castoff clothes. London's *Times* imagined that clothing recycled in Houndsditch was "about to set out on their travels, to enter new circles of society, and to see life both savage and civilized under a thousand new phases." Nov. 3, 1864, 6.

101. Mayhew, *London Labour*, 2:30–31.

102. For export figures, see *Parliamentary Papers: Accounts and Papers Relating to Customs and Excise, Imports and Exports, Shipping and Trade*, vol. 34 (London, 1832), 32; *Tait's Edinburgh Magazine*, June 1832, 375; John McCulloch, *A Dictionary, Practical, Theoretical, and Historical of Commerce and Commercial Navigation*, vol. 2 (Philadelphia: A Hart, 1852), 30, 34. By contrast, Parisian clothing dealers shipped large quantities of secondhand clothing to the countries neighboring France and less to the United States. See Charpy, "Scope and Structure," 134–135.

103. Sala, *Dutch Pictures*, 330. The export of secondhand clothing to the Levant continued into the twentieth century, with Jewish firms in New York assuming a dominant role once held by those in London. See *Levant Trade Review* 4, 4 (1915): 418; 16, 10 (1928); 16, 12 (1928): 451–452. My thanks to Uri M. Kupferschmidt for bringing this to my attention. On exports to Paris, Leipzig, and the Cape Colony, see *Times*, Nov. 3, 1864, 6.

NOTES TO CHAPTER 2

1. Quotes from James Fenimore Cooper, *The Redskins* (New York: Burgess and Stringer, 1846), 54; and Washington Irving to Mrs. Van Wart, Aug. 29, 1847, in Washington Irving, *The Life and Letters of Washington Irving*, ed. Pierre M. Irving, vol. 4 (New York: G. P. Putnam, 1864), 25. On New York's growth see Sean Wilentz, *Chants Democratic: New York City and the Rise of the American Working Class, 1788–1850* (New York: Oxford University Press, 1984), 109. For New York in the middle decades of the century see Edward K. Spann, *The New Metropolis: New York City, 1840–1857* (New York: Columbia University Press, 1983), 1–22; Kenneth T. Jackson and David S. Dunbar, eds., *Empire City* (New York: Columbia University Press, 2002), 143–254. On filth in city streets, see Tyler Anbinder, *Five Points* (New York: Free Press, 2001), 82–83. On grand retail emporia, see Robert Hendrickson, *The Grand Emporiums* (New York: Stein and Day, 1979), 25–149; Deborah S. Gardner, " 'A Paradise of Fashion': A. T. Stewart's Department Store, 1862–1875," in Jensen and Davidson, *A Needle, a Bobbin, a Strike*, 60–80.

2. O. S. Fowler, "Hereditary Descent," *American Phrenological Journal and Miscellany* 10 (1848): 117. Such urban commercial clusters were not unusual. Nassau Street, for example, gained notoriety as the city's "smut district."

3. Horatio Alger, Jr., *Ragged Dick; or, Street Life in New York with the Boot Blacks* (Boston: A. K. Loring, 1868), 45–49 (quote on 45).

4. Edwin G. Burrows and Mike Wallace, *Gotham: A History of New York City to 1898* (New York: Oxford University Press, 2000), 437–439; Dell Upton, *Another City: Urban Life and Urban Spaces in the New American Republic* (New Haven: Yale University Press, 2008), 149–150; Michael Zakim, "Producing Capitalism: The Clerk at Work," in *Capitalism Takes Command*, ed. Michael Zakim and Gary J. Kornblith (Chicago: University of Chicago Press, 2011), 237 (quote); Claudia B. Kidwell and Margaret C. Christman, *Suiting Everyone: The Democratization of Clothing in America* (Washington, DC: Smithsonian Institution Press, 1974), 57–58.

5. For a selection of these depictions, see *New York Herald*, July 8, 1841; George Foster, *New York in Slices* (New York: W. H. Graham, 1849), 13–16, 30, 32–33; Professor Ingraham, "Glimpses at Gotham," *Ladies Companion* 10 (1839): 291; *The Family of the Seisers* (New

York: J. M. Elliott, 1844), 32, 147; Cornelius Mathews, "The Ghost of New York," *United States Democratic Review* 16 (1845): 10; Henry Morford, *The Days of Shoddy* (Philadelphia: T. B. Peterson, 1863), 182; Fowler, "Hereditary Descent," 117; *Literary World* 4 (Feb. 17, 1849): 157; Charles Loring Brace, *The Dangerous Classes of New York* (New York: Wynkoop and Hallenbeck, 1872), 195–196; *Hunt's Merchants Magazine and Commercial Review* 20 (1849): 669; Walt Whitman, "Our City," *Aurora*, Mar. 28, 1842, in *Walt Whitman of the New York Aurora*, ed. Joseph Jay Rubin and Charles H. Brown (State College, PA: Bald Eagle, 1950), 18; Richard Stott, *Workers in the Metropolis* (Ithaca: Cornell University Press, 1990), 186n50; Irving Allen, *The City in Slang* (New York: Oxford University Press, 1993), 201; Frederic Jaher, *A Scapegoat in the Wilderness: The Origins and Rise of Anti-Semitism in America* (Cambridge: Harvard University Press, 1994), 222; Rudolf Glanz, *Jews in the Old American Folklore* (New York: Waldon, 1961), 100–103, 147–165; Louise A. Mayo, *The Ambivalent Image* (Cranbury, NJ: Fairleigh Dickinson University Press, 1988), 111–112.

6. The *Asmonean*, cited in Hyman B. Grinstein, *The Rise of the Jewish Community of New York, 1654–1860* (*Philadelphia: Jewish Publication Society, 1947*), 342. On urban tourism and contemporary writing about American cities, see Catherine Cocks, *Doing the Town: The Rise of Urban Tourism in the United States, 1850–1915* (Berkeley: University of California Press, 2001), 9–40.

7. For evocative descriptions, see Virginia Penny, *Employments of Women: A Cyclopaedia of Women's Work* (Boston: Walker, Wise, 1863), 135–136; David W. Mitchell, *Ten Years in America: Being an Englishman's View of Men and Things in the North and South* (London: Smith, Elder, 1862), 58–59 (my thanks to Shari Rabin for sharing this with me); R. P. Forster, *A Collection of the Most Celebrated Voyages & Travels* (Newcastle upon Tyne, UK: Mackenzie and Dent, 1818), 209; William Whitecar, *Four Years aboard the Whaleship* (Philadelphia: Lippincott, 1864), 31, 190; Arthur Hertzberg, *The Jews in America* (New York: Columbia University Press, 1997), 93; Rowena Olegario, "'That Mysterious People': Jewish Merchants, Transparency, and Community in Mid-Nineteenth Century America," *Business History Review* 73, 2 (June 1999): 165–166; Hasia Diner, *The Jews of the United States, 1654–2000* (Berkeley: University of California Press, 2006), 102. For Chatham Street abroad, see Martha Williams, *A Year in China* (New York: Hurd and Houghton, 1864), 194; Isaac Wiley, *China and Japan* (Cincinnati: Hitchcock and Walden, 1879), 194.

8. See Ira Rosenwaike, *On the Edge of Greatness: A Portrait of American Jewry in the Early National Period* (Cincinnati: American Jewish Archives, 1985), 140–170; Jonathan S. Mesinger, "Peddlers and Merchants: The Geography of Work in a Nineteenth Century Jewish Community" (Department of Geography, Syracuse University Discussion Paper Series 38, 1977), 9; Jerome Rosenthal, "A Study of Jewish Businessmen in New York City as Reflected in City Directories, 1776–1830" (term paper, American Jewish Archives, 1977); John Stevens, "New York in the Nineteenth Century," *American Historical Magazine* 1, 5 (1906): 412.

9. Bertram Korn, *The Jews of Mobile, Alabama, 1763–1841* (Cincinnati: Hebrew Union College Press, 1970), 40.

10. Quoted in Anbinder, *Five Points*, 121. On the importance of such stereotypes in maintaining ethnic niches, see Model, "Ethnic Niche," 166.

11. Anbinder, *Five Points*, 119; Peter P. Hinks, *To Awaken My Afflicted Brethren: David Walker and the Problem of Antebellum Slave Resistance* (University Park: Pennsylvania State University Press, 1997), 66–68. On the Jewish population in Boston, see "Appendix A: The Jewish Population of Boston," in *The Jews of Boston*, ed. Jonathan D. Sarna, Ellen Smith, and Scott-Martin Kosofsky (New Haven: Yale University Press, 2005), 343.

12. See John Marshall, *Jews in Nevada: A History* (Reno: University of Nevada Press, 2008), 107. On Chinese immigrants and the clothing trade, see Special Committee on Chinese Immigration, *Chinese Immigration: Its Social, Moral, and Political Effect*, report to the California State Senate (Sacramento: State Printing Office, 1876), 147; Otis Gibson, *The Chinese in America* (Cincinnati: Hitchcock and Walden, 1877), 55.

13. For the growth of New York, see Burrows and Wallace, *Gotham*, 434; Wilentz, *Chants Democratic*, 24–27, 108–110; Stott, *Workers in the Metropolis*, 7–24; William Pencak, "Introduction: New York and the Rise of American Capitalism," in *New York and the Rise of American Capitalism*, ed. William Pencak and Conrad Edick Wright (New York: New York Historical Society, 1989), xii–xiii. On vessels docking and the South Street quote, see Spann, *New Metropolis*, 2, 105. For Greenwich quote, see Charles Lockwood, *Manhattan Moves Uptown* (Boston: Houghton Mifflin, 1976), 6.

14. On the efforts of drummers to lure out-of-towners, see Timothy B. Spears, *100 Years on the Road: The Traveling Salesman in American Culture* (New Haven: Yale University Press, 1997), 29–30, 35 (quote on 29).

15. Quote from Glanz, *Jews in the Old American Folklore*, 153.

16. Quote from James Inglis, *Our Australian Cousins* (London: Macmillan, 1880), 172–173.

17. *Harper's New Monthly Magazine* 19, 113 (Oct. 1859): 676. For colorful descriptions of the overlap between the trades of Chatham Street, see Brace, *Dangerous Classes of New York*, 195–196.

18. Jews were also accused of "duffing," employing fraudulent means to deceive pawnbrokers. See Tebbutt, *Making Ends Meet*, 82.

19. *Scientific American* 2 (1847): 349. Quote from Burrows and Wallace, *Gotham*, 638. On mock auctions, see Corey Goettsch, "Pinchbeck Capitalism: Mock Auctions in Nineteenth-Century America" (unpublished conference paper, 2012). For earlier regulations governing secondhand dealers in New York, see *A Law to Regulate Pawn-Brokers, and Dealers in the Purchase or Sale of Second-Hand Furniture, Metals or Clothes: Passed July 13th, 1812*, New-York Historical Society.

20. On the overlap between pawnbroking and secondhand dealing, see Woloson, *In Hock*, 62–64, 71–73. On Mandelbaum, see Rona L. Holub, "Fredericka 'Marm' Rosenbaum, 'Queen of Fences': The Rise and Fall of a Female Immigrant Criminal Entrepreneur in Nineteenth-Century New York City" (PhD diss., Columbia University, 2007). On the inadequacies of policing, particularly across jurisdictional boundaries, see Stephen Mihm, *A Nation of Counterfeiters* (Cambridge: Harvard University Press, 2007), 209, 223.

21. In eighteenth-century Charleston imported woolen clothing was blamed for outbreaks

of smallpox. *South Carolina Gazette*, Aug. 31, 1738; Oct. 18, 1738; Nov. 2, 1738. For similar concerns about clothing and disease, see Allerston, "Market in Second-Hand Clothes and Furnishings in Venice," 276–285. See also Ilja Van Damme, "Second-Hand Dealing in Bruges and the Rise of an 'Antiquarian Culture,' c. 1750–1870," in Stobart and Van Damme, *Modernity and the Second-Hand Trade*, 75; Mortier, "Introduction into the Used-Clothing Market," 123; Charles Rosenberg, *The Cholera Years: The United States in 1832, 1849, and 1866* (Chicago: University of Chicago Press, 1987).

22. Quote from *Philadelphia Inquirer*, Nov. 10, 1838 (my thanks to Robert J. Gamble for sharing this with me). On clothing as a mark of respectability, see John F. Kasson, *Rudeness and Civility: Manners in Nineteenth-Century America* (New York: Hill and Wang, 1990), 117–121, 130; Mihm, *Nation of Counterfeiters*, 226–227. For women's clothing, see Karen Halttunen, *Confidence Men and Painted Women: A Study of Middle-Class Culture in America, 1830–1870* (New Haven: Yale University Press, 1982), 56–91. On fears about urban anomy, see Robert J. Gamble, "Promiscuous Commodities: The Cultural Landscape of Secondhand in the Antebellum Mid-Atlantic" (unpublished paper, Capitalism by Gaslight conference, June 2012), 6–7; Paul A. Gilje, "Culture of Conflict: The Impact of Commercialization on New York Workingmen, 1787–1829," in Pencak and Wright, *New York and the Rise of American Capitalism*, 249–267; Spann, *New Metropolis*, 18–19.

23. Quote from Penny, *Employments of Women*, 135–136; for average wages, see ibid., xiii.

24. *One Hundred Years' Progress of the United States* (Hartford, CT: L. Stebbins, 1870), 309, 313–315.

25. Quoted in Penny, *Employments of Women*, 135–136.

26. *Northern Monthly*, June 1867, 117; Jesse Pope, *The Clothing Industry in New York* (Columbia: University of Missouri, 1905), 7; Susan Strasser, *Waste and Want* (New York: Metropolitan Books, 1999), 51, 60; Judith Greenfield, "The Role of Jews in the Development of the Clothing Industry in the United States," *Yivo Annual* 2 (1948): 181; Feldman, "Jews in the Early Growth of New York City's Men's Clothing Trade," 5–7.

27. On homespun, see Zakim, *Ready-Made Democracy*, 11–36; Stott, *Workers in the Metropolis*, 38.

28. Leo Hershkowitz, "Some Aspects of the New York Jewish Merchant and Community, 1654–1820," *American Jewish Historical Quarterly* 66 (1977): 10–34.

29. On Broadway, see Spann, *New Metropolis*, 3, 95–99; quote from *Putnam's Monthly* 3, 15 (Mar. 1854): 242.

30. The best analysis of "metropolitan industrialization" is provided by Wilentz, *Chants Democratic*, 12–13; Richard Stott, "Hinterland Development and Differences in Work Setting: The New York City Region, 1820–1870," in Pencak and Wright, *New York and the Rise of American Capitalism*, 46–59; Stott, *Workers in the Metropolis*, 38–41.

31. On the ideology of homespun, see Zakim, *Ready-Made Democracy*, 11–36. On the market for cloth for home production, see Stott, *Workers in the Metropolis*, 38. On imported slops, see Kidwell and Christman, *Suiting Everyone*, 21–22, 31.

32. Zakim, *Ready-Made Democracy*, 38, 41–44, 47, 53–53, 60, 70, 77–81; Wilentz, *Chants Democratic*, 28, 31–34, 45–47; Stott, *Workers in the Metropolis*, 23–30, 112, 119; Kidwell and Christman, *Suiting Everyone*, 53, 61–63.

33. Clothing firms in New York were relatively slow to invest in machinery—in 1850, not a single of the fifty-five clothing firms sampled by Stott used steam power. See Stott, "Hinterland Development," 53; Stott, *Workers in the Metropolis*, 25, 42.

34. Zakim, *Ready-Made Democracy*, 57–60; Wilentz, *Chants Democratic*, 115, 404–405; Robert Ernst, *Immigrant Life in New York City, 1825–1863* (Syracuse: Syracuse University Press, 1994), 214–217; Stott, *Workers in the Metropolis*, 28; Waldinger, *Through the Eye of the Needle*, 19–39;

35. Stott, *Workers in the Metropolis*, 37, 40, 53, 69, 107; Wilentz, *Chants Democratic*, 118; Stott, "Hinterland Development," 62, 65. On the population of New York City, see Ira Rosenwaike, *Population History of New York City* (Syracuse: Syracuse University Press, 1972), 38–48. For William Bobo's account, see *Glimpses of New York City by a South Carolinian* (*Who Had Nothing Else to Do*) (Charleston, SC: J. J. McCarter, 1852), 107–108. On the composition of the female workforce, see Ava Baron and Susan E. Klepp, " 'If I Didn't Have My Sewing Machine . . .': Women and Sewing Machine Technology," in Jensen and Davidson, *A Needle, a Bobbin, a Strike*, 23; Stott, "Hinterland Differences," 62, 65.

36. On early efforts to organize, see Wilentz, *Chants Democratic*, 59, 168–169, 219–223, 231, 244–245, 248, 377–386. On the strikes of 1836, see ibid., 286–296. Female needleworkers were far from passive, striking in 1825 and organizing again in 1831 and 1836.

37. Wilentz, *Chants Democratic*, 117, 119 (quote), 124.

38. For the tariff rates imposed on imported ready-made clothing, see Feldman, *Fit for Men*, 20; for wages, see Robert A. Margo, "The Labor Force in the Nineteenth Century," in *The Cambridge Economic History of the Nineteenth Century*, ed. Stanley L. Engerman and Robert E. Gallman, vol. 2 (New York: Cambridge University Press, 2000), 221–222.

39. For cotton exports, see Brian Schoen, *The Fragile Fabric of Union* (Baltimore: Johns Hopkins University Press, 2009), 122–123.

40. Craig T. Friend, "Merchants and Markethouses: Reflections on Moral Economy in Early Kentucky," *Journal of the Early Republic* 17, 4 (Winter 1997): 566.

41. Although the national population increased by 36 percent during the 1850s, growth varied dramatically. South Carolina grew by a sedate 5 percent; the population of Illinois more than doubled. The enslaved population of Louisiana and Mississippi grew from roughly 100,000 in 1800 to 750,000 in 1860. On the cotton boom, see William J. Cooper Jr. and Thomas E. Terrill, *The South: A History* (Lanham, MD: Rowman and Littlefield, 2009), 199–201; Roger L. Ransom, *Conflict and Compromise: The Political Economy of Slavery, Emancipation and the Civil War* (New York: Cambridge University Press, 1993), 55–58; John Majewski, *Modernizing a Slave Economy: The Economic Vision of the Confederate Nation* (Chapel Hill: University of North Carolina Press, 2009), 44–45; "Taking Stock of the Nation in 1859," in *America on the Eve of the Civil War*, ed. Edward L. Ayers and Carolyn R. Martin (Charlottesville: University of Virginia Press, 2010), 18; D. Clayton James, *Antebellum Natchez* (Baton Rouge: Louisiana State University Press, 1968), 159, 161; Walter Johnson, *River of Dark Dreams: Slavery and Empire in the Cotton Kingdom* (Cambridge: Harvard University Press, 2013), 4, 32. On the Jews of antebellum Natchez, see Leo Turitz and Evelyn Turitz, *Jews in Early Mississippi* (Jackson: University Press of Mississippi, 1995), 11; Wendy Machlowitz, *Clara Lowenburg Moses: Memoirs of*

a Southern Jewish Woman (Jackson, MS: Museum of the Southern Jewish Experience, 2000), 4, 6.

42. Quote from Eugene D. Genovese, *Roll, Jordan, Roll: The World the Slaves Made* (New York: Vintage Books, 1976), 551; Roderick A. McDonald, *The Economy and Material Culture of Slaves* (Baton Rouge: Louisiana State University Press, 1993), 153–161; Fred Bateman and Thomas Weiss, *A Deplorable Scarcity: The Failure of Industrialization in the Slave Economy* (Chapel Hill: University of North Carolina Press, 1981), 22; Zakim, *Ready-Made Democracy*, 50–52; Christine Stansell, *City of Women: Sex and Class in New York, 1789–1860* (Urbana: University of Illinois Press, 1987), 109; Stuart Ewen and Elizabeth Ewen, *Channels of Desire: Mass Images and the Shaping of American Consciousness* (Minneapolis: University of Minnesota Press, 1992), 121–122; Elliott Ashkenazi, *The Business of Jews in Louisiana, 1840–1875* (Tuscaloosa: University of Alabama Press, 1988), 116.

43. Quoted in Feldman, *Fit for Men*, 48.

44. Ibid., 11–17; Burrows and Wallace, *Gotham*, 439, 873.

45. Carville Earle, "Beyond the Appalachians, 1815–1860," in *North America: The Historical Geography of a Changing Continent*, 2nd ed., ed. Thomas F. McIlwraith and Edward K. Muller (Lanham, MD: Rowman and Littlefield, 2001), 173–174; James Belich, *Replenishing the Earth: The Settler Revolution and the Rise of the Anglo-World, 1783–1939* (New York: Oxford University Press, 2009), 82, 224–234 (quote on 229); Jeffrey S. Adler, *Yankee Merchants and the Making of the Urban West* (New York: Cambridge University Press, 1991), 69–70.

NOTES TO CHAPTER 3

1. Jones, for all his contemporary fame, is best known today for a diary that he kept as a clerk in the Confederate War Department during the Civil War. The diary's casual prejudice against Jews suggests that his earlier animus had not dissipated.

2. Luke Shortfield [John Beauchamp Jones], *The Western Merchant: A Narrative* (Philadelphia: Grigg, Elliot, 1849), iii. On Jones, see Misty Cates, "Jones, John Beauchamp (1810–1866)," in *Dictionary of Missouri Biography* (Columbia: University of Missouri Press, 1999), 439.

3. Shortfield, *Western Merchant*, 128–129, 133, 204.

4. On "German" immigration, see Avraham Barkai, *Branching Out: German-Jewish Immigration to the United States, 1820–1914* (New York: Holmes and Meier, 1994); Hasia Diner, *A Time for Gathering: The Second Migration, 1820–1880* (Baltimore: Johns Hopkins University Press, 1992); Naomi W. Cohen, *Encounter with Emancipation: The German Jews in the United States, 1830–1914* (Philadelphia: Jewish Publication Society, 1984); Brinkmann, *Sundays at Sinai*, 24–30. On peddling, see Hasia Diner, "Entering the Mainstream of Modern Jewish History," in *Jewish Roots in Southern Soil: A New History*, ed. Marcie Cohen Ferris and Mark Greenberg (Lebanon, NH: Brandeis University Press, 2006), 86–108; Maxwell Whiteman, "Notions, Dry Goods, and Clothing: An Introduction to the Study of the Cincinnati Peddler," *Jewish Quarterly Review* 53, 4 (1963): 306–321; Lee Friedman, "The Problems of Nineteenth Century American Jewish Peddlers," *American Jewish Historical Quarterly* 44 (1954): 1–7.

5. See Todd Endelman, "German-Jewish Settlement in Victorian England," in *Second Chance: Two Centuries of German-Speaking Jews in the United Kingdom*, ed. Werner Mosse (Tübingen, Germany: Mohr Siebeck, 1991), 37–56; for comparison of those who settled in England with those who went to America, see ibid., 41–43; Stanley Chapman, "Merchants and Bankers," in Mosse, *Second Chance*, 341–343; Harold Pollins, "German Jews in British Industry," in Mosse, *Second Chance*, 364–367. On the Jewish population of Britain at midcentury, see Petra Laidlaw, "Jews in the British Isles in 1851: Birthplaces, Residence and Migrations," *Jewish Journal of Sociology* 53 (2011): 32–47.

6. The case is discussed in Rudolf Glanz, *The Jews of California: From the Discovery of Gold until 1880* (New York: Waldon, 1960), 87–89.

7. For the ubiquity of peddling and hawking in central Europe and its eventual decline, see David S. Landes, "The Jewish Merchant: Typology and Stereotypology in Germany," *Leo Baeck Yearbook* 19 (1974): 11–12. For an overview of the changing economic and social position of Jews in the German states in nineteenth century, see Steven M. Lowenstein, "The Rural Community and the Urbanization of German Jewry," *Central European History* 13, 3 (Sept. 1980): 218–236; Kaplan, *Jewish Daily Life in Germany*, 130–143; Monika Richarz, "Occupational Distribution and Social Structure," in *German-Jewish History in Modern Times*, vol. 3, *Integration in Dispute, 1871–1918*, ed. Michael A. Meyer and Michael Brenner (New York: Columbia University Press, 1997), 35–67; Usiel O. Schmelz, "Die demographische Entwicklung der Juden in Deutschland von der Mitte des 19. Jahrhunderts bis 1933," *Zeitschrift für Bevölkerungswissenschaft* 8 (1982): S. 31–72; Wilhelm Kreutz, "Die pfälzischen Juden der napoleonischen Ära: Bevölkerungsentwicklung, regionale Ausbreitung und Sozialstruktur," in *Pfälzisches Judentum Gestern und Heute: Beiträge zur Regionalgeschichte des 19. und 20. Jahrhunderts*, ed. Alfred Hans Kuby (Neustadt a.d. Weinstraße, Germany: Pfälzische Post, 1992), 33–83. My thanks to Anton Hieke for his help with this literature.

8. On Yankee peddlers, see Joseph T. Rainer, "The 'Sharper Image': Yankee Peddlers, Southern Consumers, and the Market Revolution," in *Cultural Change and the Market Revolution in America, 1789–1860*, ed. Scott C. Martin (Lanham, MD: Rowman and Littlefield, 2005), 89–110; David Jaffee, "Peddlers of Progress and the Transformation of the Rural North, 1760–1860," *Journal of American History* 78, 2 (1991): 511–535. On the "new culture of domestic consumption" that peddlers helped to birth, see David Jaffee, *A New Nation of Goods: The Material Culture of Early America* (Philadelphia: University of Pennsylvania Press, 2011).

9. For a detailed discussion of rural economic growth before the Civil War, see Thomas Weiss, "U.S. Labor Force Estimates and Economic Growth, 1800–1860," in *American Economic Growth and Standards of Living before the Civil War*, ed. Robert E. Gallman and John Joseph Wallis (Chicago: University of Chicago Press, 1992), 19–24.

10. Patricia Kelly Hall and Steven Ruggles, " 'Restless in the Midst of Their Prosperity': New Evidence of the Internal Migration of Americans, 1850–2000," *Journal of American History* 91, 3 (2004): 844.

11. Robert Gudmestad, *Steamboats and the Rise of the Cotton Kingdom* (Baton Rouge: Louisiana State University Press, 2011), 10 (quote), 18, 24. The challenges of travel in

nineteenth-century America are described in John H. White Jr., *Wet Britches and Muddy Boots: A History of Travel in Victorian America* (Bloomington: Indiana University Press, 2013); for the parlous state of America's roads, see 31–37.

12. Friedrich Gerstäcker, *Adventures and Hunting Expeditions in the United States of North America*, in *Gerstäcker's Louisiana*, ed. Irene S. Di Maio (Baton Rouge: Louisiana State University Press, 2006), 36; Joseph Austrian, "Autobiographical and Historical Sketches," 14–15, SC-598, American Jewish Archives, Cincinnati, Ohio (hereafter cited as AJA). For an example of a peddler who used boat, rail, and stagecoach to reach his customers, see William Frank, *Autobiography of William Frank*, SC-3596, AJA.

13. The numbers probably did not reflect shopkeepers who peddled occasionally, intermittently, or seasonally and those who did not describe themselves as peddlers to census officials. For figures, see Jaffe, "Peddlers of Progress," 522; Lewis Atherton, "Merchandising in the Ante-bellum South," *Bulletin of the Business Historical Society* 19, 2 (1945): 52–53.

14. For the perils of wagon peddling, see Isaac Wolfe Bernheim, *The Story of the Bernheim Family* (Louisville, KY: John P. Morton, 1910), 37–41. A Scottish commentator described much the same trajectory for peddlers in Britain in the eighteenth century; see Spufford, *Great Reclothing*, 45–46.

15. Marc Lee Raphael, *Jews and Judaism in a Midwestern Community: Columbus, Ohio, 1840–1975* (Columbus: Ohio Historical Society, 1979), 161.

16. Account book, 1849–1861, BV Ulster County peddler, New-York Historical Society (hereafter cited as Ulster County peddler). The peddler was probably Solomon Shears.

17. These figures are for the years before 1857, when his volume of business and profits rose dramatically. Sales Book, S. Halle Sons, Inc. Collection, Archives of the Jewish Museum of Maryland, Baltimore. Here amounts have been calculated according to the historical standard of living using MeasuringWealth (http://www.measuringworth.com/uscompare/relativevalue.php).

18. See Judith A. McGaw, *Most Wonderful Machine: Mechanization and Social Change in Berkshire Paper Making, 1801–1885* (Princeton: Princeton University Press, 1987), 127–147.

19. Charles Peters, *The Autobiography of Charles Peters* (Sacramento: LaGrave, 1915), 138. Isaac Mayer Wise offered a more elaborate hierarchy in his *Reminiscences* (Cincinnati: Leo Wise, 1901), 38. For violence directed at peddlers, see Richard Welch, "The Assimilation of an Ethnic Group: German-Jewish Peddlers in the Upper Ohio Valley, 1790–1840" (MA thesis, Michigan State University, 1972), 72–73; Marshall, *Jews in Nevada*, 10; Atherton, "Merchandising in the Ante-bellum South," 41–43; Jeffrey Gurock, *Orthodox Jews in America* (Bloomington: Indiana University Press, 2009), 57–59. Albert O. Hirschman argued for the unanticipated value of adversity in his famous essay "The Principle of the Hiding Hand," in *Development Projects Observed* (Washington, DC: Brookings Institution, 1967), chap. 1.

20. This argument draws heavily on Majewski, *Modernizing a Slave Economy*, 17, 39–40, 170. On Yankee peddlers in the South, see Rainer, "Sharper Image," 89–110. On Jewish peddlers in the South, see Diner, "Entering the Mainstream," 86–108. Quotes from Witold

Rybcynski, *A Clearing in the Distance: Frederick Law Olmsted and America in the 19th Century* (New York: Simon and Schuster, 2000), 109.

21. Julius Weis, *Autobiography of Julius Weis* (New Orleans: Goldman's Printing Office, 1908), 9.

22. See Jeff Forret, "Slaves, Poor Whites, and the Underground Economy of the Rural Carolinas," *Journal of Southern History* 70, 4 (Nov. 2004): 785–786.

23. At times these tropes became intertwined with those of the folkloric wandering Jew. Rainer, "Sharper Image," 97, 101–102, 105; Louis Schmier, "Hellooo! Peddlerman! Hellooo!," in *Ethnic Minorities in Gulf Coast Society*, ed. Jerrell Shofner and Linda Ellsworth (Pensacola, FL: Gulf Coast History and Humanities Conference, 1979), 79. On modern iterations of this mythology, see Richard I. Cohen, "The 'Wandering Jew' from Medieval Legend to Modern Metaphor," in *The Art of Being Jewish in Modern Times*, ed. Barbara Kirshenblatt-Gimblett and Jonathan Karp (Philadelphia: University of Pennsylvania Press, 2008), 147–175. On peddlers in American folklore, see Jaffe, "Peddlers of Progress," 527–531.

24. One correspondent to the *North American* groused that "not one out of fifty of the pedlers who overspread the State like a plague has a license." *North American*, Feb. 18, 1847; Rainer, "Sharper Image," 105; Atherton, "Merchandising in the Ante-bellum South," 36, 45; Richardson Wright, *Hawkers and Walkers in Early America* (Philadelphia: Lippincott, 1927), 88–95, 229–242. For license fees and taxation of peddlers, see Wright, *Hawkers*, 55n55, 57; Jaffe, "Peddlers of Progress," 531–533. For an example of the new licensing regime having a counterproductive effect, see Weis, *Autobiography of Julius Weis*, 12.

25. Charles Segal, "Isachar Zacharie: Lincoln's Chiropodist," *Publications of the American Jewish Historical Society* 43, 1 (1953): 86–87.

26. Weis, *Autobiography of Julius Weis*, 7–9.

27. Quote from Frederick Law Olmsted, *The Cotton Kingdom*, vol. 1 (New York: Mason Brothers, 1862), 46. On slave clothing, see Genovese, *Roll, Jordan, Roll*, 550–561; Shane White and Graham White, "Slave Clothing and African-American Culture in the Eighteenth and Nineteenth Centuries," *Past & Present* 148 (1995): 159–160, 168, 178; Fine and Leopold, "Consumerism and the Industrial Revolution," 174; Diner, "Entering the Mainstream," 100; Lynn Kennedy, "Out of Whole Cloth? Sewing and Family in the Old South," in *Family Values in the Old South*, ed. Craig Thompson Friend and Anya Jabour (Gainesville: University Press of Florida, 2010), 114–119. For peddlers enabling women to keep up with shifting fashions, see Neil McKendrick, John Brewer, and J. H. Plumb, *The Birth of a Consumer Society: The Commercialization of Eighteenth-Century England* (Bloomington: Indiana University Press, 1982), 77–78.

28. Mary Reynolds, in WPA, *Slave Narratives: A Folk History of Slavery in the United States from Interviews with Former Slaves*, vol. 16, Texas Narratives, part 3.

29. Olmsted, *Cotton Kingdom*, 55, 252; *Harper's Magazine* 7 (1853): 767; Glanz, *Jews in the Old American Folklore*, 129–133. On Olmsted's southern travels, see Rybcynski, *Clearing in the Distance*.

30. Bertram Korn, "Jews and Negro Slavery in the Old South, 1789–1865," *Publications of the*

American Jewish Historical Society 50, 1–4 (1961): 156–157; Morton Borden, *Jews, Turks, and Infidels* (Chapel Hill: University of North Carolina Press, 1984), 113–114; Jonathan D. Sarna and David G. Dalin, *Religion and State in the American Jewish Experience* (Notre Dame: University of Notre Dame Press, 1997), 147–148; Herbert T. Ezekiel and Gaston Lichtenstein, *The History of the Jews of Richmond from 1796 to 1917* (Richmond, VA: H. T. Ezekiel, 1917), 98; Richard and Belinda Gergel, "'A Bright New Era Now Dawns upon Us': Jewish Economic Opportunities, Religious Freedom and Political Rights in Colonial and Antebellum South Carolina," in *The Dawn of Religious Freedom in South Carolina*, ed. James Underwood and William Burke (Columbia: University of South Carolina Press, 2006), 107. In Charleston shopkeepers who sold to slaves may have contravened the thick layering of laws passed to suppress such illicit trade. See George B. Eckhard, *A Digest of the Ordinances of the City Council of Charleston from the Year 1783 to October 1844* (Charleston, SC: Walker and Burke, 1844), 171, 221, 224; my thanks to Michael D. Thompson for sharing this with me.

31. McDonald, *Economy and Material Culture of Slaves*, 68; Forret, "Slaves, Poor Whites, and the Underground Economy," 788; Benjamin L. Carp, *Rebels Rising: Cities and the American Revolution* (New York: Oxford University Press, 2007), 156.

32. John Andrew Jackson, *The Experience of a Slave in South Carolina* (London: Passmore and Alabaster, 1862), 25–26.

33. *Harper's Magazine* 7 (1853): 767.

34. This preference for colorful clothing was echoed among laborers in England in the early nineteenth century. After the ending of slavery in the British Empire, the demand for cloth increased in Jamaica, presumably as emancipated slaves purchased fabric of their own choosing. Toplis, "Stolen Garment," 60; Magee and Thompson, *Empire and Globalisation*, 161, 164; Robert Montgomery Martin, *The British Colonies: Their History, Extent, Condition and Resources*, vol. 4 (London: London Printing and Publishing, 1851), 105, 184. On missionaries and clothing, see Robert Ross, "Cross-Continental Cross Fertilization in Clothing," *European Review* 14, 1 (2006): 140–141.

35. On clothing purchases by slaves, see McDonald, *Economy and Material Culture of Slaves*, 68–81, 146–152 (quotes on 68 and 152). Helen Foster, *"New Raiments of Self": African American Clothing in the Antebellum South* (New York: Berg, 1997), 77–79, 130nn2–3, 136; White and White, "Slave Clothing and African-American Culture," 176, 178; Genovese, *Roll, Jordan, Roll*, 557; Olmsted, *Cotton Kingdom*, 45–46, 252. The sculptor Moses Ezekiel described how his grandparents' store in Richmond contained a closet "filled with ready-made dresses of all sizes to fit any Negro woman or girl": "Every Negro who was brought to Richmond from the South to be sold at auction [was brought] . . . to our house to be dressed." Ezekiel, *Memoirs*, 89–92.

36. Quoted in Foster, *"New Raiments of Self,"* 77.

37. Frederick Law Olmsted, *The Cotton Kingdom*, vol. 2 (New York: Mason Brothers, 1862), 165.

38. Philip Kahn, *A Stitch in Time: The Four Seasons of Baltimore's Needle Trades* (Baltimore: Maryland Historical Society, 1989), xvii–xviii.

39. Ulster County peddler. See also William J. Parish, "The German Jew and the

Commercial Revolution in Territorial New Mexico, 1850–1900," *New Mexico Histori-cal Review* 35, 1–2 (1960): 322. Springfield quote from Rowena Olegario, "Credit and Business Culture: The American Experience in the Nineteenth Century" (PhD diss., Harvard University, 1998), 42; Los Angeles quote from William Toll, "The Jewish Mer-chant and Civic Order in the Urban West," in *Jewish Life in the American West*, ed. Ava F. Kahn (Seattle: University of Washington Press, 2002), 90. For similar arrangements between Jews and rural customers in Europe, see Kaplan, *Jewish Daily Life in Germany*, 58, 140.

40. See Richard Howitt, *Impressions of Australia Felix, during Four Years of Residence in That Colony* (London: Longman, Brown, Green, and Longmans, 1845), 233–234.

41. *Chamber's Edinburgh Journal* 1 (1844): 334–335; Samuel Jubb, *The History of the Shoddy Trade* (London: Houlston and Wright, 1860), 99–102; Lemire, "Consumerism in Prein-dustrial and Early Industrial England," 7.

42. Jane Austin, "Rags," *Atlantic Monthly*, Mar. 1867, 365; S. M. Hunt, "Old Days in the Rag Trade," *Paper Trade Journal*, June 27, 1912; Jubb, *History of the Shoddy Trade*, 24–25, 32, 52, 113–115; *One Hundred Years' Progress*, 309, 313–315; John Ramsay McCulloch, *A Statistical Account of the British Empire*, vol. 1 (London: Charles Knight, 1839), 629; McGaw, *Most Wonderful Machine*, 66–67, 191–192, 195; Strasser, *Waste and Want*, 80–82, 85–87, 90, 95, 107–108; Edwin Perkins, "Antebellum Importers: The Role of Brown Bros. & Co. in Bal-timore," *Business History Review* 45, 4 (1971): 446; "Parliamentary Reports on the Rag Trade of Foreign Countries," *Practical Magazine* 6, 5 (1875): 222; Rachel Worth, *Fashion for the People: A History of Clothing at Marks and Spencer* (Oxford, UK: Berg, 2007), 18. "The Army Sutler and His Profits," Sept. 1861, in *Writing and Fighting the Civil War: Soldier Correspondence to the New York Sunday Mercury*, ed. William B. Styple (Kearny, NJ: Belle Grove, 2000), 51.

43. Strasser, *Waste and Want*, 13, 70–71, 73, 78–81; Horace Greeley, *The Great Industries of the United States* (Hartford, CT: J. B. Burr and Hyde, 1873), 588–589; Pope, *Clothing Industry in New York*, 6–7. See, for example, Ulster County peddler; Account book, John Sheneman Collection, Western Michigan University Library, Kalamazoo; Kahn, *Stitch in Time*, xvii–xviii; Hunt, "Old Days in the Rag Trade"; Jonathan Z. S. Pollack, "Success from Scrap and Secondhand Goods: Jewish Businessmen in the Midwest, 1890–1930," in Kobrin, *Chosen Capital*, 93–112.

44. Henry Seessel, for example, devoted less than a paragraph to his time as a clerk but many pages to his peddling career in *Memoirs of a Mexican Veteran* (Memphis: Jos. M. Samfield, 1897?), 22. For an example of the same pattern in biographies, see Leon Harris, *Merchant Princes: An Intimate History of Jewish Families Who Built Great Department Stores* (New York: Kondasha, 1994).

45. Quoted in Brinkmann, *Sundays at Sinai*, 21.

46. Brian Luskey, *On the Make: Clerks and the Quest for Capital in Nineteenth-Century America* (New York: NYU Press, 2010); Zakim, "Producing Capitalism".

47. Bernheim, *Story of the Bernheim Family*, 42–43.

48. Zakim, "Producing Capitalism," 224–231; Luskey, *On the Make*, 5–6; Wilentz, *Chants Democratic*, 403; Margo, "Labor Force," 215.

49. Horace Greeley, *Art and Industry as Represented at the Exhibition at Crystal Palace* (New York: Redfield, 1853), 231.

50. See Anton Hieke, "The Transregional Mobility of Jews from Macon, Ga., 1860–1880," *American Jewish History* 97, 1 (Mar. 2011): 21–38.

51. Census data is an imperfect measure of Jewish economic activity given that returns relied on self-reporting. As transients, peddlers may be underrepresented. The numbers for Charleston and Boston are extrapolated from large samples extracted from census data. See Kenneth D. Roseman, "The Jewish Population of America, 1850–1860: A Demographic Study of Four Cities" (PhD diss., Hebrew Union College, 1971), table 13 (for Boston); Stephen G. Mostov, "A 'Jerusalem' on the Ohio: The Social and Economic History of Cincinnati's Jewish Community" (PhD diss., Brandeis University, 1981), 107–108 (for Cincinnati); James William Hagy, *This Happy Land: The Jews of Colonial and Antebellum Charleston* (Tuscaloosa: University of Alabama Press, 1993), 193–197 (for Charleston); Lee Shai Weissbach, "Disappearing Jewish Communities in the Era of Mass Migration," *American Jewish Archives Journal* 49 (1997): 43 (for small towns). For data on clerking in a variety of Western towns, see Toll, "Jewish Merchant and Civic Order," 92–93. On clerking by Jews in Europe, see Kaplan, *Jewish Daily Life in Germany*, 134, 136–137.

52. Hieke, "Transregional Mobility"; Zakim, "Producing Capitalism," 229; Margo, "Labor Force," 222.

53. Luskey, *On the Make*, 2, 8, 36; Zakim, "Producing Capitalism," 227–228, 234.

54. Jacob Rader Marcus, *United States Jewry, 1776–1985*, 2 vols. (Detroit: Wayne State University Press, 1991), 2:90, 2:107; Peter M. Ascoli, *Julius Rosenwald* (Bloomington: Indiana University Press, 2006), 1–3; Olegario, "Credit and Business Culture," 242–243. In New York Julius boarded with his uncle and aunt Samuel and Emelia Hammerslough; Emelia's brother was the banker Samuel Sachs.

55. This phenomenon is discussed at length in Adam D. Mendelsohn, "Tongue Ties: Religion, Culture and Commerce in the Making of the Anglophone Jewish Diaspora, 1840–1870" (PhD diss., Brandeis University, 2008), 174–218. For the role of economic life in fostering Jewish group identity, see Kuznets, "Economic Structure and Life of the Jews," 1601; Penslar, *Shylock's Children*.

56. Isaac Mayer Wise, *Israelite*, Oct. 2, 1857, 102. For a similar complaint, that the "younger men, engaged as clerks, were invisible in synagogue" in Chicago in 1850, see Brinkmann, *Sundays at Sinai*, 36.

57. Mark I. Greenberg provides a useful listing of these studies; the data on Savannah is drawn from his work as well. See Greenberg, "Creating Ethnic, Class, and Southern Identity in Nineteenth-Century America: The Jews of Savannah, Georgia 1830–1880" (PhD diss., University of Florida, 1997), 95–96.

58. On peddling in England, see Felix Folio, *The Hawkers and Street Dealers of the North of England Manufacturing Districts* (Manchester, UK: Abel Heywood, 1859), 13–15; Laurence Fontaine, *History of Peddlers in Europe* (Durham: Duke University Press, 1996), 41, 136–137; John Benson and Laura Ugolini, "Beyond the Shop: Problems and Possibilities," *Journal of Historical Research in Marketing* 2, 3 (2010): 257–261; Mitchell, "Retailing

Innovation," 289–290; McKendrick, Brewer, and Plumb, *Birth of a Consumer Society*, 86–90; Woodbridge, "Peddler and the Pawn," 144–146; Spufford, *Great Reclothing*; Nancy Cox, *The Complete Tradesman: A Study of Retailing, 1550–1820* (Aldershot, UK: Ashgate, 2000), 32–33, 193–194; Spears, *100 Years on the Road*, 24–25. On Jewish peddlers in England, see Naggar, *Jewish Pedlars and Hawkers*, 13–76; Lloyd P. Gartner, *Jewish Immigrant in England, 1870–1914* (London: Allen and Unwin, 1960), 58–62; Pollins, *Economic History*, 76–80. On the improvement of roads and travel times in Britain, see Judith Flanders, *Consuming Passions: Leisure and Pleasure in Victorian Britain* (London: Harper, 2006), 71–72.

59. See Pollins, *Economic History*, 106; Naggar, *Jewish Pedlars and Hawkers*, 93–94.

60. Raphael, *Jews and Judaism in a Midwestern Community*, 35–36.

61. For an example of a peddler paid a monthly wage, see Philip Sartorius, "Small-Town Southern Merchant," in *Memoirs of American Jews, 1775–1865*, ed. Jacob Rader Marcus, 2 vols. (Philadelphia: Jewish Publication Society, 1955), 2:27.

62. Quoted in Glanz, *Jews of California*, 53.

63. The problems associated with this close connection with the agricultural cycle are described in Olegario, "Credit and Business Culture," 41; for examples of branch stores in Louisiana, see Scott P. Marler, "Merchants and the Political Economy of Nineteenth-Century Louisiana: New Orleans and Its Hinterlands" (PhD diss., Rice University, 2007), 134–135.

64. Daniel Aaron, *Cincinnati, Queen City of the West* (Columbus: Ohio State University Press, 1992), 69.

65. Ibid., 28; Olegario, "Credit and Business Culture," 34; Marler, "Merchants and the Political Economy," 111.

66. Adler, *Yankee Merchants*, 71–85.

67. Mostov, " 'Jerusalem' on the Ohio," 94–96, 138, 140; Peter Decker, *Fortunes and Failures: White-Collar Mobility in Nineteenth-Century San Francisco* (Cambridge: Harvard University Press, 1978), 91–93; Marler, "Merchants and the Political Economy," 117–119.

68. Olegario, "Credit and Business Culture," 29–30, 227–230, 241–244. Quote from Spears, *100 Years on the Road*, 28. According to Barry Cohen, R. G. Dun credit ledgers follow no consistent approach in noting religious affiliation; identification varies by religion, region, and time period, as did the attitudes expressed toward religious minorities. There is no evidence that the Mercantile Agency officially requested that credit reporters collect this information. In terms of religious identifications, Jews are most prevalent, followed by Catholics (to a much lesser degree), and an occasional Baptist. Antagonistic attitudes were routinely expressed toward peddlers regardless of their religious background. Reporters often reflected the views of the local mercantile community, which regarded itinerant traders as competitors. My thanks to Barry Cohen for his insights into this issue.

69. Isaac Leeser, *Occident* 9, 1 (Apr. 1852): 59.

70. Zakim, "Producing Capitalism," 231. See also Decker, *Fortunes and Failures*, 97–105; Gerald Tulchinsky, " 'Said to Be a Very Honest Jew': The R. G. Dun Credit Reports and Jewish Business Activity in Mid-19th Century Montreal," *Urban History Review* 18,

3 (1990): 200–209; Gerald Tulchinsky, *Taking Root: The Origins of the Canadian Jewish Community* (Hanover, NH: Brandeis University Press, 1993), 61–81; Stephen Mostov, "Dun and Bradstreet Reports as a Source of Jewish Economic History; Cincinnati, 1840–1875," *American Jewish History* 72, 3 (1983): 333–353; Ashkenazi, *Business of Jews in Louisiana*, 22–24, 29, 93–100, 151–153; William Toll, *The Making of an Ethnic Middle Class: Portland Jewry over Four Generations* (Albany: SUNY Press, 1982), 12–13, 17–18; David Gerber "Cutting Out Shylock: Elite Anti-Semitism and the Quest for Moral Order in the Mid-Nineteenth-Century American Marketplace," in *Anti-Semitism in American History*, ed. David A. Gerber (Urbana: University of Illinois Press, 1987), 211–225; Marler, "Merchants and the Political Economy," 121–123.

71. For a case study of how economic connections can bolster ethnic identity, see Edna Bonacich and John Modell, *Economic Basis of Ethnic Solidarity: Small Business in the Japanese American Community* (Berkeley: University of California Press, 1980).

72. Mostov, "'Jerusalem' on the Ohio," 122, 134.

73. Quoted in Robert E. Levinson, *The Jews in the California Gold Rush* (New York: Ktav, 1978), 24.

74. *Gleaner*, May 31, 1861.

75. *Gleaner*, Mar. 2, 1860.

76. For a description of industrial and mercantile development in Cincinnati, see Aaron, *Cincinnati*, 32–37; Allan Pred, *Urban Growth and City Systems in the United States, 1840–1860* (Cambridge: Harvard University Press, 1980). Quote from Maria A. Varney, "Letters from the Queen City," *Herald of Truth* 2 (1847): 84.

77. *New York Daily Times*, Dec. 10, 1852, quoted in Belich, *Replenishing the Earth*, 232.

78. On Jewish wholesalers in Cincinnati, see Mostov, "'Jerusalem' on the Ohio," 109, 114. On their rivals, see Adler, *Yankee Merchants*, 71–85, 110.

79. Jacob Seasongood, SC-11130, AJA; *The Biographical Encyclopaedia of Ohio of the Nineteenth Century* (Cincinnati: Galaxy, 1876), 408–409, 439.

80. Alfred D. Chandler Jr., *The Visible Hand: The Managerial Revolution in American Business* (Cambridge: Belknap Press of Harvard University Press, 1993), chapter 7; see also Glenn Porter and Harold C. Livesay, *Merchants and Manufacturers: Studies in the Changing Structure of Nineteenth-Century Marketing* (Chicago: Elephant, 1989), 130, 163; Spears, *100 Years on the Road*, 31 (quotes), 35, 43.

81. Porter and Livesay, *Merchants and Manufacturers*, 27–28; Margaret Walsh, "Industrial Opportunity on the Urban Frontier: 'Rags to Riches' and Milwaukee Clothing Manufacturers, 1840–1880," *Wisconsin Magazine of History* 57, 3 (1974): 181, 190; Mostov, "'Jerusalem' on the Ohio," 92, 110–111, 136; Zakim, *Ready-Made Democracy*, 48; Olegario, "Credit and Business Culture," 243.

82. Leonard Rogoff, *Down Home: Jewish Life in North Carolina* (Chapel Hill: University of North Carolina Press, 2010), 53; Ashkenazi, *Business of Jews in Louisiana*, 68, 72, 88–89, 93–95, 100–101, 108–109, 127; Atherton, "Merchandising in the Ante-bellum South," 48, 52; Peter Decker, "Jewish Merchants in San Francisco: Social Mobility on the Urban Frontier," in *The Jews of the West, the Metropolitan Years*, ed. Moses Rischin (Waltham, MA: American Jewish Historical Society, 1979), 15.

NOTES TO CHAPTER 4

1. Mrs. Biddell had been driven into debt by a two-pound deposit she paid to receive the trousers. The deposit was designed to safeguard manufacturers and contractors against losses by sewers who sold or pawned the fabric. The episode and its aftermath is described in detail in *Times*, Oct. 27, 1843, 4; Oct. 28, 1843, 7; Oct. 31, 1843, 3; Nov. 8, 1843; *Punch*, Nov. 4, 1843; *Morning Chronicle*, Nov. 8, 1843, 4; Nov. 9, 1843, 4; Nov. 13, 1843, 3; and in Sheila Blackburn, *A Fair Day's Wages for a Fair Day's Work?* (London: Ashgate, 2007), 17–20. See also Sarah Levitt, *Victorians Unbuttoned* (London: Allen and Unwin, 1986), 16, 181, 186; and Wechsler, "Jewish Garment Trade," 41–42. For Dickens's comment on Moses, see Charles Dickens to Frederick Dickens, n.d., in *The Letters of Charles Dickens*, ed. Madeline House, Graham Storey and Kathleen Tillotson, 12 vols. (Oxford, UK: Clarendon, 1974), 3:610. For wages paid to needleworkers, see *Parliamentary Papers, Great Britain, House of Commons*, 1864, vol. 22 (reports, vol. 7), cmd. 3414, 1864, "Second Report of the Royal Commission on Children's Employment," lxix–lxx; Leone Levi, *Wages and Earnings of the Working Classes* (Shannon: Irish University Press, 1971), 131–132. Henry's eldest son and business partner, Edward, was married to Isaac Moses's eldest child, Julia. Insurance records for Samuel Moses for 1779, 1794, and 1802 and letters of administration from the London Commissary Court, May 1806, in the collection of George Rigal.

2. Charles Dickens to Johann Kuenzel, July? 1838, in *Letters of Charles Dickens*, 1:423. Sailors were promiscuous in their use of the word "Jew," often using the term as a blanket description for traders who offered them credit in advance of their wages. See Geoffrey L. Green, *The Royal Navy and Anglo-Jewry, 1740–1820* (London: G. L. Green, 1989), 40, 132–133, 138–139.

3. On the presence and roles of Jews in naval towns, see Geoffrey L. Green, "Anglo-Jewish Trading Connections with Officers and Seamen of the Royal Navy, 1740–1820," *Transactions of the Jewish Historical Society of England* 29 (1982–1986): 99–108.

4. These examples are drawn from the British Navy's Covey Crump dictionary of slang. See http://webarchive.nationalarchives.gov.uk/20090127182544/http://royalnavy.mod .uk/training-and-people/rn-life/navy-slang/covey-crump-(a-to-aye)/jago-jutland/ (accessed March 8, 2012).

5. Quoted in Henry Lawrence Swinburne, *The Royal Navy* (London: Adam and Charles Black, 1907), 345. Clothing requirements were different for ships traveling to warm climates. *London Saturday Journal* 11 (May 25, 1839): 321.

6. On the role of military orders in the early development of the clothing trade, see Lemire, *Dress, Culture, and Commerce*, 2, 9–32. On slop sellers searching for alternative markets after previous lulls in military orders, see ibid., 20. For slop sellers in London, see Wechsler, "Jewish Garment Trade," 30; James Greenwood, *Unsentimental Journeys; or, Byways of the Modern Babylon* (London: Ward, Lock, and Tyler, 1867). *Pigot's* may well have undercounted the number of slop sellers. For evidence of its imperfections, see Flanders, *Consuming Passions*, 42. For the growth of the British navy between 1795 and 1815, see Roger Morris, *The Foundations of British Maritime Supremacy* (Cambridge:

Cambridge University Press, 2010), 131–132. On slop sellers selling used clothing, see Lambert, "Cast-Off Wearing Apparel," 6, 10–11. For quote, see *Times*, Oct. 1, 1858, 8.

7. On Elias Moses's career, see Andrew Godley, "Moses, Elias (1783–1868)," in *Oxford Dictionary of National Biography*, http://www.oxforddnb.com/view/article/57650 (accessed May 28, 2014); Stanley Chapman, "The Innovating Entrepreneurs in the British Ready-Made Clothing Industry," *Textile History* 24 (1993): 5–25; Chapman, "The 'Revolution' in Ready-Made Clothing 1840–1860," *London Journal* 29, 1 (2004): 44–61.

8. On the economic value of clusters, see Philip Cooke, *Knowledge Economics: Clusters, Learning, and Cooperative Advantage* (London: Routledge, 2002).

9. For examples of those who continued to sell to sailors, see *London Saturday Journal* 11 (May 25, 1839): 321; Levitt, *Victorians Unbuttoned*, 11, 95; Lambert, "Cast-Off Wearing Apparell," 4.

10. *Jewish Chronicle*, Oct. 27, 1854; Apr. 27, 1855; "Second Report of the Royal Commission on Children's Employment," q. 237; *Times*, Aug. 8, 1854, 9; Jan. 2, 1855, 10; Mar. 24, 1855, 3; July 11, 1855; Records of the Sun Fire Office, MS119326/506/1047246, 507/1061100, 519/1094478, Guildhall Library. For advertisements of the sale of surplus slops, see *Times*, Dec. 3, 1814, 2; Nov. 16, 1831, 1; Aug. 3, 1833, 7; July 29, 1834, 2; Apr. 23, 1859. For advertisements by merchants for "left-off military and plain-wearing apparel," see *Times*, Aug. 10, 1839, 8; Oct. 12, 1839, 8; June 27, 1843, 11. For the role of military uniforms in the secondhand trade in Paris, see Charpy, "Scope and Structure," 132–133.

11. In Manchester in 1800 a third of all slop sellers were female. Lambert, "Cast-Off Wearing Apparell," 5.

12. For a sampling of advertisements, see *Times*, Sept. 7, 1829, 1; Apr. 26, 1830, 1; Feb. 14, 1831, 1; Dec. 18, 1835, 1; May 1, 1839, 2; Dec. 18, 1839, 2; Nov. 23, 1840, 2; Nov. 28, 1846, 10; Sept. 27, 1858, 6.

13. On the economic geography of East London, see John Marriott, *Beyond the Tower: A History of East London* (New Haven: Yale University Press, 2011), 104–122; on economic clusters in London, see Roy Porter, *London: A Social History* (Cambridge: Harvard University Press, 1995), 197; Giorgio Riello, "Strategies and Boundaries: Subcontracting and the London Trades in the Long Eighteenth Century," *Enterprise and Society* 9, 2 (2008): 252; White, *London in the Nineteenth Century*, 176–178.

14. James Schmiechen, *Sweated Industries and Sweated Labor* (Urbana: University of Illinois Press, 1984), 6–9; L. D. Schwarz, *London in the Age of Industrialization* (Cambridge: Cambridge University Press, 2003), 189–194; F. W. Galton, ed., *Select Documents Illustrating the History of Trade Unionism: I. The Tailoring Trade* (London: Longmans, Green, 1896), 175–223. For an astute analysis of the gendered division between tailoring and ready-made manufacturing, see Lemire, *Dress, Culture, and Commerce*, 4–5, 71–74.

15. See *Times*, Oct. 31, 1843.

16. For analyses of the sweating system, see Schwarz, *London in the Age of Industrialization*, 179–208; Schmiechen, *Sweated Industries*, 16; David Feldman, *Englishmen and Jews* (New Haven: Yale University Press, 1994), 195, 203–204; Riello, "Strategies and Boundaries," 518–522; Duncan Bythell, *The Sweated Trades: Outwork in Nineteenth-Century Britain* (New York: St. Martin's, 1978), 65–105. On the number of large firms, see Porter,

London, 198. For average factory sizes, see John Garrard, *Leadership and Power in Victorian Industrial Towns, 1830–1880* (Manchester: Manchester University Press, 1983), 10; Harold Perkin, *The Origins of Modern English Society* (London: Routledge, 2002), 88–90. On patents by E. Moses & Son, see Levitt, *Victorians Unbuttoned*, 96, 99–100, 192, 225.

17. On subcontracting, see Giorgio Riello, "Boundless Competition: Subcontracting and the London Economy in the Late Nineteenth Century," *Enterprise and Society* 13, 3 (2012): 504–537; Riello, "Strategies and Boundaries," 243–280; David Green, "The Nineteenth-Century Metropolitan Economy: A Revisionist Interpretation," *London Journal* 21 (1996): 18–19.

18. For a discussion of this process, see Feldman, *Englishmen and Jews*, 197–204. For firsthand testimony by needleworkers and others involved in the sweating system, see "Second Report of the Royal Commission on Children's Employment," 152–153.

19. For cases of this type of demand, see *Times*, Oct. 26, 1843; Nov. 3, 1843; *Old Bailey Proceedings*, Jan. 27, 1868, 17–22.

20. The Marist fathers of Spitalfields griped in the 1860s that their flock was being dispersed by railroad construction and the settlement of Jewish immigrants. See Lees, *Exiles of Erin*, 60. For a contemporary discussion of the gender dynamics of the tailoring trade, see "Second Report of the Royal Commission on Children's Employment," lxviii; Marriott, *Beyond the Tower*, 115–118. For an example of subcontracting to immigrants from Posen, see *Morning Chronicle*, Nov. 18, 1849, 5–6.

21. By 1861, 107,000 women worked in the different branches of the clothing trade in London, but only 30,000 men did. See David Green, *From Artisans to Paupers* (Hants, UK: Scolar, 1995), 164–165; P. G Hall, *The Industries of London since 1861* (London: Hutchinson University Library, 1962), 60; Bythell, *Sweated Trades*, 75. On the occupational structure of eastern European Jewry, see Ezra Mendelsohn, *Class Struggle in the Pale* (Cambridge: Cambridge University Press, 1970), chapter 1. On immigration and poverty in the mid-nineteenth century, see Todd Endelman, *The Jews of Britain, 1656–2000* (Berkeley: University of California Press, 2002), 81–82; J. H. Stallard, *London Pauperism amongst Jews and Christians* (London: Saunders, Otley, 1867), 9; Lipman, *Social History*, 27; Pollins, *Economic History*, 117–119. For population figures and residence patterns, see Laidlaw, "Jews in the British Isles," 34–41. On the Jewish share of the workforce in the tailoring trade, see Wechsler, "Jewish Garment Trade," 46.

22. For a lengthy contemporary description of sweating that pinned part of the blame for low wages on Jews, see *Morning Chronicle*, Nov. 18, 1849, 4–6. The best discussions of the emergence and evolution of critiques of the sweating system are in Blackburn, *Fair Day's Wages*, 15–68; and Feldman, *Englishmen and Jews*, 186–190. For the same in America, see Daniel E. Bender, *Sweated Work, Sweated Bodies: Anti-Sweatshop Campaigns and Languages of Labor* (New Brunswick: Rutgers University Press, 2004). For Mayhew's description of sweating, see Henry Mayhew, *The Unknown Mayhew*, ed. Eileen Yeo and E. P. Thompson (New York: Pantheon, 1971), 116–218. For a revisionist interpretation of Mayhew's account, see Green, "Nineteenth-Century Metropolitan Economy," 19.

23. *Times*, Oct. 31, 1843; Nov. 3, 1843.

24. *Jewish Chronicle*, Jan. 28, 1859. For a discussion of the ills of the sweating system, see

Schmiechen, *Sweated Industries*, 2–18; Wechsler, "Jewish Garment Trade," chapters 3 and 4; Feldman, *Englishmen and Jews*, 197–204. On workers collecting old clothing during slow periods, see Zoë Josephs, *Birmingham Jewry* (Birmingham, UK: Birmingham Jewish History Research Group, 1984), 42.

25. On London's labor force in 1861 and the number of tailors recorded on census returns, see *Parliamentary Papers, Great Britain, Parliament, House of Commons*, 1861, "Census of England and Wales," 53-I, cmd. 3221; Katrina Honeyman, *Well Suited: A History of the Leeds Clothing Industry, 1850–1990* (Oxford: Oxford University Press, 2000), 12; Hall, *Industries of London*, 37–42. Hyam quote from the *Economist*, May 10, 1856, 528.

26. On Hyam's sale of machine-made and sweated clothing, see Green, *From Artisans to Paupers*, 164; Green, "Nineteenth-Century Metropolitan Economy," 18–19. On the symbiotic relationship between factory production and outwork, see "Second Report of the Royal Commission on Children's Employment," lxviii. On the advantages of large government contracts, see D. J. Smith, "Army Clothing Contractors and the Textile Industries in the 18th Century," *Textile History* 14, 2 (1983): 162–163.

27. Figures for railway traffic cited in White, *London*, 41–42. For the unreliability of these figures, see Dyos, "Railways and Housing," 12. On Hyam, see Sharpe, "Cheapness and Economy," 204–207; Josephs, *Birmingham Jewry*, 36; *Jewish Chronicle*, Aug. 30, 1850, 368; Oct. 8, 1858. On railway workers and their clothing allowance, see Levi, *Wages and Earnings*, 83.

28. On residential patterns in 1851, see Laidlaw, "Jews in the British Isles," 41.

29. For a contemporary estimate of the investment needed to become a wholesaler, see Nathaniel Whittock, *The Complete Book of Trades* (London: T. Tegg, 1842), 143.

30. Zakim, *Ready-Made Democracy*, 70.

31. Several scholars have argued that these innovations can be traced to the eighteenth century. John Styles and Jan de Vries have demonstrated that Englishmen in search of inexpensive clothing had a broadening spectrum of choices in that century. See Styles, *Dress of the People*, 167–178; de Vries, *Industrious Revolution*, 133–144. For useful overviews of this debate, see Jon Stobart, "A History of Shopping: The Missing Link between Retail and Consumer Revolutions," *Journal of Historical Research in Marketing* 2, 3 (2010): 342–349; and Cox, *Complete Tradesman*, 2–14, 76–115. According to one estimate, the growth of the number of shops in England over the first half of the nineteenth century outpaced population growth by a factor of ten. See Flanders, *Consuming Passions*, 44. On the development of "show shops," see *Parliamentary Papers, Great Britain, Parliament, House of Commons*, 1833, vol. 6 (reports, vol. 2), cmd. 690, "Report from the Select Committee on Manufacturers, Commerce, and Shipping," q. 1493. On the percentage of income spent on clothing, see W. Hamish Fraser, *The Coming of the Mass Market, 1850–1914* (London: Macmillan, 1981), 58. Middle-class consumers spent an even higher percentage of their income on clothing. See Levi, *Wages and Earnings*, 61. Quote from Charles Dickens, *Sketches by Boz* (London: Chapman and Hall, 1894), 104.

32. Ernest Jones, *Notes to the People*, vol. 1 (London: J. Pavey, 1851), 366. On Jones, see Miles Taylor, *Ernest Jones, Chartism, and the Romance of Politics, 1819–1869* (Oxford: Oxford University Press, 2003). Mayhew estimated that show shops and slop shops directly and

indirectly employed eighteen thousand needleworkers in 1849. See Mayhew, *Unknown Mayhew*, 182.

33. For the Moseses' innovations within the clothing business, see E. Moses & Son, *The Growth of an Important Branch of British Industry* (London: E. Moses & Son, 1860), 4–7; Chapman, " 'Revolution' in Ready-Made Clothing," 46–52, 57–58; Chapman, "Innovating Entrepreneurs," 5–25; John Weale, *The Pictorial Handbook of London* (London: Henry G. Bohn, 1854), 533–534. For the Hyams, see Sharpe, "Cheapness and Economy," 204–207; Josephs, *Birmingham Jewry*, 36; *Jewish Chronicle*, Aug. 30, 1850, 368; Wechsler, "Jewish Garment Trade," 38.

34. Weale, *Pictorial Handbook of London*, 533; Chapman, "Innovating Entrepreneurs," 16. The store was also praised in poetry: see William Thackeray, *Ballads and Songs* (New York: Scribner, 1906), 116–119.

35. E. Moses & Son, *British Industry*, 8; E. Moses & Son, *The Dressing Room Companion or Guide to the Glass* (London: E. Moses & Son, 1848), 24; E. Moses & Son, *The Library of Elegance* (London: E. Moses & Son, 1852), 25.

36. Prior to the 1840s and 1850s, most of these migrants came from the counties south and east of the city, but they were soon joined by those fleeing famine in Ireland.

37. Francis Sheppard, *London: A History* (Oxford: Oxford University Press, 1998), 289–290, 362–363 (quote on 291); Porter, *London*, 186; Ben Fine and Ellen Leopold, "Consumerism and the Industrial Revolution," *Social History* 15, 2 (May 1990): 171; Dyos, "Railways and Housing," 11–12.

38. For discussion of wages, disposable income, and the standard of living, see K. Theodore Hoppen, *Mid-Victorian Generation, 1846–1886* (Oxford, UK: Clarendon, 1998), 56–58, 75–76, 83–84. For an overview of debates about changes in the standard of living, see ibid., 72–90. On stores profiting by being located close to markets, see Cox, *Complete Tradesman*, 125.

39. This data is drawn heavily from Sheppard, *London*, 292, 302–303; Fine and Leopold, "Consumerism and the Industrial Revolution," 170.

40. For the "racial conquest" that made this possible, see Johnson, *River of Dark Dreams*.

41. For discussion of the cost of clothing relative to household budgets, see Hoppen, *Mid-Victorian Generation*, 348. For an explanation of the falling cost of cotton cloth, see Donald McCloskey, "The Industrial Revolution 1780–1860: A Survey," in *The Economics of the Industrial Revolution*, ed. Joel Mokyr (Totowa, NJ: Rowman and Allanheld, 1985), 59–60.

42. J. C. Flügel memorably described the changes in male fashions as the "Great Masculine Renunciation." See Flügel, *The Psychology of Clothes* (London: Hogarth, 1930), 110–111. For the rapidity of changes of fashion in the eighteenth century, see McKendrick, Brewer, and Plumb, *Birth of a Consumer Society*, 55–56, 63–64, 92. For fashions in the nineteenth century, see C. Willett Cunnington and Phillis Cunnington, *Handbook of English Costume in the Nineteenth Century* (Boston: Plays, 1970).

43. E. Moses & Son, *The Past, the Present, and the Future: A Public Address on the Opening of the New Establishment of E. Moses and Son* (London: E. Moses & Son, 1846), 6; *Spectator*, Jan. 26, 1861, 93; quote from Josephs, *Birmingham Jewry*, 36. Women's riding habits could

be mass-produced because their cut was similar to men's clothing. On the importance of aspiration and emulation among people purchasing clothing, see McKendrick, Brewer, and Plumb, *Birth of a Consumer Society*, 38–43, 52–53.

44. Chapman, "Innovating Entrepreneurs," 17. For similar lease arrangements, see Lambert, "Cast-Off Wearing Apparell," 11.

45. On early fashion advertising, see McKendrick, Brewer, and Plumb, *Birth of a Consumer Society*, 47–49; Berg, "French Fancy and Cool Britannia," 553. On mass printing, see Richard Altick, *The English Common Reader: A Social History of the Mass Reading Public, 1800–1900* (Columbus: Ohio State University Press, 1998), 99–128; Paul Boyer, *Urban Masses and Moral Order in America, 1820–1920* (Cambridge: Harvard University Press, 1978), 22–33.

46. *Chambers's Edinburgh Journal* 86 (Aug. 25, 1855): 128. A firm specializing in hair oil and another in cod-liver oil also reputedly spent £10,000 a year on advertising.

47. *Sidney's Emigrant's Journal*, Dec. 14, 1848, 81. For a typical example of the firm's pamphlets, see the illustrated thirty-two-page *The Pride of London: A Poem* (London: E. Moses & Son, 1850), written entirely in verse; the twenty-four-page *The Dressing Room Companion or Guide to the Glass* (London: E. Moses & Son, 1848); *The Philosophy of Dress, with a Few Notes on National Costumes* (London: E. Moses & Son, 1864), which contained a discussion of Chinese, Siberian, and Turkish fashions; and *The Tercentenary; or, The Three Hundredth Birthday of William Shakespeare* (London: E. Moses & Son, 1864), which mused about the clothing described in the Bard's plays.

48. *Times*, July 3, 1841, 8; May 13, 1842, 11.

49. *Illustrated London News*, Oct. 22, 1842. For contemporary praise of their advertising techniques, see William Smith, *Advertise: How? When? Where?* (London: Routledge, Warne, and Routledge, 1863), 36.

50. Quotes from Andrew Wynter, *Subtle Brains and Lissom Fingers* (London: Robert Hardwicke, 1863), 41, 44. See also James Dawson Burn, *The Language of the Walls* (Manchester, UK: Abel Heywood, 1855), 113; *Quarterly Review* 97 (1855): 212; and Mayhew, *Unknown Mayhew*, 196–198.

51. On the firm's advertising in Dickens, see Bernard Darwin, ed., *The Dickens Advertiser: A Collection of the Advertisements in the Original Parts of Novels by Charles Dickens* (New York: Macmillan, 1930), 140–155.

52. Dave Hollett, *Fast Passage to Australia* (London: Fairplay, 1986), 31.

53. See *Punch* 14 (1848): 127.

54. See PP 1847, q. 462.

55. Max Schlesinger, *Saunterings in and about London* (London: Nathaniel Cooke, 1853), quoted in Nead, *Victorian Babylon*, 58.

56. P. E. Razzell and R. W. Wainwright, *The Victorian Working Class: Selections from the Morning Chronicle* (New York: Routledge, 2013), 96, see also 216; White, *London*, 191.

57. Burn, *Language of the Walls*, 113.

58. Nead, *Victorian Babylon*, 89. Cunningham's guidebook to London identified one of Moses's "showy" shops as a landmark in the Minories. Cunningham, *Handbook for London*, 561. For other impressions of Moses's stores, see Beth Harris, "All That Glitters

Is Not Gold: The Show-Shop and the Victorian Seamstress," in *Famine and Fashion: Needlewomen in the Nineteenth Century*, ed. Beth Harris (Burlington, VT: Ashgate, 2005), 123; George Sala, *Gaslight and Daylight, with Some London Scenes They Shine Upon* (London: Chapman and Hall, 1859), 257–258. For the view that gas- and candlelight could serve as stage props used to gull customers, see PP 1847, q. 1786. Gas lighting may have been intended to counter the common trope that Jewish stores were "black, ugly and airless," "dangerous and deceptive," "disturbing [and] tomb-like." See Nead, *Victorian Babylon*, 177.

59. Riello, "Strategies and Boundaries," 260–261.

60. David Richardson, *The Anglo-Indian Passage Homeward and Outward* (London: James Madden, 1849), 202–203; James Barber, *The Overland Guide-Book* (London: Wm. H. Allen, 1850); E. Moses & Son, *Library of Elegance*, 6.

61. *The Merchant Shippers of London, Liverpool, Manchester, Birmingham, Bristol, and Hull*, 1868, 1878.

62. Benjamin Godwin, *Godwin's Emigrant's Guide to Van Diemen's Land* (London: Sherwood, Jones, 1823).

63. For two such extensive lists of recommended items of clothing, see *Sidney's Emigrant's Journal*, Dec. 7, 1848, 78; Feb. 22, 1849, 165.

64. Ibid., Jan. 25, 1849, 130; June 28, 1849, 309.

65. Margaret Maynard, *Fashioned from Penury: Dress as Cultural Practice in Colonial Australia* (New York: Cambridge University Press, 1994), 139–140; Chapman, "Innovating Entrepreneurs," 6; Levitt, *Victorians Unbuttoned*, 77. For the firm's advertisements aimed at emigrants, see *Sidney's Emigrant's Journal*, Dec. 28, 1848, 104; Jan. 11, 1849, 120. For prices of different immigration outfits, see E. Moses & Son, *Library of Elegance*, 22.

66. Quoted in Chapman, " 'Revolution' in Ready-Made Clothing," 45–46.

NOTES TO CHAPTER 5

1. *Sydney Monitor and Commercial Advertiser*, Mar. 19, 1841, 2. Lyons appeared to have had frequent run-ins with the law in the 1840s. See, for example, *Australian*, Mar. 6, 1847, 3. This account draws heavily on that provided in Kirsten McKenzie, *Scandal in the Colonies: Sydney and Cape Town, 1820–1850* (Melbourne: Melbourne University Press, 2005), 60–61.

2. Magee and Thompson, *Empire and Globalisation*, 18, 160. For an analogue in popular culture in America during the early national period, see Larzer Ziff, *Writing in the New Nation: Prose, Print, and Politics in the Early United States* (New Haven: Yale University Press, 1991), 56.

3. For other examples, see J. S. Levi and G. F. J. Bergman, *Australian Genesis: Jewish Convicts and Settlers, 1788–1850* (Adelaide, Australia: Rigby, 1974), 122–141; Charles Van Onselen, *The Fox and the Flies: The Secret Life of a Grotesque Master Criminal* (New York: Walker, 2007); and Van Onselen, "Jewish Police Informers in the Atlantic World, 1880–1914," *Historical Journal* 50, 1 (2007): 119–144.

4. On colonial self-reinvention, see McKenzie, *Scandal in the Colonies*, 1–4, 9, 51 (quote).

5. On the value of British clothing exports, see Schmiechen, *Sweated Industries*, 14. On

exports to the colonies, see Board of Trade (Alien Immigration), *Reports on the Volume and Effects of Recent Immigration from Eastern Europe into the United Kingdom* (London: Her Majesty's Stationery Office, 1894), 208–211; D. A. Farnie, *The English Cotton Industry and the World Market, 1815–1896* (Oxford: Oxford University Press, 1979), 84–86. For an overview of the economic relationships between Britain and its empire, see P. J. Cain, "Economics and Empire: The Metropolitan Context," in *The Oxford History of the British Empire*, vol. 3, *The Nineteenth Century*, ed. Andrew Porter (Oxford: Oxford University Press, 1999), 31–52; and B. R. Tomlinson, "Economics and Empire: The Periphery and the Imperial Economy," in ibid., 53–74.

6. The scale of the emigration is quantified in Magee and Thompson, *Empire and Globalisation*, 68–69. For an overview of migration from Britain to its colonies in the nineteenth century, see Marjory Harper, "British Migration and the Peopling of the Empire," in Porter, *Oxford History of the British Empire*, 75–87.

7. Magee and Thompson, *Empire and Globalisation*, 36, 117, 118 (quote), 120, 124–125, 135, 166.

8. Ibid., 133–134; Green, "Nineteenth-Century Metropolitan Economy," 11.

9. On the importance of personal reputation in the colonial environment and litigation to defend it, see McKenzie, *Scandal in the Colonies*, 84–86; Magee and Thompson, *Empire and Globalisation*, 50, 203. For court cases involving Jewish businessmen in Cape Town and Sydney, see McKenzie, *Scandal in the Colonies*, 69–89.

10. See Francesca Trivellato, *The Familiarity of Strangers: The Sephardic Diaspora, Livorno, and Cross-Cultural Trade in the Early Modern Period* (New Haven: Yale University Press, 2009), 11–16. For a contrasting view, see Avner Greif, "Reputation and Coalitions in Medieval Trade: Evidence of the Maghribi Traders," *Journal of Economic History* 49, 4 (1989): 857–882; Greif, "Contract Enforceability and Economic Institutions in Early Trade: The Maghribi Traders' Coalition," *American Economic Review* 83, 3 (June 1993): 525–548.

11. Quote from Richard Bickell, *The West Indies as They Are* (London: J. Hatchard, 1825), 66–67; John Stewart, *A View of the Past and Present State of the Island of Jamaica* (Edinburgh: Oliver and Boyd, 1823), 200; Frederic Bayley, *Four Years' Residence in the West Indies* (London: W. Kidd, 1831), 31; Hannah Adams, *History of the Jews* (London: London Society, 1840), 458.

12. On peddlers in South Africa, see Milton Shain, " 'Vant to Puy a Vaatch': The Smous and Pioneer Trader in South African Jewish Historiography," *Jewish Affairs*, Sept. 1987, 111–128.

13. Ross, *Clothing*, 69; Naggar, "Old Clothes-Men," 175; John Levi, *These Are the Names* (Melbourne: Melbourne University Publishing, 2006), 829–831.

14. Quote from William Shaw, *Golden Dreams and Waking Realities* (London: Smith, Elder, 1851), 313–314; Maynard, *Fashioned from Penury*, 131; Hilary Rubinstein, *Chosen: The Jews in Australia* (Sydney: Allen and Unwin, 1987), 68; *London Saturday Journal*, Apr. 3, 1841, 158.

15. For contemporary descriptions of Sydney and Melbourne, see Martin, *British Colonies*, 453–457, 598–600. On early Melbourne and its economy, see Geoffrey Serle, *The Golden*

Age: A History of the Colony of Victoria, 1851–61 (Melbourne: Melbourne University Press, 1977), 2–8. For population figures in Melbourne and its hinterland, see Lynette J. Peel, *Rural Industry in the Port Phillip Region, 1835–1880* (Melbourne: Melbourne University Press, 1974), 18, 57; Serle, *Golden Age,* 382.

16. See Howitt, *Impressions of Australia Felix,* 118; Hilary Rubinstein, *The Jews in Australia: A Thematic History,* vol. 1, *1788–1945* (Port Melbourne, Victoria: Heineman, 1991), 87.

17. Maynard, *Fashioned from Penury,* 39, 118, 124. On local clothing manufacturing, see ibid., 120. On the sale of stock from London, see Lazarus Morris Goldman, *The Jews in Victoria in the Nineteenth Century* (Melbourne, Australia: L. M. Goldman, 1954), 45; Rubinstein, *Jews in Australia,* 85.

18. Henry Mayhew, letter 45, in *Voices of the Poor: Selections from the "Morning Chronicle" "Labour and the Poor,"* ed. Anne Humphries (London: Frank Cass, 1971), 20. This view was echoed in *Sidney's Emigrant's Journal,* July 12, 1849, 323.

19. Ira Cohen, "The Auction System in the Port of New York, 1817–1837," *Business History Review* 45, 4 (1971): 489, 495–496, 498; Zakim, *Ready-Made Democracy,* 45.

20. Kinahan Cornwallis, *A Panorama of the New World* (London: T. C. Newby, 1859), 55–59, 63–66; McKenzie, *Scandal in the Colonies,* 69–79; Rubinstein, *Jews in Australia,* 104–105. For clothing auctions in Australia, see Maynard, *Fashioned from Penury,* 40.

21. On this accusation in London, see Burn, *Language of the Walls,* 39–44; Andrew Wynter, *Our Social Bees* (London: Robert Hardwicke, 1861), 35–42; Cowen and Cowen, *Victorian Jews,* 8–10. On New York, see *New York Herald,* July 8, 1841; Foster, *New York in Slices,* 33–36; George Foster, *New York by Gas-Light and Other Urban Sketches* (Berkeley: University of California Press, 1990), 209–211; Feldman, *Fit for Men,* 25; Goettsch, "Pinchbeck Capitalism."

22. William Kelly, *Life in Victoria,* 2 vols. (London: Chapman and Hall, 1859), 1:118–119; see also John Stewart, *An Account of Jamaica* (London: Longman, Hurst, Rees, and Orme, 1808), 151.

23. See, for example, the effort to standardize store hours reported in Goldman, *Jews in Victoria,* 38–39.

24. Records of the Sun Fire Office, MS 11936/457/879744, MS 11936/479/966353, MS 11936/506/1045585, MS 11936/555/1250004, MS 11936/517/1098528, MS 11936/563/1031882, Guildhall Library; *Old Bailey Proceedings,* Oct. 30, 1816, 35; Apr. 16, 1817, 42; Mar. 1835, 144; *Pigot & Co. London Commercial Directory,* 1826–1827; insurance records for Samuel Moses for 1779, 1794, and 1802 and letters of administration from the London Commissary Court, May 1806, in the collection of George Rigal.

25. See Levi, *These Are the Names,* 369–371 (quote on 370).

26. Lawrence Nathan, "Thirty-Eight Presidents," *Australian Jewish Historical Society* 9, 7 (1984): 487–501; "Appendix 3: Records of Jewish Deaths in Tasmania 1804–1954: A Consolidated List," *A Few from Afar: Jewish Lives in Tasmania from 1804,* ed. Peter Elias and Ann Elias (Hobart, Australia: Hobart Hebrew Congregation, 2003): 232; Lawrence Nathan, *As Old as Auckland: The History of LD Nathan & Co. Ltd and of the David Nathan Family, 1840–1980* (Auckland, New Zealand: Benton Ross, 1984), 17–19, 53–54, 62, 125, 146; Kelly, *Life in Victoria,* 1:147; Goldman, *Jews in Victoria,* 92; Levi

and Bergman, *Australian Genesis*, 213, 249, 268, 295; *Official Descriptive and Illustrated Catalogue of the Great Exhibition*, part 4: "Colonies–Foreign States" (London: Spicer Brothers and W. Clowes, 1851), 990–991; Chapman, "Innovating Entrepreneurs," 10.

27. Levi, *These Are the Names*, 86.

28. Insurance records reveal a significant jump in his insured property in the 1830s. For sales to clothiers in England, see *Draper and Clothier* 1 (1860): 45.

29. Records of the Sun Fire Office, MS 11936/557/1234829, Guildhall Library; *Furniture Gazette*, Oct. 11, 1879, 246; *Old Bailey Proceedings*, Aug. 23, 1841, 16; Feb. 3, 1845, 78; Oct. 27, 1845, 109–110; May 5, 1861, 13; 1851 census, HO 107/1532 175, National Archives; Sharpe, "Cheapness and Economy," 207.

30. Henry Mayhew and John Binny, *The Criminal Prisons of London* (London: Griffin, Bohn, 1862), 195, 254, 476; *Times*, Feb. 25, 1825, 4.

31. Chapman, "Innovating Entrepreneurs," 23.

32. Martin, *British Colonies*, 6; *Official Descriptive and Illustrated Catalogue*, 991. Moses was identified in the 1850 census as a colonial merchant.

33. On the paucity of credit in the colonies, see McKenzie, *Scandal in the Colonies*, 84–86; John Darwin, "Imperialism and the Victorians: The Dynamics of Territorial Expansion," *English Historical Review* 112, 447 (1997): 627.

34. Goldman, *Jews in Victoria*, 48.

35. Quoted in Rubinstein, *Jews in Australia*, 68–69.

36. John Askew, *A Voyage to Australia & New Zealand* (London: Simkin, Marshall, 1857), 327.

37. Goldman, *Jews in Victoria*, 45.

38. Magee and Thompson, *Empire and Globalisation*, 58, 157.

39. Ibid., 24, 155.

40. For examples, see Ava F. Kahn, "Looking at America from the West to the East, 1850–1920s," in Kahn, *Jewish Life in the American West*, 18; Glanz, *Jews of California*, 75.

41. Maynard, *Fashioned from Penury*, 169; Levi and Bergman, *Australian Genesis*, 310. On travel between Australia and California, see Serle, *Golden Age*, 65, 76; Charles Bateson, *Gold Fleet for Australia* (East Lansing: Michigan State University Press, 1963), 142. For Jewish merchants who shipped supplies to San Francisco from Australia, see Bateson, *Gold Fleet*, 24–25, 38, 97, 116–118, 156.

42. For the excitement in Britain, see Serle, *Golden Age*, 37–47. For immigration statistics, see ibid., 46, 383–385; Belich, *Replenishing the Earth*, 83. Serle estimates that two-thirds of all migration from Britain in the 1850s and 1860s was to the United States. For technological change in transportation, see Daniel Headrick, *The Tools of Empire: Technology and European Imperialism in the Nineteenth Century* (New York: Oxford University Press, 1981), 144–148; Robert Kubicek, "British Expansion, Empire, and Technological Change," in Porter, *Oxford History of the British Empire*, vol. 3, 249–251; *Jewish Chronicle*, Feb. 24, 1854. On immigration schemes, see Magee and Thompson, *Empire and Globalisation*, 71.

43. Between 1840 and 1861 the total Australian Jewish population grew from approximately 1,183 to around 5,486. Men made up roughly two-thirds of the community. See

Rubinstein, *Jews in Australia*, 90; Suzanne D. Rutland, *Edge of the Diaspora: Two Centuries of Jewish Settlement in Australia* (New York: Holmes and Meier, 1997), 50.

44. George W. Peck, *Melbourne, and the Chincha Islands* (New York: Charles Scribner, 1854), 105–106.

45. Quoted in Serle, *Golden Age*, 67.

46. *United States Economist* 2 (Nov. 6, 1852): 44. On the economic impact of the gold rush, see Peel, *Rural Industry*, 57–59, 154–155; Weston Bate, *Victorian Gold Rushes* (Ballarat, Australia: Sovereign Hill Museums Association, 1999), 8–24; M. Z. Forbes, "The Jews of NSW and the Gold Rushes," *Australian Jewish Historical Society Journal* 12, 2 (1994): 282–326. On the demographic impact, see Bate, *Victorian Gold Rushes*, 25–33.

47. On Edward, David, and Lawrence Moss in Montreal, see General Railroad Celebration Committee, *Montreal in 1856: A Sketch Prepared for the Celebration of the Opening of the Grand Trunk Railway of Canada* (Montreal: John Lovell, 1856), 46; Gerald Tulchinsky, *The River Barons* (Toronto: University of Toronto Press, 1977), 219–220; Tulchinsky, *Canada's Jews* (Toronto: University of Toronto Press, 2008), 43–44; Tulchinsky, *Taking Root*, 70; Tulchinsky, "Said to Be a Very Honest Jew," 206. On the expense of clothing in Canada, see *Sidney's Emigrant's Journal*, Nov. 23, 1848, 59. For tariffs, see Martin, *British Colonies*, 141, 144.

48. *Port Phillip Herald*, Dec. 2, 1842; Dec. 19, 1843; *Jewish Chronicle*, July 30, 1897; Bill Williams, *The Making of Manchester Jewry, 1740–1875* (Manchester: Manchester University Press, 1985), 321–323; Pollins, *Economic History*, 98–101; Rodney Benjamin, "David Benjamin of Launceston, Melbourne and Bayswater (London), 1815–1893," in Elias and Elias, *Few from Afar*, 61–62.

49. See *Hobart Courier*, Feb. 22, 1853, 1; *Melbourne Argus*, Feb. 12, 1856, 7; Feb. 20, 1856, 2; Mar. 19, 1856, 2; Apr. 8, 1856, 8; Kelly, *Life in Victoria*, 1:147, 2:341. The firm only appears to have reentered the Australian market—without a local store—in the mid-1860s.

50. *United States Economist* 2 (Nov. 6, 1852): 43, 45; Goldman, *Jews in Victoria*, 28; Maynard, *Fashioned from Penury*, 122, 148–149, 161–162, 173, 184. On the economic crisis of 1854 and 1857, see Serle, *Golden Age*, 239–241.

51. *Punch* 27 (1854): 132; John Timbs, *Walks and Talks about London* (London: Lockwood, 1865), 1–2. For advertisements for clothing, see *Ecclesiastical Gazette*, May 8, 1860, 289; Jacob Larwood and John Hotten, *The History of Signboards* (London: John Camden Hotten, 1867), 486; *Times*, Dec. 17, 1856, 14; June 11, 1858, 13; June 14, 1864, 16; May 11, 1869, 14; June 1, 1869, 14.

52. *Law Times*, June 21, 1873, 154.

53. Benjamin Godwin, *Godwin's Emigrant's Guide*; quote from Sidney Smith, *The Settler's New Home* (London: John Kendrick, 1850), 51.

54. Kelly, *Life in Victoria*, 1: 53; *Melbourne Punch*, Apr. 14, 1859; "Canvass Town," *Anglo-American Magazine* 3 (Sept. 1853): 265–266; Arthur Polehampton, *Kangaroo Land* (London: Richard Bentley, 1862), 123; Henry Turner, *A History of the Colony of Victoria* (London: Longmans, Green, 1904), 371; M. Riley, "Cast-Offs: Civilization, Charity or Commerce? Aspects of Second Hand Clothing Use in Australia 1788–1900," in Palmer and Clark, *Old Clothes, New Looks*, 58–59; Les Hughes, *Henry Mundy: A Young*

Australian Pioneer (Brisbane, Australia: Next Century Books, 2003), 174; Serle, *Golden Age*, 66–67.

55. Quote from Rubinstein, *Jews in Australia*, 69; Goldman, *Jews in Victoria*, 163.

56. Maynard, *Fashioned from Penury*, 40, 132, 146; Serle, *Golden Age*, 72.

57. William Howitt, *Land, Labour, and Gold*, vol. 2 (London: Longman, Brown, Green, Longmans, and Roberts, 1858), 138. For an evocative description of life in the early mining camps, see Serle, *Golden Age*, 29–31, 74–76, 218.

58. A census conducted in 1861 found that trading (merchants, shopkeepers, bankers, clerks, shop assistants) constituted the third-most-common occupation for employed adult men on the Victorian gold fields; a little over half as many men worked in this field as did in manufacturing. Gold mining claimed by far the largest share. See Bate, *Victorian Gold Rushes*, 37. For the population shift, see ibid., 51–52, 56; Levi and Bergman, *Australian Genesis*, 237–238, 252, 258; Rubinstein, *Jews in Australia*, 89–94. On the more reliable rewards of provisioning the miners, see Serle, *Golden Age*, 86.

59. *Medical Times & Gazette*, Oct. 15, 1859, 394; "Pre-Registration Deeds of Title," LBL/DALS/12/8, Lambeth Archives Department, London; Frederick Pollock, *The Law Reports: Chancery Division*, vol. 1 (London: William Clowes and Son, 1902), 100–103; Chapman, "Innovating Entrepreneurs," 14.

60. Records of the Sun Fire Office, MS 11936/464/899316, MS 11936/536/1154989, MS 11936/537/1148723, Guildhall Library; "The Life of Jacob Frankel," *Australian Jewish Historical Society Journal* 13, 3 (1996): 401; Levi, *These Are the Names*, 556–557; Levi and Bergman, *Australian Genesis*, 249–250, 295, 312; Last Will and Testament of Jacob Moses, dated Mar. 20, 1845, and Last Will and Testament of Moses Moses, dated Mar. 20, 1845, photocopies in the possession of George Rigal.

61. Mills, *British Jews*, 264. Weale made a similar assessment in *Pictorial Handbook of London*, 533.

NOTES TO CHAPTER 6

1. For numbers of Jewish clothiers in 1816, see Hershkowitz, "Some Aspects of the New York Jewish Merchant," 32–34; for the 1830 census, see Rosenwaike, *On the Edge of Greatness*, 147–150. For the size of the Jewish population of New York, see Howard Rock, *Haven of Liberty: New York Jews in the New World, 1654–1865* (New York: NYU Press, 2012), 155. For New York's advantages as a manufacturing hub, see Wilentz, *Chants Democratic*, 111; John Lauritz Larson, *The Market Revolution in America* (New York: Cambridge University Press, 2010), 37, 50–51.

2. Feldman, *Fit for Men*, 35; James M. McPherson, *Battle Cry of Freedom* (New York: Oxford University Press, 2003), 9; Stott, *Workers in the Metropolis*, 35, 38.

3. George Templeton Strong, *The Diary of George Templeton Strong: Young Man in New York, 1835–1849* (New York: Macmillan, 1952), 131.

4. On cotton and slave prices, see Jenny Wahl, "*Dred*, Panic, War," in *Congress and the Crises of the 1850s*, ed. Paul Finkelman and Donald R. Kennon (Athens: Ohio University Press, 2012), 177–178. On the panic of 1837, see Jessica Lepler, "1837: Anatomy of a Panic" (PhD diss., Brandeis University, 2008).

5. Quoted in Andrew Goodheart, *1861: The Civil War Awakening* (New York: Knopf, 2011), 315.
6. Johnson, *River of Dark Dreams*, 257.
7. The Mississippi's share of Midwestern trade declined dramatically during the three decades preceding the Civil War. See Pred, *Urban Growth and City Systems*, 103–104. On Louisiana's boom during the 1850s, see Marler, "Merchants and the Political Economy," 18, 49–50, 92–93. For cotton shipped through New Orleans, see Gudmestad, *Steamboats and the Rise of the Cotton Kingdom*, 144; Johnson, *River of Dark Dreams*, 256–257. On commercial shipping along the Mississippi, see White, *Wet Britches*, 179–191; Johnson, *River of Dark Dreams*, 6–8, 73–96. On New York's cotton exports, see Spann, *New Metropolis*, 5.
8. Quote from Belich, *Replenishing the Earth*, 244. Scott Marler estimates that Louisiana had the highest per capita investment in retailing in the United States, nearly twice that of New York. See Marler, "Merchants and the Political Economy," 31–33. On the composition of the city, see ibid., 10–14. On trade, see ibid., 48–50, 76, 148; Johnson, *River of Dark Dreams*, 2, 6–7; "Historical Census Browser," Geospatial and Statistical Data Center, University of Virginia: http://mapserver.lib.virginia.edu/collections/ (accessed August 3, 2012). On the population bordering the Mississippi, see Gudmestad, *Steamboats and the Rise of the Cotton Kingdom*, 5. For journey times along the Mississippi, see Johnson, *River of Dark Dreams*, 104–106. For the extent of steam-navigable river way, see Johnson, *River of Dark Dreams*, 87.
9. *The Commercial Agency Record, January 1861, Dry Goods, Fancy Goods, Cloths, Clothing, Hats, Caps, Furs, Straw Goods, Etc.* (New York: McKillop & Co. Commercial Agency, 1861), HG3751.7.M45 1861, New-York Historical Society; Ashkenazi, *Business of Jews in Louisiana*, 104–108.
10. Quote from Feldman, *Fit for Men*, 29; Ashkenazi, *Business of Jews in Louisiana*, 18, 105, 109–110, 113, 117, 197n32; Feldman, "Jews in the Early Growth of New York City's Men's Clothing Trade," 8–9; Bennett Wall, "Leon Godchaux and the Godchaux Business Enterprise," *American Jewish Historical Quarterly* 66 (1977): 56.
11. Gerstäcker, *Adventures and Hunting Expeditions*, 37–38.
12. Ashkenazi, *Business of Jews in Louisiana*, 105–108, 116. The classic study of cotton factorage is Harold D. Woodman's *King Cotton and His Retainers* (Lexington: University of Kentucky Press, 1968), 5–96; see also Johnson, *River of Dark Dreams*, 271–278. For descriptions of peddling in rural Mississippi, see Seessel, *Memoirs of a Mexican Veteran*, 18–19; Julius Weis, "Peddler in the Deep South," in Marcus, *Memoirs of American Jews*, 2:51. For a discussion of the ratio of planters to small farmers in Mississippi, see John Hebron Moore, *The Emergence of the Cotton Kingdom in the Old Southwest* (Baton Rouge: Louisiana State University Press, 1988), 116–155. On the proliferation of country stores, see Marler, "Merchants and the Political Economy," 107–151; John C. Willis, *Forgotten Time: The Yazoo-Mississippi Delta after the Civil War* (Charlottesville: University Press of Virginia, 2000), 82; Michael Stuart Wayne, "Ante-Bellum Planters in the Post-Bellum South: The Natchez District, 1860–1880" (PhD diss., Yale University, 1979), 235–236.

13. *Asmonean*, 1, 26 (Apr. 19, 1850): 208; Polk quoted in J. S. Holliday, *The World Rushed In* (Norman, OK: Red River Books, 2002), 48.

14. *Asmonean*, 14 (Jan. 25, 1850): 109; *Asmonean*, 1, 15 (Feb. 1, 1850): 117; Glanz, *Jews of California*, 20.

15. For an overview of the rush, see Malcolm Rohrbough, "No Boy's Play: Migration and Settlement in Early Gold Rush California," *California History* 79, 1 (2000): 25–43. On the image of Jews relative to other groups, see Decker, *Fortunes and Failures*, 116, 118; Ellen Eisenberg, Ava F. Kahn, and William Toll, *Jews of the Pacific Coast* (Seattle: University of Washington Press, 2009), 19. On tolerance and segregation, see Robert Phelps, " 'All Hands Have Gone Downtown': Urban Places in Gold Rush California," *California History* 79, 1 (2000): 131; Sucheng Chan, "A People of Exceptional Character: Ethnic Diversity, Nativism, and Racism in the California Gold Rush," *California History* 79, 1 (2000): 58–60. On criminality, see Mary Floyd Williams, ed., *Papers of the San Francisco Committee of Vigilance of 1851* (Berkeley: University of California Press, 1919).

16. Stott, *Workers in the Metropolis*, 253; Belich, *Replenishing the Earth*, 307.

17. Figures extracted from Jacob Rader Marcus, *To Count a People: American Jewish Population Data, 1585–1984* (Lanham, MD: Rowman and Littlefield, 1990), 20–31; Glanz, *Jews of California*, 5; on Jews in California before the gold rush, see Glanz, *Jews of California*, 18.

18. Julius Weis, *Autobiography of Julius Weis*, 11; see also Ashkenazi, *Business of Jews in Louisiana*, 14.

19. For the techniques and profit margins of miners, see Keith L. Bryant Jr., "Entering the Global Economy," in *The Oxford History of the American West*, ed. Clyde A. Milner II, Carol A. O'Connor, and Martha A. Sandweiss (New York: Oxford University Press, 1996), 199–208. On the decision to become a merchant rather than a miner, see Decker, *Fortunes and Failures*, 9–11. For a profile of San Francisco's merchant class, see Decker, *Fortunes and Failures*, 24–25, 33.

20. Theodore Seligman, *In Memoriam: Jesse Seligman* (New York: Philip Cowen, 1894), 10–12; Harriet Rochlin and Fred Rochlin, *Pioneer Jews: A New Life in the Far West* (New York: Houghton Mifflin, 2000), 54–55; quote from Decker, *Fortunes and Failures*, 12. For the dispersion of Jews in California and their commercial activities, see Moses Rischin, "The Jewish Experience in America: A View from the West," in *Jews of the American West*, ed. Moses Rischin and John Livingston (Detroit: Wayne State University Press, 1991), 34; Levinson, *Jews in the California Gold Rush*, 20, 29–32, 39–40; Glanz, *Jews of California*, 53–61, 85. On Jews and gambling in California, see Albert M. Friedenberg, "Letters of a Californian Pioneer," *Publications of the American Jewish Historical Society* 31 (1928): 159; Glanz, *Jews of California*, 29, 34; on the mutual-aid society for clerks, see Glanz, *Jews of California*, 35.

21. Ava Kahn, personal communication, 2013.

22. Decker, *Fortunes and Failures*, 91–93. See also ibid., 147–149, 164. For data on mobility, see Jeffrey Haydu, *Citizen Employers: Business Communities and Labor in Cincinnati and San Francisco, 1870–1916* (Ithaca: Cornell University Press, 2008), 62–64.

23. For an early description of San Francisco as New York of the Pacific, see *Letter from Albert H. Campbell to Hon. Guy M. Bryan, of Texas, in Relation to the Pacific Railroad* (Washington, DC, 1858), 7. John C. Calhoun predicted in 1844 that a city built on the San Francisco Bay would become "the New York of the Pacific Coast"; Joseph Carey, *By the Golden Gate* (Albany, NY: Albany Diocesan Press, 1902), 290. Rischin, "Jewish Experience in America," 35 (synagogues).

24. Hinton Helper, *The Land of Gold* (Baltimore: Henry Taylor, 1855), 51–55.

25. Cited in Decker, "Jewish Merchants in San Francisco," 403n10. On the composition of the city's population in 1860, see William Issel and Robert W. Cherny, *San Francisco, 1865–1932: Politics, Power, and Urban Development* (Berkeley: University of California Press, 1986), 14. For a breakdown of the occupations of Jews, see Seth Bernstein, "The Economic Life of the Jews in San Francisco during the 1860's as Reflected in the City Directories," *American Jewish Archives Journal* 27, 1 (1975): 70–75.

26. J. D. Borthwick, *Three Years in California* (Edinburgh: William Blackwood, 1857), 116, 120. On Jewish-owned clothing stores in mining camps see, Levinson, *Jews in the California Gold Rush*, 27–30, 45–48.

27. Quote from Chan, "People of Exceptional Character," 57; Phelps, "All Hands Have Gone Downtown," 124; Norton B. Stern, "Trouble from a Charitable Gift at Rough and Ready, California, 1856," *Western States Jewish History*, April 1, 1985, 265–268.

28. Eliza W. Farnham, *California, In-Doors and Out* (New York: Dix, Edwards, 1856), 365 (tradesmen quote); Lulu May Garrett, "San Francisco in 1851, as Described by Eyewitnesses," *California Historical Society Quarterly* 22, 3 (Sept. 1943): 254; Diary of Dr. Thomas Massie of Nelson County, VA, Mss1 M3855 e 64, Virginia Historical Society, Richmond. My thanks to Shari Rabin for sharing this source with me.

29. Helper, *Land of Gold*, 51–55; see also Fred Rosenbaum, *Cosmopolitans: A Social and Cultural History of the Jews of the San Francisco Bay Area* (Berkeley: University of California Press, 2009), 9.

30. The agency assessed 1,676 businesses in New York City. *Commercial Agency Record 1861*.

31. Decker estimates that German-born traders constituted the largest single group among foreign-born petty and general merchants in the city; of these, "well over half" were Jews. He was incorrect, however, to assume that German Jews lacked access to sources of credit. Decker, *Fortunes and Failures*, 66–86, 96–97.

32. For a firsthand account of doing business in San Francisco, see Caspar T. Hopkins, "The California Recollections of Caspar T. Hopkins," *California Historical Society Quarterly* 26, 1 (Mar. 1947): 63–75. On imports, see Belich, *Replenishing the Earth*, 314.

33. "A Sonora Suicide," *Sonora Union Democrat*, 1869, in *Jewish Voices of the California Gold Rush*, ed. Ava F. Kahn (Detroit: Wayne State University Press, 2002), 343–344 (Ritzwoller quote). On Norton, see Benjamin Lloyd, "Joshua Abraham Norton I, an Emperor and an English Jew," 1876, in ibid., 447–450; Albert Evans, *Our Sister Republic: A Gala Trip through Tropical Mexico in 1869–70* (Hartford, CT: Columbian, 1873), 377–379 (Norton quote on 377); Rochlin and Rochlin, *Pioneer Jews*, 169–170; Louis Herrman, "The Fantastic Career of Joshua Abraham Norton," in *Essays in Honour of the Very Rev. Dr. J. H. Hertz*, ed. Isidore Epstein (London: E. Goldston, 1942). For Mark

Twain's comments on Norton, see Lawrence Howe, *Mark Twain and the Novel* (New York: Cambridge University Press, 1998), 234n1.

34. Decker, *Fortunes and Failures*, 95.

35. Quotes from New York Trade Agency Reports 1851, BV New York Trade Agency, New-York Historical Society; *Gleaner*, May 31, 1861; Friedenberg, "Letters of a Californian Pioneer," 159–160 (quote about death by fire). Seligman, *Jesse Seligman*, 12. On fires, see Decker, *Fortunes and Failures*, 92; Friedenberg, "Californian Pioneer," 153–154, 157–158. For an account of claiming delinquent debt, see Friedenberg, "Letters of a Californian Pioneer," 148, 151. On the rate of business failure in San Francisco, see Decker, *Fortunes and Failures*, 90–94.

36. Friedenberg, "Letters of a Californian Pioneer," 139–143; see also "Samuel Oscar Alexander: California Merchant," *American Jewish Archives Journal* 7, 1 (1955): 85–89.

37. On credit and the costs of doing business, see Decker, *Fortunes and Failures*, 13–19, 37–44.

38. Friedenberg, "Letters of a Californian Pioneer," 146.

39. Ibid., 150, 158. By June Mayer had suffered further losses because of fire. His wish was "only to bring back Again" what he had "lossed by the Two fires" (158).

40. For comparison of Australia and California, see Walter Nugent, "Comparing Wests and Frontiers," in Milner, O'Connor, and Sandweiss, *Oxford History of the American West*, 821–823; Philip Ross May, "Gold Rushes of the Pacific Borderlands: A Comparative Survey," in *Provincial Perspectives: Essays in Honour of W. J. Gardner*, ed. Len Richardson and W. David McIntyre (Christchurch, New Zealand: University of Canterbury, 1980), 97–98; Belich, *Replenishing the Earth*. On travel, see Aims McGuiness, *Path of Empire: Panama and the California Gold Rush* (Ithaca: Cornell University Press, 2008), 6–7.

41. Friedenberg, "Letters of a Californian Pioneer," 144.

42. Williams, *Manchester Jewry*, 119; New York Trade Agency Reports 1851. For an example of fraud by an English Jew in 1850, see T. A. Barry and B. A. Patten, *Men and Memories of San Francisco in the "Spring of '50"* (San Francisco: A. L. Bankroft, 1873), 244–245. On travel to California, see White, *Wet Britches*, 28–31; Bryant, "Entering the Global Economy," 208–212. On freight rates, see Decker, *Fortunes and Failures*, 93; on merchants who had failed elsewhere, see Decker, *Fortunes and Failures*, 98. For a firsthand account of travel across Panama by a Jewish merchant, see Friedenberg, "Letters of a Californian Pioneer," 135–139. On Texas, see Belich, *Replenishing the Earth*, 241 (quote).

43. Friedenberg, "Letters of a Californian Pioneer," 143, 150–151.

44. For the unpredictability of business cycles and the importance of information, see Decker, *Fortunes and Failures*, 34–44. For an example of how commercial information was relayed, see the extensive correspondence in Friedenberg, "Letters of a Californian Pioneer."

45. Haydu, *Citizen Employers*, 62–64; Issel and Cherny, *San Francisco*, 25, 27, 29; Lynn Downey, "Levi Strauss Invented Western Work Clothes for Miners, Cowboys, and Engineers," in *The American Frontier: Opposing Viewpoints*, ed. Mary Ellen Jones (San Diego: Greenhaven, 1994), 272–276.

46. *Asmonean*, Oct. 30, 1857; *Commercial Agency Record 1861*.

47. *Asmonean* 17 (Oct. 16, 1857): 1; Oct. 30, 1857.

48. *Occident* 15, 10 (Jan. 1858): 462–469. For the impact of the crisis, see Belich, *Replenishing the Earth*, 229, 317.

49. Calculated using the *Commercial Agency Record 1861*. It does not necessarily mean that the remainder failed—they may have added or removed partners, moved to other cities, or escaped the attention of credit-agency reporters.

50. Lockwood, *Manhattan Moves Uptown*, 256.

51. Edward K. Spann, *Gotham at War: New York City, 1860–1865* (Wilmington, DE: SR Books, 2002), 6–7, 10, 135–136; Burrows and Wallace, *Gotham*, 864–868; Goodheart, *1861*, 73–74. On bank failures, see Benjamin J. Klebaner, *American Commercial Banking: A History* (Washington, DC: Beard Books, 2005), 257n6. On Straus, see Isidor Straus, "A Young Confederate Businessman," in Marcus, *Memoirs of American Jews*, 2:316–319 (quote on 318).

52. *Jewish Messenger*, Dec. 5, 1862. For a description of this section of Broadway, see Lockwood, *Manhattan Moves Uptown*, 96.

NOTES TO CHAPTER 7

1. On Mordecai, see Stanley L. Falk, "Divided Loyalties in 1861: The Decision of Major Alfred Mordecai," in *Jews and the Civil War: A Reader*, ed. Jonathan D. Sarna and Adam Mendelsohn (New York: NYU Press, 2011), 207. Myers's tenure is described in Harold S. Wilson, *Confederate Industry* (Jackson: University Press of Mississippi, 2002), 3–92. For the obstacles facing Myers and Gorgas, see Wilson, *Confederate Industry*, 39, 102–103; Richard D. Goff, *Confederate Supply* (Durham: Duke University Press, 1969), 67–68; McPherson, *Battle Cry of Freedom*, 91, 95, 318.

2. Edward C. Anderson, *Confederate Foreign Agent: The European Diary of Major Edward C. Anderson*, ed. Stanley W. Hoole (University, AL: Confederate Publishing, 1976), 3, 39, 23, 43; John D. Bennett, *The London Confederates* (Jefferson, NC: McFarland, 2008), 54.

3. See Michael Jolles, *Samuel Isaac, Saul Isaac and Nathaniel Isaac* (London: Jolles, 1998), 44–45. For Samuel Isaac and his family, see ibid., 3–6, 11, 14–16, 43–46, 207. For a more detailed discussion of the firm's activities before and during the Civil War, see Adam Mendelsohn, "Samuel and Saul Isaac: International Jewish Arms Dealers, Blockade Runners, and Civil War Profiteers," *Southern Jewish History* 15 (2012): 41–79.

4. See David Waller, "Northampton and the American Civil War," *Northamptonshire Past & Present* 8, 2 (1990–1991): 137–139; *Jewish Chronicle*, Feb. 1, 1856; *Parliamentary Papers, Great Britain, Parliament, House of Commons*, 1858, "Fifth Report from Select Committee on Contracts (Public Departments)," q. 6864.

5. The most thorough account of the episode is provided in C. L. Webster, *Entrepôt: Government Imports into the Confederate States* (Roseville, MN: Edinborough, 2009), 21–27; and Mendelsohn, "Samuel and Saul Isaac."

6. For Samuel Isaac's account of the contract and his trip to Naples, see *Northampton Mercury*, Jan. 5, 1861, 8. On the British Legion, see George Macaulay Trevelyan, *Garibaldi and the Making of Italy* (London: Longmans, Green, 1912), 98–99, 259–260.

7. McPherson, *Battle Cry of Freedom*, 324.

8. Philip Scranton, *Proprietary Capitalism: The Textile Manufacture at Philadelphia, 1800–1885* (New York: Cambridge University Press, 2003), 281.

9. Mark Wilson, *The Business of the Civil War: Military Mobilization and the State, 1861–1865* (Baltimore: Johns Hopkins University Press, 2006), 1, 5–6, 9, 11, 13, 19–22, 91; Wilson, "The Business of the Civil War: Military Enterprise, the State, and Political Economy in the United States, 1850–1880" (PhD diss., University of Chicago, 2002), 436, 444–445. To see total wartime purchases, see United States War Department, *War of the Rebellion: A Compilation of the Union and Confederate Armies* (*Washington, DC: Government Printing Office, 1880–1901*), ser. 4, vol. 5, 284–285.

10. *New York Times*, Nov. 10, 1861, 8, quoted in Spann, *Gotham at War*, 52.

11. For a more detailed account, see Adam Mendelsohn, "Beyond the Battlefield: Reevaluating the Legacy of the Civil War for American Jews," *American Jewish Archives Journal* 64, 1–2 (2012): 82–111. For examples of opportunistic subcontracting, see Bruce S. Bazelon and William F. McGuinn, *A Directory of American Military Goods Dealers and Makers, 1785–1915* (Manassas, VA: W. F. McGuinn, 1990), 45, 47, 71, 126.

12. *Documents of the Assembly of the State of New York, Fifty-Eight Session, 1862, Volume 7* (Albany, NY: Charles Van Benthuysen, 1862), 378 (hereafter after cited as *Documents 1862*).

13. On Murphy, see S. R. Harlow and H. H. Boone, *Life Sketches of the State Officers, Senators, and Members of the Assembly of the State of New York, in 1867* (Albany, NY: Weed, Parsons, 1867), 125–127; *Documents 1862*, 62, 378.

14. *Documents 1862*, 62, 138, 393.

15. Wilson, "Business of the Civil War," 183.

16. Wilson, *Business of the Civil War*, 262n25. For other examples in the cap business, see *Documents 1862*, 375, 380–381, 388, 390–392.

17. *Journal of the Assembly of Wisconsin Annual Session of 1862, Volume 2* (Madison, WI: Smith and Cullaton, 1862), 1445–1447 (hereafter cited as *Wisconsin 1862*).

18. *Documents 1862*, 31–32, 179–180, 285, 342–343, 380.

19. Ibid., 386.

20. Ibid., 388.

21. The firm won contracts to supply 533,000 forage caps in 1864 alone. Ibid., 378; *Report of the Minority of the Select Committee to Investigate the Transactions of the State Military Board*, April 17, 1862, reprinted in William A. Jackson, *Memoir of William A. Jackson* (Albany, NY: Joel Munsell, 1862), 88; 131; Bazelon and McGuinn, *Directory of American Military Goods Dealers*, 131.

22. *Documents 1862*, 31–32, 108, 121–129, 458.

23. Ibid., 466; Bazelon and McGuinn, *Directory of American Military Goods Dealers*, 148.

24. *Documents 1862*, 276, 330, 567; Wilson, "Business of the Civil War," 450. On the Seligmans' efforts to sell war bonds, see Ross L. Muir and Carl J. White, *Over the Long Term: The Story of J. & W. Seligman & Co.* (New York: J. & W. Seligman, 1964), 28–29.

25. Sykes claimed that Mrs. Fountain paid for the sewing machine. *Documents Accompanying the Journal of the Senate and House of Representatives at the Biennial Session of 1863* (Lansing, MI: John A. Kerr, 1863), 10, 18–21.

26. Wilson, "Business of the Civil War," 191.

27. *Wisconsin 1862*, 1439–1447; Bazelon and McGuinn, *Directory of American Military Goods Dealers*, 78.

28. McPherson, *Battle Cry of Freedom*, 217, 225, 260, 324. For a summary of contracting scandals during the war, see Stuart D. Brandes, *Warhogs: A History of War Profits in America* (Lexington: University Press of Kentucky, 1997), 67–107.

29. These cities were joined by St. Louis, Washington, DC, and Louisville as sites of major depots. Wilson, *Business of the Civil War*, 6, 108; Burrows and Wallace, *Gotham*, 872.

30. *Documents 1862*, 193–194; Spann, *Gotham at War*, 46–47; Burrows and Wallace, *Gotham*, 875; Brandes, *Warhogs*, 70–73.

31. *Journal of Mining and Manufactures*, Dec. 1861, 627–628; "Army Sutler and His Profits," 51; Scranton, *Proprietary Capitalism*, 289–291.

32. *Journal of Mining and Manufactures*, Dec. 1861, 627–628. Some of these reports smacked of more than a little exaggeration. See, for example, *Supplement to the Hartford Courant*, Jan. 11, 1862, 5.

33. McPherson, *Battle Cry of Freedom*, 323.

34. See J. H. Robinson, *Barnaby, the Sandhiller, or the Planter's Ruse* (New York: Frederic A. Brady, 1862), 47; Burrows and Wallace, *Gotham*, 877–878; Wilson, *Business of the Civil War*, 149–150, 180; Brandes, *Warhogs*, 69–73; Michael Thomas Smith, *The Enemy Within: Fears of Corruption in the Civil War North* (Charlottesville: University of Virginia Press, 2011), 15–36; Strasser, *Waste and Want*, 96; *Times*, Nov. 16, 1863.

35. The mayor unsuccessfully sued an Albany editor for libel for writing that "George Opdyke has made more money upon army contracts than any fifty Jew sharpers in New York." Wilson, *Business of the Civil War*, 180–181.

36. Mary Chesnut, *Mary Chesnut's Civil War*, ed. C. Vann Woodward (New Haven: Yale University Press, 1983), 288–289; Jane Ridley, *Young Disraeli, 1804–1846* (New York: Crown, 1995), 200–203.

37. On the antisemitic dimensions of the term *contractor*, see Gary Bunker and John Appel, "Shoddy, Anti-Semitism, and the Civil War: The Visual Image," *American Jewish History* 82 (1994): 43–71.

38. Wilson, *Business of the Civil War*, 3, 103 (quote), 148–190.

39. Wilson, "Business of the Civil War," 209.

40. Wendy Jean Katz, *Regionalism and Reform: Art and Class Formation in Antebellum Cincinnati* (Columbus: Ohio State University Press, 2002), 5; Jonathan D. Sarna and Nancy H. Klein, *The Jews of Cincinnati* (Cincinnati: Center for the Study of the American Jewish Experience, 1989), 38; Charles Cist, *Cincinnati in 1841* (Cincinnati, 1841), 54–57; Charles Cist, *Sketches and Statistics of Cincinnati in 1859* (Cincinnati, 1859), 271, 363–364; Isaac Lippincott, "A History of Manufactures in the Ohio River Valley to 1860" (PhD diss., Chicago University, 1914), 91; *Israelite*, June 13, 1856, 399; Jun. 20, 1856, 407; Dec. 24, 1858, 196. Production figures for 1860 are from US Bureau of the Census, *Manufactures of the United States in 1860 Compiled from the Original Returns of the Eighth Census* (Washington, DC: Government Printing Office, 1865), lxi. For conflicting statistics, see Harry N. Scheiber, *Ohio Canal Era* (Athens: Ohio University Press, 2012), 339; Charles R. Wilson,

"Cincinnati a Southern Outpost in 1860–1861?," *Mississippi Valley Historical Review* 24, 4 (1938): 478; Cist, *Sketches and Statistics of Cincinnati*, 271. For an explanation of the statistical anomaly, see Pred, *Urban Growth and City Systems*, 257n150.

41. *Wisconsin 1862*, 1439–1444; Wilson, *Business of the Civil War*, 127–131. On the Seligman's financial predicament, see Muir and White, *Over the Long Term*, 26–27.

42. Wilson, "Business of the Civil War," 429, 449, 462. For Seasongood and Heidelbach's New York operation, see Bazelon and McGuinn, *Directory of American Military Goods Dealers*, 62.

43. *Israelite*, Dec. 12, 1861; Ohio, vol. 78, 1533, R.G. Dun & Co. Credit Report Volumes, Baker Library Historical Collections, Harvard Business School, Cambridge, MA. For Max Glaser's and Henry Mack's description of the contracting process, see "Government Contracts," Part 2, House Report 2, 37th Congress, 2nd session, ser. 1143, 765–767, 917–924.

44. On Henry Mack, see *Biographical Encyclopaedia of Ohio*, 186–187; Michael Rich, "Henry Mack: An Important Figure in Nineteenth-Century American Jewish History," *Stammbaum* 23 (2003): 1–10. On Grant's order, see Jonathan D. Sarna, *When Grant Expelled the Jews* (New York: Nextbook, 2012), chapter 1.

45. See Max Glaser interviewed Dec. 31, 1861, "Government Contracts," Part 2, House Report 2, 37th Congress, 2nd session, ser. 1143, 766; Wilson, *Business of the Civil War*, 17, 124, 126, 235; Wilson, "Business of the Civil War," 449, 463; "Clothing for the Army of the Union," *American Jewish Archives* 13 (1961): 174–175. For a rival consortium in Cincinnati (Henderson, Fecheimer, Krause, Frankel & Co.), see Bazelon and McGuinn, *Directory of American Military Goods Dealers*, 43.

46. *Brevier Legislative Reports Embracing Short-Hand Sketches of the Journals and Debates of the General Assembly of the State of Indiana, Volume 5* (Indianapolis: Daily Indiana State Sentinel, 1861), 147; Wilson, "Business of the Civil War," 192; Wilson, *Business of the Civil War*, 17.

47. George Clark interviewed March 11, 1862, "Government Contracts," Part 2, House Report 2, 37th Congress, 2nd session, ser. 1143, 974.

48. Wilson, *Business of the Civil War*, 121, 436; Wilson, "Business of the Civil War," 198; Spann, *Gotham at War*, 152–153.

49. Henry Mack interviewed March 10, 1862, "Government Contracts," Part 2, House Report 2, 37th Congress, 2nd session, ser. 1143, 923–924.

50. For a detailed discussion of this subject, see Mendelsohn, "Samuel and Saul Isaac."

51. In Indianapolis clothier Joseph Kohn advertised "military goods constantly on hand." Memphis had at least fifteen Jewish merchants selling military clothing in 1863. Bazelon and McGuinn, *Directory of American Military Goods Dealers*, 78; Robert N. Rosen, *The Jewish Confederates* (Columbia: University of South Carolina Press, 2000), 263.

52. See Louis Gratz, "From Peddler to Regimental Commander," 1861–1862, in *The Jew in the American World: A Source Book*, ed. Jacob Rader Marcus (Detroit: Wayne State University Press, 1996), 223.

53. J.S.H. of the 12th Regiment, NYSM, writing from Harper's Ferry, August 15, 1862, in Styple, *Writing and Fighting*, 116.

54. David Michael Delo, *Peddlers and Post Traders: The Army Sutler on the Frontier* (Salt Lake City: University of Utah Press, 1992), 103–110. For the prescribed list of wares, see Francis A. Lord, *Civil War Sutlers and Their Wares* (New York: Thomas Yoseloff, 1969), 39, 67. For the regulations governing sutlers, see United States War Department, *War of the Rebellion*, ser. 3, vol. 1, 938–940. For contemporary descriptions of (and complaints about) sutlers, see Styple, *Writing and Fighting*, 50–51, 69–70, 308, 319, 349.

55. For a fuller account of Jewish sutlers, see Mendelsohn, "Beyond the Battlefield," 99–103.

56. Lord, *Civil War Sutlers*, 68–69. This was a frequent complaint among soldiers. See Styple, *Writing and Fighting*, 56, 69–70, 116, 137, 163.

57. A——, color guard writing from camp near Falmouth, VA, Feb. 3, 1863, in Styple, *Writing and Fighting the Civil War*, 163.

58. For examples of complaints about sutler's wares, see Sam, Fortieth (Mozart) Regiment, N.Y.V., writing from near Brandy Station, VA, Apr. 9, 1864, in Styple, *Writing and Fighting*, 250.

59. See Huse Audit Series: S. Isaac Campbell and Co. Subseries of the Colin J. McRae Collection at the South Carolina Confederate Relic Room and Military Museum, Columbia, SC.

60. Using the retail price index as a measure, the sum of £515,000 is roughly equivalent to £37,500,000 ($58,000,000) today. When calculated to reflect changes in average earnings, the sum is equivalent to £330,000,000 ($517,000,000). For the scale of orders, see Bell Irvin Wiley, *The Life of Johnny Reb: The Common Soldier of the Confederacy* (Baton Rouge: Louisiana State University Press, 1978), 110–111; Wilson, *Confederate Industry*, 160, 176–179; Richard Lester, *Confederate Finance and Purchasing in Great Britain* (Charlottesville: University Press of Virginia, 1975), 180, 188; Bennett, *London Confederates*, 57. On the sums expended by the purchasing agents, see Frank Lawrence Owsley, *King Cotton Diplomacy* (Chicago: University of Chicago Press, 1959), 368; Bennett, *London Confederates*, 61.

61. Lester, *Confederate Finance*, 167.

62. Quoted in Wilson, *Confederate Industry*, 106. This was confirmed by the Confederate Quartermaster General. Ibid., 155.

63. J. B. Jones, *A Rebel War Clerk's Diary*, vol. 2 (Philadelphia: Lippincott, 1866), 98. See also ibid., 77, 101, 235.

64. W. C. Corsan, *Two Months in the Confederate States: An Englishman's Travels through the South* (1863; repr., Baton Rouge: Louisiana State University Press, 1996), 61. For a similar complaint in wartime Richmond, see *Richmond Examiner*, Dec. 20, 1862. On nativism in the antebellum South, see Andrea Mehrländer, *The Germans of Charleston, Richmond and New Orleans during the Civil War Period, 1850–1870* (Berlin: Walter de Gruyter, 2011), 61–76.

65. Goff, *Confederate Supply*, 16; Wilson, *Confederate Industry*, 156–157.

66. United States War Department, *War of the Rebellion*, ser. 4, vol. 2, 539–547, 646–647; Wilson, *Confederate Industry*, 166; Stephen R. Wise, *Lifeline of the Confederacy: Blockade Running during the Civil War* (Columbia: University of South Carolina Press, 1991), 102–104; Bennett, *London Confederates*, 51, 58; Charles S. Davis, *Colin J. McRae: Confederate Financial Agent* (Tuscaloosa: Confederate Publishing, 1961), 37–40, 46.

67. Jones, *Rebel War Clerk's Diary*, 2:53.
68. See Balance Sheet, June 1863–Aug. 1863, G11; McRae to SIC, Oct. 28, 1863, K75; McRae to Huse, Dec. 10, 1863, K37; S. Isaac Campbell correction of Interest Account, G17; M. H. Bloodgood to McRae, Apr. 27, 1864, K28, all in Financing the Confederacy Series, Colin J. McRae Collection, South Carolina Confederate Relic Room and Military Museum, Columbia, SC; Anderson, *Confederate Foreign Agent*, 37. See also Owsley, *King Cotton Diplomacy*, 368; Bennett, *London Confederates*, 61; Wilson, *Confederate Industry*, 167; Lester, *Confederate Finance*, 167; United States War Department, *War of the Rebellion*, ser. 4, vol. 2, 646–647.
69. See Anderson, *Confederate Foreign Agent*, 62; David G. Burt and Craig L. Barry, *Supplier to the Confederacy: S. Isaac, Campbell & Co. London* (Bedfordshire, UK: Bright Pen, 2010), 65.
70. United States War Department, *War of the Rebellion*, ser. 4, vol. 2, 890. On the difficulty of disposing of the bonds, see Davis, *Colin J. McRae*, 38–40.

NOTES TO CHAPTER 8

1. Leslie Meyers Zomalt, "An Exercise in Caution: The Business Activities of the Joseph Seligman Family in the 19th Century American West" (PhD diss., University of California, Santa Barbara, 1979), 52–60 (quotes on 58); Muir and White, *Over the Long Term*, 46–48.
2. *New York Times*, Apr. 14, 1912, 12.
3. Seligman, *In Memoriam Jesse Seligman*, 4; *New York Times*, Apr. 14, 1912, 12 (quote); Zomalt, "Exercise in Caution," 9–51. Zakim, *Ready-Made Democracy*, 61–62; Muir and White, *Over the Long Term*, 24–43.
4. Quoted in Decker, *Fortunes and Failures*, 149. On the purchasing power of gold, see Wesley C. Mitchell, *Gold, Prices, and Wages under the Greenback Standard* (Berkeley: University of California Press, 1908), 4; Hugh Rockoff, "Banking and Finance, 1789–1914," in Engerman and Gallman, *Cambridge Economic History*, 657–659.
5. Zomalt, "Exercise in Caution," 53–55; Decker, *Fortunes and Failures*, 149–151; J. Matthew Gallman, *Mastering Wartime: A Social History of Philadelphia during the Civil War* (New York: Cambridge University Press, 1990), 268; Elliott Ashkenazi, "Jewish Commercial Interests between North and South: The Case of the Lehmans and the Seligmans," in *Dixie Diaspora: An Anthology of Southern Jewish History*, ed. Mark K. Bauman (Tuscaloosa: University of Alabama Press, 2006), 198–203.
6. Wilson, "Business of the Civil War," 745–747, 757, 766.
7. Raphael, *Jews and Judaism in a Midwestern Community*, 39. For a similar description at the end of the Mexican-American War, see Sartorius, "Small-Town Southern Merchant," 2:26.
8. Wilson, "Business of the Civil War," 450, 747; Spann, *Gotham at War*, 192–195; Olegario, "Credit and Business Culture," 24. On postwar prices, see Mitchell, *Gold, Prices, and Wages*, 26 (quote), 264–267; Rockoff, "Banking and Finance," 659. Figures in Margo, "Labor Force," 223, present a less flattering picture of wage growth.
9. Gallman, *Mastering Wartime*, 228, 258–261, 263, 300–301; Stott, *Workers in the Metropolis*,

21; Stott, "Hinterland Development," 51; Judith Greenfield, "The Role of Jews in the Development of the Clothing Industry in the United States," *Yivo Annual* 2 (1948): 182–183; Stanley Nadel, *Little Germany: Ethnicity, Religion, and Class in New York City, 1845–80* (Urbana: University of Illinois Press, 1990), 65.

10. These conclusions are derived from a comparison of *Wilson's Business Directory of New York City* for 1866 with those from 1848, 1854, and 1856. See also Moses Rischin, *The Promised City: New York's Jews, 1870–1914* (Cambridge: Harvard University Press, 1962), 52.

11. *New York Tribune*, c. 1859, quoted in Kidwell and Christman, *Suiting Everyone*, 79.

12. Ibid., 77–78; Godley, *Jewish Immigrant Entrepreneurship*, 97–98.

13. On consolidation, see Fraser, "Combined and Uneven Development," 525–546; Green, *Ready-to-Wear and Ready-to-Work*, 57. On variation, see Kidwell and Christman, *Suiting Everyone*, 93–96.

14. The impressionistic number appears to originate in an essay written by Ely Pilchik ("Economic Life of American Jewry, 1860–1875" [1934], 2) while he was a student at Hebrew Union College. It was picked up by Allan Tarshish, who wrote one of the earliest scholarly studies of American Jewish economic life ("The Rise of American Judaism" [PhD diss., Hebrew Union College, 1938], 86–87), then by Naomi W. Cohen in *Encounter with Emancipation: The German Jews in the United States 1830–1914* (Philadelphia: Jewish Publication Society of America, 1984), 29; and Hertzberg in *Jews in America*, 125.

15. Styles, *Dress of the People*, 177; Kahn, *Stitch in Time*, 33; Green, *Ready-to-Wear and Ready-to-Work*, 30. On Jewish-owned department stores, see Harris, *Merchant Princes*.

16. Margo, "Labor Force," 214, 223–224, 229; Fraser, "Combined and Uneven Development," 527; Godley, *Jewish Immigrant Entrepreneurship*, 98.

17. Peter George, *The Emergence of Industrial America* (Albany: SUNY Press, 1982), 18–20; Alfred D. Chandler Jr., *Scale and Scope: The Dynamics of Industrial Development* (Cambridge: Harvard University Press, 2004), 52. For comparison of economic development in Britain with the United States, see Oliver M. Westall, "The Competitive Environment of British Business, 1850–1914," in *Business Enterprise in Modern Britain: From the Eighteenth to the Twentieth Century*, ed. M. W. Kirby and Mary B. Rose (London: Routledge, 1994), 207–235.

18. Mesinger, "Peddlers and Merchants," 11, 23; Barkai, *Branching Out*, 125–134.

19. Greenberg, "Creating Ethnic, Class, and Southern Identity," 97, 103–104, 114–115, 133; Steven Hertzberg, *Strangers within the Gate City* (Philadelphia: Jewish Publication Society, 1978), 40–41; Raphael, *Jews and Judaism in a Midwestern Community*, 40–46; Brinkmann, *Sundays at Sinai*, 86.

20. Charles Gavan Duffy, *Conversations with Carlyle* (London: Sampson Low, Marston, 1892), 218–219.

21. Figures from Steven E. Woodworth and Kenneth J. Winkle, *Oxford Atlas of the Civil War* (New York: Oxford University Press, 2004), 336; McPherson, *Battle Cry of Freedom*, 818.

22. E. Merton Coulter, *The South during Reconstruction, 1865–1877*, vol. 8 (Baton Rouge: Louisiana State University Press, 1975), 220.

23. For prices, see C. Mildred Thomas, *Reconstruction in Georgia* (New York: Columbia University Press, 1915), 300; Roger L. Ransom and Richard Sutch, *One Kind of Freedom: The Economic Consequences of Emancipation* (New York: Cambridge University Press, 2001), 64.

24. In 1860 a fifth of the free population of the county in which Natchez is located were foreign-born, the highest percentage in the state. Aaron D. Anderson, *Builders of a New South* (Jackson: University Press of Mississippi, 2013), 60 (quote), 112–141; Anderson, "The Builders of a New South: Merchant Capital, and the Making of Natchez, 1865–1914" (PhD diss., University of Southern Mississippi, 2009), 61–63, 78; Marler, "Merchants and the Political Economy," 137; Willis, *Forgotten Time*, 83–87, 207; Wayne, "Ante-Bellum Planters," 227–231, 236, 242–248; Burrows and Wallace, *Gotham*, 906–907; Thomas Clark, "The Post–Civil War Economy in the South," *American Jewish Historical Quarterly* 55, 1–4 (1965–1966): 432.

25. See Anton Hieke, "Some among the Few: The German Jewish Immigrants of Reconstruction Georgia and the Carolinas" (PhD diss., Martin Luther University of Halle-Wittenberg, 2011); Hertzberg, *Strangers within the Gate*, 33; Hieke, "Transregional Mobility," 34; Wayne, "Ante-Bellum Planters," 239–241, 248 (quote).

26. Weis, *Autobiography of Julius Weis*, 18–27; Machlowitz, *Clara Lowenburg Moses*, 9, 43; Anderson, "Builders of a New South," 75, 77–79, 82–90; Turitz and Turitz, *Jews in Early Mississippi*, 16; Wayne, "Ante-Bellum Planters," 171 (quote), 250.

27. Quoted in Wayne, "Ante-Bellum Planters," 237.

28. Bernheim, *Story of the Bernheim Family*, 43.

29. Eagle, One Hundred and Thirty-Ninth Regiment N.Y.V., writing from Camp Westman, Williamsburg, VA, Aug. 19, 1863, in Styple, *Writing and Fighting*, 211.

30. Quoted in Wayne, "Ante-Bellum Planters," 228n18.

31. Stephen Powers, *A Foot and Alone* (Hartford, CT: Columbian, 1872), 42–44; Jeffrey Strickland, "Ethnicity and Race in the Urban South: German Immigrants and African-Americans in Charleston South Carolina during Reconstruction" (PhD diss., Florida State University, 2003), 64.

32. For accusations, see *Pennsylvania Freedmen's Relief Association Report* (Philadelphia,1864), 1–2; G. K. Eggleston, "The Work of Relief Societies during the Civil War," *Journal of Negro History* 14, 3 (1929): 278–279. For explanations of the role of merchants in facilitating sharecropping, see Wayne, "Ante-Bellum Planters," 222–224, 251–266; Anderson, *Builders of a New South*.

33. Wayne, "Ante-Bellum Planters," 232–233.

34. Weis, *Autobiography of Julius Weis*, 20–21 (quote on 21); Anderson, "Builders of a New South," 80–81; Melvin Urofsky, *Louis D. Brandeis: A Life* (New York: Pantheon, 2009), 3l.

35. Ashkenazi, *Business of Jews in Louisiana*, 114; Ashkenazi, "Jewish Commercial Interests," 198, 203–205; Wall, "Leon Godchaux," 59; Anderson, *Builders of a New South*, 117, 124–125; Wayne, "Ante-Bellum Planters," 283–286.

36. Quoted in Muir and White, *Over the Long Term*, 53. The best description of the firm's entry into banking is provided by Zomalt, "Exercise in Caution," 61–83.

37. Barry Supple, "A Business Elite: German-Jewish Financiers in Nineteenth-Century New York," *Business History Review* 31, 2 (1957): 152–155, 172; Vincent P. Carosso, "A Financial Elite: New York's German-Jewish Investment Bankers," *American Jewish Historical Quarterly* 66, 1–4 (Sept. 1976): 67–87; Whiteman, "Notions," 313; Ashkenazi, *Business of Jews in Louisiana*, 114, 127–130.

38. On the wealth of the Bernheimers and other leading Jews in New York, see *The Income Record: A List Giving the Taxable Income of Every Resident of New York* (New York: American News Company, 1865). On the profits from slum properties, see Elizabeth Blackmar, *Manhattan for Rent, 1785–1850* (Ithaca: Cornell University Press, 1991); Godley, *Jewish Immigrant Entrepreneurship*, 95, 158nn18–19.

39. For examples of Jews opening banks, see Levinson, *Jews in the California Gold Rush*, 53; Parish, "German Jew and the Commercial Revolution," 323–324; Rosenbaum, *Cosmopolitans*, 40–41; Clark, "Post–Civil War Economy," 428–429.

40. Henry Vere Huntley, *California: Its Gold and Its Inhabitants*, vol. 1 (London: Thomas Cautley Newby, 1856), 67–70.

41. Willis, *Forgotten Time*, 86–87, 98. On participation in local government, see Lee Shai Weissbach, *Jewish Life in Small-Town America: A History* (New Haven: Yale University Press, 2005), 222–223.

42. See Naomi W. Cohen, "Antisemitism in the Gilded Age: The Jewish View," *Jewish Social Studies*, Summer–Fall 1989, 187–189. For one particularly vituperative attack on Jews for supposed wartime misdeeds, see *American Israelite*, Oct. 12, 1866, 4.

43. On exports, see the following in *Parliamentary Papers, Great Britain, Parliament, House of Commons*, 1873–1914: "Trade and Navigation" (Annual Statement); Board of Trade, *Reports on the Volume and Effects of Recent Immigration from Eastern Europe into the United Kingdom*, C.7406, 1894, 208–211; *Report of the Royal Commission on Alien Immigration* (London: HMSO, 1903), CD 1741-I: 30. For the Jewish occupational profile in London in 1880, see Lipman, *Social History*, 79–82.

44. Beatrice Webb, "The Tailoring Trade," in *Life and Labour of the People in London*, ed. Charles Booth, 1st ser., vol. 4 (London: Macmillan, 1902–1903), 46–66; Gartner, *Jewish Immigrant in England*, 84; Pollins, *Economic History*, 105–106, 146, 173, 177, 200; Magee and Thompson, *Empire and Globalisation*, 160, 164–165; Joseph Jacobs, *Studies in Jewish Statistics, Social, Vital and Anthropometric* (London: D. Nutt, 1891), 33–38; Godley, *Jewish Immigrant Entrepreneurship*, 97–98.

45. For the impact of technological change, see Feldman, *Englishmen and Jews*, 192–193; Schmiechen, *Sweated Industries*, 25–28. For typical tasks, see Wechsler, "Jewish Garment Trade," 54. On the reputation of early machine-made clothing, see Wechsler, "Jewish Garment Trade," 53, 64. On the development of the clothing industry in Leeds, see Honeyman, *Well Suited*, 1–33. On the speed of piecework orders, see Edward Smith, "Sanitary Circumstances of Tailors in London," in *Sixth Report of the Medical Officer of the Privy Council* (London: Eyre and Spottiswoode, 1864), 425.

46. For examples of how earlier immigrants facilitated the entry of the new immigrants, see Hadassa Kosak, *Cultures of Opposition: Jewish Immigrant Workers, New York City, 1881–1905* (Albany: SUNY Press, 2000), 70–72; Daniel Soyer, "Cockroach Capitalists: Jewish

Contractors at the Turn of the Twentieth Century," in *A Coat of Many Colors: Immigration, Globalization, and Reform in New York City's Garment Industry*, ed. Daniel Soyer (New York: Fordham University Press, 2005), 106–107, 110–111.

NOTES TO THE CONCLUSION

1. For figures, see Godley, *Jewish Immigrant Entrepreneurship*, 106; Pollins, *Economic History*, 144; Green, *Ready-to-Wear and Ready-to-Work*, 202. For participation rates outside New York, see Joel Perlmann, "Beyond New York: The Occupations of Russian Jewish Immigrants in Providence, R.I. and in Other Small Jewish Communities, 1900–1915," *American Jewish History* 72, 3 (Mar. 1983): 388–389. See also Daniel Soyer, "Introduction: The Rise and Fall of the Garment Industry in New York City," in Soyer, *Coat of Many Colors*, 4; Annie Polland and Daniel Soyer, *Emerging Metropolis: New York Jews in the Age of Immigration, 1840–1920* (New York: NYU Press, 2012), 118. On Jewish women within the sweatshop economy, see Susan A. Glenn, *Daughters of the Shtetl: Life and Labor in the Immigrant Generation* (Ithaca: Cornell University Press, 1990), chapter 2.

2. The view that Jews arrived well prepared for tailoring is made forcefully in Kuznets, "Immigration of Russian Jews to the United States," particularly pages 215–216. See also Nancy L. Green, "The Modern Jewish Diaspora: East European Jews in New York, London, and Paris," in *Comparing Jewish Societies*, ed. Todd Endelman (Ann Arbor: University of Michigan Press, 1997), 127. For the contrary position, see Lederhendler, *Jewish Immigrants*, 3–18, 42–54; Gartner, *Jewish Immigrant in England*, 57–58; Feldman, *Englishmen and Jews*, 213; Wechsler, "Jewish Garment Trade," 61–62; Joel Perelman, "Selective Migration as a Basis for Upward Mobility? The Occupations of the Jewish Immigrants to the United States, ca. 1900" (Working Paper 172, Bard College, October 1996); Green, *Ready-to-Wear and Ready-to-Work*, 180–181.

3. See Model, "Ethnic Niche," 162–163, 166, 176; Ivan Light, Parminder Bhachu, and Stavros Karageorgis, "Migration Networks and Immigrant Entrepreneurship," in *Immigration and Entrepreneurship: Culture, Capital, and Ethnic Networks*, ed. Ivan Light and Parminder Bhachu (New Brunswick, NJ: Transaction, 1993), 37–39; Green, *Ready-to-Wear and Ready-to-Work*, 183–184. On skills and the length of time it took to acquire them, see Green, *Ready-to-Wear and Ready-to-Work*, 176–177, and on interethnic workplaces, see 287–290.

4. Webb, "Tailoring Trade," 60.

5. For Webb's tart critique of clothing made by Jews, see ibid., 43, 56, 64.

6. Beatrice Webb, "The Jewish Community," in *Life and Labour of the People in London*, ed. Charles Booth, 1st ser., vol. 3 (London: Macmillan, 1902–1903), 185–186.

7. Soyer, "Cockroach Capitalists," 94; for an evocative description of workplace conditions, see ibid., 100–102; for the employment cycle see ibid., 105–108. See also Fraser, "Combined and Uneven Development," 536–537; Model "Ethnic Niche," 168; Hadassa Kosak, "Tailors and Troublemakers: Jewish Militancy in the New York Garment Industry, 1889–1910," in Soyer, *Coat of Many Colors*, 118. For street markets in London, see H. Llewellyn Smith, ed., *New Survey of London Life and Labour*, vol. 3 (London: P. S. King & Son, 1932); on New York, see *Report of the Mayor's Push-Cart Commission* (New York:

City of New York, 1906); Andrew Heinze, "Jewish Street Merchants and Mass Consumption in New York City, 1880–1914," *American Jewish Archives Journal* 42, 2 (1989): 199–213. On secondhand dealing, see *Jewish Chronicle*, Aug. 16, 1895.

8. Godley, *Jewish Immigrant Entrepreneurship*, 55–59. For similar figures, see Chiswick, "Occupational Attainment and Earnings."

9. See Godley, *Jewish Immigrant Entrepreneurship*.

10. On the impact of antisemitism on patterns of labor, see Feldman, *Englishmen and Jews*; Godley, *Jewish Immigrant Entrepreneurship*, 112–113; Gartner, *Jewish Immigrant in England*, 86; Model, "Ethnic Niche," 176.

11. Godley, *Jewish Immigrant Entrepreneurship*, 104–106; Green, *Ready-to-Wear and Ready-to-Work*, 50. On trade unionism in the garment industry, see Green, *Ready-to-Wear and Ready-to-Work*, 51–66; Bythell, *Sweated Trades*, 116; Pollins, *Economic History*, 152–164; Kosak, "Tailors and Troublemakers," 115–139.

12. Soyer, "Introduction," 6–7; Green, *Ready-to-Wear and Ready-to-Work*, 48; Fraser, "Combined and Uneven Development," 525–546; Kahn, *Stitch in Time*, 96; Naomi R. Lamoreaux, "Entrepreneurship, Business Organization, and Economic Concentration," in Engerman and Gallman, *Cambridge Economic History*, 403, 424.

13. Green, *Ready-to-Wear and Ready-to-Work*, 45–48; Phyllis Dillon and Andrew Godley, "The Evolution of the Jewish Garment Industry, 1840–1940," in Kobrin, *Chosen Capital*, 46–53; Waldinger, *Through the Eye of the Needle*, 50; Baron and Klepp, "If I Didn't Have My Sewing Machine," 28; Anne J. Kershen, "Morris Cohen and the Origins of the Women's Wholesale Clothing Industry in the East End," *Textile History* 28, 1 (1997): 39–46; Soyer, "Introduction," 6–7; Wall, "Some Implications of the Earnings, Income and Expenditure Patterns," 312–335. On the history of the Garment District, see Andrew S. Dolkart, "From the Rag Trade to Riches: Abraham E. Lefcourt and the Development of New York's Garment District," in Kobrin, *Chosen Capital*, 62–92.

14. Pollins, *Economic History*, 187–202; Godley, *Jewish Immigrant Entrepreneurship*, 38–41, 56–59, 112–115; Susan Cotts Watkins and Arodys Robles, "Appendix B: A Tabular Presentation of Immigrant Characteristics, by Ethnic Group," *After Ellis Island: Newcomers and Natives in the 1910 Census*, ed. Susan Cotts Watkins (New York: Russell Sage Foundation, 1994), 376–377. Thomas Kessner provides even higher figures for white-collar employment; see "New Yorkers in Prosperity and Depression: A Preliminary Reconnaissance," in *Educating an Urban People*, ed. Diane Ravitch and Ronald K. Goodenow (New York: Teachers College Press, 1981), 94–100.

15. Pollins, *Economic History*, 106; Godley, *Jewish Immigrant Entrepreneurship*, 38–34, 100–101; Barry R. Chiswick, "The Billings Report and the Occupational Attainment of American Jewry, 1890," *Shofar* 19, 2 (Winter 2001): 63. On the vacancy chain in ethnic economies, see Roger Waldinger, "Immigration and Urban Change," *Annual Review of Sociology* 15 (1989): 221–222.

16. These processes are described in Waldinger, *Through the Eye of the Needle*, 1, 30, 54–56; Green, *Ready-to-Wear and Ready-to-Work*, 37–40, 57–58, 67–70, 145–146, 204; Soyer, "Introduction," 17; Soyer, "Cockroach Capitalists," 106–114; Kosak, "Tailors and Troublemakers," 115–122; on Howe, see Soyer, "Cockroach Capitalists," 94, 109.

17. The early stages of this diversification—and its limitations—are evident in a much-cited feature in *Fortune* 13, 2 (Feb. 1936): 79–133, reprinted as *Jews in America* (New York: Random House, 1936), particularly 34–71. On England, see Pollins, *Economic History*, 202–205.

18. Kessner, *Golden Door*, 65. The impact of the interwar years is explored in much more detail in Deborah Dash Moore, *At Home in America: Second Generation New York Jews* (New York: Columbia University Press, 1981); Diner, *Jews of the United States*, 230–232, 239–258.

19. These communities are discussed in Jeffrey Gurock's *Jews in Gotham: New York Jews in a Changing City, 1920–2010* (New York: NYU Press, 2012).

20. Barry A. Kosmin and Nigel Grizzard, *Jews in an Inner London Borough: A Study of the Jewish Population of the London Borough of Hackney Based on the 1971 Census* (London: Board of Deputies of British Jews, 1975), 25–30; Ernest Krausz, "Occupation and Social Advancement in Anglo-Jewry," *Jewish Journal of Sociology* 4, 1 (1962): 82–90; Krausz, "The Edgeware Survey: Occupation and Social Class," *Jewish Journal of Sociology* 11, 1 (1969): 75–95; S. J. Prais and M. Schmool, "The Social Class Structure of Anglo-Jewry, 1961," *Jewish Journal of Sociology* 27, 1 (1975): 5–16; Pollins, *Economic History*, 209–217, 220; William Rubinstein, *A History of the Jews in the English-Speaking World: Great Britain* (New York: St. Martin's, 1996), 106, 227–228; Endelman, *Jews of Britain*, 196–198.

21. Temin, "Elite Minority," 252–254; Brenner and Kiefer, "Economics of the Diaspora," 525–526; Muller, *Capitalism and the Jews*, 101; Sarachek, "Jewish American Entrepreneurs," 359–360; Simon Kuznets, "Economic Structure of U.S. Jewry: Recent Trends," in *Jewish Economies: Development and Migration in America and Beyond*, vol. 1, *The Economic Life of American Jewry*, ed. Stephanie Lo and E. Glen Weyl (New Brunswick, NJ: Transaction, 2012), 107–124; Model, "Ethnic Niche," 174–176.

22. This analysis draws heavily on Waldinger, *Through the Eye of the Needle*, 44–45 (quote on 44). For his arguments about immigrant clusters within city government, see Waldinger, "The Making of an Immigrant Niche," *International Migration Review* 28, 1 (Spring 1994): 3–30.

23. The classic studies are Kessner, *Golden Door*; and Nathan Glazer and Daniel Patrick Moynihan, *Beyond the Melting Pot* (Cambridge: MIT Press, 1970). For Kessner's findings on Jewish mobility, see *Golden Door*, 52, 60, 110. For a wealth of comparative data, see Model, "Ethnic Niche," 177, 180.

24. On Italians in the garment industry, see Nancy C. Carnevale, "Culture of Work: Italian Immigrant Women Homeworkers in the New York City Garment Industry, 1890–1914," in Soyer, *Coat of Many Colors*, 141–167. On their earning power relative to Jews, see Model, "Ethnic Niche," 177–180. On Italian and Jewish entrepreneurship in Texas, see Stacy D. Bondurant, "Gone to Texas: Eastern-European Jewish and Italian Immigrants in Urban Texas, 1900–1924" (PhD diss., George Washington University, 2012), 105.

INDEX

Page numbers in italics refer to illustrations.

Aaron, Elizabeth, 28, 34

Adler, Jeffrey, 82

Advertising: for Australian clothing, 123, 126; from E. Moses & Son, 108–9, 264n47; expense of, 108, 264n46; in London, 109–10; in Melbourne, Australia, 108; status in, 107–8

Agriculture, 80. *See also* Cotton

Alabama, 39, 184

Aldgate (London), 20–21

America compared to England, 187; in clothing industry success, 130, 133–34; clothing prices in, 121; competition in, 215–16; distribution in, 220, 227; in 1860 and 1870s, 203–6; foreign markets for, 112, 121; geography of, 45–46, 79; *hazer mark* in, 212; immigrants to, 205–8; Jewish immigrant entrepreneurs in, 210–16; Jewish peddlers in, 89–90; labor system in, 43–44; legislation in, 214–15; menswear trade in, 207, 215–16; middlemen in, 97; networks in, 132; opportunities in, 219–20, 226–28; partnerships in, 131; post–Civil War economy in, 192; ready-made trade in, 104, 227; secondhand-clothing trade in, 3–5, 15–16, 35–36, 43, 46, 227; self-employment in, 212–13; sewing machines in, 203–4; shoddy industry in, 72; status in, 218–19; subcontracting in, 96–97; sweating system in, 214, 227–28; timing for, 135, 227–28; unions in, 215; wages in, 215; womenswear in, 217–18, *218*; working-class Jews in, 223–24

American clerks: American peddlers compared to, 72–73, 75–76, 255n44; desirability of, 73–76; developments for, 73–74; education of, 76–77; future for, 75–77;

networks for, 76; society of, 77–78. *See also* Jewish clerks

American clothing trade, Jews: banking from, 201–2; capitalism of, 7; domination in, 7–8; dry goods and, 6; exodus from, 221–22; expansion from, 6, 201–2; immigrants' trajectory and, 4, 210–14; innovations in, 4–5; Jews and clothing trade in England, 3–5, 15–16, 35–36, 43, 46; quantification of, 191, 281n14; self-employment for, 211–13; skills from, 5, 222. *See also* America compared to England; Jewish immigrant entrepreneurs

American Jewish migration, 83

American Jewish peddlers: barter for, 70–71; benefits for, 60–61; careers of, 63–64, 66; ethnic ecosystem for, 79–80; information from, 68; Jewish storekeepers and, 85; partnerships for, 65–66; in post–Civil War economy, 193–94; profits of, 65; proportion of, 75; regions for, 61; regulations for, 67–68; role of, 60; rural expansion and, 62; seasons and, 64–65; slaves' clothing and, 68–69; in South, 66–72, 140; stereotype of, 64, 67; stigma of, 61–62, 67; transportation for, 62–63; wholesalers and, 80

American peddlers, 252nn13–14, 253n23, 256n51; American clerks compared to, 72–73, 75–76, 255n44; in Civil War, 177–78; sales of, 64, 252n16

America's clothing trade: competition in, 56–57; England's clothing trade compared to, 44–45; in South, 53, 55–56

America's population, 54–55, 249n41

Anderson, Edward, 180

Antipodes. *See* Australia and New Zealand

287

ABOUT THE AUTHOR

Adam D. Mendelsohn is Director of the Pearlstine/Lipov Center for Southern Jewish Culture and Associate Professor of Jewish Studies at the College of Charleston. He specializes in the history of the Jewish communities of the United States and British Empire in the century prior to eastern European mass migration.